Managing the Global Firm

Managing the Global Firm

Edited by
Christopher A. Bartlett, Yves Doz
and
Gunnar Hedlund

ROUTLEDGE
London and New York

First published 1990
by Routledge
11 New Fetter Lane, London EC4P 4EE
Simultaneously published in the USA and Canada
by Routledge
a division of Routledge, Chapman and Hall, Inc.
29 West 35th Street, New York NY 10001

Typeset by Pat and Anne Murphy, Highcliffe-on-Sea, Dorset
Printed and bound in Great Britain by
Biddles Ltd, Guildford and King's Lynn

British Library Cataloguing in Publication Data

Managing the global firm.
  1. Multinational. Companies. Management
  I. Bartlett, Christopher A.   II. Doz, Yves, L.   III. Hedlund,
  Gunnar, *1949–*
  658'.049

  ISBN 0-415-03711-5

Library of Congress Cataloging in Publication Data

Managing the global firm / edited by Christopher A. Bartlett,
Yves Doz, and Gunnar Hedlund.
    p.   cm.
  Bibliography: p.
  Includes index.
  ISBN 0-415-03711-5
  1. International business enterprises—Management.
I. Bartlett, Christopher A., 1943–   . II. Doz, Yves L.
III. Hedlund Gunnar.
HD62.4.M37   1990   89-34004 CIP
658'.049—dc20

Contents

Contents

List of contributors

Editors: **Christopher A. Bartlett**, Harvard Business
School
Yves Doz, INSEAD
Gunnar Hedlund, Stockholm School of
Economics, Institute of International Business

Other Authors: **E. Ralph Biggadike**, Becton Dickinson
Sumantra Ghoshal, INSEAD
Peter Hagström, Stockholm School of
Economics, Institute of International Business
Lars Håkanson, Stockholm School of
Economics, Institute of International Business
Gary Hamel, The London Business School
Bruce Kogut, The Wharton School, University
of Pennsylvania
Donald R. Lessard, Sloan School of
Management, MIT
Håkan Ledin, Millicom International
Peter Lorange, The Wharton School, University
of Pennsylvania
Nitin Nohria, Sloan School of Management,
MIT
Ikujiro Nonaka, Institute of Business Research,
Hitotsubashi University
Thomas A. Poynter, Sloan School of
Management, MIT
C. K. Prahalad, University of Michigan
Gilbert Probst, Institut für Betriebswirtschaft,
St Gallen
Dag Rolander, Stockholm School of Economics,
Institute of International Business
D. Eleanor Westney, Sloan School of
Management, MIT

List of contributors

Other Authors: **Roderick E. White**, School of Business
Administration, University of Western Ontario

Preface

The present volume attempts to chart the state of the art concerning the management of global firms. The editors conceived the idea of inviting a selected group of academics and reflective business leaders in late 1986. A conference on the theme was convened at the European Institute for Advanced Studies in Management (EIASM) in Brussels during June, 1987. The contributions to the book were presented in their preliminary form at the conference, and have since undergone several revisions. All papers are original and have not been published elsewhere.

The initiative was taken as a part of a series of activities by the European International Business Association (EIBA). Financial support for the conference was received from EIASM and from the Institute of International Business (IIB) at the Stockholm School of Economics. Mr Peter Hagström and Mrs Vanja Ekberg at IIB have helped greatly in the planning and administration of the seminar and the production of the book. We the editors wish to express our warmest thanks to the organizations and individuals mentioned. Also, our thanks to the authors, who have taken our anxious and repeated calls for revision and addition with admirable good humour.

Chris Bartlett, Yves Doz, Gunnar Hedlund
Boston, Fontainebleau, and Stockholm

Acknowledgements

Chapter 1

Gunnar Hedlund and Dag Rolander wish to thank participants at the EIASM conference in Brussels, 9–10 June 1987, and colleagues at the Institute of International Business, Stockholm School of Economics, for helpful comments. In particular, we have benefited from discussions with Yves Doz, Peter Hagström, Bruce Kogut, and Sumantra Ghoshal.

Chapter 2

Bruce Kogut would like to acknowledge Christopher Bartlett, Yves Doz, Peter Hagström, and Gunnar Hedlund for comments on the paper, Don Lessard for stressing the functional underpinnings, Joe Zycherman for his admonition to write more simply, and Stephen Oresman for many useful discussions. Funding was provided through a grant from Booz Allen and Hamilton and AT&T.

Chapter 3

Ikujiro Nonaka expresses special thanks for constructive criticism to his colleagues and friends, among others to Gunnar Hedlund and Johnny K. Johansson, and also to Takaya Kawamura and Munehiko Matsumaya, graduate students of Hitotsubashi University who assisted in the preparation of the paper.

Chapter 4

Roderick E. White and Thomas A. Poynter would gratefully like to acknowledge the support of the 'Plan for Excellence', School of Business Administration, University of Western Ontario, and the 'Business in the 1990s Project', Sloan School of Management,

MIT. An earlier version of this paper was presented to the Managing the Multinational Conference, Brussels, June 1987.

Chapter 6

Peter Lorange and Gilbert Probst wish to thank Gunnar Hedlund of IIB and Edgar Vincent of ICI for helpful comments. They also express their thanks to the senior executives of eleven European-based multinationals who gave them, and their students, generously of their time to discuss the issues reported in the paper.

Chapter 7

Comments on previous versions of this paper by Lars Håkanson, Gunnar Hedlund, Bruce Kogut, and Yves Doz are gratefully acknowledged by Peter Hagström.

Chapter 8

The initial version of this paper was presented at the conference of the Management of the Multinational Corporation, Brussels, 10 June 1987.

This research was supported by the MIT research project on 'Management in the 1990's'. Special thanks go to those firms that provided access for interviews and funds to participate in the 1986–87 and 1988–89 Masters' Thesis Workshops on coping with volatile exchange rates.

Chapter 9

Christopher Bartlett and Sumantra Ghoshal gratefully acknowledge the comments and suggestions of Professors Joseph Bower and Louis Wells of the Harvard Business School, and of Gunnar Hedlund, IIB.

This paper presents part of the findings from a broader study sponsored by the Division of Research at Harvard Business School. It represents an early draft of a chapter from a forthcoming book *Managing across Borders: The Transnational Solution* (Harvard Business School Press) in which the full findings of the project will be presented.

Acknowledgements

Chapter 10

Valuable comments from Yves Doz, Gunnar Hedlund and Bruce Kogut are gratefully acknowledged by Lars Håkanson.

Chapter 12

E. Ralph Biggadike gratefully acknowledges Professors Bartlett and Beer of the Harvard Business School, and Ray Gilmartin and Wilson Nolen of Becton Dickinson for their helpful suggestions. Discussions with several of the contributors of this book helped his thinking. He would like to thank all the managers who provided data.

Introduction
The changing agenda for researchers and practitioners

Chris Bartlett, Yves Doz, and Gunnar Hedlund

International business is an ancient phenomenon. Indeed, the promise of new trade routes and trading partners provided the motivation for much of the world's geographical exploration. With the establishment of world-wide networks of trading posts, entire cultures were often brought in contact with each other for the first time through travelling merchants. The changing patterns of international trade and finance shaped the world's political economy for centuries, with the wealth and power of nations being directly tied to their ability to establish and manage effective trading links and financing arrangements within their widespread empires and networks of partners.

Yet it has only been during the last century that the truly multinational corporations (MNCs) have emerged. In both structure and operation such organizations differed substantially from the trading companies or investment houses that had historically dominated international trade. Unlike the trading companies, the MNC's operations were based on foreign direct investment (FDI), and in contrast to the international financial houses, these investments were managed as an integrated operating unit rather than as a passive portfolio.

Exporting to other countries is, of course, still the dominant form of conducting international business. However, trade is increasingly carried out among the various units of individual MNCs, as companies import goods manufactured in their off-shore plants or export products to be sold by wholly owned foreign subsidiaries. In 1982, for example, 38 per cent of all United States exports was trade internal to American-based MNCs.

Thus, in today's international environment the MNCs command vast resources and are often the dominant actors in the economics of the home and host countries in which they operate. Yet, despite the fact that the quality of their management is of vital importance for global welfare and for the health and robustness of the international economy, surprisingly little academic research has focused on this complex and fast-changing field until comparatively recently. Most scholars have been more interested in defining the forces at work in the international business environment than in probing the complexities of managing the primary tool of such activity — the MNC. It is this latter agenda that provides the focus for the contributions to this volume.

The challenge is a daunting one, for not only is the management task highly complex, it is also evolving rapidly with the continual changes occurring in the international economy. To provide a backdrop for the discussion that follows, we will provide a brief, and clearly oversimplified view of the changing organizational tasks and management perspectives that marked the spread and development of the MNC over the past century, and particularly in the post-World War II era. We will then show how the evolving challenges faced by MNCs and their management shaped the research agenda of academics. Again, taking a grossly oversimplified approach, we will trace the emergence of the nascent field of international management — the field from which the contributions to this book were solicited.

The practitioners' challenge: evolving MNC tasks

The birth of the modern MNC in the late nineteenth century was associated with the rapid industrialization of western society in general. The Industrial Revolution gave rise to new technologies of production and distribution that required much larger scale operations than firms had previously managed. On the one hand, the new mass production technologies demanded a constant and reliable flow of inputs, and the quest for new low-cost, long-term sources of materials and supplies was the motivation that drove many companies abroad. (For example, the internationalization of companies in the rubber, aluminium, and oil industries was driven primarily by this need.) Other companies were driven by the need for assured markets for the new high-volume output needed to achieve scale efficiencies not available in their domestic markets. These companies were encouraged to move offshore to capture the huge and often untapped potential of overseas markets. (The rapid international expansion of companies in the machinery, transporation, and drug industries was due primarily to these forces).

Underlying both these international expansion thrusts, was a clear common motivation — a company's need to build and defend its competitiveness in the home market. The overseas operations were managed primarily to protect that business's continuity of supply, cost efficiency, and market share. The predominant mentality was one that Perlmutter described as 'ethnocentric' (Perlmutter 1965) in both the strategic and organizational sense.

Gradually, however, the extraordinary success of these large sophisticated MNCs in national markets around the world began to stimulate more effective local competition. Many MNCs were forced to transfer more resources, technology, and personnel abroad, as they established more integrated local operations to protect export sales that had often become of vital strategic importance. This trend towards greater offshore investment was greatly accelerated in the late 1920s and 1930s, when protectionist sentiments caused trade barriers to rise to their highest levels of the century and blocked many previously accessible export markets.

Isolated by local differences in consumer practices and preferences, inefficient and expensive international communications and transportation, and high-tariff and non-tariff barriers, individual national markets now became the logical focal point for most MNC managers. Furthermore, because of their size and growth rate, overseas markets were increasingly viewed as important in their own right, not just as appendages to the home country operation, and the key task shifted to understanding how to manage within these different foreign environments.

As overseas subsidiaries became larger and more self-sufficient, their role expanded from simply selling products developed and manufactured by the parent company to adapting designs and producing for local needs. In this era of decentralized federations (Bartlett 1986), as management's attention was focused on the task of managing foreign subsidiaries, the mentality shifted to a predominantly 'polycentric' one in Perlmutter's terms.

In this period of rapid international expansion, the parent company typically viewed its key task as one of administering the expansion. The installation of formal information, planning, and control systems allowed managers in parent companies to develop a better understanding of the growing foreign operations, but most subsidiaries were managed as individual free-standing entities rather than as part of an integrated global organization. This strategic posture and management mentality endured well into the post-war era, with managers concentrating on exploiting the numerous market opportunities triggered by the reconstruction boom of the 1950s.

But changes emerged in the 1960s that were to have profound effects on the structure and operations of MNCs in the following decades. With the lowering of trade barriers (particularly through successive rounds of GATT agreements) and the revolution in international transport and communications (notably, the impact of containerization, international jet air travel, and world-wide telecommunication linkages), companies were able to — and often forced to — treat the world in a much more integrated manner. These early triggers of an era of 'globalization' were reinforced by a new wave of competitors, particularly from Asia, who capitalized on falling tariffs and efficient global distribution to leverage their country-specific comparative advantages.

A new global competitive game emerged that put those who were locked into the old country-by-country approach at a serious disadvantage. Global market segments were recognized — or, more often, created; technology was imitated rapidly and diffused world-wide almost instantaneously; and scale economies were captured to exploit the benefits of the multiple market segments and the free trade access.

Progressively, the key management requirement was for global integration and cross-market co-ordination. The strategic mentality and organizational capability had shifted to a mode that Perlmutter termed 'geocentric'. And in doing so, MNC managers, particularly in the United States and Europe, were challenged to develop an entirely new approach to managing their world-wide operations.

The academic response: a shifting research focus

Because it is such a dynamic and contemporary phenomenon, the nature and operation of the MNC has attracted a good deal of academic attention, particularly in the last fifty years. Most of the early studies of the expansion of MNCs were dominated by neo-classical economists in terms of international capital theory and international trade theory. The focus was primarily on the macro-economic flows between nation states, with the MNC being of interest only as the primary instrument of these flows.

Later, the contribution of industrial economists shifted the focus to the industry level and particularly to the source of competitive advantage. The path-breaking work of Stephen Hymer (Hymer 1960) showed how foreign direct investment was based on the exploitation of imperfect markets. Subsequent work by other economists refined and elaborated on this approach (e.g. Kindleberger 1969; Caves 1971; Knickerbocker 1973; and Graham 1974).

As practitioners adjusted to changes in their external environment, so too were researchers forced to develop new paradigms to explain the shifting behaviour. A literature that had been dominated by economists increasingly became populated by students of management; and a research perspective that had been predominantly macro began to focus more on the internal operations at the level of the individual MNC. Among economists, the work of Oliver Williamson (Williamson 1975) led to a new interest in the economic value of information and the implications for companies that were able to lower transaction costs. Streams of research developed under such banners as internationalization theory (e.g. Buckley and Casson 1976; Dunning 1977), appropriability theory (e.g. Magee 1977), and technology transfer (e.g. Teece 1977).

Equally important was the fact that the new focus on the firm, and even the manager, as an appropriate unit of analysis gave new impetus to researchers focusing more directly on management aspects. Drawing from an emerging body of literature and theory in fields such as business policy and organization behaviour, a growing network of researchers began to shed new light on the internal management issues that had begun to intrigue the economists. For the first time, researchers began to understand that management's ability to build and manage an effective internal organization process was a primary source of competitiveness for MNCs.

Some early pioneering managerial researchers used a clinical methodology to examine the FDI process from a more managerial perspective (Aharoni 1966; Carlson 1966, 1975). Others built on the seminal work of Chandler (1962), defining the archetypical strategies and structures that had allowed MNCs to expand (Stopford and Wells 1972; and Franko 1976).

More recently, a body of research has begun to appear that draws from and builds upon the business policy research at Harvard Business School and elsewhere in the 1960s and early 1970s. Under Professor Joseph Bower, several doctoral dissertations were written which examined the nature of the management process in MNCs (Prahalad 1975; Doz 1976; Bartlett 1979). Simultaneously, a group of researchers at the Stockholm School of Economics was researching the organization and control of European MNCs, particularly those based in Sweden. Over time, this group focused on the nature of headquarters–subsidiary relationship and provided new insights into how world-wide operations were co-ordinated and controlled (Otterbeck 1981; Hedlund 1978, 1980; Leksell 1981).

As the complexity of the MNC's management task continued to increase in the competitive and turbulent international environment of the 1980s, more and more researchers in the broad field of international business have become aware of the importance of this emerging stream of managerial research. Economists like Bruce Kogut and international finance theorists like Don Lessard increasingly highlighted the managerial implications of their analysis. (See Kogut 1983; Lessard 1986.) Similarly, those studying issues as diverse as competitive strategy, technology transfer, manufacturing management, and human resource management were also drawn to this rich and rapidly developing research arena.

Background for this book

It was in this context that the editors of this volume met in Singapore in the autumn of 1986 to plan a conference that would address some of the emerging questions and issues facing managers of MNCs, and evaluate some of the concepts and conclusions being proposed by academics. Our idea was to bring together a relatively small number of leading academics currently doing research in this area with a group of thoughtful senior level managers from large MNCs. The objective was not only to allow the researchers to share their latest thinking, but also to elicit feedback from the practitioners regarding the appropriateness of the topics being studied and the relevance of the conclusions.

Under the aegis of the European Institute for Advanced Studies in Management (EIASM), and with the additional support and sponsorship of the Institute of International Business (IIB) at the Stockholm School of Economics, an international seminar was held in June 1987 at the EIASM facilities in Brussels. For two full days, forty scholars and managers exchanged views on the current and future challenges facing managers of MNCs, and debated the appropriateness of various guidelines and solutions. The papers presented in this book were selected to represent the major thrust of the issues raised and proposals presented.

A brief outline and overview

The agenda addressed at the conference was a broad one, and while there are many themes, issues, and conclusions that connected or related the various papers to one another, we decided to present them in four fairly simple groups:

● The four papers that comprise the first part of the book challenge some of the basic concepts about the nature and purpose of global management, providing a broad base for the chapters that follow.
● The second section is comprised of four views of the different

administrative systems, organizational processes and management practices required to manage the successful MNC in the 1990s.

- In part three, papers focus on the challenge of creating global innovations, and the critical role that international R&D management has to play.
- The final section of the book is devoted to the application and evaluation of the concepts and ideas as two practitioners present views on applicability and appropriateness of the emerging ideas.

In the following paragraphs we will outline some of the thoughts and themes presented in each of the chapters. Rather than attempting to present a pre-digested summary of the main conclusions, our aim is simply to give a flavour of each of the papers. For full nourishment, we encourage the reader to dig into the smorgasboard of offerings laid out in the chapters that follow.

Part I Conceptions of global management

A common theme binding the first four chapters is the view of the modern MNC as an organization that has outgrown the stage in which managers at the centre co-ordinate a set of peripheral subsidiaries, largely independent of each other. The utilization of the multinational network as an integrated and interdependent whole is presented as the basis for successful global business.

Hedlund and Rolander suggest that a genuinely global MNC can better be thought of as what they term a heterarchy rather than a classic hierarchy. They define this new form as a set of reciprocally interdependent and geographically dispersed centres, held together largely by shared strategies, norms, and information. Through the use of the metaphor of the organization as a hologram, they are able to suggest the wide distribution of strategic information necessary to operate such an organization.

Kogut introduces the concept of sequential advantages of the MNC to indicate the shift of competitive advantage subsequent to the initial penetration of foreign markets. In his view, it is the management of a company's global network that eventually becomes the source of advantage, allowing it to achieve economies of scale and scope, to learn about foreign conditions, and to achieve the operating flexibility inherent in such a network. Duplication of activities and differentiation of roles and tasks are two partly contradictory organizational properties critical to the implementation of sequential strategies.

Introduction

Nonaka argues that a shift from an information processing to an information creation paradigm is necessary in order to understand the globalization of Japanese firms. He also emphasizes the interplay between corporate level articulated information, and local tacit information, and the important intermediating role of entrepreneurial middle management. Nonaka points to multiple headquarters in several geographical regions, and the establishment of R&D units abroad by Japanese MNCs as evidence of the qualitative changes brought about by the self-renewal of globalizing firms.

White and Poynter focus on the horizontal organization of an MNC. They describe how lateral processes with widely distributed and shared responsibilities replace the groupings of sets of functional activities under strict hierarchies with unity of command. In their view, strongly held and shared decision premises and values protect the organization from disintegrating.

Part II Management processes and systems

The second section contains discussion of more specific management processes and systems needed to co-ordinate and control the new more complex organization forms. In spite of the various foci, there is some common ground and several common themes that run through all the chapters. Like their colleagues whose contributions appeared in the first section, all the authors in this section also emphasize the importance of 'indirect' means of co-ordination, rather than large formal systems. The need for flexible information processing underlines much of the analysis.

Doz and Prahalad address the issue of co-ordination and control of global strategic alliances. After providing a framework for understanding the required strategic management capabilities — strategic control, strategic change and strategic flexibility — the authors then show how traditional tools and approaches used by MNC managers in establishing such processes may not be effective when projects, responsibilities and relationships span historical corporate boundaries. The complexity of the management process leaves the authors pessimistic about the long-term viability of such partnerships.

Lorange and Probst conclude that MNCs should re-examine their strategic planning processes. Because of the complexity of the international environment, many companies have developed approaches that are overly formal and complicated, and the authors stress the need to keep systems simple and flexible. They suggest that the centrifugal tendencies inherent in the increased complexity require strong integration and direction through central strategic vision.

The emphasis should be on managing people and *ad hoc* teams rather than on increasingly sophisticated systems and procedures.

Hagström discusses the effects of new information technology on the structure and management of the MNC. He shows how such technologies open radically new possibilities to unbundle and rebundle activities geographically and organizationally. The effect of the new technology also extends beyond the MNC's traditional organizational boundaries, facilitating the establishment of new links to customers and suppliers, for example. The net effect is to make the MNC a more permeable but at the same time more co-ordinated system. Hagström suggests that the impact of the new information technology will be to encourage the development of MNCs in which organization structures are mixed, and functional specialization is encouraged.

Lessard and Nohria also emphasize functional expertise in their discussion of managing in an environment of volatile exchange rates. Because information exchange between the managers and functional specialists is crucial, the authors suggest that the division of responsibilities not be specified in rigid organizational terms. Instead, they propose an emergent matrix in which networked and interlinked actors share expertise and negotiate between different perspectives, in a more flexible manner than in a formal matrix.

Part III   Innovation and R&D in the MNC

A recurring theme in the conference was the growing importance of R&D management, technology transfer, and the broader issue of innovation in the MNC. The third section of the book focuses on three papers that look at various aspects of this issue. The common thread that binds the chapters in this section is a belief that MNCs must attempt to utilize their world-wide networks as a source of innovation, and not only for the penetration of distant markets — a theme that picks up on some of the broad issues of organizational learning raised in Part I.

Bartlett and Ghoshal analyse how a transactional organizational model can lead to a much richer and more effective innovation process, by explicitly differentiating roles and responsibilities of the different national subsidiaries. The authors describe how companies can develop multiple simultaneous processes of innovation by linking and leveraging existing organizational assets and capabilities. They argue that it is not necessarily the amount of money expended on R&D or other sources of innovation that is the key success factor for MNCs, but the ability to develop an organizational capability that allows the four basic processes of innovation they describe to flourish and coexist.

Håkanson discusses in detail the role changes for staff at the centre, in product divisions, and in foreign subsidiaries as a consequence of international decentralization of R&D. More general conceptions and models of the MNC (geocentrism, heterarchy, transnationality, etc.) are found to be useful. However, they need to be made more specific to give effective guidance to practising managers faced with the organizational challenges of multinational R&D. To fill the gap, the author proposes some changes in the roles and tasks of R&D managers in today's more complex MNCs.

Westney analyses the intricacies of balancing the needs for internal and external linkages in MNCs R&D networks. R&D subsidiaries in Japan constitute an important case, since the linkages with the internal Japanese environment are quite specific and differ from the situation in most Western countries. A number of factors influencing the effective organization design of R&D units in Japan are analysed, and responses to the dilemmas of linking into both internal (the MNC) and external (the host environment) networks are suggested.

Part IV The concepts in use

The fourth and final section of chapters reflects on experiences in specific firms and on the totality of approaches taken in the book. Here we present some views that are both applied and specific, as two practitioners reflect on the applicability of some of these concepts and prescriptions to their particular firms and industries.

Biggadike reports on the organizational evolution of Becton Dickinson, and the use of research on MNC management in this process. Although helpful in diagnosing problems and setting the basic direction, the author feels that such research needs to be complemented by more tools and specific approaches to facilitate change and organizational learning. In his company's experience, rapid communication of core ideas and organizational changes to employees at lower levels, and a clear task orientation are desirable to move more rapidly to globally effective organization.

Ledin draws on his experience as a senior manager in the Swedish telecommunications giant, Ericsson, to draw an analogy between the design of a telecommunications network and the characteristics of an appropriate organization structure and process for an MNC. He concludes that MNCs increasingly have to function as networks of intelligent nodes, rather than as traditional hierarchies or matrix structures, and that the quality and integrity of the informal organization will become the main determinant of success or failure.

The conclusion of those attending the conference — academic and practitioner alike — was that the papers and the discussion they stimulated were extremely worthwhile. Our hope is to share these views with a wider audience through this volume of collected papers. We recognize that many of the ideas presented here are not yet widely accepted, nor even completely formed in the authors' minds. By presenting such early stage thinking of researchers who are exploring the frontiers of international management issues, our objective is to provide a stimulating and provocative set of ideas that will help to set the agenda for managers and students of management wresting with the challenges facing the global firm in the 1990s.

References

Aharoni, Y. (1966) *The Foreign Investment Decision Process*, Boston: Harvard UP.

Bartlett, C. A. (1979) *Multinational Structural Evolution: The Changing Decision Environment in International Divisions*, doctoral dissertation, Harvard Business School.

—— (1986) 'Building and managing the transnational: the new organizational challenge', in Porter, M. E. (ed.) *Competition in Global Industries*, Boston: Harvard Business School Press.

Buckley, P. J. and Casson, M. (1976) *The Future of the Multinational Enterprise*, London: Macmillan.

Carlson, S. (1966) 'International business research', *Studie Oeconomica Negotiorum*, 1, Uppsala.

—— (1975) 'How foreign is foreign trade? A problem in international business research', *Studie Oeconomica Negotiorum*, 11, Uppsala.

Caves, R. E. (1971) 'International corporations: the industrial economics of foreign investment', *Economica*, pp. 1–27. Reprinted in Dunning, J. H. (ed.) (1972) *International Investment*, Harmondsworth: Penguin Books.

Chandler, A. P. (1962) *Strategy and Structure*, Cambridge, MA: MIT Press.

Doz, Y. (1976) *National Policies and Multinational Management*, doctoral dissertation, Harvard University.

Dunning, J. H. (1977) 'Trade, location of economic activity and the multinational enterprise. A search for an eclectic approach', in Ohlin, B., Hesselbom, P. O., and Wiskman, P. J. (eds) *The International Allocation of Economic Activity*, London: Macmillan.

Franko, L. G. (1976) *The European Multinationals*, Greenwich, CT: Greylock Press.

Graham, E. M. (1974) *Oligopolistic Imitation and European Direct*

Investment in the US, doctoral dissertation, Harvard Business School.

Hedlund, G. (1978) 'Organization as a matter of style', in Mattsson, L-G. and Widersheim-Paul, F. (eds) *Recent Research on the Internationalization of Business*, Uppsala.

—— (1980) 'The role of foreign subsidiaries in strategic decision-making in Swedish multinational corporations', *Strategic Management Journal*, 9.

Hymer, S. (1960, 1976) *The International Operations of National Firms: A Study of Direct Foreign Investment*, MIT Press. (Originally published as doctoral dissertation in 1960).

Kindleberger, C. P. (1969) *American Business Abroad: Six Lectures on Direct Investment*, New Haven, Conn: Yale UP.

Knickerbocker, F. T. (1973) *Oligopolistic Reaction and the Multinational Enterprise*, Boston, MA: Harvard UP.

Kogut, B. (1983) 'Foreign Direct Investment as a Sequential Process', in Kindleberger, C. P. and Andretsch, D. (eds), *Multinational Corporations in the 1980s*, Cambridge: MIT Press.

Leksell, L. (1981) *Headquarters–Subsidiary Relationships in Multinational Corporations*, Stockholm: EFI/IIB.

Lessard, D. (1986) 'Finance and global competition: exploiting financial scope and coping with volatile exchange rates', in Porter, M. E. (ed.) *Competition in Global Industries*, Boston, MA: Harvard Business School Press.

Magee, S. P. (1977) 'Information and the multinational corporation: an appropriability theory of direct foreign investment', in Bhagwati, J. N. (ed.) *The New International Economic Order*, Cambridge, MA: MIT Press.

Otterbeck, L. (ed.) (1981) *The Management of Headquarters–Subsidiary Relationships in Multinational Corporations*, Aldershot, England: Gower.

Perlmutter, H. V. (1965) 'L'enterprise internationale — trois conceptions', *Revue Economique et Sociale*, No. 23.

Prahalad, C. K. (1975) *The Strategic Process in a Multinational Corporation*, doctoral dissertation, Harvard University.

Stopford, J. M. and Wells, L. T. (1972) *Managing the Multinational Enterprise*, New York: Basic Books.

Teece, D. J. (1977) 'Technology transfer by multinational firms: the resource cost of transferring technological know-how', *Economic Journal 87*, June.

Williamson, O. E. (1975) *Markets and Hierarchies: Analysis and Antitrust Implications*, New York: Free Press.

Part one

Conceptions of global management

Chapter one

Action in heterarchies — new approaches to managing the MNC

Gunnar Hedlund and Dag Rolander

New developments in the international business environment pose exciting challenges for the management of multinational corporations (MNCs). More ambitious global strategies necessitate closer co-ordination of activities. The diffusion of technological and managerial competence internationally gives rise to more vigilant competition, but also creates opportunities for scanning for new ideas by MNCs. As the task of managing becomes more complex, there are signs that currently prevailing models for organizing and controlling international operations do not suffice. Most experienced MNCs wrestle with striking a balance between straightforward but perhaps simplistic structures, on the one hand, and sophisticated but perhaps unwieldy ones, on the other. The dominating archetype in terms of formal organization structure — the global product division — shows signs of weakness.

A reassessment of current notions is needed in managerial practice as well as in research and theory. This chapter contains some suggestions for new approaches to two issues of crucial importance. First, it will be argued that the organizational structure and mode of control in highly international MNCs is shifting, and should shift, towards a model which we call heterarchy. This entails a geographical diffusion of core strategic activities and co-ordinating roles, a break with the notion of one uniform hierarchy of decisions as well as organizational positions, and an increased focus on normative control mechanisms. Second, frames of reference for the understanding of the MNC's relationship to its environment are proposed. Traditional views of strategy as building on analysis of given strengths and weaknesses, with a strong focus on the immediate competitive environment, are discussed and found to be too restrictive. It will be argued that stronger emphasis should be put on learning and the search for opportunities, and on action aimed at reshaping the environment. With this emphasis, our conception of 'strategy' is different from some predominant views in the strategy field. Elements of an alternative framework will be put forth.

The chapter is divided into four parts. The first section summarizes and discusses an important stream of research which originates in the hypothesis that 'structure follows strategy'. We group this research under the label of the strategy–structure paradigm (SSP). This paradigm has been very influential in both research and MNC practice, sometimes through intermediation by academics and consultants, but largely in an implicit, unconscious way. We will debate some basic characteristics and critical assumptions inherent in the approach. The subsequent section outlines an alternative framework and discusses, in turn, 'structure', 'strategy' and 'environment'. In spite of a wish to depart from relational logic (Angyal 1941), an attempt is also made to discuss the complex relationships between these three parts. The third section gives illustrative empirical support for our theoretical arguments. Most of the examples are taken from Swedish MNCs. Finally, the chapter is summarized and avenues for further research are suggested.

The strategy–structure paradigm

The kind of business history research pioneered by Chandler (1962) has been an important basis for much thinking on international business management. One basic concluion was that changes in the environment of the firm lead to changes in its strategy, which in turn generated changes in the internal structure of the corporation. Each step required time, and the lag in response was often long, sometimes too long to secure survival of the firm. 'Strategy' was conceived of in terms of four main dimensions: growth, degree and type of vertical integration, geographical extension, and degree of product diversification. The definition of 'structure' encompassed both formal and informal aspects, and the focus was on lines of authority and communication on the one hand, and information and data flows on the other. Environmental developments mentioned by Chandler are changes in population, income, and technology. The weaving together of the elements of the framework provided a rich, vivid and convincing picture of the emergence of the giant multi-divisional corporation in the United States. The story is further documented and refined in *'The Visible Hand'* (1977).

Chandler's work, it should be noted, is not normative, but a description and explanation of business developments in the US over a period of a century. The causal relationships suggested are observations in the history of managerial capitalism and important as such. When we join in the following debate with the strategy–structure paradigm, it is a debate with the notion that a firm should act as if there was a clear causal chain from the environment, over strategy to structure; and with the notion that the firm should conceptualize its 'strategy' and 'structure' along the dimensions chosen by Chandler.

Later works, such as Teece (1977), Caves (1980), Chandler and Daems (1980), Williamson (1981), and Chandler (1987), analyse also non-US firms, concentrating on the emergence of MNCs, and provide theoretical arguments from (mainly) the transaction cost tradition.

Before turning to applications in the area of multinational business strategy and management, it is of interest to highlight some aspects of Chandler's (1962) work which are important for the further discussion and of particular relevance for understanding the MNC.

- First, there is a definite sequence in time and with regard to causality. Environment leads strategy, which leads structure. Empirical evidence suggested that the reverse order of causality was not common.
- Second, there were significant time lags in adapting to new realities.
- Third, developments were uniform, in the sense that similar environmental and strategic factors impacted on all firms, and in the sense that a given set of such factors tended to produce similar structural responses in different firms.
- Fourth, the strategy dimensions were all 'expansionary': growth, not decline; vertical integration, not disintegration; diversification, not concentration; geographical expansion, not contraction.
- Fifth, and reflecting a mode of analysis as well as practice and thinking in corporations, strategy and environment were broken down into separate dimensions or variables, and archetypes of structure adapted to the combined changes along these dimensions were formulated (such as the functional structure and the divisionalized structure.)

These points will be discussed below, and it will be argued that the reality of the modern MNC can be interpreted in ways radically different from the reality documented by Chandler. Consequently, a conceptual framework for describing and understanding strategic processes of the MNC can be developed along lines different from those underlying the SSP.

17

A stream of thoughts related to the SSP is the 'contingency school'. The basic idea is that management systems and corporate structures do and should depend on environmental and strategic 'contingencies'. The literature abounds with suggestions of critical contingencies, and no summary will be attempted. Suffice it here to note that one important part of research focuses on the degree of uncertainty and complexity of the environment. The causal link implied is often from environment straight to structure, conceived of in terms rather different from Chandler's (organic-mechanistic, such as in Burns and Stalker 1961; or mechanisms of differentiation and integration, such as in Lawrence and Lorsch 1967). Corporate strategy as an intervening variable has also been introduced, however, and managerial choice of strategy is emphasized by some writers (Child 1972).

A good summary of developments in the SSP and contingency paradigms is found in Galbraith and Nathanson (1978). The importance of the nature of information flows for the design of organizational structure, in the broad sense of the words, is emphasized here. The informational complexity facing the firm, rather than broader environmental or strategic factors, is seen as determining the way the firm is managed. (Thompson [1967] is an important source and developer of such ideas.) The hypothesis of consistency between structural elements as crucial is also discussed. The consistency view gives a less deterministic picture of corporate structure than the SSP (including contingency) views.

In international business research, Stopford and Wells (1972) is an example of the adoption of the SSP. The most important strategy dimensions, geographical spread and product diversification, are related to structural archetypes such as the mother-daughter structure, the international division structure and the global product division. Many studies have followed similar paths. Franko (1976) is one of the most important. Egelhoff (1984) is interesting in that the volume of foreign manufacturing (not only sales) is explicitly considered as a strategy dimension.

Although some injustice is done to the authors within the field, we think it is fair to say that international business research has dealt with a fairly low number of strategic dimensions. There is not much to be found on two of Chandler's four variables — growth and vertical integration — as far as more detailed implications for managerial practice are concerned. Theoretical work on the reasons for the existence of MNCs does focus on these dimensions. (See, for example, the literature inspired by transaction cost theory, such as Buckley and Casson 1976.) Later conceptions of strategy dimensions and 'generic strategies' (such as in Porter 1980) have not really been discussed thoroughly as to the structural implications in MNCs. Fombrun (1983) investigates the association between Porter's generic strategies and structural solutions, but does not find any strong relationships.

The problems of deriving appropriate structures from given strategies is illustrated already in Stopford and Wells' (1972) discussion of what happens when both geography and product scope is very diversified. A number of responses are suggested, but no clear archetype emerges. Practising managers also often find reasoning in SSP terms somewhat restrictive, and often — in our experience — claim 'historical' or 'personal' factors as equally important. They also find living with supposedly ill-adapted structures easier than the theorists of strategic 'fit' would expect. (See Hedlund 1978, 1984 for illustrations in the Swedish context.)

Recent contributions to the discussion of management of the MNC tend to stress the indeterminacy of structural response. Bartlett (1986) emphasizes that national administrative heritage, in addition to task demands, influences the structure. He also argues for a more flexible organizational form and more flexible management systems in general. Work by Doz and Prahalad (1986) also emphasizes the importance of organizational capability to deal simultaneously with global and local challenges, in a way stressing internal over — but not unrelated to — external factors. Furthermore, they stress the importance of 'balance' and 'balanced individuals'. Thus, there are indications both from practice and in academic writings that there are some fundamental problems in applying the strategy–structure framework to the task of effectively managing the MNC. Four such important sets of problems can be identified and are discussed below. (Most of the points have been made by other authors. Good discussions of the issues involved are found in, for example, Weick 1969; Miles and Snow 1978; Hall and Saias 1980; Child and Kieser 1981; Peters 1984. Rarely, however, are MNCs the prime object of analysis.)

Problems with the SSP approach

First, the SSP approach leads to contradictory contingencies. 'On the one hand, you need to co-ordinate over product lines, on the other over geographical territories . . . .' There are no clear predictions of structural solutions, and in practice a multitude of patterns can be observed. This may have to do with a too narrow interpretation of strategic demands. Some of the contingency school's conceptions give less ambiguous predictions. Returning to analysis of the effects of environmental uncertainty may therefore prove fruitful. However, the conclusions are rather abstract (like proposing organic vs mechanistic structures), and the empirical support from MNCs is not overwhelming. Environmental hetero-geneity also gives contradictory signals to managers who try to adapt their structure according to the SSP. Growth is not to be found everywhere, vertical integration makes sense in some countries and industries and not in others, the degree of environ-mental uncertainty varies over the globe, etc.

Second, the dimensions of strategy and structure covered by the SSP do not easily capture important aspects of the reality of MNCs. There are frequent calls for richer conceptualization of strategy and structure (see, for example, Caves 1980), but actual research is more limited. There are many issues for which few clear answers exist.

The 'informal structure' of the MNC is one example of this. It has frequently been noted that the formal organization chart (which can be classified using archetypical structures) does not reflect the management processes considered most important. How to relate different models of the 'informal structure' to strategies and environmental conditions is a task so far only marginally addressed.

Yet another issue is how to set up an organization that can work with heterogenous buyer and supplier relationships: that is, simul-taneously handle various degrees of vertical integration within one organization. For example, how should a firm manage a distribu-tion network consisting of a mixture of sales subsidiaries, agents, and other contractual arrangements such as joint ventures. Related to this are questions concerning what structures and organizational processes accommodate and support changes in the form of estab-lishment abroad (see Kogut 1989, in this volume, Chapter 2), such as the transition from a joint sales venture to a wholly owned manufacturing and sales subsidiary; and which management pro-cesses support more rapid internationalization processes, such as annual doubling of foreign sales over a few years.

Scanning is another important area. The 'scientification' of knowledge raises the question of which strategies and structures deal effectively with search for information and fast combination of information from different fields, in terms of both geography and substance, into opportunities for the firm. Major changes in information technology, such as real on-line direct horizontal communication between nodes in the organization's 'periphery', imply that basic structural forms will be, and can be, affected. (See Hagström 1989 and Ledin 1989, in this volume, Chapters 7 and 13.)

In oligopolistic highly international industries, firms have designed 'global' strategies emphasizing mutual hostage positions and oligopolistic imitation. In such a setting what is the real role of a small subsidiary on your global competitor's home ground, and how should a unit be managed? Bartlett and Ghoshal (1986) have provided some answers and fruitful ideas.

Third, empirical research seems to indicate less determination in the choice of structural solutions than rigid adherence to the SSP would imply. The mother–daughter structure has survived much longer than 'reasonable' in Europe, for example. Even with environmental and strategic factors approximately constant, different firms successfully appear to be able to live with different structures, including the 'softer' sides of structure. The impression of freedom of choice is strengthened when one considers that concepts such as 'the mother–daughter structure' mask a great variety of practices. Consistency arguments about 'fit' between elements of structure, rather than between strategy and structure only, have been put forth by many authors. (See, for example, Hedlund 1978; Galbraith and Nathanson 1978; Leksell 1981.) However, often the question of what constitutes a 'fit' is not really answered. Even if such answers could be given, the logic of the argument is hardly reconcilable with a clear prediction of the entire structure of the firm from single elements of the same.

The structural voluntarism observed in practice is probably one of the reasons for the re-emergence of analysis of culture as a mechanism of integration. Whatever the formal organization and systems used, a common corporate culture may tie the firm's members together and focus efforts intangibly but forcefully. This return of the normative is, in our view, of great importance in the study of organizations. The complexities of interaction between national and corporate cultures in MNCs gives rise to interesting problems. (See Adler and Jelinek 1986.)

Fourth, SSP implies a rather passive and reactive approach on the part of managers. Environment is leading, and before any structural change is initiated, it should be scrutinized in terms of the strategic imperatives. When things are changing fast, this may be too slow an approach.

Furthermore, there is an assumption of an almost epistemological character involved here. The environment is seen as something given outside the organization, not as something defined and created by the latter. The recent advances along lines of reasoning developed from the industrial organization literature are one example. The relevant environment is defined as the 'industry', which is seen as common to all members of the same. This severely constrains the understanding of, particularly, strategies in scientifically and industrially new fields (See Rolander 1989.) This is recognized by proponents of the competitive strategy school (see Porter 1980, Chapter 10), but in our view the difficulties are encountered also in analysing and acting in 'mature industries'.

Strategy is thus seen as largely derived from environment. In the same way, structure is derived from strategy. In spite of the criticism of a passive view of structure by many authors, the logic of starting with strategy — or some more encompassing concept such as 'task demands' (Bartlett 1986) or 'information processing demands' (Kagono 1981) is prevalent. Davis (1982) argued that this must be so since one has to know what to do (strategy) before one can concentrate on how to do it (structure). However, one may retort, what one sets out to do depends on the given structure. Furthermore, increasingly the modern MNC has to select what environment to be in and discover what to do, and intelligent design and use of the structure of the firm is crucial in this respect. We will return to this argument later.

Outlines of an alternative framework

The foregoing discussion indicates that a guiding paradigm for understanding and informing action in the modern MNC is lacking. Valuable insights have been gained from the SSP approach, and from criticism of it in the organization theory and strategy fields. However, there is a need for synthesis and integration. Below, we will suggest the outlines of such a synthesis.

A sketch of the directions of change is provided by discussing Figure 1.1 which depicts the logic of the SSP approach and elements of an alternative view. SSP conceives of the environment as given constraints, common to actors in the (given) field, such as an industry. Strategy emerges as deduced action programmes. Structure is a logical response to the demands for action, and conceived of as alternative hierachical structures, with other co-ordinating mechnisms subordinated to the selected basic structure.

In an alternative logic, which we argue is both more descriptively realistic and more useful in practice, things do not necessarily start in the environment. The structure of the corporation is seen as embodying strong elements of heterarchy, where many centres of several different kinds (e.g. in terms of functional, geographical, or product responsibility) are co-ordinated increasingly through normative means. The structure is designed in order to utilize the symbiotic potential in the environment (Perlmutter 1984), which is seen as something to a large extent created by the firm, and unique to it. To avoid the connotations of calculated premeditation

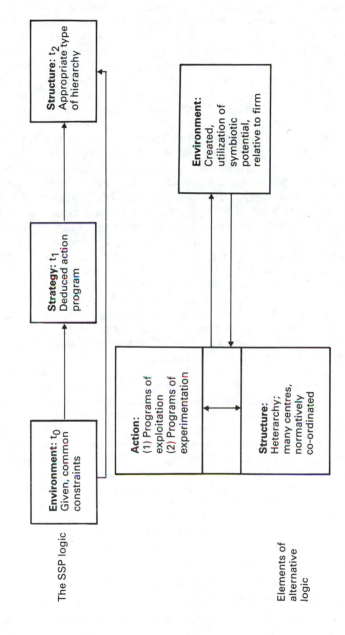

Figure 1.1 The SSP logic and elements of an alternative logic

The SSP logic

Environment: t_0
Given, common constraints

Strategy: t_1
Deduced action program

Structure: t_2
Appropriate type of hierarchy

Elements of alternative logic

Action:
(1) Programs of exploitation
(2) Programs of experimentation

Structure:
Heterarchy; many centres, normatively co-ordinated

Environment:
Created, utilization of symbiotic potential, relative to firm

inherent in the concept of 'strategy', what the firm does is seen as action, involving both programmes of exploitation of given (in the short run) environments, capabilities and resources and programmes of experimentation, changing relationships to the external world as well as internally. These programmes of experimentation embody a heuristic search orientation, deliberately adopted to escape the tyranny of inordinate time lags of response to changing conditions. (For an interesting and related distinction between 'autonomous' and 'induced' strategic behaviour, see Burgelman 1983.)

The reluctance to separate strategy and structure in our alternative scheme, will be explained in detail later. Here, two initial points will be made. First, structure–strategy–environment are so closely intertwined that relationships between them are almost definitional. In fact, not seeing the strong 'strategic' choices involved in setting the structure of a firm is one of the dangers of the 'classical' approach. Other things than focusing upon the articulated strategy dimensions happen, so the structure almost becomes the strategy. Disregarding such interlinkages would be to sacrifice truth for simplicity. Miller's (1987) discussion of 'configurations' of strategy and structure aspects represent a desirable complexification.

Second, the need to identify logical and causal primacy is perhaps less pronounced in practice than in theory. For a manager the important thing is to know something about what is likely to happen when certain things are initiated. One is likely to have to do things in all three 'realms' to be successful, and waiting for the environment to decide is no good. Although, of course, environment and task agendas will affect the internal working of the firm, in a way the structure is the foundation upon which environment and strategy are 'resting'. An often forgotten point is that the notion of an environment is relative to that of a focal system. Consequently, every environment is uniquely defined by one particular such system. A rigorous model of the kind described in the upper part of Figure 1.1 is thus a logical impossibility, and structure must be tied back to environment, unless one selects to let 'evironment' stand for something very broad. The model has to be recursive.

Recognizing the difficulties of starting from a model we are criticizing in outlining an alternative, we shall still in turn discuss each of the components in Figure 1.1 and try to sketch how they could be interpreted.

Structure as heterarchy

The concept of the heterarchical MNC is proposed in Hedlund (1986). While this structure obviously is not a prerequisite for acting and relating to the environment, even in daring ways, as conceived in Figure 1.2, we believe that heterarchical elements in organizations support, in particular, programmes of experimentation and an active stance *vis-à-vis* the environment. In general, the main characteristics of the heterarchical MNC are:

1. *Many centres, of different kinds.* 'Headquarter functions' are geographically diffused, and no dimension (product, country, function) is uniformly superordinate. There may be, for a Swedish MNC: a financial centre in Brussels; the largest division HQ in London; an R&D centre with group responsibility for certain products in India; a regional unit in Hong Kong with a role of co-ordinating activities in that whole area; a strategic project *ad hoc* group on integrating global manufacturing; and an Italian unit with global responsibility for component supply. (All these are real examples from Swedish MNCs, although all of them are not found together, yet, in similar form in any single firms.) The overlap of responsibility following from multi-centredness is seen as an advantage.

   Thus, the heterarchical firm does not worry too much about logical inconsistency, but instead focuses on practical coherence. The structure is flexible over time: at a certain moment, global product management is most important; next year perhaps integration of total R&D resources is paramount. The flexibility and multidimensionality goes beyond what is possible in a formal matrix organization, which often tends to rigidify rather than — which is the intention — allow fast and flexible response. (See Hedlund 1986, pp. 22–33 for further discussion of the difference between heterarchy and matrix).

2. *A strategic role for foreign subsidiaries,* not only for 'their' company, but for the corporation as a whole. Corporate level strategy has to be both formulated and implemented in a geographically scattered network.

3. *A wide range of governance modes,* between pure market and hierarchy. A heterarchical MNC use joint ventures in one area, externalizing transactions and handling in-house business on an arms-length basis in another, and internalizing and insisting on governance by management fiat in a third context. This flexibility in governance mode makes the heterarchical MNC a meta-institution, whose unique role is the effective design, on the basis of experience, of institutional arrangements for specific tasks.

4. *Integration primarily by normative integration,* rather than by calculative or coercive mechanisms (Etzioni 1961). 'Corporate

culture', 'management ethics', 'style' and ..ilar concepts become critical in understanding why a heterarchy does not break down into anarchy.

5. *Coalitions with other firms* and with other types of actors. This will often be necessary in order to utilize potentials for synergy in the global environment.

6. *Radical problem orientation*, rather than starting from existing resources, or from competitive positions in narrow fields of business.

7. *Holographic organization*, in the sense that information about the whole is stored in each part of the company. The basic strategy, guiding principles of behaviour, and access to detailed information are widely shared in the organization. Information technology is of crucial importance here, and is likely to be one of the forces leading companies to heterarchy. (See Hagström 1989, Chapter 7 in this volume.) Corporate culture may be seen as the analogue of the laser light which gives 'meaning' to a hologram.

8. *A 'firm as a brain' model of action*, rather than a 'brain of the firm' model. The entire firm is supposed to think, and act directly on thinking. Thought informs action, but action in each part of the firm is also seen as an experiment informing thought.

9. *Action programmes for seeking and generating new firm-specific advantages* through global spread. Exploitation of given, home country based advantages is emphasized in the theory of the MNC, but this bias should not entrap the MNC in its action.

Obviously, the heterarchical model has precursors and analogues in the suggestions by, for example, Mintzberg (1973) for 'anarchic organization', Hedberg *et al.* (1976) for 'organizational tents', and Starbuck (1985) for 'acting first and thinking later'. We feel, however, that the totality of elements of the heterarchy model entails a new conception. Furthermore, we argue that the 'messy' structure is relevant for large, geographically dispersed organizations, whereas most of the proponents for anarchy-looking structures reserve them for smaller units, and for particular kinds of environments characterized by rapid change, or strong professional norms.

Most of the characteristics of heterarchy have to do with structure, but a few of them are intimately linked to strategy. (Points 3, 5, 6 and 9 above, in particular.) This is an indication that it is possible, and perhaps unavoidable, to think in terms of packages of strategy and structure characteristics. A main point, however, is that the structural items are most important and necessities in order to carry out the broad types of action indicated.

Obviously, the need for heterarchical structure varies. Although one strong force for it is that it conforms to demands for autonomy and structuring of work life around self-selected values, there is scope for more rigidly and permanently defined structures. Thus, the degree of heterarchy becomes an interesting variable. Note that functional and (product) divisionalized structures are both low on heterarchy, in spite of mapping different kinds of hierarchy.

There is also scope for distinguishing between different action programmes based on global reach. (See Kogut 1983, for an interesting discussion of types of globality advantages, and Vahlne and Nordström 1986, for an effort to analyse 'advantage cycles'.) At least three types, all supported by heterarchical structures, can be distinguished:

(a) Action programmes aiming at market creation. This applies mostly in new or rapidly changing fields of business.
(b) Action programmes for the exploitation of comparative advantages between countries and regions, and the co-ordination of activities to optimize on such, rather long-run, possibilities. This applies acutely for companies in 'mature industries', where global restructuring is taking place.
(c) Action programmes for flexible global arbitrage. This is most relevant in the financial field, but also in trading firms. ([b] could be seen as a subset of [c], but then 'arbitrage' would stand for something very broad. We have chosen to use it in the sense of exploiting relatively short-run differences in prices between locations and actors.)

Strategy as action: heuristic search orientation and exploitation of current potential

Previous research within the SSP has not been clear on how correct strategies can be carved out of an environmental analysis. Some critical issues are identified, but the indeterminacy of the choice is also emphasized. It is, for example, by no means clear how one deduces the adequate levels of diversification, in terms of products and geographical markets served, from an analysis of the competitive environment; nor is it straightforward to infer from an industry analysis what generic strategy a given firm should choose. Thus, the frameworks based on SSP fail to provide statements on exactly how the strategy of the firm depends on the environment. Finding the, or at least one, correct strategy is a crucial step left rather vague.

Our view is that this hesitation is very sound. Strategy should be conceptualized at another level of abstraction. Basically, we suggest that strategy be seen as action patterns over time, of which there are two intertwined aspects. Firstly, there are programmes of experimentation, where the primary aim is to seek opportunities. Key words in experimentation are search and learning. Secondly, there are programmes of exploitation, where the primary focus is on the effective utilization of given resources and the appropriation of value stemming from current activities. Exploitation aims at capturing the current potential; experimentation aims at changing the future potential.

Exploitation and experimentation should not be confused with a call for increased emphasis on innovation and entrepreneurship on the part of MNCs, although we do not in general disagree with these calls. Experimentation is not the responsibility of the R&D department. We argue that experimentation and exploitation are aspects of actions taken in any activity of the firm, and that the emphasis on either one of these processes varies, and should vary, from one activity to another and over time for the organization as a whole. Both processes are present on the assembly line as well as in the encounter between a salesman and his customer. Activities differ in terms of degree of experimentation — it is not either one or the other. It is an organization-wide responsibility to ensure that adequate levels of experimentation are upheld in all activities.

The GM/Toyota joint venture to manufacture Toyota designed cars in Fremont, California, sold under the Chevrolet brand name, is a clear example of the two intertwined processes. To Toyota, the joint venture was a first experience of the operation of a US assembly plant for cars, which tested, in the US context, the viability of organizational abilities developed in Japan. It was also (and still is) a business venture which exploited Toyota resources which were transferred from Japan and enabled Toyota to increase its share of the US car market. If performance is measured only in terms of successful exploitation (financial performance of the joint venture, increased market share and the like) the venture may appear to be of limited significance. If, however, the less easily quantifiable value of the experience gained in Fremont is taken into account, Toyota may be able to avoid costly mistakes in its future US plants, operated independently of GM, and thus significantly enhance future financial performance. To the extent that this experience can also be exploited in the trucks business, the Fremont experiment will be immensely successful financially even if it can be shown to be less profitable as an isolated activity. Strategically speaking, the joint venture was probably above all an experiment and its mission was learning.

Similarly, GM's concerns can be put in terms of experimentation (with Japanese plant organization) and exploitation (filling a gap in its product range and exploiting distribution capacity already in place). Obviously, an organization's capability to learn from experience is as crucial as the initial design of the experiment. For example, it seems that US automobile manufacturers have benefited relatively little historically from the know-how in their European subsidiaries (Ford Europe, Opel, Talbot), although the potential for realistic experimentation with small car and performance car production certainly was there. Our hypothesis is that ambitions for learning are best served by heterarchical design of the corporation.

An admitted travesty of 'standard' strategy literature is to say that it rather consists of algorithms for analysis of given problems. (At least this goes for the normative literature. Much of the more descriptive research does emphasize learning and experimentation.) An example from research on ants, inspired by Prigogine's (1976) theories of dissipative structures and the emergence of higher levels of order in physical systems, serves to illustrate further the dichotomy of action into experimentation and exploitation.

Ant colonies need to find and exploit food sources. If one ant finds a good source, he (let us assume he is male) communicates this to his comrades by repeatedly walking up and down a track between the source and the antheap, in the process leaving a chemical substance with a characteristic smell behind him. The more he, and his comrades, walk the food trail, the stronger is the smell, and more of his friends are inclined to follow it. We have here a simple positive feedback system, allowing success to multiply and the food source to be fully exploited.

However, if all ants followed the track, it would be over-crowded and too many would continue to dwell on it even after the dead hare (or whatever) was devoured. Therefore, the ants are pro-grammed to deviate from the beaten track now and then, and so to increase the likelihood of finding new food sources. The degree of deviancy is an important parameter, setting the balance between exploitation of the known environment and the investment in search in new fields. If the goodies and baddies of ant life change very fast, the proportion of deviant behaviour should be high. In more stable conditions, perhaps it is better to have more con-formists.

Fast experimentation in multiple directions, and systems enabling the firm to learn from experience, are crucial in a global environment where change is fast and competition virulent. The is, however, one other aspect of action programmes which needs to be stressed. The 'food sources' of MNCs are not so much lying around as created. Global reach means that there are opportunities for utilizing the synergistic potential by combining elements hitherto not combined. Adding one technology to another, or taking product A to country B to serve demands for a new application C of the basic technology, or investing in building a system of distribution for products of a certain kind together with the prospective customers; these are all examples. The environment does not 'hang around' to be analysed. Rather, it is a canvas to be painted, and this makes experimentation the relevant approach.

The discussion above is relevant for all firms, but of course more so for some than for others. Why bring it up in the context of an analysis of MNCs? In our view, there ar three main reasons. First, the environment and the strategic options are more open to an MNC than to a domestic firm. It is necessary to select action programmes, since not all continents and product areas can be concentrated upon. The possibilities of deciding on the basis of a priori analysis are furthermore more limited, wherefore experimentation is the favoured course of action. Second, the strategic turbulence is greater for an MNC. To have a great number of experiments going ensures against being trapped strategically, and generates opportunities which cannot be analysed into existence. Third, a potent rationale for the modern MNC is exactly to utilize the slumbering potential for economic progress by combining resources with different national origins in new ways. Finding these opportunities requires non-trivial levels of experimentation. Bringing them to successful completion of course also requires cross-border mechanisms for exploitation.

Environment as the creative utilization of symbiotic potential

The point that environment is a relative concept was stressed above. The firm defines, selects, and creates its environment. Our contention is that it is not fruitful to consider the environment solely in terms of given constraints. Particularly on a global scale, the scope for creating new opportunities by combining elements so far unconnected, and to select the structure of the firm's environment, is very large. This posture implies environmental scanning systems very different from those directed at 'early warnings' concerning existing product markets, competitors, etc. Good systems for this latter purpose require more heterarchical organizations. The implications of the much more ambitious aim of creating new markets are even more radical.

Supporting viewpoints are provided by several authors. Vernon (1979) discusses the changing nature of the relationship between the MNC and the global environment in his review of the product cycle theory. His view of 'global scanners' includes active search for new technologies. Bartlett and Ghoshal (1986) analyse the role of foreign subsidiaries of MNCs in generating information about the competitive as well as other aspects of the environment. In organization theory, Weick's (1969) emphasis on the 'enacted environment' is close to our argument, although we want to stress even more the actual creation of domains. Nonaka's (1987) conception of information creation — rather than just information processing — is also consistent with our reasoning.

The standard analysis of the environment of MNCs includes a strong focus on competitors. No doubt this is healthy, but there are also dangers in this approach. Just following what others are doing may leave a company as an eternal second. Others are innovating and reaping first mover advantages. Opportunities for novelty from within the firm are neglected. One antidote to such dangers is to spend energy also on analysing units in the environment actually or potentially complementing the firm. For research oriented companies, perhaps universities are as much part of the relevant milieu as competitors, who are anyway by definition at the moment selling products based on yesterday's technology. Thus, focusing upon different types of actors, rather than on a homogenous industry, is one consequence of a more active stand towards the environment. (On a theoretical level, the discussion in Emery and Trist (1965), on associations between dissimilar organizations as a response to turbulence is of great interest here.)

As a final note on the interpretation of the environment, we would like to point to the structuring of industrial progress in 'development blocks' (Dahmén 1950) or 'growth poles' (Perroux 1961). Dahmén belongs to the institutionalist school in economics and was highly influenced by the works of Schumpeter (1911, 1942). This line of thought criticizes economics for paying too much attention to static theories — the results of economic transformation rather than the transformation process itself — and for providing taxonomic theory rather than an analysis of economic developments in time.

Dahmén identified and described how a business potential thanks to advances in technology (whether in production, management or distribution), could not be profitably utilized before complementary advances had been made in other areas. The problem could be of a fundamental nature, meaning that the missing pieces were beyond reasonable reach for scientific or other reasons, or simply due to a time-lag because attention was directed at more urgent opportunities. In any case, bringing a development block to a successful completion required an ability to conceive the environment in broad terms and a capacity to participate in or stimulate parallel development and expansion of key parts of the system. Dahmén found that growth patterns were cumulative following a breakthrough for a development block. When missing links in one area had been found, and complemented with necessary management skills and financing, possibilities opened up also for earlier advances, which had so to say been stocked in inventory. Business historians in other countries have made similar observations. For a review, see Freeman (1982).

'New technology' seems to entail a lot of combining developments in seemingly unrelated fields, and building a human and social infrastructure enabling the realization of such synergies. The enlargement of perspective to the global arena means a quantum jump in possibilities for creating development blocks, and the MNC is one of the critical actors with a catalytic role in this respect.

Thus, the environment is not a mess of randomly scattered elements, but is ripe with 'cluster embryos', awaiting development. Location in the total system and intensity of interaction with critical components become of prime importance in order to take part in the fruition of such processes.

The relationship between environment, action, and structure

The most elusive part of our argument probably has to do not with any new aspects on each of the parts of the environment–strategy–structure model, but with the relationships between the parts. A few of the stipulations below can easily be understood in the language of the standard SSP, but some of the latter points require departing quite radically from the relational logic of the paradigm. We see seven main differences between a new model and the traditional one:

1. Structure is the final derivation in SSP, and in a sense fundamental and primary in our model. It determines what strategies can be carried out, and defines what environment is considered. It is the more permanent aspect of the triad, and it sets the values which guide action. These values are not seen as instruments in achieving some strategic objective. (Like hiring miserly managers to implement a cost-leadership strategy.) Instead, the values guide what strategy is contemplated. In fact, one hypothesis about the functioning of heterarchies is

that the engineering of 'strategies' is much easier than the engineering of values, and that therefore the former should follow from the latter.

One of the critical assets of a well-functioning MNC is its cadre of internationally experienced personnel, well versed also in the intricacies of intra-firm communication. This, together with the hardware and software of information management, constitutes the nervous system of the firm — its perceptive apparatus, information processing systems, and activators for response to opportunities and problems. This human system, even more than in the case of a national company, is the really fixed asset and sunk cost with very company bound use (cf. the analysis by Polanyi 1969, on 'tacit knowledge' and Arrow 1974). In Williamson's (1975) terms, these are the activities with an extreme degree of idiosyncracy. There is no market for these systems; they are valuable only to the firm that created them, and losing the carriers of the corporate nervous system is dramatic for any firm. This is not to say that a few individuals in top management cannot be replaced. In our view, one of the reasons for historical success of Swedish MNCs is the relatively broad-based, almost 'underground' network of personal international contacts and experience.

It is obvious from the above that the most important part of structure is, not the formal organization, but the less easily describable management systems, communication processes, and the corporate culture. This conforms to an emerging consensus in the study of MNCs. (See Galbraith and Nathanson 1978; Bartlett 1981; Kagono 1981; Doz and Prahalad 1986; and many others.)

2. The relationship is not deterministic in the sense that a given structure goes with a certain strategy, in terms of traditional strategy classifications. Only a broad correspondence, relating degree and type of heterarchy to degree of experimentation in strategy and type of global advantage sought, can be stated.

    Indeed, we may have to give up the idea of prediction based on causal undirectional influence. Rather, we have to adopt the view that evolution as complex as that of an MNC is subject to the openness characteristic of Prigogine's dissipative structures. In a way, it is not surprising that the structural–strategic development of an MNC is at least as difficult to predict as that of a chemical substance. (See Prigogine 1976).

3. The relationship is not best interpreted as a deductive chain but as a system of learning, with negative and positive feedback

loops at several levels (Works by Bateson 1972, Watzlawick *et al.* 1974, Argyris 1976, Argyris and Schön 1981, are of great interest here). The important question for a manager becomes what 'strategy' is most conducive to fast learning and change of action, not what strategy is logically related to the structure of the environment, as presently perceived. There is a fallacy in believing that the basis for strategy can be identified in the present situation. Chances are that if you do something 'stupid' you may at least learn something interesting which can be applied in a different context. A degree of 'illogicality' is even necessary in order to break the constraints on learning imposed by clear definitions of relevant environment, strategies, and internal structure (cf. March's 1971 discussion of the 'technology of foolishness'). Particularly in a multinational context, efforts to deduce an optimal structure from explicit strategic priorities easily leads to neglect of opportunities, at the local level particularly. (See the conclusions of Davidson and Haspeslagh (1982) on the weaknesses of the global product division.)

4. The relationship is dynamic, rather than static. The main purpose of action on structure is not to adapt to external events, but to enable change in action and the segments of the environment explored. It is not assumed that 'fit' between the three elements at one certain point in time is very interesting. The core leadership of the company has as one of its most important tasks to ensure a degree of short-term instability, which over time amounts to stability. (Cf. the argument by Klein (1977) about the positive correlation between macro-stability and micro-instability.)

   Because best practice changes with innovations, 'fit', however conceived, will be an occasional phenomenon. Innovations and change may appear either gradually or in leaps, and organizational response, or adaptation to these circumstances, may be more or less radical. Timing of the organizational response is obviously a crucial issue. How much 'unfit' is accepted before major actions are carried out? A period of 'unfit' during which freedom of action is being built up can be followed by major, unexpected competitive thrusts over short time periods. This type of response can be contrasted with gradual, and perhaps obvious (for competitors), adaptation patterns in which a close 'fit' is continuously sought. An action programme can have more ambitious objectives than merely accomplishing a 'fit'. Parts of the game-plan can be redefined — the firm can be creative *vis-à-vis* its environment.

5. The relations are subject to a logic of creation, in addition to a logic of exploitation. This need not be taken in a mystic (or Marxist) sense. We simply mean that firms which aspire to survive in internationally integrated societies have to design their internal structure with a view to creating new markets, through interaction with their environment and with lots of experimentation. It will not suffice to exploit given positions, in a geographical, competitive, or other sense. Any strategy in product/ market terms will soon become outdated, so it would be very dangerous to lock one's structure into such frames.

6. Structure is not an instrument, but primarily a giver of meaning. This is the most esoteric of the points, but we find it difficult to avoid arriving at. If normative integration is the most powerful and flexible way of guiding an organization embarking on experimental strategies and efforts at global opportunity creation; if rather basic values and deeply embedded action orientations define the norms; and if such norms have to grow organically and are very hard to engineer in a predetermined direction (which all evidence indicates is the case): then it follows that structure is primary in a more profound sense than in terms of causality. We touched on the same point under point 1 above. An extension of the reasoning leads to the conclusion that environments and strategies should also harmonize in terms of the core beliefs of the organization.

    It is interesting to note that managers often find it easy to talk about whether businesses are compatible or not with their corporate culture. Large oil companies debated whether they did not need diversification projects on the scale of space exploration to function well, having failed with many smaller scale non-oil businesses. Exxon's problems with office automation are well known. Research into such 'mentalities' of corporations and industries may prove very interesting. (Perhaps the French historians can contribute in terms of methodology?)

    A radical position is to see the relationship between environment, strategy, and structure as aesthetical. Members of the organization, in order to function and feel well, must 'see' (hear?) the resonance between what they do, who they are, and what arena they are active in. The evolution over time, the company's history and vision for the future, should also make sense. This puts management scientists in the perhaps uncomfortable position of being more like art critics than expert engineers in commenting upon corporate life.

7. Finally, a system of dynamic processes of the kind described does not have the same bias for growth as one built on hierarchy. Promotion in a heterarchy could as well be horizontally as vertically, so the social and individual urge to grow is not there to the same extent. The trauma of projects spinning off from the core is not so great either. In fact, this is part of normal developments. Successes which do not fit well into the guiding thrust of the firm take on their own life in the periphery of the company, or completely outside it. Thus, although aiming for dynamism and change, heterarchically structured learning does not try to internalize all new developments. The focus on normative control sets limits for the size of the organization. The double hypothesis of a tight core, bound together by strong and shared values, on the one hand, and flexible cooperation with a periphery of units and individuals with looser attachment to this core, on the other, implies a sort of 'dual organization'. (See Hedlund (1986) for further elaboration of this point.) On a theoretical note, such solutions again indicate that the leadership of a large, modern MNC is meta-institutional, in the sense of elaborating systems of governance forms, where the simplistic, rigid, line between 'hierarchy' (inside the firm, to be managed) and 'market' (outside, to be dealt with at arm's length) is abandoned.

Examples in MNC practice

The discussion so far has been theoretical and speculative. In order to clarify the points and provide an indication of where the ideas come from empirically, we will report on some aspects of practice in Swedish MNCs. These facts are of course not randomly selected, and we do not pretend that they mirror average behaviour. Indeed, the hypothesis is that a few leading firms are now finding and inventing approaches to the new global challenges, and that there is no reason — given the inertia of organizational change — to expect tight conformity between practice and our conclusions concerning effective behaviour. Instead, the hypotheses have to be tested looking explicitly at performance. Therefore, the examples should be seen as illustrations only. They are, however, supported by previous research. (See Horvath 1975; Hedlund 1981, 1984; Hedlund and Åman 1984; Leksell 1981; Otterbeck 1981.)

Using Swedish examples has both advantages and disadvantages. MNCs from small countries face high degrees of environmental heterogeneity earlier in their development, and also cannot rely on one dominant market, which provides the backbone for the structure and action of the firm. On the other hand, the possibilities to draw conclusions for companies in other circumstances may be restricted. Since we put emphasis upon the structural characteristics, we will devote most of the discussion to these. So, is there any evidence of heterarchy around?

The diffusion of strategic functions can easily be observed. A few examples:

- Atlas Copco (rock drilling equipment, compressors, tools, etc.), through an acquisition years ago, has the headquarters of its largest division in Antwerp, Belgium. This has dramatically complexified flows of products, money, and people in the direction of an 'integrated network' model (Bartlett 1986).
- Esselte (office equipment, conglomerate) has its largest division headquartered in London. (It is listed on the New York stock exchange and is valued almost at par with the whole group.)
- SKF (ball bearings) has its central research laboratories in Holland. It also has built up a system for international product responsibility in the foreign units within the Global Forecasting and Supply System. This system started at a European level and is now expanding to include the US.
- Electrolux (white goods) has assigned to one of its European acquired companies a global co-ordinating role for component manufacturing and supplies, which is strategically critical in this industry.
- The merged operations of ASEA (electrical engineering) and Brown Boveri (Swiss, electrical engineering) are organized into business areas located in different countries.
- Several companies have created finance centres in Brussels, London or other cities outside Sweden to co-ordinate global financial flows.
- Datatronic (computer software) acquired much larger Victor Technologies (US), which will be an important know-how base.
- Tetra Pak (packaging) is headquartered in Switzerland, but has most of its R&D and manufacturing in Sweden.

If one includes less dramatic projects, the picture of geographical diffusion of 'central' functions, coupled with global integration from a scattered network of points, becomes quite convincing. There is still a research task to be done to thoroughly document this development, and we state it as a very strong hypothesis.

Concerning the importance of normative integration, the spectacular turn-arounds of SAS (airline) and ASEA include pronounced elements of installing a strong corporate culture. The most potent illustration, however, is perhaps found in Pharmacia (pharmaceuticals, biotechnology).

Pharmacia has instituted a unit called 'Personnel and Business Culture' (PBC). It exists on the group as well as on the division level. Its role is to uphold and articulate the strong identity of the firm, particularly in relation to acquired units abroad. It is given support by top management, which also insists on the use of an internally created language for strategic discussions and manage-ment decisions. PBC has formulated guiding corporate principles and spreads its message with substantial zeal.

Another mechanism used to hold together parts of the firm is that Pharmacia deliberately builds in overlap between divisions. This contrasts sharply with pratice in most MNCs trying to carve out clearly defined global product divisions. The need for cross-fertilization of ideas at the research stage as well as in marketing is seen as so great that total separation of responsibility areas would be dangerous. Thus, the formal structure is designed to be a bit fuzzy, in order to increase chances of creative synergy.

The total empirical picture is mixed, however. Many firms are busy trying to create global product divisions. Furthermore, historical reliance on normative and personal control is giving way to more financially oriented systems (Hedlund and Åman 1983). Our view is that, although it may make sense to many firms to decentralize international operations to divisions and other sub-units, there is a clear risk of an 'ethnocentric backlash', and of losing the rather unique global networks of loyalties and internal communication paths that carried Swedish MNCs internationaliza-tion historically.

Regarding flexibility of governance system, the tradition has been not to engage in joint ventures and coalition strategies. Historically, greenfield strategies were used, but lately acquisitions have become the favoured mode of international expansion. A very recent trend is that the reluctance to engage in collaborative schemes is breaking down. Ericsson is involved in co-operation with Honeywell as well as with Digital Equipment and IBM. Alfa-Laval acquired an early share of Genentech (USA), partly in order to benefit from technological developments in the genetical engineering field.

However, it is still fair to say that Swedish MNCs so far have not been leaders in the global alliance market. This could be seen partly as a reflection of strength; they have not had to enter into such arrangements (cf. the argument by Doz *et al.* 1986). It could also be a reflection of reluctance to accept foreign bodies into the delicate informal global structure, not yet having learnt to work in a 'dual system'. We have to conclude that the evidence is mixed on this point.

Holographic information processing has always been a, relatively, strong part of managing Swedish MNCs. The sharing of strategic information has gone further than in MNCs from most other home countries. (See Hedlund 1981, for comparative measures.) Lately, efforts at communicating the corporate credo have intensified. The most well-known campaign is the one at SAS, where detailed analysis of competitors was distributed to all employees. Furthermore, information technology is increasingly being used to facilitate horizontal communication, and to allow on-line distributed access to a wide range of data in all corners of the corporation (Hagström 1987).

Volvo's several gigantic internal educational programmes stress the importance of everybody knowing the basic thrust of the company, including its history. Also, investment in information technology is large, and there is an ambitious programme to bring broad cadres of managers up to date in knowledge of modern technology in general. Specialization of function, and of information access, is not seen as a viable overall strategy.

Volvo is interesting also with reference to radical problem orientation. Several of its top managers have taken leading roles in the debate and activities concerning Europe's fragile economic and technological position in the world. On a more local scale, the sponsoring of the Gothenburg Symphony Orchestra is seen more as an effort to improve the cultural environment for its employees than as promotion of products.

The fundamental distinction between exploitation of given advantages and creation of new advantages, on the basis of global reach, can also be illustrated. There are several versions of globalizing. One dramatic example of international restructuring of industries is Electrolux within white goods. Largely through acquisitions, Electrolux is now the only firm with a strong presence in the three crucial regions: Europe, North America and Japan. A key idea is transnational, and later transcontinental, integration and rationalization. Another clear exponent of this strategy is ESAB (welding), which today is the world's largest welding firm, dominating in Europe and having smaller but important positions also in the US.

Such active rationalization of industry structures is the most obvious global role, and need not be expressed in terms of heterarchy and other new concepts. Industry analysis (Porter 1980) does most of the analytical trick. However, it is striking to what extent the success of the campaigns mentioned above seems to depend on small, tightly knit teams of extremely dedicated individuals. The supported association between mature industries and formal control systems is not borne out in the Electrolux case, however. According to its present president, Electrolux does not have a formal organization chart. There is a clear emphasis on individual responsibility, doing things quickly, and in an Electrolux way of not complicating things and being very lean on overhead costs. In fact, the firm has an entrepreneurial image, 'maturity' notwithstanding. (Disregarding the gloom of diagnosed maturity, for example by stubbornly investing in R&D, seems to be one characteristic of so far very successful Swedish MNCs. See Sölvell 1987).

The more complex task of global scanning and development of new advantages through creation of new products and markets is harder to exemplify. The pharmaceutical companies do invest heavily in decentralized R&D. Pharmacia has concentrated on the US, for example through a large laboratory in La Jolla, California. They are also extremely active in Japan, building up R&D capacity in addition to marketing resources. Astra is also, emphasizing Japan. ASEA Robotics exhibits a clear pattern of heavy investment in technological capacity in the US and Japan, in addition to Sweden. In automobiles, Volvo has for long sourced important components in Japan, as have many other firms. Indeed, internationalizing on the basis of purchasing, rather than sales only, seems to be an emerging trend. Opportunities for internationalizing arise in all functional areas, and advanced firms are not tied to their marketing network, which historically has been a clear bias.

Unorthodox, more active approaches towards the environment can be found in Ericsson's development of the AXE public telecommunication switching system. This effort was set up together with the Swedish PTT as a joint company, Ellemtel. It was really a project organization, which took a very radical approach in rethinking what a telephone exchange really was. (See Ledin 1989, chapter 13 of this volume.) A joint venture with an important customer was one ingredient of the success, a flexible organizational solution outside the main structure was another.

Pharmacia's very close relations to Uppsala University is another indication of the importance of the complementors, in addition to the competitors, in the environment. In new, fast-moving, science-driven fields, it may even be impossible to know who the competitors of tomorrow (literally) will be. Exclusive focus on competitive strategy and industry analysis leads to paranoia and neglect of crucial success factors, which, in Pharmacia's case, have to do with the nurturing of the capacity for fast and creative utilization of scientific knowledge, combined with a solid understanding of customer needs.

Summary and conclusions

The strategy–structure paradigm (SSP) served to describe the historical evolution of the large, multidivisional firms. It was natural to use it in analysing the emergence of MNCs, and useful knowledge was generated and structured in this fashion. However, there are problems intrinsic to the SSP which are particularly pronounced in an analysis of the modern MNC. The needs for organizational innovation go beyond the scope of SSP so far conceived. Dimensions of both strategy and structure need to be enriched, and the relationship between them needs to be reassessed.

An approach can be sketched, and the direction of conceptual as well as practical development can be identified. The clear articulation of the trends is so far only to be seen in a minority of firms, but our hypothesis is that they will set the example for the future. The elements of such a revision in the MNC context include:

- Building strategy on advantages inherent in global coverage rather than in narrowly defined technology or product areas.
- A view of 'structure' as a complex heterarchy of geographically diffused but globally co-ordinated core functions, tied together primarily through normative integration mechanisms.
- A holographic quality characterizing information processing and storage, so that the actions and state of the entire organization are intimately known at each node in the communication network constituting the nervous system of the firm.
- Corporate action as programmes of experimentation, entailing heuristic search for opportunities and fast learning, and programmes of exploitation of historical strengths.
- Exploration of the environment in terms of its synergistic potential where an active, selective, catalytic stance replaces a passive defensive one.

Many examples of structures and action consistent with our model can be found, and together they amount to empirical support for continued research along the lines suggested. Future efforts in two areas are particularly needed.

First, the pioneering efforts to create a new type of MNC, building on global presence rather than historical and nationally derived strengths, need to be closely assessed. Probably, clinical methods are necessary, and perhaps action research approaches are also desirable. The fact that the hypotheses involved are really normative, rather than pertaining to average behaviour of MNCs, makes explicit consideration of performance effects necessary.

Second, the hypotheses in our framework are so far only loosely phrased, and need to be stated in less ambiguous terms. A modified 'contingency view', explicating the conditions under which heterarchy, learning and search, and other proposed approaches are most fruitful, is required. A number of factors need to be taken into account. Examples are: the character of the knowledge base (involving many or only one basic technology); the geographical dispersion of country comparative advantages over functions in the industrial arena explored; the rate of technical change, and the intrinsic culture-generating capacity of the end product.

References

Adler, N. J. and Jelinek, M. (1986) 'Is "organization culture" culture bound?, *Human Resource Management*, vol. 25, 1.

Angyal, A. (1941) 'Foundations for a science of personality', Cambridge: Harvard University Press.

Argyris, C. (1976) 'Single-loop and double-loop models in research on decision-making', *Administrative Science Quarterly* 21(3).

Argyris, C. and Schön, D. A. (1981) *Organizational Learning*, Boston, Mass: Addison-Wesley.

Arrow, K. J. (1974) *The Limits of Organization*, New York: W. W. Norton.

Bartlett, C. A. (1981) 'Multinational structural change: evolution versus reorganization', in Otterbeck, L. (ed.) *The Management of Headquarters-Subsidiary Relationships in Multinational Corporations*, Aldershot: Gower.

    (1987) 'Building and managing the transnational: the new organizational challenge', in Porter, M .E. (ed.) *Competition in Global Industries*, Boston: Harvard Business School Press.

Bartlett, C. A. and Ghoshal, S. (1986) 'Tap your subsidiaries for global reach', *Harvard Business Review*, November–December.

Bateson, G. (1972) *Steps Towards an Ecology of Mind*, New York: Ballantine.

Buckley, P. J. and Casson, M. (1976) *The Future of Multinational Enterprise*, New York: Holmes and Meyer.

Burgelman, R. A. (1983) 'A model of the interaction of strategic behaviour, corporate context, and the concept of strategy', *Academy of Management Review*, vol. 8, No. 1.

Burns, T. and Stalker, G. M. (1961) *The Management of Innovation*, London: Tavistock.

Caves, R. E. (1980) 'Industrial organization, corporate strategy and structure', *Journal of Economic Literature*, 18.

Chandler, A. D., Jr. (1962) *Strategy and Structure*, Boston, Mass: MIT Press.
— (1977) *The Visible Hand*, New York: McGraw-Hill.
— (1987) 'The evolution of modern global competition', in Porter, M. E. (ed.) *Competition in Global Industries*, Boston: Harvard Business School Press.
Chandler, A. D., Jr. and Daems, H. (eds) (1980) 'Managerial hierarchies', Cambridge, MA, and London, England: Harvard University Press.
Child, J. (1972) 'Organizational structure, environment and performance: the role of strategic choice', *Sociology*, 6.
Child, J. and Kieser, A. (1981) 'Development of organizations over time', in Starbuck, W. H. and Nystrom, P. C. (eds) *Handbook of Organization Design*, Oxford University Press.
Dahmén, E. (1950) 'Svensk Industriell Företagarverksamhet' ('Entrepreneurial activity in Swedish Industry in the period 1919–1939', with an English summary), Stockholm: Industriens Utredningsinstitut.
Davis, S. M. (1982) 'Transforming organizations: the key to strategy is context', *Organization Dynamics*, Winter.
Davidson, W. H. and Haspeslagh, P. (1982) 'Shaping a global product organization', *Harvard Business Review*, July–August.
Doz, Y., Hamel, G., and Prahalad, C. K. (1986) 'Strategic partnerships: success or surrender?', Paper presented at the 1986 AIB-EIBA meeting (unpublished).
Doz, Y., and Prahalad, C. K. (1986) 'Controlled variety: a challenge for human resource management in the MNC', *Human Resource Management*, 25, 1.
Egelhoff, W. G. (1984) 'Patterns of control in US, UK and European multinational corporations', *Journal of International Business Studies*, Fall.
Emery, F. E. and Trist, E. L. (1965) 'The causal texture of organizational environments', *Human Relations*, 18.
Etzioni, A. (1961) *A Comparative Analysis of Complex Organizations*, New York: Free Press.
Fombrun, C. J. (1983) 'Corporate culture, environment and strategy', *Human Resource Management*, vol. 22–1/2.
Franko, L. G. (1976) *The European Multinationals*, Greenwich, CT: Greylock Press.
Freeman, C. (1982) 'Innovation as an engine of economic growth: retrospect and prospect', in Giersch, H. (ed.) *Emerging technologies: Consequences for economic growth, structural change and employment*, Tübingen: Mohr.
Galbraith, J. R. and Nathanson, D. A. (1978) *Strategy Implementation: The Role of Structure and Process*, West Publishing Co., Minnesota.
Hagström, P. (1987) 'New information systems and the changing structure of MNCs', Institute of International Business, Stockholm School of Economics. IIB research paper series 87/3, Stockholm.
Hall, D. and Saias, M. (1980) 'Strategy follows structure', *Strategic Management Journal*, 9.

Hedberg, B. L. T., Nystrom, P. C., and Starbuck, W. H. (1976) 'Camping on seesaws: prescriptions for a self-designing organization', *Administrative Science Quarterly*, 21.

Hedlund, G. (1978) 'Organizations as a matter of style', in Mattsson, L-G and Wiedersheim-Paul, G. (eds) *Recent Research on the Internationalization of Business*, Uppsala.

——— (1981) 'Autonomy of subsidiaries and formalization of headquarters-subsidiary relations in Swedish MNCs', in Otterbeck, L. (ed.) *The Management of Headquarters-Subsidiary Relationships in Multinational Corporations*, Aldershot: Gower.

——— (1984) 'Organization in-between: the evolution of the mother-daughter structure of managing foreign subsidiaries in Swedish MNCs', *Journal of International Business Studies* Fall, vol. 15, 2.

——— (1986) 'The hypermodern MNC — a heterarchy?', *Human Resource Management*, Spring, vol. 25, 1.

Hedlund, G. and Aman, P. (1984) *Managing Relationships with Foreign Subsidiaries — organization and control in Swedish MNCs*, Stockholm: Sveriges Mekanförbund.

Horvath, D. (1975) *Administration av utlandsverksamhet i divisionaliserade företag*, Malmö: Liber.

Kagono, T. (1981) 'Structural design of headquarters-division relationships and economic performance: an analysis of Japanese firms', in Otterbeck, L. (ed.) *The Management of Headquarters-Subsidiary Relationships in Multinational Corporations*, Aldershot: Gower.

Klein, B. (1977) *Dynamic Economics*, Cambridge, Mass: Harvard University Press.

Kogut, B. (1983) 'Foreign direct investment as a sequential process', in Kindleberger, C. P. and Andretsch, D. (eds) *Multinational Corporations in the 1980s*, Cambridge: MIT Press.

Lawrence, P. R. and Lorsch, J. W. (1967) *Organization and environment: Managing Differentiation and Integration*, Cambridge, Mass: Harvard University Press.

Leksell, L. (1981) 'Headquarters-subsidiary relationships in multinational corporations', doctoral thesis, Stockholm: IIB and EFI.

Lorange, P. (1986) 'Human resource management in multinational co-operative ventures', *Human Resource Management*, Spring, vol. 25, 1.

March, J. G. (1971) 'The technology of foolishness', *Civiløkonomen*, (Copenhagen), 18 (4).

Mattsson, L-G. and Wiedersheim-Paul, G. (eds) (1978) *Recent Research on the Internationalization of Business*, Uppsala.

Miles, R. E., Snow, C. C., and Pfeffer, J. (1974) 'Organization — environment: concepts and issues', *Industrial Relations*, vol. 13.

Miles, R. E. and Snow, C. C. (1978) *Organizational Strategy, Structure and Process*, New York: McGraw Hill.

Miller, D. (1987) 'The genesis of configuration', *Academy of Management Review*, vol. 12, No. 4.

Mintzberg, H. (1973) 'The nature of managerial work', New York: Harper & Row.

Nonaka, I. (1987) 'Managing the firm as an information creation process'. Unpublished research paper, Institute of Business Research, Hitotsubashi University.

Otterbeck, L. (ed.) (1981) *The Management of Headquarters-Subsidiary Relationships in Multinational Corporations*, Aldershot: Gower.

Perlmutter, H. V. (1984) 'Building the symbiotic societal enterprise', *World Futures*, 19.

Perroux, F. (1961) 'La firme motrice dans une région et la région motrice', Cahiers de l'Institut de Science Economique Appliqué, Suppl. No. 111, March.

Peters, T. J. (1984) 'Strategy follows structure; developing distinctive skills', *California Management Review*, 26 (3).

Polanyi, M. (1969) *Knowing and Being*, London: Routledge & Kegan Paul; Chicago: University of Chicago Press.

Porter, M. E. (1980) *Competitive Strategy: Techniques for analyzing industries and competitors*, New York: Free Press.

Prigogine, I. (1976) 'Order through fluctuation: self-organization and social system', in Jantsch, E. and Waddington, C. H. (eds), *Evolution and Consciousness*, Reading, Mass: Addison-Wesley.

Rolander, D. (1989) 'Action patterns in emerging industries', Institute of International Business, Stockholm School of Economics, Stockholm: IIB.

Schumpeter, J. (1911) *Theorie der wirtschaftlichen Entwicklung*, Jena.
  (1942) *Capitalism, Socialism and Democracy*, New York: Harper and Brothers.

Starbuck, W. H. (1985) 'Acting first and thinking later: theory versus reality in strategic change', in Pennings, J. M. (ed.), *Organizational Strategy and Change*, San Francisco.

Stopford, J. M. and Wells, L. T. (1972) *Managing the Multinational Enterprise*, New York: Basic Books.

Sölvell, Ö. (1987) 'Entry barriers and foreign penetration', Institute of International Business, Stockholm School of Economics (doctoral thesis), Stockholm: IIB.

Teece, D. J. (1977) 'Technology transfer by multinational firms', *Economic Journal*, 87 (June).

Thompson, J. D. (1967) *Organizations in Action*, New York: McGraw-Hill.

Vahlne, J-E. and Nordström, K. A. (1986) 'Global oligopolies and the advantage cycle', Institute of International Business, Stockholm School of Economics, IIB Research Paper series 86/15, Stockholm.

Vernon, R. (1979) 'The product cycle hypothesis in a new international environment', *Oxford Bulletin of Economics and Statistics*, 41.

Watzlawick, O., Weakland, J. H., and Fisch, R. (1974) *Change: Principles of Problem Formation and Problem Resolution*, New York: Norton.

Weick, K. E. (1969) *The Social Psychology of Organizing*, Reading, Mass: Addison-Wesley.

Conceptions of global management

Williamson, O. E. (1975) *Markets and Hierarchies — Analysis and Antitrust Implications*, New York: Free Press.

(1981) 'The modern corporation: origins, evolution, attributes', *Journal of Economic Literature*, 19, December.

Chapter two

International sequential advantages and network flexibility

Bruce Kogut

There is a common tendency in studies on international competition and foreign investment to emphasize the conditions leading to the initial entry into a foreign market. Yet, a cursory glance at foreign direct investment data for the United States shows that reinvested earnings far outweigh new capital flows. For American corporations, current investment is largely channeled through an already existing multinational network.[1]

Because of the establishment of these networks, there is a significant distinction between the initial motivations for foreign direct investment and the sequential advantages of the co-ordinated multinational system. For the initial investment across borders, the motivations for a firm are three-fold: to access raw materials, to exploit cost and skill differentials across countries, or to penetrate markets based on some product, process, or brand-label advantage. Over time, the establishment of internationally dispersed assets generates subsequent advantages through the co-ordination of the individual subsidiaries. In this sense, the benefits of multinational co-ordination are sequential to the initial entries.

The need to analyse competition in terms of international networks is underscored not only by the formation of dispersed subsidiaries, but also by the convergence in technical capabilities across countries. Foreign direct investment frequently reflects, as numerous studies show, the extension of new product and process innovations to overseas markets.[2] The rapid growth of US investments after the war has been shown to stem from that country's technological leadership. However, data from the past decade have shown a remarkable convergence in R&D expenditures as a percentage of business expenditures among the major industrial countries. To a multinational corporation, the convergence of technological capabilities among countries shifts the dependence on the headquarter's location as the source of innovation towards the acquisition and management of technology throughout the international network.[3]

The expanding use of subsidiaries for gaining strategic leverage is, in part, an outcome of the maturation of many industries founded in the after-war period. For US firms, their early strategies were based on the transfer of technology and superior organizational abilities to overseas markets. Though US overseas growth is no longer in excess of other countries, US firms have been able to maintain a strikingly stable share of world trade where their investment positions are strongest, primarily in Europe.[4]

The transition from competing on the transfer of technological and organizational knowledge to strengthening already established subsidiary positions raises the issue of what is the competitive advantage of a multinational firm in a mature market. In recent years, the answer to this question has been sought through analysing the advantages of multinational co-ordination and network flexibility. In short, multinationality itself can be a source of advantage.

Little attention, however, has been paid to how a firm builds advantages in the process of its development from the initial investments to network co-ordination. The first part of this chapter examines international strategies as they unfold through the development of economies of scale and scope, learning, and operating flexibility. These four sources of advantage are paired with four derived strategies. For each strategy, an example is provided. The intent is not to develop a model for the purpose of competitive analysis but rather of describing a few, among possibly many, patterns in the expansion of the international firm.

The second part of the paper turns briefly to showing how the organization and co-ordination of the multinational corporation gradually evolve to support the passage of foreign direct investments from initial entries to sequential investments. The organizational structure and operating systems of early multinational corporations were designed for the management of dyadic relationships between headquarters and subordinate subsidiaries. To benefit from multinationality has required the development of new systems for managing the international network. These systems are dependent upon mechanisms of organizational learning and the evolution of the international firm towards acquiring some of the traits of a professional organization.

I. Multinationality and competitive advantage

Most studies on the motives for investing for overseas, other than for reasons of material or component sourcing, have found that the initial foreign investment reflects the extension of products for the domestic market. In turn, these products stem from specialized investments in technology and brand labels. The dilemma facing the firm at this time is whether the additional revenues of foreign market penetration are offset by the requirements of adapting products to national markets. In this sense, the conflict between standardized products and national differentiation represents the fundamental and initial trade-off of domestic and international strategies (Doz, Bartlett, and Prahalad 1981). The resolution of the conflict between standardization and national differentiation is not only a question of marketing adaptation, but also of production and research. Indeed, an international strategy frequently rests upon national differentiation of the downstream links of the value-added chain coupled with upstream economies of scale or scope.[5]

Over time, however, as a firm establishes mutiple subsidiaries throughout the world, subsequent advantages are realized through the co-ordination of the multinational network. It could well be that the initial advantage of proprietary technology and brand labels declines in competitive significance. Instead, the strategy of the firm shifts increasingly to the exploitation of country differences through four sources of competitive advantage: economies of scale and scope, learning, and operating flexibility. The process by which these sources are strategically developed is described in turn.

Economies of scale, national segmentation, and international aggregation

Much has been made, and often rightly so, of the importance of economies of scale. The significance of economies of scale in producing for world markets is closely linked to the advocacy of standardized products and global rationalization (Doz 1978; Levitt 1983). Critical to this analysis is the determination at what point economies of scale are exhausted. In production, for example, even if average unit manufacturing costs decline with increased output, transportation costs increase as markets in the greatest proximity are saturated. Scherer *et al.* (1973) found for the United States that plant economies are exhausted at relatively moderate volume relative to the size of the US market. Clearly, for companies targeting a market the size of the US (or of Europe and, in most cases, of Japan), the incremental gain of the world market is insignificant in terms of further scale economies at the single plant level.[6]

For R&D, studies tend to show that overseas research subsidiaries are primarily development oriented (Mansfield *et al.* 1979). This trend suggests that economies of scale in research are potential sources of competitive advantage in international markets, whereas development incurs substantial incremental investments in order to adapt products to country markets. For marketing, the evidence for scale economies has been ambiguous. The scale advantage of a sales force tends to end at the border. If scale economies are derived from global brand labeling, this relationship is likely to be robust for only a few industries.[7]

To accept the findings on scale in the US market is not to reject that scale can play an important role in international competition during a period of industry evolution or new product launches. There are two important considerations in this regard. First, access to the international market may be critical when there are important scale economies and the product life cycle is short. In this case, foreign penetration may not only serve to amortize fixed costs, but also to deprive potential competitors of the necessary scale.

Second, most of the studies on scale assume that the market is identical for similar products. Clearly, however, as any standard textbook on marketing and industrial economics shows, firms actively segment markets by the physical or psychological differentiation of their products. A policy of segmentation is costly; if not, then segments could be easily addressed by competitors. A strategic issue is the balance between sharing costs across segments (thereby risking competitors' entry) and dedicating investment to a specific segment.

In the international market, firms confront the analogous issue of balancing shared and dedicated costs across countries.[8] However, the separation of national markets creates unusual opportunities for firms to develop new products addressed to market segments which vary across countries. Through the aggregation of demand, an investment in specialized fixed assets — which could not be supported by a domestic competitor — is amortized. Contrary to received wisdom, international firms may be, consequently, better able than local firms to address small national segments due to market aggregation. Frequently, such a strategy requires downstream differentiation and upstream scale or scope economies and the utilization, sequential to the initial entry, of existing national market positions. Scale economies are exploited not through simple standardization of product design, manufacturing, and advertising, but through a segmentation of national markets.

The AE-1 camera

Takeuchi and Porter's (1986) discussion of the development of the AE-1 camera provides a good example of international aggregation backed by economies of scale. The AE-1 is a single lens reflex camera with a standardized design for the world market. Its development required considerable co-ordination between marketing and production engineering and investment in machining dedicated to its manufacture. Of great interest, Canon sourced externally the intelligence of the camera, using a customized chip manufactured by Texas Instruments. There was a clear decision made as to which internal resources to develop and which components, no matter how critical, to procure.

Central to the success of the product was the capturing of sufficient volume to justify the significant investments in customizing the chip and manufacturing equipment. Sales volume was achieved through a careful segmentation within targeted countries. In Japan, the camera served as a replacement for mid-income buyers; in the United States, the served market was for first time users of 35 mm cameras; in Germany, the targeted market was older consumers with experience in sophisticated products. Through the international aggregation of these segments, sufficient scale economies were realized to justify the high fixed costs of investment dedicated to the production of the AE-1. The success of this strategy relied, in a sequential sense, on the existing network of Canon marketing and sales subsidiaries throughout the world.

Economies of scope and product line broadening and upgrading

Economies of scope can serve either to augment or negate a global advantage. By economies of scope, it is meant that the cost of producing two products together is less than the sum of the costs of producing these products individually. Because of economies of scope, the benefits of an international strategy riding on a scale advantage can sometimes be nullified. A purely domestic firm may be able to achieve full-scale economies in some link by competing in several product markets.[9]

Certain links are particularly susceptible to economies of scope which favour encumbent national firms, especially in the area of brand label creation and distribution. An international firm might counter local advantages in brand labeling or distribution by relying on large retailers or by downstream investments. The economics of such a decision depend on whether the market share supports the fixed investment or the appropriability hazards in selling through large retailers are not prohibitive.[10] On the other hand, economies of scope can often serve in the interests of a global strategy. Information on one regional product market can be used to benefit another market. For firms where international transportation and global sales force are important, economies in information and logistics can be a critical source of advantage. Moreover, as a firm builds its position overseas, scope economies with existing overseas products can benefit the introduction of other lines internationally.

Because of these shared benefits, market penetration by foreign firms is frequently characterized by a strategy of product line broadening. Davidson (1980), for example, found that new product lines are likely to be introduced in countries where a firm already has operations. From anecdotal evidence, a common Japanese policy has been product line upgrading, whereby the introduction of smaller volume but higher quality goods benefits from previous investments in brand labeling and distribution.[11]

The pattern appears to rest on two reasons. One, dynamic changes in a country running an export surplus lead to a shedding of lower value-added activities. Persistent export surpluses lead in the long run to an appreciation in the home currency, thereby increasing imports and decreasing exports. From this perspective, international competition is between national firms who seek to upgrade their products and improve their productivity in order to offset an appreciating currency. The irony in this struggle is that the more the exporters succeed, the more the exchange rate must appreciate, forcing exports to go overseas, to upgrade further, or to divest.

Two, the initial product entry might exploit a low-cost and volume production strategy in order to justify the high initial costs. Sequential product entries can, then, be targeted for smaller segments, though sharing some fixed costs with the volume line. Such a dynamic suggests that the initial entry by a firm will be characterized by investments that may not be justified by current returns, but lays the foundation for the introduction of higher margin products.

This latter strategy reflects the importance of future options on previous decisions. The dependence of future opportunities on current asset positions may warrant investments that provide the option, at a cost, for product line upgrading and broadening. For example, a firm might invest in quality brand labeling rather than in a specific product advertisement in order to retain the option to upgrade in the future. Or plants might be designed to be retooled easily in order to produce more sophisticated products in the future.[12] Economies of scope can be seen not only in terms of static joint economies, but also as affecting the costs of sequential product entries. By lowering the costs of future entries, dynamic scope economies permit the introduction of global products whose volume alone may not justify the costs of entry.

Honda Motors

Honda's entry into the US market reveals an interesting choice of differentiating the exploitation of scope economies along the value chain. Its remarkable success in the US was built up through the sequential entry of upgraded products over time and the strong pull of the Honda name. Moreover, Honda, like other Japanese producers, frequently relied on contracting out of US model designers, building their strategy on internal manufacturing and engine design know-how.

Given the strong quality reputation of the Honda name, it should be expected that future product entries would ride upon dynamic scope economies in marketing and advertising. Yet, its top of the line cars were introduced under the brand label of the Acura; no mention of the Honda name was made in the television or printed advertising. Furthermore, the Acura dealerships have been either separated from the Honda distributors or placed on different lots.

The Honda strategy bears similarities to the strategy followed by Hattori in differentiating brand labels for different market segments: Pulsar for the lower-mid end, Seiko for the mid- to upper-mid segment, and Lasale for the top end. Both the Honda and Seiko strategies are based on the differentiation of the downstream links of the value chain at the loss of scope economies, while gaining such economies upstream in design know-how and, at least in the case of Honda, some component commonalities. The danger of such strategies is that larger national competitors may respond by fragmenting the national market into segments too narrow to be supported by the market shares of foreign entrants. It is interesting that Honda appears to be anticipating such a trend — if not promoting it as an offensive strategy against other non-US competitiors — by the construction of assembly plants with smaller capacity than traditionally recommended. Through the fragmentation of national markets, Honda apparently seeks to address intra-country segments while maintaining scope economies in the upstream links of design and component production.

Learning and information updating

The benefits of learning rely on market share in much the same way as economies of scale do, except that costs fall with units of time rather than with units of output in any one production period (Spence 1981). To the extent that market expansion is not offset by product adaptation or inhibited by tariff-induced fragmentation of resources, international participation potentially results in lower costs through increasing cumulative volume, whether this be achieved through segment aggregation or product line broadening. This advantage is especially important when product life cycles are short and diffusion is relatively slow.

In addition to the case where unit costs decline with cumulative volume, learning is frequently organizational in nature, that is, it represents the transfer of organizational practices and know-how across the firm. Examples are the transfer across borders of managerial skills or innovations acquired through new subsidiary establishments. Though the transfer of organizational knowlege may occur infrequently, such learning may drop set-up costs by discrete quantities, providing significant advantages to firms who establish an early position in international markets.

Consider, for example, international marketing. Much of the controversy over international marketing has been centred on whether international brand labeling can serve as a source of global competitive advantage. The emphasis on brand labeling has led to a neglect of the importance of learning as a form of information updating in international marketing, especially in regard to reducing the costs of new product launches. Yet, a multinational corporation accumulates significant information on the covariance of demand characteristics among countries. Hence, the outcome of a product launch in one country serves (in a Bayesian sense) to provide a better forecast of the success of sequential launches in other countries, permitting alterations in the marketing programme and lowering the probability of costly failures. In fact, without learning and information updating of the estimated covariance structure among countries, the existence of international marketing firms appears inexplicable.

Proctor and Gamble

Many examples exist of the use of information updating across countries. Considerable marketing research is usually dedicated to the analysis of pilot tests in order to launch new products. Companies frequently find it worthwhile to make trial launches in restricted geographical areas and, then based on results, adjust the campaign for the launch in the wider market. In international markets, Canada is often used, as it has been by Hyundai of Korea and IKEA of Sweden, as a trial for penetrating the US. For such a trial to be effective, the correlation in demand characteristics of the two countries must be implicitly or explicitly known.

An example of the use of country-specific knowledge to inform new product launches is provided by Bartlett and Ghoshal (1986) in their discussion of Proctor and Gamble's Vizir (a liquid detergent) entry in the European market. An earlier attempt was made to launch Pampers (a disposable diaper) when centralizing marketing and advertising under a single manager located in Brussels. For Vizir, P&G relied upon a 'Eurobrand' team which assigned lead roles to country managers and co-ordinated marketing and advertising, using a common theme. Moreover, subsequent launches were modified based on results in earlier countries.

The Vizir and Pampers comparison illustrate how sensitive learning and information updating within a corporation are to the organizational infrastructure. Effective use of knowledge required the delegation of marketing responsibilities to country managers on a flexible assignment basis. Both the Vizir and Pampers launches utilized common advertising and marketing programs. Where they differed was in the cross-application of country-specific knowledge and an understanding of the correlation in demand across Europe.

Multinational dispersion: comparative advantage and operating flexibility

Studies on international competition have concentrated on the determinants of foreign entry without considering how once the entry is accomplished, subsequent advantages are achieved through the ownership of a multinational network. The multinational dispersion of the firm presents opportunities of profitable arbitrage through the ownership of options written on movements in real factor and product prices, competitors' moves, or government policy.

From this point of view, competitive advantage is equivalent to the exploitation of strategic options. As compared to a domestic firm, the ownership of the assets around the world provides the multinational corporation with the ability to shift production to more favourable locations in the event of adverse exchange rate movements or to minimize taxes through various mechanisms. Multinationality provides, then, a unique benefit in the form of the possibility to gain from uncertainty. In this kind of world, variance implies profit opportunities.

55

In short, one of the key strengths of the multinational corporation is its capability to respond to country variance, whether source of the variance be exchange rate movements, tax and financial distortions, competitors' overseas positioning, or new innovations. The exercise of such options rests, however, upon the creation of complex organizational routines involving the co-ordination of intra-firm activities across the borders. Since it is likely that firms differ in their abilities to co-ordinate contingent routines in response to stochastic environmental events, an enduring source of advantage is the quality of international managerial control and information.

General Motors

Potentially, one advantage of the multinational corporation is the shifting of production between countries. Ford has tended, in recent years, to design its manufacturing around internationally dispersed plants for the production of components, while relying relatively more on local assembly in its large national or regional markets. General Motors, in comparison, has tended to be a collection of country-oriented companies, stressing local production for local sales. In theory, dispersed manufacturing plants producing identical components, provide the opportunity to co-ordinate production flows across countries. In practice, GM has either earmarked certain plants for production at full economy of scale without shifting, or relied on local manufacturing for local sales.[13]

The evaluation of the costs of such a country-based strategy should include the loss of the option to shift production in response to exchange rate movements. GM has engine plants in Australia, Brazil, and at one time, South Africa to supply Opel in Germany. If wages in Australia were to increase more than wages in Brazil when evaluated in a common currency, GM could shift some or all production to the Brazilian plant. To do so, it would need to build excess capacity into its plants and arrive at labour contracts to permit overtime or layoffs. However, the greater the uncertainty in exchange rates or in relative wages, the more valuable is the option to shift.

It could well be that GM's decision not to invest in such real options reflects considerations of costs or fears over an erosion of its local country-oriented reputation. Another explanation is that the shifting of production is organizationally complex. It requires, first, a set of transfer prices which fluctuate with exchange rates and, thus, gives an incentive to shift internal suppliers. (In the absence of transfer pricing rules, an internal committee could administratively order the shift.) Second, it requires the co-operation of the plants to reduce or increase production. There must be, then, an alignment of incentives so that plant managers are not penalized for failing to meet output targets. Working out a set of transfer prices and incentives for international production shifting requires a capable organizational infrastructure.

Summary

The above discussion is summarized in Table 2.1. All of these strategies depend upon previous entry investments. National segmentation and international aggregation rides upon the acquisition of knowledge of local markets and sales subsidiaries; product-line broadening upon prior product introductions; information updating on accumulated learning of the covariance of demand across countries; and operating flexibility on plant or market positions in multiple countries. They represent, therefore, strategic options acquired in the establishment of an international network of subsidiaries.

Table 2.1 International sequential advantages and strategies

Source of advantage	Implicit strategy
Economies of scale	National segmentation and international aggregation
Economies of scope	Product-line broadening Product-line upgrading
Learning	Information up-dating
Multinational dispersion	Low-cost sourcing Operating flexibility

II. Sequential strategy and organizational evolution

The implementation of sequential strategies is dependent upon the two organizational properties of duplication and differentiation, backed by an international competence in terms of both management and operating systems at the functional level. There is, however, an inherent structural tension in sequential strategies which impedes the development of international competence. The process of moving from a domestic to an international firm is often accompanied by structural change, usually in stages from the creation of an international division to world product lines or areas.[14] However, the international structures designed for the transfer of home

57

advantages to overseas markets are not necessarily suited for competing on network co-ordination.

Though the significance of leveraging the international firm on its subsidiaries has been often noted, the persistence of traditional organizational structures, as many studies have shown, has impaired the creation of multinational flexibility.[15] Franko's (1976) study of European multinational corporations described not only the adoption of US principles of management, but also the endurance of subsidiary independence and looser financial controls. More detailed corporate case studies carried out at the Stockholm School of Economics have also shown the persistence of organizational characteristics despite the adoption of US-type restructuring (Otterbeck, ed. 1981; Hedlund and Åman 1984). Bartlett's (1986) description of how the 'administrative heritage' of the multinational corporation encumbers organizational evolution is a reflection of this line of thinking. It is not surprising, therefore, that the organizational capability of the multinational corporation to exploit the inherent sequential advantages is impaired by relatively inert structures and management systems.

Heterarchy and the professional organization

In this sense, the international development of multinational corporations shares the characteristics of what Mintzberg and Waters (1985) have described as 'emergent strategies'. It is likely, as Aharoni's study (1966) shows, that the initial foreign direct investment decision is not part of a larger international strategy, but rather is frequently a response to unexpected market opportunities. Indeed, much of the planning literature suggests that investments overseas were controlled as part of a dyadic relationship between headquarters and each subsidiary. Over time, the value of managing the international network as for the exploitation of sequential advantages emerged as a recognized strategy. Organizationally, this evolution implies that the multinational corporation — having succeeded in the initial entries overseas — reaps further incremental value by moving from a dyadic relationship with its subsidiaries to the profitable management of its international network.

Hedlund (1986) views this evolution as tending towards holographic subsidiaries, namely, that every part of the organization reflects the entire organization. In his view, the internal hierarchy of the corporation is replaced by balance interdependence, or what he calls a heterarchy. Bartlett (1986) also sees the multinational corporation moving from a hierarchical control to a more co-operative relationship between headquarters and subsidiaries.

In some ways, these themes are familiar. Prahalad and Doz (1981), in particular, noted the importance of formulating strategy 'in the context of reciprocal dependence between HQ and subsidiaries.' Edstrom and Galbraith (1977) also underlined the important role played by socializing managers in a common culture through rotation across different country assignments to create shared norms.

The difference lies in the greater emphasis placed on the autonomy of country subsidiaries and symmetry in responsibilities across horizontal and vertical divisions.[16] Hedlund's (1986) and Hedlund's and Rolander's (1987) thesis is particularly instructive in setting the limiting case of this argument. In their view, the firm learns about its environment and its own resources through a radical delegation of responsibilities to multiple centres. Organizational structure does not only channel information and delegate authority; it, in fact, provides a system by which information and organizational knowledge are created. As Nonaka (1987) argues, short-term instability in the organization is a prerequisite to organizational evolution.

The emphasis by Hedlund, Rolander, and Nonaka on learning points out the fundamental importance of developing international competence, both at the individual and organizational levels. The desire to resolve conflicts and anxieties over the process of learning as a firm internationalizes can easily lead to premature decisions. An example of such decisions is the eradication of international divisions before product line managers are sufficiently educated in, and committed to, the international business of their firm. The work of Davidson and Haspelagh (1982) suggests that an evolution to global product structures impedes the transfer of technology and new products from headquarters to subsidiaries. It would not be surprising if similar evidence should be found for the impediment of technological transfer across subsidiaries. In effect, a too hasty evolution to world structures weakens the development of international commitment and competence.

The emphasis on systemic learning leads to the view of the international firm as tending towards the development of characteristics frequently associated with the professional firm. These characteristics are principally the loosening of formal control systems in favour of greater managerial autonomy and lateral communication across departments or subsidiaries.[17] Moreover, both greater autonomy and lateral communication have been found to be encouraged under highly uncertain environments. For the international firm, it is not surprising that the growing complexity of its internal network and the interdependence across markets should lead to an increased dependence on the professional competence of its managers.

However, the heterarchy as a professional firm is a poor model unless the mechanisms by which the system is stabilized and co-ordinated are delineated. System stability is particularly critical given that the country subsidiary is squeezed between the pull of the internal corporate network, on the one hand, and its position in the external national network of customers, suppliers, and other groups, on the other. Much like a Byzantine Empire, a multi-national corporation may slowly deteriorate by the entropy stemming from the need of the country subsidiaries to adapt to, and draw resources from, the local environments.

A strategy riding upon dynamic economies of scope exemplifies this dilemma by raising the question which resource should serve as the basis of further product line expansion. Though the initial entry into a country may be based on a corporate product innovation, the country subsidiary may decide to launch further products on a local basis which draw upon unused capacity in distribution channels. Such entrepreneurial activity should be tolerated, if not encouraged, by headquarters. Local entrepreneurship provides not only motivational incentives, but also, the possibility that innovations in response to local market demands may be internationally useful. The drawback is that local entrepreneurship will not only deflect managerial attention from corporate-wide products, but also that the evolution of country subsidiaries' capabilities will deter the development of an internationally co-ordinated network.[18]

Localized learning and entrepreneurship must be evaluated in light of the contribution to, and stability of the corporate system. Heterarchy is itself no more than entropy towards internal market competition, unless there is a definition of the value of the system and how this value is managerially achieved. Entropic decline, as the recent history of ITT might suggest, is not an unreasonable possibility. Ultimately, the viability of a heterarchy rests on the operating systems of network management.

Duplication and differentiation

A strategy which utilizes the international network of subsidiaries presumes that the value in the co-ordination of activities across borders is worth its costs. To achieve sequential advantages through network co-ordination, two structural properties of duplication and differentiation are necessary. Duplication is a way to achieve gains through the arbitrage of factor, product, and technological markets. Differentiation permits the utilization of the variation in subsidiary and national resources for the benefit of the wider network.

Consider both in further detail. Duplication of resources is the organizational requisite to exploiting operating flexibility. For example, production shifting requires construction of two or more plants in different country sites producing identical products or components. Similarly, the transfer of innovations across countries necessitates the duplication of R&D efforts if these innovations reflect national capabilities and are not purchasable through market transactions.

Network management also consists of differentiation of tasks among subsidiaries.[19] This differentiation may stem simply from the acquisition of foreign companies. Davidson (1982) reports that during the period between 1951 and 1976 some 69.5 per cent, 59.5 per cent, and 45 per cent of new US subsidiaries in Canada, the United Kingdom, and Continental Europe were established by acquisitions. Often, these acquisitions contribute not only marketing and distribution channels, but capabilities in research and development and manufacturing. Differentiation may also reflect the allocation of different capabilities to national subsidiaries. Available data show clearly that Asian subsidiaries to both US and Japanese firms tend to be sourcing sites for sales to third countries. Jacque (1986) found that US joint ventures in Japan have tended to expand to become functionally the regional headquarters serving Asian markets. Jacque's data also suggest that differentiation may reflect national variations, with the US being the source of product innovation, Japan for manufacturing. By differentiation of tasks, subsidiaries are assigned world-wide responsibilities for selected product development, manufacturing, or marketing.

International competence and integrative systems

Through duplication of resources and differentiation of subsidiary tasks, headquarters plays a major role as the co-ordinating centre for the management of the multinational network. This co-ordination has been facilitated by the gradual emergence of global organizational structures, which have been particularly well suited to the requirements of dyadic control between headquarters and subsidiary or regional managers. Global geographic or product line structures (or any combination of the two) cannot eradicate the trade-off between the benefits of utilizing subsidiaries' knowledge of the local environment and the costs of acquiring and the information in product development and delivery. Indeed, the conflict is inherently irresolvable.

However, structural solutions can be augmented by designing integrative systems to permit the co-ordination of network activities (Kogut 1985). Integrative systems include not only international human resource management, but also pricing rules, environmental scanning, and decentralized incentives attached to planning and control. Pivotal to the operation of the international network is the delineation of cross-country functional roles and development of international competence.

The use of such systems can be further clarified by considering the design of a planning and control system under fluctuating exchange rates. A fundamental dilemma of a multinational corporation is that for planning and review purposes, country managers are frequently tracked against forecasted earnings. Fluctuating exchange rates denigrate, however, the significance of such a comparison, unless the tracking is adjusted for currency movements. Early solutions to this problem were addressed at the selection of the appropriate exchange rate (Lessard and Lorange 1977). The proposed solutions reveal, quite clearly, that the problem was formulated as one of dyadic control between the headquarters and subsidiary.

The issue is more than just one of monitoring performance. As shown in the earlier discussion, exchange rate fluctuations present profitable opportunities for the shifting of production. Lessard and Lightstone (1986) also note that fluctuating exchange rates have implications for investments in flexible manufacturing and in product mix, as the capability to change the material/labour inputs or product with different degrees of price sensivity is more valuable the greater the exchange rate uncertainty. But a dyadic planning and control system with locked in sales forecasts and forecasted exchange rates reduces the incentive for managers to exploit these capabilities.[20]

The proposal by Lessard and Sharp (1984) has, in this light, far-reaching consequences. They suggest the use of contingent planning, by which country managers are asked to work out market share and profit goals based for different exchange rate scenarios. To move from a dyadic relationship requires, furthermore, the iteration of these plans across countries or regions, so that a movement in the dollar rate leads to enacting a plan which shifts sales to higher margin goods or production to plants located in countries benefiting by currency trends.

To enact such plans by delegation under structured incentives may be too slow and costly under conditions of rapid change. An alternative is the use of administered co-ordination over international production. This co-ordination can be exercised through the creation of task forces or committees. It is, thus, through lateral communication across borders and an enhancement of the functional authority of production managers that co-ordination is achieved.

Through integrative operating systems, the international competence of the corporation is functionally developed. Strategic implementation has long stressed the importance of organizational structures and product lines. For a strategy resting on sequential advantage and operating flexibility, the value of an international network is critically dependent upon the integration of functions across borders.

III. Conclusions

The above analysis suggests that the effective utilization of a co-ordinated network requires a reciprocal but asymmetrical dependence between headquarters and subsidiaries. Whereas localized learning may be fruitful, there are significant opportunity costs in allowing subsidiaries to evolve along unco-ordinated paths. These costs stem from the failure to exploit operating flexibility and the development of subsidiary, as opposed to corporate, resources and knowledge in the long run. Both the management of operating flexibility and the corporate development of the option value inherent in multinational resources require a strong and activist role for headquarters and the creation of integrative operating systems.

For many American and some European firms, there currently exists a window of opportunity to develop the capability to compete on network flexibility relative to Japanese competitors. Prior to 1940, the US was one among a few countries which dominated overseas investment. The post-war period has been largely characterized by the expansion of US firms overseas and the gradual catch-up of European and, more recently, Japanese firms.

In this gradual balancing of the economic fortunes of countries, it is unlikely that US and European multinational firms can count any longer on their technological and organizational skills to dominate world markets as previously. Rather, a central source of advantage lies in the cumulative experience of operating dispersed multinational resources. The economic potential is already at hand; the strategic question is whether the organizational support can be effectively designed and implemented.

Notes

1 This data is provided in Kogut 1983.
2 For a review, see Caves 1982.
3 For an incisive and early discussion of these issues, see Ronstadt 1978, who distinguishes between technology units operating for local adaptation and those serving world markets. For an empirical study of the development of Swedish overseas R&D facilities, see Håkanson and Zander 1986.
4 See Lipsey and Kravis 1986.
5 See Kogut 1984, and Porter 1986.
6 Small firms may, however, require the international market. Indeed, there is some evidence that small Japanese firms were frequently the first to invest abroad (Tsurumi 1976) and, more generally non-dominant firms led their industries in overseas expansion (Mascarenhas 1985). But neither of these cases suggests that international competition led to enhanced economies of scale relative to dominant firms.
7 See Mueller and Hamm 1980, and Scherer 1980, for a discussion of scale economies and marketing.
8 An excellent analytical description of this balance is given by Ghemawat and Spence 1986.
9 For analyses of economies of scope, manufacturing flexibility, and national strategies, see Fuller, Nicholaides, and Stopford 1987, on the white goods industry in the UK and the rest of Europe, and Solvell 1987, on world-wide competition.
10 By appropriability hazards, it is meant the potential that the (excess) profits accruing to a firm due to its ownership of some proprietary skill or factor may be captured by imitators, suppliers, buyers, or other competitors.
11 In an article laying down some of the theoretical groundwork for the value-added chain, Wernerfelt 1984, describes the Japanese strategy in similar terms.
12 Sushil Vachani has, in a presentation at the Wharton School, February 1986, described a policy of flexible tooling and brand identification as characteristic of multinational corporations in India which face continual competitive pressures on the lower end of their product offerings.
13 To adopt the language of Flood and Lessard (1986), Ford is following a policy of global to global, i.e. global manufacturing for global sales, whereas GM is following a local to local strategy. Production shifting treats manufacturing as local in costs but global in production.
14 Stopford and Wells (1972) remains the seminal piece on this transformation.
15 Many of the recent ideas of the distributed intelligence and authority among subsidiaries is incipient in Perlmutter's (1969) notion of the 'geocentric' multinational corporation. Other writings which explicitly discussed the international firm as a network include Root (1973), Vernon (1979), Dunning (1981), and Kogut (1983).
16 The importance of autonomy (if not instability) and learning has filtered

slowly, if not always consciously, from mainstream organizational theory into the writings on the international firm. See Burns and Stalker (1961: 5–6) for an early discussion of holography; March (1976) on the complexity of means and end relationships; Ouchi (1980) on the use of solidarity when formal controls are weak; and Mintzberg and McHugh (1985) on management by an 'adhocracy'.

17 An excellent analysis is given in Scott 1987: 219–39.

18 For a case description of this problem, see Paul Browne, *Vick International Division*, Harvard Business School, 179–268.

19 For an early discussion of the differentiation of subsidiaries, see Hedlund 1980. See also Bartlett and Ghoshal 1986, and Ghoshal and Nohria 1987.

20 See Sharp (1987) for a detailed analysis.

References

Aharoni, Y. (1966) *The Foreign Direct Investment Process*, Boston: Division of Research, Graduate School of Business, Harvard University.

Bartlett, C. A. (1981) 'Multinational structural reorganization: evolution versus reorganization', in *The Management of Headquarters-Subsidiary Relationships in Multinational Corporations*, ed. L. Otterbeck, UK: Gower.

(1986) 'Building and managing the transnational: the new organizational challenge', in *Competition in Global Industries*, ed. M. E. Porter, Boston: Harvard Business School Press.

Bartlett, C. A. and Ghoshal, S. (1986) 'Tap your subsidiaries for global reach', *Harvard Business Review*, November–December, 87–94.

Browne, P. *Vick International Division*, Harvard Business School, Boston.

Burns, T. and Stalker, G. (1961) *The Management of Innovation*, London: Tavistock.

Caves, R. E. (1982) *Economic Analysis and Multinational Enterprise*, New York: Cambridge University Press.

Davidson, W. H. (1980) 'The location of foreign direct investment activity: country characteristics and experience effects', *Journal of International Business Studies*, 11.

(1982) *Global Strategic Management*, New York: Wiley.

Davidson, W. H. and Haspelagh, P. (1982) 'Shaping a global product organization', *Harvard Business Review*, July–August.

Doz, Y. L. (1978) 'Managing manufacturing rationalization within multinational corporations', *Columbia Journal of World Business*.

Doz, Y. L., Bartlett, C. A., and Prahalad, C. K. (1981) 'Global competitive pressures and host country demands: managing tensions in MNCs', *California Management Review*.

Dunning, J. H. (1981) 'Explaining outward direct investments of developing countries: in support of the eclectic theory of international production', in *Multinationals from Developing Countries*, Lexington, MA: Maxwell G. McLeod.

Edstrom, A. and Galbraith, J. (1977) 'Transfer of managers as a control strategy in multinational organizations', *Administrative Science Quarterly*.

Flood, E. and Lessard, D. (1986) 'On the measurement of operating exposure to exchange rates: a conceptual approach', *Financial Management*.

Franko, L. (1976) *The European Multinationals*, Stamford, CT: Greylock.

Fuller, C. B., Nicholaides, P., and Stopford, J. (1987) 'National or global? The study of company strategies and the European market for major domestic appliances', Working Paper Series, London Business School.

Ghemawat, P. and Spence, A. M. (1985) 'Learning curve spillovers and market performance', *Quarterly Journal of Economics*, 100.

Ghemawat, P. and Spence, A. M. (1986) 'Modelling global competition', in M. E. Porter (ed.) *Competition in Global Industries*, Boston: Harvard Business School Press.

Ghoshal, S. and Nohria, N. (1987) 'Multinational corporations as differentiated networks', working paper, INSEAD.

Håkanson, L. and U. Zander (1986) *Managing International Research and Development*, Stockholm: Mekanpublikation.

Hedlund, G. (1980) 'The role of foreign subsidiaries in strategic decision-making in Swedish multinational corporations', *Strategic Management Journal*, 1.

(1986) 'The hypermodern MNC — a heterarchy?', *Human Resource Management*, 25.

Hedlund, G. and Åman (1984) *Managing Relationships with Foreign Subsidiaries*, Stockholm: Sveriges Mekanforbund.

Hedlund, G. and Rolander, D. (1987) 'The strategy-structure paradigm in international business research and practice', paper presented to seminar on 'Management of the MNC' at EIASM, 9–10 June.

Jacque, L. (1986) 'A morphology of joint ventures in Japan', working paper, Reginald H. Jones Center, Wharton School.

Kogut, B. (1983) 'Foreign direct investment as a sequential process', in *The Multinational Corporation in the 1980s*, C. P. Kindleberger and D. Audretsch (eds) Cambridge, MA: MIT Press; reprinted in *International Finance and Management*, Donald Lessard (ed.), New York: Wiley, 1984.

(1984) 'Normative observations on the international value-added chain and strategic groups', *Journal of International Business Studies*, 16.

Lessard, D. and Lightstone, J. (1986) 'Volatile exchange rates can put operations at risk', *Harvard Business Review*, July–August.

Lessard, D. and Lorange, P. (1977) 'Currency changes and management control: resolving the centralization/decentralization dilemma', *Accounting Review*, 52.

Lessard, D. and Sharp, D. (1984) 'Measuring the performance of operations subject to fluctuating exchange rates', *Midland Corporate Journal*, 2.

Levitt, T. (1983) 'The globalization of markets', *Harvard Business Review*.

66

Lieberman, M. (1987) 'The learning curve, diffusion, and competitive strategy', *Strategic Management Review*, 8.

Lipsey, R. E. and Kravis, I. B. (1986) 'The competitiveness and comparative advantage of US multinationals', working paper no. 2051, National Bureau of Economic Research, Inc.

Mansfield, E., Teece, D., and Romeo, A. (1979) 'Overseas research and development by US-based firms', *Economica*, 46.

March, J. (1976) 'The technology of foolishness', in *Ambiguity and Consent in Organizations*, J. G. March and J. P. Olsen (eds) Bergen, Norway: Universitetsforlaget.

Mascarenhas, B. (1985) 'International strategies of non-dominant firms', *Journal of International Business Studies*, 16.

Mintzberg, H. and McHugh, A. (1985) 'Strategy formulation as an adhocracy', *Administrative Science Quarterly*, 30.

Mintzberg, H. and Waters, J. (1985) 'Of strategies, deliberate and emergent', *Strategic Management Journal*, 6.

Mueller, W. F. and Hamm, L. G. (1980) 'Trends in industrial market concentration: 1947 to 1970', *Review of Economics and Statistics*, 56.

Nonaka, I. (1987) 'Managing globalization as a self-renewing process', paper presented to seminar on 'Management of the MNC' at EIASM, 9–10 June.

Otterbeck, L. (ed.) (1981) *The Management of Headquarters-Subsidiary Relationships in Multinational Corporations*, UK: Gower.

Ouchi, W. G. (1980) 'Markets, bureaucracies and clans', *Administrative Science Quarterly*, 25.

Perlmutter, H. (1969) 'The tortuous evolution of the multinational corporation', *Columbia Journal of World Business*, 4.

Porter, M. E. (1986) 'Competition in global industries: a conceptual framework', in *Competition in Global Industries*, M. E. Porter (ed.) Boston: Harvard Business School Press.

Prahalad, C. K. and Doz, Y. L. (1981) 'An approach to strategic control in MNCs', *Sloan Management Review*, 22.

Ronstadt, R. C. (1978) 'International R&D: the establishment and evolution of research and development abroad by seven US multinationals', *Journal of International Business Studies*, 10.

Root, F. R. (1973) *International Trade and Investment*, fifth edition, Cincinnati, OH: Southwestern Publishing Co.

Scherer, F. M. (1980) *Industrial Market Structure and Economic Performance*, Boston: Houghton Mifflin Company.

Scherer, F. M., Beckstein, A., Kaufer, E., and Murphy, R. (1973) *The Economics of Multi-Plant Operations: An International Comparison Study*, Cambridge, MA: Harvard University Press.

Scott, W. R. (1987) *Organizations, Rational, Natural, and Open Systems*, second edition, New Jersey: Prentice-Hall.

Sharp, D. (1987) *Control Systems and Decisionmaking in Multinational Firms: Price Management under Fluctuating Exchange Rates*, unpublished Ph.D. thesis, Sloan School, MIT.

Solvell, O. (1987) *Entry Barriers and Foreign Penetration*, Stockholm:

Institute of International Business, Stockholm School of Economics.

Spence, M. (1981) 'The learning curve and competition', *Bell Journal of Economics*, 12.

Stopford, J. and Wells, L. (1972) *Managing the Multinational Enterprise*, New York: Basic Books.

Takeuchi, H. and Porter, M. E. (1986) 'Three roles of international marketing in global strategy', in M. E. Porter (ed.) *Competition in Global Industries*, Boston: Harvard Business School Press.

Tsurumi, Y. (1976) *The Japanese are Coming: A Multinational Interaction of Firms and Politics*, Cambridge, MA: Ballinger Publishing Co.

Vernon (1979) 'The product cycle hypothesis in a new international environment', *Oxford Bulletin of Economics and Statistics*, 41.

Wernerfelt, B. (1984) 'A resource-based view of the firm enterprise', *Strategic Management Journal* 5, New York: Basic Books.

Chapter three

Managing globalization as a self-renewing process: experiences of Japanese MNCs

Ikujiro Nonaka

Introduction

After World War II, globalization posed a major challenge for Japanese firms that lagged far behind advanced western firms in terms of management resources, technology, and management systems. Some Japanese firms have been utilizing globalization as a lever towards self-renewal. Their globalization process is quite different from that of advanced western multinational corporations (MNCs).

A typical model for the globalization of these western MNCs is the Product Life Cycle Model which shows that western firms first develop products for the domestic market, then launch them into the global market, as the domestic market matures.[1]

Another typology classifies globalization strategies into three models: the multinational strategy, the multidomestic strategy, and the global-supplier strategy.[2] Most of the US MNCs have executed the multinational strategy that allows the global headquarters to control its 'subordinate' subsidiaries down to the most minute detail. The global headquarters first determines a world-wide strategy and a plan for execution from a global point of view. Then, headquarters orders its subsidiaries to execute the plan as prescribed in the manual. The MNC that adopts this strategy is highly structured and maintains its tight hierarchy through an owner-owned relationship.

The MNC that has adopted the second, multidomestic strategy consists of a loose network of national subsidiaries. The network is maintained chiefly through stable financial relations between the global headquarters and national subsidiaries, rather than through strong, centralized control wielded by the global headquarters. Individual national subsidiaries are virtually independent, and adapt themselves to the business environment of the countries in which they operate. This multidomestic strategy has been adopted mainly by European MNCs.[3]

The third globalization strategy, that of global supplier, is one of export-centered global expansion and has been typically used by Japanese manufacturing firms during the post-war era. All systems such as R&D, procurement, sales and marketing, distribution, and the organizational structure are designed so as to enhance exports of products manufactured in the home country. This strategy has been remarkably effective thus far for Japanese firms trying to globalize. Yet Japanese firms are now required to re-examine this traditional strategy under severe business conditions such as a stagnant domestic economy, rapid appreciation of the yen, worsening trade conflicts, etc.

This chapter intends to show the self-renewal processes of those Japanese firms that are actively seeking a new style of globalization which differs from the global supplier strategy, the multidomestic strategy, and the multinational strategy. Here, the key concept is world-wide organizational information creation. I hope that bringing to light this new style of globalization will offer a new perspective on the planning and evaluation of globalization strategies of MNCs throughout the world.

Globalization as a challenge

As explained above, relatively globalized Japanese firms have been using globalization as a challenge for their self-renewal. Their self-renewal process can be conceptualized as consisting of the following four phases.[4]

Figure 3.1 The self-renewing process of the organization

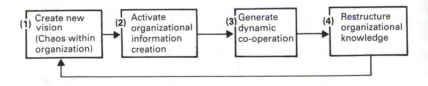

Self-renewal of a company often starts with the creation of strategic vision (domain and/or mission). Such a vision may create an entirely new meaning or organizational direction for the firm, which radically transforms the organizational perspective used up until now. It frequently includes a proactive assertion containing a strong sense of purpose to challenge the new environment.

The second process involved in the self-renewal of a firm consists of the activation of information creation through the amplification of chaos and the focusing on contradictions. Generating chaos is not enough; it has to be amplified. To begin with, formation of a new order is pulled back to the inertia of the organization unless it is far removed from its state of equilibrium. As the organization moves in the direction of innovation, creative chaos is amplified so as to focus on the specific contradictions that need to be resolved in order to actualize the new vision. These contradictions produce a continuous and fluctuating demand for new information or a new perspective.

The third process involved in the self-renewal of the firm is the stimulation of dynamic co-operation within an organization for resolving problems. When the chaos makes employees change their way of looking at a given situation and when new information is created, dynamic co-operation between the members of the entire organization must take place. An important result of the generation of dynamic co-operation is to produce cross-functional synergy within the organization. As long as the process of creating information is constrained to certain levels or to a particular department or division, no change of organizational viewpoint throughout the total organization will take place. A dynamic cross-functional interaction across functional specializations (development, manufacturing, and sales functions at the minimum) and divisions must occur all at once.

The fourth process in the self-renewal of the firm is the transformation of accumulated information into knowledge. The three processes of information creation discussed above are conceived with the idea of promoting the activation of information creation. In addition to these, a continuously evolving organization is a learning organization. A learning organization transforms the flow of information into a stock of knowledge, and at the same time, spreads it to other departments and stimulates the systematic transfer of information which has been generated and stored. The information generated is shared by all the members of the organization and becomes knowledge at the organizational level. Once organizational knowledge becomes too obsolete to cope with new environment, it has to be renewed. Self-renewal must progress irreversibly as existing knowledge is restructured to create new visions. Thus, the self-renewing process goes on.

Based on this self-renewing model, the globalization process of relatively advanced Japanese companies is demonstrated. These companies may be characterized as leaders of the global-supplier strategy, but now have begun to develop a new style of globalization. The next section describes how the globalization of Japanese companies corresponds to the four phases of the self-renewing process of organizations.

1. Creation of chaos

There are two types of corporate self-renewal. One is an endogeneous self-renewal achieved by setting challenging tasks in order to cast off the firm's old structure irrespective of environmental conditions. The other is an exogeneous type of renewal achieved by responding to challenges from the environment. In either case, some sort of 'chaos' or fluctuation is necessary for the initiation of self-renewal. Chaos generates redundancy, uncertainty, tension, and challenge *vis-à-vis* the established organizational order, and it may even include the intentional creation of a crisis.

One of the maxims of Koji Kobayashi, chairman of Nippon Electric Co. Ltd (NEC), is 'Stability in instability'. This paradoxical quote suggests that a stable firm is unstable and vice versa, because the instability in the environment is a stimulus creating the chaos necessary for the development of stability within a firm. Accordingly, a corporation must have the dynamism to respond constructively to unstable influences. The globalization of NEC began with the plan to de-stabilize NEC's short-run security derived from its high degree of dependence on Nippon Telegraph & Telephone Public Corporation (NTTPC), and to make NEC itself stable in the long run. As a major supplier of equipment to NTTPC, NEC enjoyed an uninterrupted profit flow at that time. Nevertheless, it started exploring the overseas market very early in order to expand its business beyond the safety of its favourable position. Kobayashi comments as follows:

> It was around 1959 when we began planning our entry into the overseas market. When I joined the company, it was blindly following technological information of foreign origin, paying royalties, and just imitating these technologies without any original creation. What was worse, the company was nothing more than a sort of factory for NTTPC, which was our largest customer at that time. This was the background that led us to the decision. My number one priority was to make the company show promise for the future.[5]

Thus, NEC's push to sell products abroad was not a scheme to demonstrate its technological ability, but rather, the company thought that by entering overseas markets, it would be able to evaluate its level of technological development *vis-à-vis* its foreign competitors.

Since its foundation, Honda has maintained as its corporate principle: 'Our company stands on a global vision. We respond to customer needs and produce superior products at a reasonable price.' When Kawashima, former president, heard about this corporate motto immediately after the World War II, he almost burst out laughing, as this was the policy of a small business from which only a few staff members had ever been abroad. In 1950, just after its foundation, Soichiro Honda used to shout out his message 'Let's be the best in the world, not just in Japan' while standing on a box of tangerines before about fifty employees, even though the company could not pay these employees at the end of the month.

In 1954, after his first study tour of the TT race held at The Isle of Man, UK, Soichiro Honda realized that such a difficult race could become an indispensable 'moving laboratory' for Honda's technological development. With the declaration of the Honda company's entry in the race to be the winner, Honda Motors took upon itself the challenge to catch up with the world level of motor-cycle technology. At that time, European manufacturers were producing engines of the same gas column volume that were three times as powerful as Honda's, and their technologies as applied to some components such as tyres and chains were far superior to those of the Japanese.

Canon's predecessor, the Seiki Kogaku Kenkyusho, was a start-up firm founded in 1933 by young camera buffs with the ambition to develop a Japanese Leica camera, which was the best camera in the world at that time. On 1 October, 1945, Takeshi Mitarai, the founder of Canon, announced the resumption of camera production at the Meguro Lens Plant in Tokyo with the following words:

It is true that the U.S. defeated Japan. However, when officers of U.S. occupation troops visited us to buy cameras, they found our products to be 'wonderful!' They also commented that 'It is not hard to understand why Japan can make such a wonderful product. The excellent technological tradition, which gave birth to Zero Fighters, still lives in the Japanese precision manufacturing industry, and has produced these high-class cameras.' We have lost the war, but it was not due to the lack of brain power. At present, many companies are manufacturing only necessities such as pans and pots, and no brain power is needed for this purpose. These Japanese skills, which astonished the Americans, are best utilized in the field of camera manufacturing,

73

which requires few raw materials. If we continue our research with redoubled efforts, the day will soon come when we can dominate the world camera market with our excellent cameras. I would like to ask those of you who agree with me to follow me from now on.

As the above cases show, globalization has been a challenging goal, which seemed almost impossible to attain even for those Japanese firms which, from today's standpoint, appear to have succeeded in globalization. This challenge made employees recognize the contradictions between the status quo and the visions, and created much chaos within these firms.

2. Activation of organizational information creation

Chaos within an organization requires the active inflow of hetero-geneous information into the established organizational order. Consequently, it generates contradictions and gaps between the status quo and the ideal. In order to overcome these contradictions and gaps, the organization initiates the generation of new informa-tion and organizational learning. It is the middle management which functions as the core group of organizational information creation activities.

It is international races that have played an important role in the process of Honda's organizational learning. Participation in a speed race, which provides the challenge of time and technological limitations, has been the best training for its engineers. In pre-paring for these races, one must take every possible measure in order to defeat the competitors. For example, one must develop new materials, and design engines never tried before. In other words, a race is a challenge to achieve the impossible. Technologies of the highest edge are tested in races, and their success or failure is determined instantly.

Canon shifted its sales style in the US market from exporting through Bell & Howell, its sales agent, to direct sales through its own subsidiary, Canon America. This enabled Canon to accumu-late hands-on knowledge of the market. In the early 1970s, the company's senior management became concerned about US camera sales. Other product lines were doing well, but camera sales had lost ground to the chief competitors. They sent three managers to the US to look into the problem. They had never been to the US before, and they were almost amateurs in marketing research. Instead of using sophisticated marketing research techniques, they visited camera stores and other retail outlets across the US. By talking with store owners, they learned that US dealers were not giving Canon much support because their sales forces were too small. They often invited the store managers to lunch to discuss cameras and whatever else happened to be on the dealers' minds. The pay-off was more than just market research. They were building lasting relationships with the dealers — an important competitive advantage. Their research determined Canon's distribution strategy: sell exclusively through specialty dealers serving an upscale, high-quality niche. The AE-1, one of Canon's best selling cameras, was successfully developed in 1976 on the basis of the knowledge derived from this direct experience in the US.[6]

3. *Dynamic co-operation*

The chaos within an organization activates organizational information creation and learning. This then induces a dynamic co-operative phenomenon throughout the entire organization. The dynamic co-operation in a firm is linked to the synchronization of dynamism in the firm, market, and technology respectively. In enlarging a business's domain by undertaking overseas marketing, a sudden sales burst of macroscopic proportions often energizes the entire corporation and sparks it to move forward. This phenomenon may be detected when export or overseas sales exceed a certain 'critical mass' (say 10 per cent to 20 per cent of total production or sales). Such a 'critical mass' can be considered the threshold of 'true globalization'. In this case the self-renewing process through globalization is accelerated.

In the 1950s, export markets seemed to hold very little promise for NEC — the company started out with only three successful export orders out of 1,000 inquiries. However, the ceaseless efforts to crack the export market were eventually rewarded. Export levels began to rise considerably around 1957. As the NEC trademark was almost unknown abroad, NEC had to start from scratch. From the latter part of the 1950s through the 1960s, NEC accumulated a wealth of knowledge about the kinds of products needed in international markets and concentrated on meeting these demands as well as the challenges posed by foreign competitors. NEC's efforts began to bear fruit around 1968. Despite daunting odds in the export business, NEC triumphed because it learned to respond to the needs of the private sector, and because it emphasized the importance of profits in the long run. For an unknown company like NEC, cost was of paramount importance in selling its products overseas. Since its export operations were not very profitable in many cases, NEC soon became acutely aware of the need for company-wide cost-consciousness in order to maintain its price-competitiveness. Over time, a growing network of NEC engineers began to accumulate considerable experience in foreign markets. As the ratio of exports to total sales of a particular division expanded, the division would have to redouble its cost-cutting efforts in order to secure profits. As the Senior Executive Director of NEC, Shozo Shimizu recalls, it was around 1968 when such continual efforts finally bore fruit. The ratio of exports to the company's total sales was then reaching about 20 per cent, which was significant enough to encourage the whole company to undertake additional globalization activities. The whole organization then changed its character to meet the new trend which accompanied the rapid increase in exports. At the product division level, a 20 per cent export ratio has also been the threshold of rapid and substantial globalization.

After its motorcycle gained world-wide recognition by challenging globalization, Honda diversified itself into the automobile business, utilizing its previous success as a marketing tool. Honda then proceeded to change from an export-centred overseas strategy to one of overseas production, proceeding one step at a time. The event which triggered the acceleration of this process was the sudden and massive opening up of the motorcycle market by the successful 'Nicest People Campaign'. This success enabled the organization to develop considerable forward momentum toward globalization.

The initiation of direct sales led to an explosive increase in the sales of the Canon AE-1 in the North American market. The AE-1 sold a tremendous number of units in the world market. It pushed up Canon, which had been only number two in the Japanese market, to become the dominant force in the world single-lens, reflex camera market.

4. The restructuring of organizational knowledge

After the dynamic co-operative phenomenon occurs, it facilitates the organization-wide transformation of new information into knowledge, and a restructuring of organizational knowledge is carried out. In other words, both the learning and unlearning of knowledge are triggered.

The driving force of NEC's self-renewal was the creation and realization of its strategic concept 'C & C' (Computers & Communications). This concept did not emerge suddenly. Rather, it has been persistently forged out of the product concepts generated at the division level. Its precursors were '4C' and '5C', which were the themes of company-wide campaigns in 1964 and 1965.

After the successful global marketing of its main lines, telephone switching systems, and microwave communication systems, NEC diversified into the area of computers. This was a natural outgrowth of its need for hardware in designing microwave filters for communication systems. The success in employing digital technology in microwave communication systems increased the similarities of the technologies embodied in both communications systems and computers. In 1977, NEC announced a digital switching system, and simultaneously, the 'C & C' concept. Koji Kobayashi, chairman, said that one of the factors that brought about the 'C & C' concept was the development of the semiconductor. He also indicated that the shift of the existing technological core to digital technology by means of semiconductor devices served as a basis for the integrated computer and communication network. In order to develop and execute a strategic concept at the corporate level, each department in an organization must accumulate a specific amount of information in order to create concepts for new products. These product concepts then interact, and the information accumulated in each department is integrated into the store of organizational knowledge of the entire corporation. In addition to the generation of creative concepts by each department in this way, a change in the consciousness of the entire organization occurred, and a restructuring of organizational knowledge took place.

After Canon recorded a loss due to the unsuccessful Synchro-Reader and its desk-top calculators, Ryuzaburo Kaku, its new president, began reconstruction of Canon as a whole. At the same time, Seiichi Takigawa, who as president of Canon US had made excellent contributions to the strengthening of its sales force in the US, took the initiative to reform the entire sales division of Canon itself. One of the reforms Takigawa derived from his experience in the US was to switch to direct domestic marketing, a move which resulted in a complete restructuring of Canon's basic business practices in the domestic market.

Continual self-renewal and global information creation

The globalization of Japanese firms is conceptualized in the self-renewal process outlined in the above four phases. These processes are, however, patterns of the past. Japanese firms today facing rising protectionism and trade conflicts, have been seeking new patterns of globalization. Consequently, the self-renewal process progresses irreversibly. The essence of this self-renewal resides in continuous organizational 'information creation'.[7]

Before proceeding to further discussions, it is necessary to explain what is meant by 'information creation' and the concept of 'information' itself.

Information can be divided into two representative types — syntactic and semantic information.

Syntactic information is a quantitative type in which no attention is given to the inherent meaning of the information. Shannon's communication theory conceptualizes the basic nature of this type of information as symbolic information measured in bits.[8] A telephone bill is not computed based on the contents of the conversation (meaning), but on the length of time the communication takes. The information-processing paradigm mainly deals with this quantitative type of information. The model for syntactic information is type of information which can be stored in a computer in a coded and quantitatively measurable form.

In contrast, semantic information examines the actual meaning of information. Although actual measurement is difficult, it is this qualitative type of information that somehow changes our perceptions and meaning association. The 'generation of information' is the generation of 'information with meaning'. As Bateson puts it, information is 'any difference that makes a difference'.[9] The new meanings provide a new standpoint for interpreting events. More simply, the creation of information means creating a new perspective or a new point of view, namely a new dimension for organizing and interpreting information. The model for semantic information is exemplified by the creation of concepts and values in strategy, new product development, marketing promotion, and production methods (e.g. 'Kanban').

One cannot, of course, create a total distinction between syntactic information and semantic information. Most syntactic information, for example, can be perceived within normal, routine information, but when it is integrated above a certain level, clues regarding new dimensions of information can be discovered. Once formed and made into a routine, semantic information, or meaning, becomes syntactic information. In this way syntactic information is gradually mechanized, and humans are able to devote more of their efforts to non-routine information. Thus, one can hope that the two types of information will actually complement each other, resulting in greater efficiency in the generation of information.

At this point, in order to summarize the special characteristics of syntactic versus semantic information, I would like to refer the reader to Table 3.1.

First of all, with respect to the uniqueness of the information, syntactic information is not 'surprising' because it does not reveal a

Table 3.1 A comparison of the characteristics of syntactic and semantic information

	Syntactic information	*Semantic information*
Novelty	1 Unsurprising 2 Meaning pre-exists — reiteration of existing concepts	1 Surprising — provides a new point of view 2 Meaning is created — a new perspective is created
Variability	1 Low context 2 Universal meaning, limited discretionary powers, and static	1 High-context 2 Meaning varies with the situation and is dynamically generated
Organizational character	1 Mechanistic — counteracts entropy 2 Self-completing (individual fact)	1 Organic — promotes entropy 2 Self-organizing (association between facts)
Methodology	1 Deductive, analytical reductionistic Hands-off (abstract, objective, logical) 2 Reduction of redundancy (requisite variety) 3 Human interaction is not essential (computer network)	1 Inductive, synthetic, holistic Hands-on (concrete, experiential, intuitive) 2 Importance of redundancy (noise, fluctuation, chaos) 3 Human interaction is essential (human network)
Type of organizational knowledge	Articulate knowledge (manuals, procedures)	Tacit knowledge (expertise of craftsman)

new angle exposure to a new perspective. This is not because syntactic information contains a meaning, but because the meaning is ultimately pre-existing, and even if new data were to appear, it could be explained by use of existing terminology. The majority of syntactic information possesses a high degree of universality due to its clearly codified nature, and its meaning does not change from one context to another. Here, the degree of contextual dependency is low. Therefore, the processing of this information requires only a modicum of ability for individual decision, and this type of function better exemplifies information processing than information creation. Since this type of information is self-contained and repetitive, it is useful in constructing physical information processing capability (hardware) to counteract the tendency toward entropy within an organization.

The methodology used in information processing is deductive. That is to say, if one analytically reconstructs the separate facts in order to clarify the premise, all of the new information can be identified and any redundancy can be eliminated so as to raise the efficiency of the information processing. It then becomes easy to enter this information into a computer network.

Semantic information, on the other hand, creates new meaning and produces 'surprise', shifting perspective, and revealing a new point of view. Therefore, meaning (concept), rather than being as given, is created. This best exemplifies the idea of information creation. Meaning varies and becomes specific depending upon the given context, and active creation is predominant. In terms of organizational characteristics, semantic information perhaps advances entropy tentatively. But when it triggers the restructuring of organizational knowledge, drastic reduction in entropy takes place. New meanings are proposed or created when existing information or knowledge is no longer able to explain effectively the novel situation. The creation of chaos or fluctuations aims at the intentional creation of such a critical situation. Various types of information are brought together in the situation in order to form new meanings that facilitate the entropy reduction. Yet, because there are many alternative ways to combine the information, more information than was initially presented is continuously produced in a chain reaction-like process. This 'information breeder' mechanism repeats the cycle, from the creation of meaning to the reduction of entropy. Semantic information which has been codified represents only a small portion of the total information. The majority of semantic information lies (untapped) within the individual. While the syntactic information is integrated into 'articulate' knowledge, the semantic information is integrated into 'inarticulate' knowledge, or what Michael Polanyi has termed 'tacit' knowledge — that is, the knowledge which cannot be completely expressed either in words or numbers.[10]

The methodology for dealing with meaning creation is basically inductive. However, there are few situations where the premise is clearly defined; the information-creating process is never free of inductive ambiguity. 'In the presence of inductive ambiguity, what propels a science is a heuristic principle which is neither unique nor necessary. It does not guarantee success.'[11] Therefore, redundancy and instability are essential in order to stimulate and support information creation. Intuitive, synthetic judgements are more important than deductive analysis for this type of conceptual creation. Meaning is therefore created in a dynamic manner, involving personal contact, dialogue, and flashes of insight.

Based on the above discussion, two methodological types of organizational information creation have been conceived: top-down management and bottom-up management. These types of organizational information creation can be extended to the management of multinational firms. For example, top-down management is utilized in a 'multi-national' corporate structure in which the centre of information creation is located at the global headquarters. Bottom-up management occurs in a 'multi-domestic' structure in which the centre of information creation is at a local office.

As for the 'global supplier' corporate structure that has been adopted by typical export-oriented Japanese firms thus far, the characteristics of the organizational information creation involved are similar to those of top-down management. In this pattern, each local agency is regarded as a satellite branch which is under the tight control of headquarters. This 'global supplier' strategy of Japanese firms is, however, in serious trouble today in regard to the changes in the global market. This strategy has been very effective in achieving rapid and intensive penetration into a targeted market through the export of universal products, manufactured in locations where the best labour and parts suppliers were available. In this scenario, unlimited openness of the global market is necessary as a basic condition. Cut-throat competition among Japanese firms that eagerly seek for larger market share has been combined with this strategy, and has resulted in 'concentrated-heavy-rain exports', which is considered to have caused serious trade friction. Japanese firms must now make rapid localization their top priority. However, localization through the construction of multi-domestic structures will result in a loss of competitive advantage against local firms. Therefore, the challenge which faces Japanese firms at present is the contradictory task of successfully localizing operations while simultaneously maintaining the advantages of globalization.

The quest for a new globalization strategy which could replace the 'global supplier' strategy has already been initiated by the above-mentioned leading Japanese MNCs, as well as other Japanese firms. The new strategy by which to realize globalization may be characterized by a third pattern of organizational information creation, different from the top-down management of the 'multi-national' strategy and the bottom-up management of a 'multi-domestic' one. I call this new pattern 'middle-up-down management'.[12] Middle-up-down management is to be found in a network structure in which information is generated by means of the dynamic co-operation between global and regional headquarters.

81

The task of 'global-localization' gives continuous motivation to keep interaction necessary for the dynamic co-operation.

Japanese firms that have succeeded in globalization tend to practise this third type of management since it enables them to carry out their continuous self-renewing process. Other Japanese firms are presently following the lead of those firms which have adopted this style of middle-up-down management. A considerable number of Japanese firms are now in the process of self-renewal through globalization; that is, creating chaos, creating organizational information, generating dynamic co-operation and restructuring organizational knowledge.

The key factor in this process is global information creation through cross fertilization of various types of organizational knowledge. Syntactic and semantic information, or rather, articulate knowledge and tacit knowledge are combined, and they fertilize each other in local offices, global headquarters, and in the dynamic synergy between the two. This new pattern of globalization of Japanese firms involves the following processes:

1. Creation of global vision,
2. Integration of overseas organizations and the establishment of multiple corporate headquarters,
3. Promotion global hybridization process, and
4. Globalization of personnel administration and cultivation of entrepreneurial middle management.

1. Creation of global vision

It is the task of the global headquarters to create a global vision. This global vision must be universally valid. From the viewpoint of information creation, it is desirable to show a broad direction but not to be too specific. This type of vision permits fluctuation in interpretation and thus activates information creation in regional headquarters. Such visions can be regarded as metaphors in the sense that the metaphor provides novel and equivocal meanings (even contradictions) which depend on indefinite patterns of associated ideas or images. Therefore, a global vision as a metaphor encourages people to search for new meaning in which to integrate these various interpretations and contradictions. It is also desirable that the vision activates the spontaneous self-renewal of regional headquarters by making those at regional offices recognize the gap between the current situation and the ambitious dreams proposed in the vision. The following strategic visions of Japanese firms reveal universal and ambitious dreams: 'NEC must become a world leader in the 2.5 industry' (NEC); 'Canon contributes to world humanity' (Canon); 'We wish to be essential to people throughout the world' (Sanyo); and 'Otsuka People Creating New Products for Better Health Worldwide' (Otsuka Pharmaceutical).

NEC's President Sekimoto envisages their corporate domain which looks forward to the twenty-first century in the following manner:

> How will secondary industry change? In the future the manufacturing sector will need to incorporate tertiary industry within secondary industry, creating a secondary industry armed with information and software. In raising secondary industry halfway to tertiary level we will gain a more sophisticated level of industrial power and development — what I call a '2.5' industry . . . NEC itself must become a 2.5 industry. To take semiconductors and ICs as an example, this transition consists of making not only standard products such as memories but also custom products that incorporate software such as custom LSIs and system LSIs or ASICs (Application Specified ICs). In other words, the important products of the future will be 2.5-industry products. The same is true of production. We must establish production methods armed with software — 2.5-industry production methods. In practice these include large variety-small-lot production systems, and the development of FMSs (flexible manufacturing systems) and unmanned factories. Thus, 'NEC must become a world leader in the 2.5 industry' by arming both our products and our production processes with software. That is clearly the direction for us to take and the identity to aim for.

Tadashi Kume, CEO of Honda, expresses the role of middle management as follows:

> I continually create dreams. . . . Top management doesn't know what the bottom is doing. The opposite is also true. For example, John at Honda Ohio is not able to see the company's overall direction. We at corporate headquarters see the world differently, think differently, and face a different environment. It is middle management which is charged with integrating these two view points emanating from top and bottom management. There can be, therefore, no progress without such integration.[13]

Honda is, in fact, a company creating continuous contradictions. They still keep firmly to their corporate vision: 'Our company stands on a global vision. We respond to customer needs and produce superior products at a reasonable price.' Meanwhile, the company also stresses the need to 'be in touch with the reality of local conditions'. Consequently, the company constantly generates conflict between dreams and reality. In order to resolve this conflict, middle management or local managers must create and actualize business and product concepts which are capable of being tested empirically.

2. Integration of overseas business organization and establishment of multiple corporate headquarters

It is imperative for corporations to redefine domestic and overseas organizational structures for the speedy deployment of global information creation. On 1 April 1987, Toshiba Corporation announced the integration of its 'International Division', which had been responsible for overseas sales along with the Electrical Home Appliances Division and other product divisions. The integration of these divisions was intended to serve as the basis for its global business deployment.[14]

Those who are proficient in English and have much experience doing business abroad have been regarded as 'internationalists' in Japanese firms, and have been given 'overseas-related jobs'. However, this simple human resource allocation pattern is no longer effective. As many as 220 people were moved from Toshiba's International Division to other product divisions in accordance with the 'big transfer'. It is hoped that these people will reform company-wide business awareness by stimulating other people who have thus far engaged only in traditional 'domestic-oriented assignments' as opposed to the more disappointing experiences in US MNCs.[15] In other words, the integration aims at 'producing new internationalists who do business with the world atlas in mind' and 'fostering staff members who are qualified to handle both domestic and overseas business'.

At the same time, in order to carry out successful middle up-down management, it is necessary to create multiple headquarters. The object is to achieve dynamic co-operation between the top global headquarters and the highly independent 'regional headquarters' that control all operations inside a specific region. The construction of a 'hererarchy' structure may represent a new pattern of globalization, one which differs from the traditional configurations and methods employed by IBM and Coca Cola.[16] Several Japanese firms are currently developing the multiple headquarters concept.

Yamaha released the 'Rules of Authority Delegation' which includes as many as eighty articles in the four months beginning in

August 1986. The Rules increase the autonomy of overseas subsidiaries to the extent that subsidiaries like YCA (Yamaha Corporation of America) can function as regional headquarters. The authority of the headquarters in Japan is supreme only in the case of: (1) changes in the rules of incorporation, (2) increases or decreases in capital, (3) merger or dissolution, and (4) authorization of account settlement and appropriation of retained earnings. Various functions and authority such as management planning and budgeting are delegated to these 'regional headquarters'.

Yamaha's multiple-headquarters system enables the firm to respond to local needs adequately and rapidly. In the Summer of 1988, YCA made two big decisions. The first was to increase piano production at the Yamaha Music manaufacturing plant in Georgia by 1989. The other was to expand its wind instrument manufacturing plant to almost twice present production capacity.

Those two plans were made under the initiative of the YCA, which is able to communicate closely with local marketing channels in the US. Divisional Headquarters in Japan only have to give the final go-ahead. One of executive officers said, 'If the global headquarters took the initiative in the strategy for North American region like we used to do, such ambitious plans would never have been proposed. Both plans would have been much more conservatively modified, and would have taken much longer for a final decision.'

Hitachi America, a subsidiary of Hitachi Ltd, started its operations in New York as Hitachi's US headquarters. Hitachi America has drastically increased its capital by 8.2 times, from $4.3 million to $35.3 million, and affiliated itself with four manufacturing companies such as Hitachi Consumer Products. 'Establish a miniature Hitachi in the U.S., which is the largest market for us,' is the strategic policy of Katsushige Mita, the President of Hitachi Ltd. A regional headquarters with a high level of authority over final decision-making can serve as an effective response to changes in exchange rates. Large financial benefits can also be obtained by consolidating the final accounts of several overseas affiliates which allows the headquarters to cover the loss of one affiliate with the profit of another.

As the number and the size of overseas affiliates increase, overall control by the headquarters in Tokyo becomes less practical and less effective. 'Product development should be localized, otherwise critical delays eventually occur. Timely decisions by local management will lead to cost reduction' says the management of Honda Motors, which founded its new US headquarters this March. As the management environment is changing very rapidly, it is necessary to respond effectively by redistributing the heaquarters' functions among subsidiaries in Japan, the US, and Europe.

However, Honda does not enforce 100 per cent the Honda way, (all the business methods of Honda in Japan) in its US head-quarters and plants. As its director, Chino, explains, mutual under-standing with local employees and business partners on the outside such as parts suppliers is critical in the localization of subsidiaries. Being a manufacturing company, Honda North America can com-municate with local employees and parts suppliers smoothly by taking pains to work together in the process of production. Chino says, 'There is no magic wand in Honda Ohio. The key is the accumulation of minor, incremental improvements attained through everyday communication.'

For Honda, establishing the regional headquarters in the US, named Honda North America, has another important aim. That is getting social recognition that 'Honda is one of the American firms managed by Americans.' Chino said, 'Such kind of localization is necessary not to get "Honda bashing" coming from the wrong image that the success of Honda in the United States is due to "fear of Japan".'

HOYA, a leading glass products manufacturer, is planning to found regional headquarters in the US and Europe in four to five years. Dainippon Ink and Chemicals, Inc., the dominant ink manu-facturer in Japan, will soon transfer a part of its headquarters' responsibilities to DIC America. Nippondenso Co., Ltd, a leading automobile parts maker, will set up a four headquarters system in Japan, US, Europe, and Asia by 1991.

It is not strange that some companies have begun to feel that their headquarters need not be located in Japan. Soichiro Honda, now the top corporate adviser of Honda, predicts, 'Our head-quarters is not in Tokyo, yet it may be possible to locate it in a space satellite in the future.'

3. Promotion of global hybridization

While a global vision creates contradictions and gaps between the current situation and the ideal at the global level, local managers function as the key producers of creative solutions to these contra-dictions and gaps. The creation of new perspectives, or new information is necessary in order to find solutions. The globaliza-tion of personnel described below produces active information creation through cross-fertilization, or global synergy of local tacit knowledge and global articulate knowledge.

(a) Hybridization

When Honda motors first went to the US, there was considerable conflict between the 'Honda way' and the American way of doing things. For example, one feature of the Honda way is to 'manufacture where your market is'. When Honda began to produce automobiles in the US, the Americans questioned its logic, as the Big Three (Chrysler, General Motors, and Ford) had all begun producing abroad. The Japanese explained their company policy as something which was 'appropriate in the long term'.

HAM President Shoichiro Irimagiri calls the conflict between the Japanese and American way of thinking 'a tug-of-war'. He feels that Japanese and Americans can accept 20 per cent of each others' ways of thinking without question, but that there was 40 per cent which could not be understood at all. Including this remaining 40 per cent, the company has a 60 per cent area within which to make policy. Whether decisions are influenced more by the American way or the Japanese way of thinking then becomes extremely important. If the Japanese were to keep quiet, Honda Ohio would turn into another 'Detroit-style' plant. If management favours the Japanese style, Honda Ohio will become another 'Suzuka' or 'Sayama', which are typical domestic plants of Honda. In either case, one side would be dissatisfied and the policy would not last long. 'By avoiding dissatisfaction on either side and by wavering between the two, I hope the distance between us will become smaller,' say Irimagiri.[17]

More importantly, the 'tug-of-war' metaphor is not only applicable to the established Honda way, it is also concerned with closing the gap between American and Japanese practices and differences in methodology used for information creation so as to create a new Honda way. This can only be accomplished through human interaction. Irimagiri emphasizes this point, noting, 'It's said that we should debate things between ourselves. If there were less debate, this company would close. As long as we're tugging away at each other, we're O.K.' Irimajiri makes it an everyday practice to visit the shop floor and to converse directly with workers so that he can enjoy the flavour of the tacit knowledge, which he brings back in his search for a 'Honda Ohio way'.

It is the global self-organizing team of across functional or inter-disciplinary nature that plays a central role in the process of organizational information creation. Such a team is formed with middle management as its core. Honda developed 'Legend', its first model, as the product of its joint development team with Leyland, UK. Fuji Xerox is developing computer software (on a twenty-four hour basis) together with the members of the Xerox Research Lab at Stanford University. Nomura Securities uses project teams consisting of the staff of its headquarters and other regional branches (mainly the New York Branch) as core groups for the development of new merchandise.

(b) Global synergy and cross fertilization

It is very important to design the global synergy between localization and globalization. This global synergy is realized by cross-fertilization of the localized, tacit knowledge and the global, articulate knowledge. It has been emphasized that the cross-fertilization of the tacit and the articulate knowledge is critically important for organizational information creation. The dynamic process of organizational information creation continuously requires a new leap that is the outcome of interaction between the tacit and the articulate knowledge. The tacit knowledge that is attained through hands-on, local experience is of limited value unless it is widely shared in a clearer form. On the one hand, even though the conversion of the tacit knowledge into the articulate knowledge has to be done through a difficult and muddling path, the effort is truly worthwhile. By repeating trials and errors in the conversion process, the tacit knowledge is integrated into the articulate one, resulting in the enrichment of the latter. On the other hand, enriched articulate knowledge provides new perspectives for the quest of more tacit knowledge in new fields, and consequently, enlarges the domain of the total organizational knowledge. Thus, both tacit and articulate knowledge are equally important, and like wheels and the drive shaft, they are indispensable to each other.

President Kume of Honda motors says that in order to expand a truly global firm beyond simple localization, the one way outflow of technology and systems from Japan must be abolished, and various types of networks and mutual information exchanges among local bases must be instituted. He also says, 'The product of each local base has its own flavour created by its own people. I feel that by condensing and purifying, that flavour becomes precious in value. It is important to create products of original local value, and then to exchange various values recognized world-wide.' As for R&D activities in general, western researchers are said to be more skilled and talented in selected fields of individual information creation than their Japanese counterparts. Globalization of MNCs generally starts with the product export phase, then proceeds to the overseas production phase, and eventually reaches the overseas R&D phase. Yet, emerging today are some Japanese firms who have begun their overseas business expansion with product development and basic research, taking advantage of global information creation.

Kao has founded a Kao Research Laboratory in West Berlin. 'Each European has unique hair colour and texture. Products for European markets must be developed there. Doing research in an entirely different environment widens the range of Kao's product development,' comments Hiroshi Fukuzaki, Administrator of the Laboratory.

Since its foundation in October 1986, the laboratory has developed as many as twelve new products in only half a year. Its initial ten research staff members (seven Germans and three Japanese) started development of such hair care products as shampoo, rinse, and hair colouring, as well as cosmetics.

Yoshio Maruta, President of Kao, indicates that 'in order to compete with Western firms dominating international markets, we must possess the unique ability to develop products closely connected with the market.' Kao is now planning to found another laboratory in Los Angeles this year, and to bring back the result of overseas product development for domestic R&D activities.

Otsuka Pharmaceutical opened a satellite laboratory in Frankfurt, West Germany in 1982, and in Maryland and in Seattle, US in 1985 and 1987 respectively. The two laboratories in the US are mainly doing basic research in such fields as immunity, sugar, and fats. Akihiko Otsuka, President, emphasizes that 'major western pharmaceutical firms have been establishing R&D bases worldwide for a long time. From now on, Japanese firms must also utilize the brain power of the world strategically.'

The standards for production licensing of pharmaceuticals differ from country to country. Consequently, it is hard to predict which medicines can be manufactured where. 'Having R&D bases in three major poles Japan — the U.S., and Europe — we can enter any market quickly, says Hideyuki Miwa, managing director, explaining the aim of the 'Simultaneous R&D in Three Countries' system. This system also facilitates the retrieval of the newest information and the elimination of fruitless research.

'British researchers are logical, whereas American are goal-pursuing, and Japanese are disposed to trial-and-error. Combining the respective advantages of these different types of researchers makes R&D much more effective.' Masahiko Morkuni, vice president of Sony emphasizes the importance of a multi-national brain complex. Currently, Sony is operating R&D bases in the US and the UK with a total of 110 researchers.

It would be necessary to remember that global hybridization

must be realized through a subtle balance between the head-quarters' initiative and local initiative. Once that balance has been broken, not only the local subsidiary, but also the parent company may face a crisis. Sony used to have a localization policy about overseas subsidiaries, and allowed them to have their own sales and pricing policies. But when a recession struck Sony in 1982, the parent company wanted to limit the corporate response, but could not prevent the overseas subsidiaries from adopting aggressive sales policies. As the result, the inventory accumulated and Sony as a whole suffered great damage in comparison to other Japanese electric appliance makers. Sony introduced a new divisional structure and moved profit centres to product divisions. As the chief of overseas sales, said, 'It is necessary to centralize at a certain stage of the process in order to achieve "true globalization".'

4. Globalization of personnel management and cultivation of an entrpreneurial middle management

Organizational information creation cannot be achieved by top-down control. Instead, subtle control methods such as global personnel administration and global information networks should be adopted.

(a) Global personnel interchange

Some Japanese firms are testing a counter-stationing system as a form of global personnel interchange. The trading companies were early pioneers of this system, Marubeni counter-stationing in 1978 and Mitsubishi Shoji in 1980. Other companies include Fuji Bank and NEC, both commencing this practice in 1986.

The NEC procedures illustrate how such a system is usually implemented. Every year one of its forty-odd subsidiaries abroad is asked to nominate a candidate. The company then selects five to six individuals who are invited to work for two years as senior management trainees at the headquarters in Tokyo. Although problems still remain, the goal of this system is to enable native executives of overseas subsidiaries to experience the corporate culture of the parent company. As the head of NEC's International Personnel Relations Department says, 'It is quite meaningful to stay in Japan for several years, to live and work together with the Japanese staff of related departments, and to be personally acquainted with them as well as with Japanese executives.' For most companies, personnel exchange between Japanese head-quarters and overseas subsidiaries thus far has been limited to the one-way outflow of staff from Japan. The counter-stationing system is the beginning of a truly global personnel interchange.

(b) Networking syntactic information

In addition to the information generated by the compiling of semantic information and tacit knowledge through personnel interchange, it is also important to form a network of syntactic information.

In January 1987, Matsushita Electric Trading Co., Ltd linked 88 points in Japan and 80 points world-wide with its computerized network 'MAXNET II'. One of the primary aims of this network is to support the global management strategies of the Matsushita Group by obtaining on-line management information from its subsidiaries inside and outside Japan. Yet, there is another important aim to note here.

Matsushita's International Procurement Representatives, who are stationed in major locations around the world, transmit information on materials and parts through the MAXNET II to the International Trading Division at the Japan Headquarters. The International Trading Division, in turn, relays the collected information to regional divisions world-wide. 'Procurement so far has been conducted with limited information. With this system, it is now possible to obtain materials and parts of the highest quality and the lowest possible price on a twenty-four hour basis from anywhere in the world.'

Other Japanese firms such as automobile makers have also initiated global inventory control and the just-in time procurement of materials and parts in response to the rapid yen appreciation and the increase of overseas production plants. The twenty-four hour system is useful not only for coping with developments in international markets, but also as an international computer information network. Such a network can collect syntactic information as widely and rapidly as possible, enabling it to support the activities of semantic information creation rooted in human nature.

(c) Cultivation of an entrepreneurial middle management

Cultivation of entrepreneural middle management is the key factor in the activation of organizational information creation.

The fact that YKK provides no education and training programmes for its employees clearly shows how much the company requires self-discipline among its employees. 'Learn through hands-on experience.' Emphasis is placed on learning rather than teaching. Only a small number of employees are assigned to respective overseas offices and YKK Sangyo (Aluminium products sales company). Those employees are expected to confront difficulties as local managers and to develop their skills and abilities through struggles and strife.

Vice President, Tadahiro Yoshida, often asks his staff members who are going abroad, 'Do you want to be controlled?' No one answers yes, so he tells them that they must control themselves, and must not control others. Once the business situation becomes unstable and ambiguous, being controlled becomes far easier than self-control. Vice President Yoshida also addresses those staff members by saying, 'You are my representatives. If you fail, who will assume the responsibility? You may say you will, but it is I who assume the final responsibility. So you do not have to worry excessively.' Those who have been sent abroad with these words from the Vice President are to manage by themselves in places far from Japan. These places are usually fiercely competitive markets, and staff must overcome all the handicaps they face in the process of new entry into the market. They need to be backed up physically as well as mentally.

More than seventy of the overseas subsidiaries of Honda have been fostering the development of managers from among the 20,000 non-Japanese employees. However, the Executive Vice President Koichiro Yoshizawa, has decided to re-examine the existing local manager fosterage system because 'the current system is not effective enough in fostering managers who possess the group-wide perspective necessary for top executives.'

Honda does not 'scout' its top executives from outside. Instead, it invites non-Japanese employees to work in its Japan offices so that they will understand Honda's corporate culture. Regular recruitment in the Japanese style helps Honda to foster local staff with a global perspective.

Conclusion

If globalization is viewed as the transfer of products originally developed for the domestic market to international markets as the domestic market matures, the dynamism of corporate growth has its own limitation. For the continued, dynamic growth of a firm, corporate strategies must be designed so that globalization is built-into the organization in order to succeed in the self-renewal process.

The basis of the self-renewal process is dynamic information creation by the entire organization. Middle up-down management is utilized rather than top-down or bottom-up management within this framework of information creation. This type of management methodology offers much promise in coping with today's turbulent environment.

The essential logic of middle up-down management consists of top management at headquarters developing a vision or dream. Local management creates and implements concrete concepts to solve and transcend the contradictions arising from gaps between what exists presently and what management hopes to create. In other words, top management conceives a grand theory of global business development, while middle management transforms this into a middle-range theory and tests it empirically within the framework of the grand theory.

It is the cross-fertilization of different types of organizational knowledge, the articulate and the tacit knowledge, that plays a critical role in this middle up-down management. The cross-fertilization can be understood as the dynamic synergy between localized, tacit knowledge and globalized, articulate knowledge, which are combined through the global hybridization of personnel. Thus, the key factor of the globalization of Japanese firms is the hybridization of personnel that is achieved through globalized personnel management. Cultivation of entrepreneurial middle management is indispensable in facilitating the cross-fertilization.

This paper has analysed the management of multinational firms from the viewpoint of managing the self-renewal process. The essence of the process resides in organizational information creation. Until now, management of multinational firms has been analysed only from the viewpoint of the information processing paradigm. Underlying this view is the problem of how to design the most efficient hierarchical structure to process information worldwide. In contrast, I have attempted to analyse it in the context of the information creation paradigm. Managing a self-renewing or information-creating process across nations is the fundamental concern here. I hope this analysis will contribute to the restructuring of the management of multinational corporations throughout the world.

Notes and References

1 R. Vernon, 'International investment and international trade in the product life cycle', *Quarterly Journal of Economics*, May 1966.
2 J. M. Livingstone, *The International Enterprise*, New York: Associated Business Programs Ltd, 1975. D. F. Channon, *Multinational Strategic Planning*, New York: Macmillan, 1979. M. E. Porter, 'Changing patterns of international competition', *California Management Review*, xxviii–2, 1986. K. Yasumuro, 'The logic of the

globalized firm', *Organizational Science*, vol. 21, No. 2, Tokyo, 1978 (in Japanese).

3 G. Hedlund, 'The role of foreign subsidiaries in strategic decision-making in Swedish multinational corporations', *Strategic Management Journal*, vol. 1, 1980.

4 For more detailed discussion on self-renewing process, see I. Nonaka, 'Creating organizational order out of chaos: self-renewal in Japanese firms', *California Management Review*, vol. 30, No. 3, Spring 1988.

5 K. Kobayashi, 'Why and how I create C&C strategy', *Business Review*, Institute of Business Research, Hitotsubashi University, vol. 31, No. 1, 1983 (in Japanese).

6 J. K. Johansson and I. Nanaka, 'Market research the Japanese way', Harvard Business Review, May–June 1987.

7 I. Nonaka, *Corporate Evolution: Managing Organizational Information Creation*, Tokyo: Nikkei Shimbunsha, 1985 (in Japanese).

8 C. E. Shannon and W. Weaver, *A Mathematical Theory of Communication*, Urbana, Ill: University of Illinois Press, 1949. Further discussion on the nature and type of information, see F. Machlup and U. Mansfield (eds) *The Study of Information*, New York: John Wiley, 1983.

9 B. Bateson, *Mind and Nature: A Necessary Unity*, New York: John Brockman Associates, 1979.

10 M. Polanyi, *The Tacit Dimension*, New York: Doubleday, 1966.

11 S. Watanabe, *Pattern Recognition: Human and Mechanical*, New York: John Wiley & Sons, 1985.

12 I. Nonaka, 'Speeding organizational information creation: toward middle up-down management', *Sloan Management Review*, vol. 29, No. 3, Spring 1988.

13 T. Kume, 'Creative chaos and humane management', *Business Review*, Institute of Business Research, Hitotsubashi University, vol. 35, No. 2, 1987 (in Japanese).

14 Unless specified the cases are based on my own interviews and on Nikkei Sangyo Shimbun (ed.) *Toward Global Management*, Tokyo: Nikkei Shimbunsha, 1987 (in Japanese).

15 H. D. Davidson and P. Haspeslagh, 'Shaping a global product organization', *Harvard Business Review*, July–August 1982.

16 G. Hedlund, 'The hypermodern MNC-A heterarchy', *Human Resource Management*, vol. 25, No. 1, 1986. For a further discussion of this trend, see C. A. Bartlett and S. Ghoshal, 'Managing across borders: new organizational responses', *Sloan Management Review*, Fall, 1987.

17 S. Irimajiri, 'Pioneering the globalization of the Japanese automobile industry: Honda, Ohio', *Business Review*, Institute of Business Research, Hitotsubashi University, vol. 34, No. 3, 1987 (in Japanese).

Chapter four

Organizing for world-wide advantage

Roderick E. White and Thomas A. Poynter

Sustained competitive advantage is a cornerstone underlying any successful strategy. However, as the international environment becomes more complex and dynamic, and competitors become increasingly adroit at deploying their resources, the straightforward pursuit of advantages with a singular focus, whether cost or differentiation, local or global, often proves inadequate for long-run survival and success. Increasingly, to gain maximum advantage requires the combination of different perspectives. Strategies must incorporate an intricate mosaic of advantages. Some elements of this mosaic are based upon the firm's global strengths, others are founded on local opportunities and competences and still others combine both. The barrier to building such a mosaic is not analytic. We have the formulation tools and concepts available. The principle impediments are organizational. This paper reports on the organizational approach used by three multinational firms with their subsidiaries: Dow, Matsushita Electric, and IBM. Able to develop and exploit a mosaic of advantages, these organizations share some common characteristics which will be described.

Recently Black & Decker found that its traditional advantage in power hand tools had been seriously eroded. With a country-centred organization oriented towards local markets B&D had developed different products for most of its geographic markets. The company had failed to balance the opportunities for locally-based advantages against those available from a more global orientation. In the face of pressure from Makita, a more globally oriented competitor, B&D has now attempted to redress this imbalance.[1]

Black & Decker exemplifies the challenge confronting many multinational businesses, to develop its world-wide potential for competitive advantage. For multinational corporations, fulfilling this goal requires a responsive organization able to identify and exploit advantages where it finds them. This may require a typical multinational business to, on one hand, have certain of its value-

95

adding activities globally rationalized and co-ordinated, in order to achieve an advantageous cost position; but on the other hand, if differentiation benefits are to be secured, it may be necessary to have other activities, typically elements of the marketing mix, tailored to local situations.[2]

On the face of it this appears to be a problem of strategic choice and balance. However, within a world-wide context exploiting the multiple and differing opportunities for advantages is principally an organizational issue. Even within the context of a single (national) market few firms are able simultaneously to achieve both cost and differentiation advantages.[13] Those businesses that do achieve such a position appear not to follow the conventional organizational prescriptions.[4] With the added complexity of international operations, developing and maintaining a mosaic of advantages requires a unique organizational solution. Some multinational companies have evolved organizations able to cope. Three of these — Dow Chemical, Matsushita Electric, and IBM — provide the grounding for this paper. Their organizations share some common characteristics; attributes of what Porter calls a horizontal organization[5] and Hedlund more precisely defines as a 'heterarchy'[6], a special case of Perlmutter's geocentric organization.[7]

Whether called a heterarchy, a geocentric or a horizontal organization this form is not for every business. Developing and maintaining a horizontal organization is a costly undertaking. It only makes sense if industry or business circumstances have significant potential for a mix, or mosaic of advantages. More conventional organizational arrangements are acceptable when sufficient advantage can be garnered from the pursuit of a singular set of advantages. Companies like Timken and SKF in the roller bearing business, where the basis for competitive advantage is global cost position, are organized with a world-wide product emphasis. Others in the retailing, consulting, and consumer food business achieve advantage with a predominantly local orientation and a geographic area organization.

As illustrated by Figure 4.1, different types of organizations are better suited to exploit one category of opportunity than another. This outcome is not at all surprising if we think about the fit between the different organizations and strategic advantage. As Davidson and Haspeslagh explain, the global product structure is able to exploit globally based advantages but often overlooks local advantages.[8] Conversely, the area structure exploits local advantages but appears unable effectively to deal with the potential for globally based advantages. A horizontal organization does bear

Figure 4.1   Strategic advantage — organization relationship

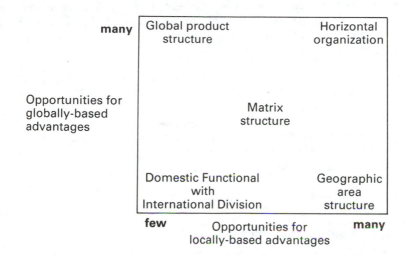

some apparent similarities to a matrix organization. However, Hedlund has pointed out important differences.[9] To paraphrase:

— the patterns of co-ordination are more mixed and flexible (for a heterarchy).
— internal, flexible processes link the different elements of the multinational system.
— conflicts are resolved laterally, not vertically.

Furthermore, other research on the matrix structure has concluded it is not, by itself, a stable, long-term solution for firms attempting to balance both world-wide product and local market concerns.[10]

Firms aspiring to the upper right-hand quadrant of Figure 4.1 must have organizations able to cope with tremendous variety — to identify, balance and exploit advantages flowing from different sources. The great strength of conventional organizations, their ability to simplify a complex decision process by emphasizing one type of advantage, in this situation becomes a weakness. Effective horizontal organizations must avoid being stuck-in-the-middle, pursuing differing sources of advantage but achieving none.

To overstate the case only slightly, conventional organizational prescriptions, product, area and even matrix — all suffer from the same root problem. The belief that information (and decisions) should flow vertically to some point within the organization, where a person or group charged with the appropriate authority decides. These decisions are based upon the application of a narrow logic incorporating a single historically-based perspective on advantage. Typically, that person is a local subsidiary or regional general manager if the business has a country-centred strategy, or a headquarter's manager if there is a more global strategy. This view holds that decision making (and co-ordinated action-taking) is simply a matter of the appropriate, one-time division and assignment of responsibilities and structuring of vertical reporting relationships within the organization. This view is not incorrect; it is contingent. As Figure 4.1 illustrates, it is contingent upon the opportunities for strategic advantage. However, the variety, interdependence and complexity of decisions that have to be made in a multinational firm pursuing a mixture of advantages precludes this type of decision making and requires a very different organizational approach.

The horizontal organization

Simultaneously achieving both global and local advantages is what effective horizontal organizations do well. Instead of referring an issue upwards through the vertical hierarchy, managers in the companies studied addressed it at their level, initiating contact and collaborating with peers in other units potentially affected by the outcome. The geographically dispersed functional units are held together not so much by the vertical chain of command as by a flexible horizontal network accompanied by lateral decision processes and, underlying it all, a common set of shared premises upon which decisions are based and actions assessed.

In our simple model of the effective horizontal organization, results flow from actions which are based upon decisions. These decisions were impacted by three key attributes of the horizontal organization:

— Lateral decision processes,
— Horizontal network,
— Shared decision premises.

As Figure 4.2 illustrates, these elements were themselves interrelated – nested one within another.

In an effective horizontal organization decisions are made through lateral processes with the input and agreement of those members of the organization representing key activities in the field most affected by the outcome. Although world headquarters may actively participate in the lateral decision making, the horizontal

Figure 4.2 The horizontal programme

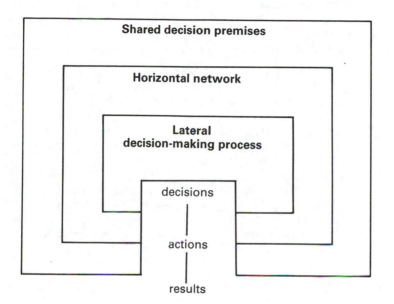

network prevents them from dominating it. These processes are facilitated by a common set of decision premises. As Herbert Simon[11] observed, when decision premises about the business are shared, individuals from diverse backgrounds can coalesce around a decision and take concerted action.

Lateral decision processes: the global glue

In a well-balanced organization, there will naturally be a mix of global and local perspectives. But it is necessary to have decision-making processes which identify critical choices and reach a resolution resulting in the greatest overall advantage to the MNC. Decisions affecting world-wide advantage are numerous, often subtle, and always complex and uncertain. Given individual cognitive limitations and information impactedness it is unrealistic to expect one or even a few decision makers located at a single point in the MNC to be able effectively to resolve these questions. Lateral decision making processes bring together in a collaborative effort around these key decisions the persons representing the activities

99

most affected by the outcome. These processes may include *ad hoc* direct contacts, liaison roles like project managers, temporary task forces, or more permanent teams.

The effect of these processes will be described with reference to several categories of decisions which relate directly to the advantage base for MNCs. These include:

— Directing product flow from the low-cost manufacturing sites to high return markets. These decisions, while perhaps operational in nature, are related to the ongoing utilization of existing resources to their maximum advantage.
— Developing and adjusting programmes with impact overlapping different geographic units. More commonly considered strategic, these decisions involve the (re)deployment of resources.
— Sharing information and knowledge generated in one geographic unit with other units. The diffusion of experience, insight and innovative ideas is a primary rationale for the MNC. When attempting to link local opportunities with global scope such exchanges are even more critical.

Product flows

Achieving maximum advantage requires manufacturing at the lowest possible cost and selling the output for the highest sustainable price. A simple concept, but a difficult problem for multinationals with multiple manufacturing sites, serving numerous markets and confronting a dynamic international environment. We observed one of the most striking examples of a lateral process for solving this problem within the Dow Chemical Company.

In a world-wide petrochemical company, one might expect coordination of production volumes among the more than 100 Dow producing locations in 29 different countries to be handled centrally. In fact they are not. Each geographic area within Dow has a commercial department (i.e. sales and marketing function) exclusively charged with supplying their territory with Dow products, while contributing to the highest possible world-wide after tax profit. These departments make sourcing decisions consistent with this corporate objective and are not bound by established relationships with manufacturing plants, even plants in their own territory. Furthermore, to ensure that lowest cost sourcing takes place continually, the internal product sourcing relationship between a manufacturing plant and a commercial department can be 'challenged' at any time. A challenge can originate from either the area commercial department or any manufacturing plant, and results in a global sourcing study.

Conducted by a special group, each sourcing study is a specific comparison of the changes in direct costs which would occur if the volume was shifted from one producing location to another. If, for example, the US market for polyethylene could be sourced at lower out-of-pocket cost (i.e. higher world-wide after tax profit) from a Dow Canada plant than from elsewhere, that adjustment would be made. Sourcing relationships within Dow can be challenged by the internal customer, or any potential alternate source of supply. In this example, the sourcing study would be requested by either the US commercial department or the Canadian manufacturing department. This internal challenge mechanism ensures that world-wide Dow is supplying its markets from the lowest cost sources. It also keeps pressure on the manufacturing plants to get costs down; otherwise volumes will shift to other producing locations.[12]

When the demand for products exceeds Dow's internal supply, as happens quite regularly in this cyclical business, sourcing studies become product allocation studies. In the allocation situation manufacturing managers are charged with directing the output of their plants to those commercial departments that can realize the largest after tax world-wide profits for Dow. The information system allows the profit realized on the sale of product to be associated with the plant of manufacture. Commercial managers who can establish strong positions for their products within their geographic area, and thereby realize a high relative price, receive output when supplies are limited. Thus, they have a long-term incentive to maximize locally available advantages.

These sourcing/allocation decisions are critical to the profit objective, and to how Dow competes world-wide. Indeed, one executive described this process as the 'global glue' holding Dow together. Products are sourced from the low-cost facility and directed towards the high margin markets. This approach provides an incentive for manufacturing plants to reduce costs, and for local marketing departments to seek meaningful differentiation in order to enhance margins and secure supply.

World headquarters' role in these decisions is minimal. As one global product director commented:

> Sourcing questions rarely reach my desk. They are resolved by the commercial departments and the producing locations. Occasionally, when a unique situation arises the rules (for sourcing/allocation studies) have to interpreted and someone from world headquaters has to become involved as referee.[13]

101

Development and adjustment of programmes

Certain types of programmes benefit from multinational co-ordination and co-operation. Often advantages can be gained if a new product is developed for more than one national market. Similarly, the marketing approach in one country can have implications for sister companies in neighbouring countries. One way in which consistency of programmes across geographic markets and amongst different functional units can be achieved is with a horizontal planning process which promotes the exchange of information and provides for the identification and resolution of differences.

IBM develops, manufactures, markets and services its large computers around the world. The interdependences are considerable. The mutual adjustment between its geographically dispersed but inderdependent development centres, manufacturing facilities, and marketing groups is accomplished through detailed planning processes, both operational and strategic, accompanied by a pre-dominantly lateral conflict resolution process.

Plans, once prepared by the operating unit, are shared with other related divisions (as well as corporate staff). These units are required to concur or disagree. As Richard Vancil explains: '. . . other units whose needs were not being met by a given unit might nonconcur with that unit's plan.'[14] In this way the planning system surfaces opportunities for collaboration as well as differences, and provides lateral processes for their resolution. Almost all 'nonconcurrences' get resolved horizontally through direct negotiations between the line managers concerned. In rare instances nonconcurrences may be appealed vertically and, if a resolution at lower levels is not possible, ultimately reach the top-level Corporate Management Committee. However, these are the exceptions, the novel or unique situations. And they provide senior management with a window on what is happening deep within their horizontal organization, giving them a mechanism to identify precedent-setting situations and establish new directions (or reaffirm old ones).

IBM's concurrence mechanism co-ordinates the allocation of resources to projects and programmes in much the same way Dow's challenge mechanism balances the operational flow of products within the multinational system. Interestingly, Dow's strategic planning process, although perhaps not as formal as IBM's, also provides for the identification resource allocation opportunities involving the co-operation of geographically diverse units.

For example, Dow Chemical Canada's polyethylene business was threatened by both low cost imports and a local competitor with a more flexible production process offering a wider variety of products to the local market. Dow's central R&D group had developed a new, efficient process to make polyethylene, but the minimum scale was more than twice the expectation for initial Canadian volume. However, Dow Canada's managers, involved in the global planning process, were aware Dow Pacific had an un-developed market for this product. They also knew the US area, while unable to provide products for the long run, did have capacity available for several years which could be allocated to develop the Pacific market while the world-scale Canadian plant was under construction. The Canadian plant would then come on stream at efficient scales by serving both the Canadian and Pacific markets.

Faced with problematic local competition, Dow Canada was able to enhance its competitive position and expand production not only by drawing upon the multinational's technological expertise, but also by being aware of market opportunities in another geographic area and the capacity situation in yet another affiliate and then getting all three areas to make mutual adjustments to Dow's overall benefit. This collaborative effort was conceived because informa-tion on markets and capacity was widely available, crossing con-ventional organizational boundaries. The project was initiated and then carried forward by the managers directly concerned, without intervention and with only limited involvement by world head-quarters.

Planning processes, like Dow's and IBM's, promote collabora-tion and mutual adjustment between related organizational units. In part this is initiated by the broad-based exchange of information amongst diverse organizational units.

Sharing of information and knowledge

The open exchange of information and knowledge is necessary for managers in one organizational unit to learn about and benefit from the experiences of other units in other markets. Such exchanges allow for (1) the diffusion of innovative ideas from the originating unit to the rest of the organization, and (2) the identi-fication of the types of collaborative activities just described.

In conventional organizations information is often zealously guarded. In the effective horizontal organizations information knows no internal boundary. Dow's information system facilitates the sourcing process described earlier by making relevant informa-tion widely available. Managers everywhere within Dow can access detailed cost, revenue, and profit data for any product category in any geographic area. Even managers not explicitly accountable for profits are expected to make decisions consistent with the primary objective of the company, which is to produce maximum long-term, world-wide profit growth. Information needed to pursue this objective is available to managers wherever they are located.

A lateral process may serve more than one purpose. For example, Dow's sourcing/allocation studies not only direct the flow of products but require the exchange of detailed cost information which, in turn, stimulates the exchange of knowledge. The detailed and specific cost information contained in sourcing studies is shared with all parties concerned. Thus manufacturing managers are familiar with the cost position of their sister plants in other areas. Other lateral processes and Dow's internal ethic require that a particular plant, which through some innovation has achieved an advantage, share this knowledge with other manufacturing sites. What begins as an exchange of cost information to make decisions about product flows often results in a sharing of knowledge about cost-reduction techniques. Thus the web of lateral processes interweaves.

The lateral processes which have been described attempt to parallel those interdependencies within the firm critical to the exploitation of world-wide advantage. If we were to apply conventional organizational design parameters then these interdependencies should form the basis for grouping and structuring organizational units.[15] However, this approach assumes that the critical interdependencies can be specified in advance. In fact it is the constant search for the interdependencies to enhance advantage that characterizes the effective horizontal organization. It is more helpful to view the horizontal organization not as having a structure of (pre)defined relationships but rather as being a network with the potential for any element of the network to be linked to any other element. The lateral processes already described provide the search routine and encourage interactions amongst elements of the network to form, dissipate and reform.

Horizontal network

In a conventional organization, the functional units for a business – R&D, purchasing, manufacturing, marketing, sales and distribution – typically report to, and are co-ordinated and directed by either a local subsidiary manager or a global product manager. As a result, the full set of functional activities for the business tend to adopt either a global or local orientation. In a horizontal organization, individual functional or value-adding activities operate on a more discrete basis. Functional activities are decoupled from the vertical hierarchy. The importance of vertical reporting relationships is intentionally diminished. Indeed, Dow refuses to draw up organization charts for fear of creating 'calcified hierarchical structures'. Matsushita has charts but in typical Japanese fashion they read horizontally, like a production flow chart, not vertically.[16]

Breaking discrete value-adding or functional activities, like marketing and sales and manufacturing, out of a strict vertical hierarchy is a hallmark of many successful MNCs. IBM World Trade Corporation was initially and is still principally an amalgamation of IBM's international sales companies. Within Dow Chemical, even though manufacturing activities may appear to report to, and be the responsibility of the area president, in fact, as one of Dow Canada's senior manufacturing managers stated, 'The production facilities really belong to Dow corporate. We have the responsibility for managing these plants in Canada for the (long-term) benefit of the whole corporation.'[17]

The Japanese multinationals are perhaps the clearest example of this kind of structural arrangement. Typically, these companies make a formal legal distinction between their sales (and marketing) companies, and their manufacturing companies. For example, Matsushita Electrical Industrial Co. has 44 different manufacturing and 34 separate sales companies world-wide. Much as within Dow, sales companies are expected to arrange with the manufacturing companies for a supply of product suitable for their market, irrespective of national boundaries. Even though sales and manufacturing companies may be separate legal entities, lateral relationships within a horizontal network still abound. As part of a regular process within Matsushita, manufacturing company personnel work closely with their sales company customers on product design and innovation, sales forecasts, and a general sharing of information. In addition, the North American general managers from all sales and manufacturing companies meet every other month to review their operations with their peers. Many Japanese companies have evolved the attributes of a horizontal organization within their domestic operations. *Nemawashi* and *ringi*, consensus processes for lateral decision making are examples.[18] Successfully translating this approach into international operations has resulted in very effective multinational operations.

A horizontal network in combination with lateral processes makes this type of organization very responsive to its external environment. Network interactions are flexible, forming and reforming as the situation(s) dictate. Adjustments from local to global focus, cost to differentiation and vice versa, can be made without restructuring of vertical reporting relationships. Vertical structures are not allowed to get in the way of the pursuit of advantage. This internal flexibility is extremely valuable when confronted with high external variety — a changing, difficult-to-predict international environment.

Common decision premises

The types of lateral processes at work in horizontal organization do not operate in isolation. In the search for advantage, people from diverse functional backgrounds, different countries, even with different languages must work together collaboratively. This would be a formula for anarchy unless accompanied by a strongly shared set of business values, resulting in a common set of premises upon which decision making is based. Consistency in these premises amongst geographically dispersed managers greatly facilitates lateral decision making within the MNC.

Konosuke Matsushita is recognized as one of the great business leaders of our time. He has instilled within his organization and its people a deeply-shared set of values, a basic management philosophy. One senior Matsushita executive described these basic business policies: '. . . the purpose of this company is to manufacture the necessities of people; constantly and in abundance. Through that effort we try to enrich people's lives.'[19]

This statement sounds hopelessly altruistic to western ears. But when translated into practice by experienced Matsushita managers who understand its operational implications, it is a powerful force. Most importantly, however, it guides lateral relationships deep within the organization. As one Matsushita executive commented:

> I can do what I like without referring to (headquarters) as long as it is in line with the basic policy. This makes it easy for us; we can be independent and creative, and we can take initiatives.

These corporate-wide philosophies contribute to a world-wide uniformity in expectations and how things work. As one IBMer stated:

> This company is the same wherever you go in the world. I could find out tomorrow I was being transferred 3,000 miles away and I would walk into that job like I had worked there all my life.[20]

This corporate identity, the feeling of oneness, is very important. As Christopher Bartlett rightly observed, 'a (lateral) process that depended upon forced alliances between reluctant colleagues, each protective of his turf, . . . would not be effective in the long run.'[21] Barriers to collaboration and co-operation created by national and cultural, as well as functional differences are greatly diminished by a strong sense of corporate purpose. Even though managers may disagree upon the specifics of a certain decision, they share the same fundamental premises upon which decisions within their firm are made. This allows the focusing of effort on the pursuit of world-wide advantage.

Making it work

Developing a horizontal organization and making it work is no simple or quickly accomplished task. And while there is no set of definitive guidelines the firms we studied did utilize certain approaches.

Creating shared values

Instilling the members of an organization with shared values which will lead to common decision premises is often viewed as an act of personal, charismatic leadership by the CEO. Although personal leadership is an important factor value infusion is a much more broadly-based socialization process. Indeed, for multinational companies operating in geographically dispersed locations with language and cultural differences, an institutional approach for socializing new members is often most feasible. This approach is consistent with Selznick's view that '(the infusion of values) involves transforming men and groups from neutral, technical units into participants who have a peculiar stamp, sensibility and commitment. This is ultimately an educational process.'[22]

Some firms have in fact established 'educational institutions'. Matsushita has an overseas training centre in Osaka, Japan. Managers and supervisors from around the world come to this centre to learn specific skills, but more importantly they are exposed to the Matsushita philosophy, in theory and in practice. The first few weeks of study are devoted to the company's history and philosophy. Only after this phase is complete do the trainees visit Matsushita facilities in Japan to see how the philosophy works in the field. Without the language differences among managers encountered by Matsushita, Dow provides a similar educational experience by posting international managers to world headquarters in Midland, Michigan early in their careers. Although the approach differs, the objective is the same: to broaden the managers' perspective and instill the corporation's basic business values.

Building a horizontal network

There is a natural tendency in any organization for vertical relationships to re(assert) themselves. Successful horizontal organizations counter this in several ways. Headquarters executives often have dual or multiple responsibilities; typically one for a geographic area, another for a ('global') product. A sort of reverse matrix structure; instead of one subordinate having two bosses, each with a different orientation, each boss has several subordinates with different orientations. In addition, these executive assignments are rotated regularly among senior managers at world headquarters. These steps help prevent the establishment of narrowly defined vertical fiefdoms with senior executives developing either a global or local bias. Furthermore, it makes it difficult for senior executives to frustrate the horizontal network by attempting to act as the primary link between their own subordinates and other parts of the MNC. Because of dual responsibilities and frequent job changes, headquarters executives must rely upon their subordinates and the lateral processes that link them with related organizational units.

Senior manager's role

Naturally a horizontal network requires different skills, attitudes and approaches from senior corporate management than conventional vertical organizations. Fundamentally, senior managers must create, maintain and defend an organizational context that promotes lateral decision making oriented towards the achievement of competitive advantage world-wide. Their primary role is to facilitate these processes, act as referee when required and, except for unique circumstances, avoid becoming involved in the substance of decisions. A process, as opposed to substantive role in decision making is counter-instinctive for many North American managers who rose to the top because of their decisiveness and action orientation. They must, however, learn to influence decisions and actions more indirectly, by inculcating members of the organization with corporate values, encouraging appropriate horizontal relationships and facilitating lateral processes.

Subsidiary manager's role

In an effective horizontal organization managers of country-based subsidiaries cannot run their organizational units as independent principalities. The subsidiary general manager must seek and exchange information with his counterparts in other countries, and using the information engage in local initiatives that draw upon global strengths and opportunities for collaboration. Further-more, he should encourage his subordinates to do likewise. Indeed, a large part of the local general manager's role, like that of his corporate counterpart, is facilitating this lateral process.

Assessing results

Assignment of performance responsibility and accountability for results within horizontal organizations is problematic. Using output measures of performance for individual geographic or product units can actually impede the pursuit of world-wide advantage. The subsidiary general manager cannot and should not defend actions that maximize local unit performance when these actions lead to lower overall performance. In one company we studied, it became advantageous for the Canadian subsidiary to source an intermediate product from the US; however, to do so would have had a detrimen-tal effect upon reported local unit performance (after absorbing plant shutdown costs and ongoing fixed costs). The overall performance impact, however, was expected to be positive. The commercial and manufacturing managers in Canada helped to identify and exploit this opportunity. This never would have happened had this unit been run simply by the local numbers.

Because of the complex interdependences a horizontal organiza-tion cannot be 'run simply by the numbers'. Overall results are obviously important and were heavily stressed in the horizontal organizations observed. However, it is understood that summary output measures for individual sub-units must be accompanied by a review of decisions and actions. Because information is so widely shared, decision premises so firmly established and peer reviews the norm, any sub-unit manager pursuing his narrow self interest was likely to be exposed. General managers at all levels must have the experience and the involvement to judge whether or not sub-ordinates are taking appropriate actions. And these actions cannot be simply tied to locally reported results. A big part of the local general manager's job is forging the link between local actions, world-wide advantage and overall results.

An effective general manager within a horizontal organization must be familiar enough with the business, close enough to the action, and involved enough in decision making to ensure sub-ordinates see the whole picture and act accordingly, even when locally reported results may suffer. Performance should not be evaluated by locally reported results but rather by the accumulation of actions consistent with the pursuit of world-wide advantage. Making such evaluations requires considerable experience in the business. Managers with backgrounds in core functions, operations and marketing, and experience in several subsidiaries as well as corporate headquarters are most likely to have developed this ability.

A different view of multinational strategy

Our conceptions of strategy and organization are linked. Just as the horizontal organization makes some unconventional assumptions about internal relationships it also requires some non-traditional assumptions about business strategy. Those who view multinational business strategy as some grand design, emanating from the senior executives of the firm, will have difficulty accepting a horizontal organization. Inherent in this organizational approach is a view of strategy that is more incremental but also more flexible, more responsive and better able to extract maximum advantage from the full set of opportunities available to the MNC worldwide.

Effective multinational strategy is not like a chess game with some grand master at world headquarters positioning the pieces on a global gameboard. Senior managers who view their role in this way will have great difficulty accepting a horizontal organizational approach. Rather the individual pieces, the discrete value-adding units, position themselves to the overall advantage of the corporation. This is done through a process of decentralized initiative, mutual co-ordination, and adherence to corporate-wide premises. Managers in effective horizontal organizations view strategy as the outcome of a collaborative process requiring the mutual adjustment and co-operation of discrete, geographically dispersed organizational units.

The foregoing does not mean senior corporate management does not have a critical role in the direction of the corporation. Richard Hamermesh makes a distinction between business strategy (how a company will compete in a given business); corporate strategy (which businesses a company will compete in); and institutional strategy (the basic character and vision of the company).[23] The corporate role lies in setting the institutional strategy within which business strategies will be formed.

Conclusion

Horizontal organizations reject a structure based upon the groupings of sets of functional activities under strict hierarchies with unity of command, and replace it with discrete units linked by a horizontal network and lateral processes where everyone is responsible. This apparent diffusion of responsibility could be a serious problem except that in successful organizations, the members have a strongly held sense of the firm's purpose, a common set of premises upon which they base decisions, take action and assess results. These widely shared values govern the conduct of members as they interact laterally and make decisions affecting their firm's strategy and competitive position.

Failure to build an effective horizontal organization, when the competitive situation demands it will, as our original Black & Decker example illustrated, result in the erosion of a firm's competitive position. The conventional, vertically organized firm will find itself continually outmanoeuvred by more nimble horizontally organized competitors. And when it attempts to replicate their strategic moves and gain similar advantages, it will fail more often than it will succeed. These failures will no doubt be blamed upon market conditions, competitor reaction, changing technologies or lack of specific capabilities, but will, in fact, be due to that vertical organization's inability to marshal its resources and utilize and deploy them flexibly to its maximum advantage, in the face of competitors who have developed horizontal organizations with this ability.

For the MNC pursuing world-wide advantage the balance between global and local orientation has to be made product by product, value-added activity by value-added activity, market by market and country by country. This complex and often ambiguous task cannot be performed by a chess master at the centre of the MNC placing the subsidiary units in position on some global-local/cost-differentiation grid. The organization must facilitate the alignment of competences with opportunities, at all levels, so geographically dispersed units can form the intricate mosaic required of a truly world-wide strategy. A horizontal organization allows these units to exercise flexibility within the bounds of the overall MNC objectives and strategy.

This paper is based upon part of a larger study examining the strategic management of foreign-owned subsidiaries in Canada. It has involved over thirty Canadian subsidiaries, principally of US parent companies. Detailed clinical studies have been conducted in seven companies in three different industries – in petrochemicals, consumer package foods and consumer electronics.

Notes

1 B. Saporito, 'Black & Decker's gamble on globalization', *Fortune*, May 14, 1984, 40–48.

2 J. A. Quelch and E. J. Hoff, 'Customizing global marketing', *Harvard Business Review*, May–June, 1980, 59–68.
   J. S. Hill and R. R. Still, 'Adapting products to LDC tastes', *Harvard Business Review*, March–April, 1984, 92–101.
3 W. K. Hall, 'Survival strategies for hostile environments', *Harvard Business Review*, September–October, 1980, 75–85.
4 R. E. White, 'Generic business strategies, organizational context and performance: an empirical investigation', *Strategic Management Journal*, vol. 7, No. 3, May–June, 1986, 217–31.
5 In Porter's Book, *Competitive Advantage*, the term was used in a different setting, related business firms, but the basic organizational form is equally, if not more, applicable to multinational businesses.
6 G. Hedlund, 'The hypermodern MNC – A heterarchy', in *Human Resource Management*, Spring, 1986, pp. 9–35.
7 D. A. Heenan and H. V. Perlmutter, *Multinational Organizational Development*, Chapter 2, Reading, MA: Addison-Wesley, 1979.
8 W. H. Davidson and P. Haspeslagh, 'Shaping a global product organization', *Harvard Business Review*, *60*, no. 4, July–August, 1982, 125–132.
9 G. Hedlund, *op. cit.*, p. 23.
10 C. K. Prahalad, 'Strategic choice in diversified MNCs', *Harvard Business Review*, July–August, 1976, 67–78.
11 H. A. Simon, *Administrative Behavior (3rd edition)*, New York: The Free Press, 1976.
12 R. E. White and T. A. Poynter, 'Dow Chemical Canada Ltd', unpublished research case study, School of Business Administration, the University of Western Ontario, 1984.
13 Ibid.
14 R. F. Vancil, 'IBM corporation: background note' in *Implementing Strategy: The Role of Top Management*, Boston: Division of Research, Harvard Business School, 1982, pp. 37–51.
15 J. D. Thompson, *Organization in Action*, New York: McGraw-Hill, 1967.
16 T. A. Poynter and R. E. White, 'Matsushita Industrial Canada Ltd', unpublished research case study, School of Business Administration, The University of Western Ontario, 1985.
17 R. E. White and T. A. Poynter, 'Dow Chemical Canada Ltd', unpublished research case study, School of Business Administration, the University of Western Ontario, 1984.
18 R. T. Johnson and W. G. Ouchi, 'Made in America (under Japanese management)', *Harvard Business Review*, September–October, 1974, pp. 61–69.
19 Harvard Business School *Bulletin*, February, 1983, p. 56.
20 Vancil, *op. cit.*, p. 38.
21 C. A. Bartlett, 'How multinational organizations evolve', *Journal of Business Strategy*, *3*, 1982, 20–32.
22 P. Selznick, *Leadership in Administration*, New York: Harper & Row, 1957.

23 R. G. Hamermesh, *Making Strategy Work*, New York: John Wiley & Sons, 1986.

Part two

Management of multinational processes and systems

Chapter five

Control, change, and flexibility: the dilemma of transnational collaboration

Yves Doz, C. K. Prahalad, and Gary Hamel

This chapter develops a logical comparison between the multi-national management challenges faced in fully-controlled businesses and the difficulties faced in businesses which rely on international partnerships for their international development. While we touch upon the well-known issues of local market-access joint ventures, our focus is elsewhere. We are concerned with partnerships that include multiple countries (e.g. Philips and DuPont in optical media) and, often, multiple product lines (e.g. AT&T and Olivetti), not so much with local market-driven partnerships (e.g. Honda and PT Astra in Indonesia for mopeds).

Based on our past research on multinational management, we first establish the need for three capabilities to develop a successful strategic management process in multinational companies. These capabilities, in turn, are rooted in the carefully orchestrated use of a series of management tools by top management. These are strategic control, strategic change, and strategic flexibility. As the argument is developed extensively elsewhere, it is only summarized below.[1]

Then for each of the key capabilities — control, change and flexibility — we analyse the likely impact of partners and partnerships on the development and maintenance of these capabilities. In particular, we consider how top management's ability to use management tools to sustain the three key capabilities, is affected by partnerships. While some tools can continue to be used successfully in partnerships, the use of others may be jeopardized by differences between the partners.

We conclude that while the use of partnerships can allow companies to dispense with the slow, patient, build-up of their own international infrastructure, and thus may offer a short cut to world markets, partnerships remain unlikely to provide the basis for stable long-term success in the face of strong competition.

117

Three key capabilities

The increasing global competition and the more sophisticated forms of government intervention faced by multinational companies put conflicting demands on their organizations. First, in most multinational businesses, becoming an effective global competitor requires the cross-border integration of selected tasks and functions, and the exercise of the degree of strategic control over subsidiary actions commensurate with the successful implementation of a global strategy. Yet, in the very same businesses, competing successfully for differentiated — or merely fragmented — national markets requires that other tasks and functions have the freedom to adapt autonomously to local demands and national success requirements. Successful global strategies do not require only the cost effective use of resources provided by cross-border integration, nor the differentiation advantages provided by responsiveness to local demands. Both are needed.

Second, the relative importance of integration across borders, and that of responsiveness to national market conditions, usually changes over time in a given business. In structuring relationships between headquarters and affiliates, managers must therefore be sensitive not only to the present responsiveness and integration needs, but also to possible changes in the underlying competitive and economic conditions of a business. Such changes will lead to new responsiveness and integration demands. Managing changes in the headquarter-subsidiary relationships in order to allow strategic redirection to respond to shifting needs for integration and responsiveness is thus as important as ensuring static strategic control at any point in time.[2]

Third, beyond control and redirection, flexibility is often required. Global competition takes place even in 'local' businesses, i.e. businesses the economics of which do not justify an integrated approach to international markets. In these international but not global businesses, where competition is for global cash flow, top managers must still have the ability to co-ordinate global strategies by assigning different strategic missions to different subsidiaries. They also need to shift these missions as the evolution of competitive conditions demands. Flexibility, thus, is also required. Further, flexibility in horizontal couplings between subsidiaries may also be required, and be left to evolve as a function of changing opportunities and requirements. In a very volatile market and competitive environment, built-in flexibility in inter-unit relationships may be critical.

The needs for flexibility are further increased by the varying extent of government influences, and differing government policies, from country to country in the same industry.[3] Finally, interdependencies between businesses, i.e. common technologies, manufacturing facilities and know-how, common distribution, and common customers, can be a source of competitive advantage for individual businesses, provided they are selectively leveraged.[4] Selective management of interdependencies calls for further flexibility.

In sum, the critical capabilities that management has to develop to compete successfully internationally are:

1. Efficiency in executing agreed-upon strategies through a process of control of subsidiary actions.
2. Ability to change the nature of the headquarter-subsidiary, and subsidiary-to-subsidiary, relationships in order to allow required changes in strategic direction to take place.
3. Flexibility to bring subsidiaries together to compete in a co-ordinated fashion, to exploit government-controlled and non-conventional markets (e.g. China), and selectively to take advantage of interdependencies across businesses (rather than to suffer from them).

Taken together, these three capabilities are the keys to the strategic management process in a multinational business. They allow corporate management, or the business unit management for a single business to vary selectively the nature and the extent of autonomous responsiveness to diverse market conditions, and the degree of co-ordination and integration across borders.

As our past research deomonstrates, developing these capabilities in the context of the evolution of a single company, and even in that of a single 100 per cent controlled business, is no mean task. The three priorities of control, change, and flexibility, put conflicting requirements on the organizational structures and management processes of MNCs, and need to be traded off. Even with full ownership, individual managers are likely to have quite different perceptions, and interests, about these trade-offs as they directly affect the success of businesses and the relative power of individual managers. Further, in diversified multinationals, the trade-offs are likely to have to be quite different from one business to another, with no single management process being appropriate across businesses, countries and even functions.[5] Successfully addressing these three priorities of control, change and flexibility is a constantly challenging balancing act. It requires the careful use of a selected repertory of management tools that allow top management to structure, and to differentiate and adapt the management process.

Rapid changes in technology, such as the impact of micro-processors on markets (e.g. the fragmentation of mass markets into more demanding 'customized' segments), and in production processes (e.g. the new opportunities offered by CADCAM), make the performance of this balancing act increasingly exacting: reaction times have to shrink.

Companies which are not yet mature MNCs, but which see their markets becoming increasingly global (e.g. telecom equipment) or increasingly related to other markets (e.g. telecom and computers) are at a strategic disadvantage to companies that have globalized earlier, that exploit interdependencies between their businesses and that have already developed the capabilities required to make the trade-offs between control, change and flexibility.[6]

Such disadvantages may result from at least three sets of factors. The most obvious and practical one is the lack of the underlying infrastructure successfully to penetrate international markets on one's own. Sales forces, local plants, market intelligence and marketing presence to understand and serve distant markets, all are lacking. Both sensing and responding mechanisms are lacking. Developing such an infrastructure on a global, or even regional scale, is costly, difficult and time consuming. To gain the full benefits of such infrastructure takes years, for instance, the development of a brand franchise is a slow process. Many companies can no longer afford to develop these capabilities from scratch in fast-moving markets. Further, in government-mediated markets (e.g. teletext, mobile radio, etc.) newcomers may not be given the opportunity to develop such infrastructure from scratch. Although they may supply equipment, brand franchises remain held by local companies. In principle, building plants for production at a low cost is easier, but again setting up effective operations in low factor cost locations is not easy, and cannot be done overnight.

Infrastructure is not all, though. It is almost worthless until it is co-ordinated in an effective management process. Building these management processes takes longer than building plants or acquiring local competitors. This is a second disadvantage to newcomers. An effective administrative and managerial infrastructure has to complement the physical infrastructure. This infrastructure is comprised of a series of management systems and tools that provide the capabilities for strategic control, change, and flexibility. Such management systems take years to put in place and begin operating effectively. For instance, a new accounting system may require three years to be operational, while a career management system is much slower to evolve and have results. Again, established global competitors have this organizational infrastructure in place, while newcomers do not.

Finally, the capability effectively to make the trade-offs outlined above requires subtlety and sophistication in the use of management systems, something that is learned over time. Managers trained in a global management system learn effective management processes over time, while managers with a primarily domestic orientation (be it in a domestic company or in a nationally responsive multinational one) do not. Again, this is a source of disadvantage for the newcomer.

Late internationalization into a global industry is thus fraught with difficulty. Similarly, industry convergence, with its need for diversification into a series of related but different businesses may be a challenge.

The strategic logic from one business — in which is steeped the experience of top management — can hardly be transferred to others. And the benefits of integration and synergies often prove elusive.[7]

To the management of companies confronted with the need for fast internationalization and related diversification, strategic alliances and partnerships provide an interesting option to access the world markets and/or to combine with adjacent technologies. Companies that have been primarily domestic (e.g. AT&T in the US, GEC and Plessey in the UK) may see in partnerships a short cut to world markets. Companies affected by converging technologies (e.g. Olivetti and AT&T, NEC and Bull) may also see in partnerships a short cut to full coverage of related markets. Partnerships provide low cost fast access to new markets, by 'borrowing' the already-in-place infrastructure of a partner. Particularly in businesses where customer interfaces are critical, and need to be local, partnerships are a very effective alternative to self-development. Both Fujitsu with ICL and NEC with Bull, may see fast low-cost entry into the European market as a major benefit. Beyond buying access and time, partnerships may also be a more effective way to acquire skills than self-development. This is true for both marketing and technical skills. As a result of these expected advantages, an increasing number of companies in global industries — such as electronics, automobiles, chemicals, and pharmaceuticals — have entered alliances and partnerships, trying to build global competitive coalitions between formerly independent companies. They see such coalitions as a short-cut towards global competitiveness.

Attractive as they are, and while these alliances indeed provide an opportunity for fast global market access, they may not allow the degree of strategic control, change and flexibility which would be needed to secure long-term competitiveness.

Exploring this issue is the central theme of this chapter: do partnerships allow for the organizational capabilities required to compete effectively in global businesses?

Strategic control

Strategic control may be considered as the sum of operational control and strategic co-ordination. By operational control in a global business we mean the ability to manage a network of operations integrated across borders, world-wide or region-wide. Typical examples of such control would include central plant loadings, global logistics, co-ordinated new product development for multiple national markets, and controlled transfer pricing policies for multiple subsidiaries. Strategic co-ordination, and thus strategic control, is more subtle; it involves the assignment of different strategic missions to different subsidiaries, depending on the nature of market and competitive demands. While profits may be a primary objective assigned to some national subsidiaries, others may, for instance, have as their main objective to block the expansion of a local competitor, or to limit the profitability of a market where a global competitor is dominant. The assignment and co-ordination of differentiated missions require a shared view of strategy between headquarters and subsidiaries, a shared interpretation of competitive situations, and an ability to develop and implement different but mutually supportive strategic missions assigned to individual subsidiaries in the context of an overall strategy for the success of the world-wide business. Neither operational nor strategic control come easily to mature multinationals, particularly when their subsidiaries are developed in protected, separate national markets.

Dependency is the essence of control. Dependency can affect either the subsidiaries' businesses or their managers. Business dependency hinges on product and knowledge flows to the subsidiary from the headquarters and from other subsidiaries in the multinational's integrated network. Product flows exist in very integrated product development and manufacturing networks (e.g. Ford and IBM in Europe) or in networks with very differentiated subsidiary roles (e.g. sourcing plants in Singapore and Taiwan for Philips). Knowledge flows exist when subsidiaries are dependent upon central technological and engineering resources (e.g. Dresser Industries' subsidiaries' dependence on US-based product engineering, as was shown during the US 'Soviet pipeline' embargo).[8] More broadly, subsidiaries are usually dependent on system-wide R&D and management skills, without which they would quickly fall behind in technology.

Managers' dependency usually stems from the use of expatriate managers, or of third country nationals, for whom running an affiliate is but a step in a career that they hope will take them to headquarters. This makes the development of a shared vision between corporate and subsidiary executives easier, and removes the strongest forms of identification to national subsidiary, rather than global network, interest. Control tools which emphasize a global perspective, for instance by rewarding managers on the basis of their contribution to a global business P&L rather than on the basis of their subsidiary's results alone, also help align managers' perceptions with a global strategic vision. A whole array of management tools, such as global product and business planning teams and co-ordinating committees, world-wide planning processes, budgeting processes, etc., can contribute to fostering and anchoring in the organization such a global strategic vision.

Not all MNCs achieve strategic control, for many reasons. First, historically, subsidiaries have a tendency to become autonomous as they grow and mature, particularly in periods of protectionism. As dependency on central know-how, and often on central funding for accelerated development, wanes, a most direct form of dependency is lost. Further, when protectionism rises, cross-shipments no longer allow the maintainance of control. Such loss of control over subsidiaries has been witnessed in many mature MNCs operating in Europe, with the 1930s depression leading to protectionism, and with the following world war which often put headquarters and subsidiaries in opposite camps. Second, as national environments are more deeply different, headquarters executives find it more difficult to contribute useful skills and know-how to local subsidiaries. A finance expertise acquired in the US or in Sweden may be of limited value in steering a subsidiary through triple-digit inflation in Brazil or Israel. Third, host government policies may also make strategic control difficult or impossible. Local content regulations, preferential buying from local suppliers or responsive MNCs, non-tariff barriers, etc., may limit the exercise of effective strategic control over national subsidiaries.[9] Finally, let-alone government policies limiting the use of expatriates in subsidiaries, putting headquarters managers on relatively short secondments to subsidiaries is occasionally a self-defeating policy: the excessive mobility of expatriate managers does prevent them from going 'native', but it also prevents them from ever being effective in the local national environment. This usually results in a layer of local managers — whose career ambitions are local only — actually running the subsidiary operations and making all critical decisions. These local managers, aggravated by the frequent moves of senior executives from and to headquarters, are likely to protect jealously their own independence, thus defeating the policy of sending trusted heaquarters executives to run subsidiaries.

Partnerships further complicate the control issues. It was noted by researchers long ago that strategic and organizational transitions towards integration across borders made joint ventures with local partners more difficult to manage, and even unlikely to survive.[10] Interests diverge between a local partner primarily concerned with a profitable development of the local market, and the multinational partner who may see priorities for local operations mainly in the context of a global stragey.

The more internationally integrated the operations of the MNC, the more its priorities towards activities in any individual country are likely to diverge from those of an independent national company in that country, the view most often taken by the joint venture partner. Tensions with local joint venture partners in the context of a global business are normal and cannot easily be avoided. Central strategic control is essentially not compatible with such partnerships.

Partnerships between less dissimilar companies than a global MNC and a local national company are not free of tensions though.

Strategic control is not an objective *per se*, rather, to most MNCs, it is a tool to allow optimization of activities across borders. Partnerships raise difficult optimization issues, and thus complex control problems. Interdependencies between operations carried out within the partnership, and operations carried out by the parent companies are at the heart of the problems. It is useful here to distinguish between scale and skill dimensions of partnerships. In scale-based partnerships, partner firms usually combine forces jointly to develop and produce some products, with some of the work being performed in the partner companies and some in a new entity, often a joint venture or a consortium, formed to run the partnership. Airbus Industrie, one of the better known pan-European partnerships, carries out the marketing of its family of airliners, but subcontracts the manufacturing and development tasks to its parent companies in various countries. In other cases, partners jointly produce some goods, but market them independently (e.g. Thomson and JVC jointly produce VCRs in Europe, but market them separately, competing with each other in distribution). Tensions in scale-based partnerships, in which operations are combined to achieve higher production and/or marketing volume are likely to result from several causes:

1. Part of the value-added structure is shared, part is not. The shared part is likely to be jointly optimized (although criteria may vary, this can be negotiated), the separate parts of value-added structure are not jointly optimized. For example, when JVC supplies components to its joint venture with Thomson, J2T, it faces the trade-off of making profits, alone, in Japan by setting component transfer prices high, or in J2T, with Thomson, by setting lower component transfer prices. The same is true downstream for the transfer of products back to the sales subsidiaries of JVC and Thomson. Since Thomson and JVC are not symmetrical suppliers to and customers of J2T, they are bound to differ in transfer pricing priorities. Even if they were symmetrical suppliers to and customers of their joint operations, they would still face different trade-offs as the rest of their operations are not similarly deployed and configured. The issue would disappear only if the partners set up the partnership as a stand-alone operation, with no product nor component (or subassembly in the case of Airbus) transshipments between themselves and the joint operations.

2. Exchange rate fluctuations affect the partners quite differently. In Airbus Industrie, for instance, the Germans have suffered from the revaluation of the Deutschmark against their partners' currencies and, above all, against the dollar (aircraft are commonly priced in dollars). This leads to higher series' lengths before breakeven estimates, and to overall lower profitability forecasts for the German partners, thus creating tensions between partners around new product launches, and product pricing to airlines.

3. Competitive conditions faced by the partners are likely to be different, for instance, the intensity of competition in their home markets may vary, leading to different priorities.

4. The relative strategic importance of a partnership, *vis-à-vis* their other operations, may differ between partners, and this, in turn, may lead them to want to exercise different levels of strategic control over the partnership's operations. Typically, the partner for whom the partnership is most central is likely to want to exercise more control than the partner(s) for whom the partnership is more peripheral.[11]

5. Resource imbalance, or asymmetries, in the relative willingness

of partners to commit resources to the partnership also creates tensions. In particular it may well be that the partner for whom the partnership is more peripheral is also the one who has the most resources, but is less willing to commit them. Conversely, the partner to whom the partnership is most central may depend on the other partner for key resources.

The asymmetries between partners outlined above make the joint exercise of strategic control difficult. It is not that the partners lack the strategic control tools, as partnerships are usually *de novo* operations, it is rather that the partners are not likely to agree easily to the joint use of these tools, since their priorities and trade-offs, in matters regarding partnership performance are likely to differ.

Skill-based partnerships between global companies raise even trickier issues than scale-based partnerships; in skill-based partnerships, asymmetrical dependency itself often becomes a goal.[12] In other words, each partner may try to maintain its influence on the partnership, and on the other partner(s) through the partnership, by making his contribution both more essential and scarcer. The partnership may be starved of know-how, each partner using its control over know-how transfer as a bargaining tool towards the other: each partner is tempted to restrict the flow of know-how it provides to the partnership in order to increase its own bargaining power. Fear of leakage into the partner's other operations, and of the partner's option to cut loose from the partnership and regain independence, usually lies behind such restrictions.[13] Such escalation of partnership dependency may drastically curtail the effectiveness of partnerships and the scope for joint activities. Only when one of the partners believes that he can maintain competititve advantage outside of the partnership, despite leakage within the partnership, are such tensions attenuated. For example, for the Toyota–General Motors joint venture, NUMMI, to work relatively smoothly, as it seems to do, it may have been necessary for Toyota not to provide its most up-to-date technology. GM too maintains options to make small cars outside the NUMMI partnership, e.g. by importing them from subsidiaries or associates in Europe, Japan or Korea. Similarly, JVC may be relatively indifferent to Thomson's learning of VCR manufacturing through their joint venture as JVC believes that it can outmanoeuvre Thomson on most geographical markets, and in particular outside the EEC, through a wider, more frequently renewed, more efficiently produced, model range.

Conflicts between the joint venture and the parents may also arise. Observers of negotiations and joint ventures stress the fact that the efficiency of the initial agreement is likely to be low. Lack of knowledge, both of the situation and of the partner(s), lack of trust, leading to partial misrepresentation of one's capabilities and true utility function, lack of a common language, uncertainty on the relative value of partners' contributions, are all likely to contribute to making the initial agreement inefficient. Yet, as the partners learn more about the situation they face, and about each other, quite considerable efficiency improvements can be achieved, provided the initial agreement is renegotiated, and partners see their joint activity as an evolving relationship, not as a once-for-all contract to be implemented as is. This is typically best achieved when the joint venture gains enough strategic autonomy from its parents to take the initiative in making its own activities evolve. To a large extent, this was achieved in the Airbus case. Yet, the need for adjustment often conflicts with the perceived need for strategic control on the part of the parents, particularly when the joint venture is active in strategically important areas for them.[14] A vicious circle may even develop, where disappointed by the low performance of the venture — which derives from the inefficient nature of the early agreement — parents reinforce control, possibly with divergent priorities, and thus make it impossible for the venture managers to make the agreements and activities evolve towards a more efficient form of collaboration.

Strategic control over partnerships without a joint venture or consortium arrangement is even more problematic. In the absence of the joint financial optimization structure provided by a joint venture, the high uncertainty and need for specialized assets make enduring co-operation difficult.[15] Partners will hesitate to commit resources or specialized assets specific to the partnership when uncertainties affect the outcome of the partnership. The temptation to undercommit, to keep options open, and not to solve conflicts jointly may take over. This is all the more important when partnerships have skill transfer rather than cost decrease or market power as their main objective: skill-transfer objectives are almost always transient rather than permanent, like cost decreases or market power increase. Shared strategic control under these circumstances is thus difficult, as partners have strategic objectives that cannot be shared — or even discussed — with the other partner(s).

Strategic control through resource dependence, the essence of strategic control in MNCs, is thus compromised in the context of joint ventures and partnerships. Heightened perceived needs for control, particularly when the partnership is strategically important, lack of trust, and the tendency to restrict skill transfer, may not allow the joint venture the autonomy required to evolve an efficient relationship over time. Rivalry for control through skill starvation may compromise the success of the venture or of the joint programme. Asymmetric balances in inputs and outputs, and in partners' leveraging capabilities for outputs, may also over-whelm the needed contributions, and thus make co-operation impossible. Such imbalance also makes the partners' agreement on joint exercise of strategic control difficult. Often the partnership is thus neither placed in a clear strategic control situation nor an autonomous one. Unless the joint venture takes the initiative and is autonomous enough to survive against its parents' desire for control, and unless the parents no longer retain an independent option after the joint venture is created, strategic control issues may compromise the success of many multinational strategic partnerships.

Strategic control through human resources management in a partnership is also fraught with problems. Employees, of either parent companies, but delegated to a partnership, or of a joint venture itself, may not be so easily controlled as employees of a fully-owned, and/or singly managed corporation.

First, the appointment of key employees to run a joint venture, or to manage a partnership, may itself be an opportunity or a problem issue. Observers have noted, for example, that MNC joint ventures with Japanese companies in Japan are usually controlled, strategically, by the local Japanese company, not by the MNC. The location of the venture, as well as linguistic and cultural barriers, and the cost of posting expatriates in Japan usually justify the decision to rely mostly on managers seconded from the local partner to run the joint activities.[16] The difficulty of recruiting senior managers locally, particularly to run a collaborative relationship between a major Japanese company and a foreign partner, also increases the reliance on managers seconded from the Japanese partner. Further, the Japanese partner may place his best or his second-rate people in the collaborative venture, depending on the strategic importance of the venture to his own interests. Similar issues arise outside Japan as well, with, for example, Toyota managing the joint venture with General Motors in California. More generally, senior appointment decisions in joint ventures and collaborative programmes have to be agreed upon jointly by both partners, and this limits the use of human resource management as a tool for strategic control by either partner.

The issue does not pertain exclusively to partnerships between western and Japanese firms. Concerns about leakage and encroach-ment may have led Japanese companies not to appoint their best scientists to collaborative R&D efforts among Japanese firms.

Imbalance issues in staffing were also observed in partnerships between internationally experienced UK firms and less experienced continental European firms. In particular, the adoption of English as the working language, and the borrowing of management systems from the UK partner lead to a major imbalance where the non-British partner finds it difficult to exercise any level of strategic control.

Further, once appointed, employees may suffer divided loyalties. Loyalties between parents and joint venture, or joint programmes may conflict. When the joint venture general manager is ambitious, whatever the reasons, to gain autonomy from the parent, he attempts to draw employee loyalties to him rather than to the parents.[17] Loyalties between parents may also conflict, in particular when the key individuals involved in the partnership partly identify with the partner, and can self-select their involvement. In several of the partnerships we studied in depth, employees appointed by one partner to run the partnerships identified closely with the values, operating modes, and culture of the other partner, to the point where they became excessively critical of their own organization, and in some cases, jumped ships! The loyalty of personnel delegated to a partnership may not be taken for granted, at least in a western company. Further, the 'window' into a partner's culture provided by a partnership may encourage employees to leave much more readily than a posting in 100 per cent owned foreign subsidiaries.

Given the doubts about loyalty that are inherent to a partnership situation, employees, once seconded to a partnership, or to a partner's organization, may no longer be fully trusted once they return to the parent company. This, in turn, once known, makes appointments to partnerships and joint ventures less attractive to successful and loyal employees, turning the loss of trust in partnership employees into a self-fulfilling prophecy.[18]

We can thus hypothesize that partnerships do not allow the degree of strategic control achievable in fully controlled operations. Resource dependence cannot be used effectively, and yet the joint activities cannot gain the autonomy required to evolve into a more effective partnership. This may perpetuate an ineffective relationship between the partners. Beyond resource dependence, other more subtle control approaches, such as the use of human resource management to make subsidiary and parent company interests converge, are also more difficult in partnerships. As a result, partnerships often may not succeed. Parents do not exercise effective strategic control, nor do they allow the degree of strategic autonomy that would allow the joint activities to succeed on their own.

Strategic change

The essence of strategic change in a global business is the capacity to anticipate, or at least to comprehend quickly changes in the market and competitive conditions affecting a business, to develop among key managers an agreement on new strategic directions and to redeploy the resources of the business toward the implementation of that new strategy. This involves changes in the perception of key executives, for instance from perceiving a plurality of discrete national markets to becoming aware of the competitive interdependencies between these markets. Such competitive changes are brought about, in the change processes we observed, through a series of steps. Usually, a newly appointed senior executive brings with him a different 'vision', not a detailed analytical blueprint, but a broad perspective on how the environment, the industry, and the business might evolve, or be made to evolve in a different way. This vision is then usually communicated, redefined, debated, and shared through a series of analytical and political steps which both bring new data and analyses and also bring a widening group of senior managers to buy into it. At that stage, managers do not commit to the new vision, but at least, they accept it as legitimate, intellectually.

Yet, for strategic change to take place, a well-justified, well-articulated, appealing vision is not enough. Actual change also needs a clear way to go, not just an end-point. Beyond a shared vision, or shared strategy, at least a few simple, do-able, and challenging first steps need to be defined in detail. Agreement on a timed sequence of conditioned steps, i.e. on a strategy to change, must also be present. Although the sequence may not be complete, but only include a few first steps, and may not be implemented in the planned order, such a sequence of practical steps, and some early successes in implementing those steps are needed to lend credibility and to allow commitment to this vision.

Third, for strategic change to be effective, vision and strategy are not enough, intellectual commitment, and emotional confidence, must be complemented by power realignments which facilitate the change. The existing distribution of relationships and power in the organization is usually inherited from the stablization of the past strategy, and, as such, it is unlikely to support, unaltered, the success of a change strategy. Strategic redirection can ultimately be accomplished only through power realignment.

Even in the context of fully-controlled global businesses, strategic redirection is often a slow and painful process, spanning several years, and facing many barriers. Typically, strategic redirection requires not only top management vision and constant leadership, but also the use of management tools in a careful sequence to shift the perceptions, the stakes and the personal priorities of key managers. Redirection requires changing the 'rules of the game' within the organization. This process is already difficult in the context of a single corporation.[19]

In some relatively clear situations, partnerships are likely to make this process impossible.

The already discussed local market access joint ventures are an obvious case where partnerships are an additional barrier to strategic redirection towards global competitiveness. There, the interests of the local partner and those of the global one may diverge so much as to make continued co-operation impossible. Partnerships in business areas subjected to intense government intervention, such as military aerospace, nuclear engineering, space exploration, network broadcasting, etc., raise somewhat similar issues, as the partners themselves cannot easily develop strategies independent from those of their major national sponsors and customers. Other partnerships may become politically salient, and fall prey to complex and evolving coalitions as their intended outcome is politically controversial.[20] Attempts at co-opting potential adversaries and required partners may fail, or even when they succeed, they may still make co-operation and joint management increasingly complex.

In simpler situations, where the interests of the partners confronted with a need for strategic change do not necessarily clash, where partners can change their strategies autonomously, and are few in number, there is no a priori reason why partnerships may not successfully achieve strategic change.

Yet, many international partnerships falter through inability to respond to changed strategic circumstances.

In the partnerships we analysed so far, lack of strategic adaptation stemmed from factors rather similar to those which prevented successful strategic redirection in single companies, with added difficulties brought by the partners' relations.

First, existing strategic logics, prior to the partnership, may be resilient and result in inertia. In some cases we observed, each partner held deep-rooted, but very different beliefs, about the nature of the market place and of the opportunities they were jointly pursuing. This was particularly true when partners were entering new areas (products or territories) with which they were not fully familiar. Managers from both partners sometimes took perspectives, attitudes, assumptions, and approaches from known territories to new ones. This blocked learning and mutual adaptation between the partners. Each clung to its own prior vision, and analyses, and found it difficult to come to a new more appropriate vision that could be common. Further, where partners had come to the partnership following the failure of independent efforts, they often clung even more strongly to a prior perspective.

For example, the same two companies, collaborating in two business areas took strikingly different approaches. In one business area, which they acknowledged was relatively new to both partners, at the inception of the partnership, they commissioned market research and competitive benchmarking studies, and thus developed a joint understanding of market conditions. This provided the basis on which to build a common strategy and from which to evolve joint product specifications. In that business area, the co-operation between the two partners quickly evolved into a close relationship. Concerns for value creation — for doing whatever would be most effective marketwise — took precedence over concerns for value-appropriation, i.e. for gaining the most benefits within the partnership.

In another business area the same two partners took a radically different approach. Each partner already had products in that business area, albeit relatively unsuccessful. Rather than acknowledge the shortcomings of their prior independent approach to the market, each tried to make his approach prevail in the partnership. This led to criticism from the partners, who were quicker to see the limits of their partner's approach than of their own. Over time, they also each lost interest, since each rightly believed that the partner's approach would probably fail, and should it not, would benefit the partner more than themselves. In that business area the relationship quickly degenerated into a set of OEM agreements, for components of the products, and into technology 'cherry picking' where each company tried to extract from the partner the technologies and skills it did not have. A few years into the partnership, the partners introduced separate competing product lines to replace their own offerings — rather than the joint product lines the partnership envisioned — and the relationship faltered. While in one business area they had quickly converged to a single vision of their market and competitive environment, and to an agreement on a joint strategy, in the other business area the strength of their different a priori vision, as well as vested interests to pursue it, led to failure.

In such situations there is a genuine conflict between the contractual terms of a partnership, defining relative power between the partners (and the desire on the part of each partner to maintain or improve its power position in the partnership), and the need to shift power (including relative power between the partners) to meet new strategic requirements. Concern for power balance, or a battle of wills, prevents the needed strategic changes from taking place. In the same way as strategic redirection in a single multinational company requires redefining the roles and contributions of various sub-units, strategic redirection in a partnership may require redefining the contributions and roles of each partner. Strategic redirection is not neutral.

Strategic adaptation, based on the development of a new shared vision in the context of a partnership, is indeed likely to be easier in new areas where vested interests, a priori perspectives, the shadow of past commitments, and 'not-invented-here' syndromes are least evident, or in very mature areas where both partners have a long similar experience and a shared understanding of market and competitive conditions. In areas that are close to existing businesses, where vested interests are already strong, but experience limited, agreement may be more difficult. Yet, as we discussed in the introduction, many partnerships may be reached in these areas. The development of a shared vision, and the commitment of managers to that vision may be impossible in many partnerships.

Similarly, the administrative systems and power distribution changes required by strategic redirection may be quite difficult to accomplish in the context of a partnership. For example, key managers may be appointed to a partnership as a way to maintain a balance of power between the partners, or to facilitate the flow of know-how acquired in the partnership back to the partner companies, or still, to slant the exercise of strategic control in favour of one partner over the other. These motives may take precedence, implicitly or explicitly, in the partners' eyes over the needs for strategic change in the partnership activities. These motives, in turn, may lead to distribution of power structures and to power relationships that are inconsistent with the strategic needs of the activities carried out jointly in the partnership. The use of the powerful management tools, such as key managers' appointments, revised measurement, evaluation procedures, and changes in budgeting processes, may thus be quite difficult in the context of a partnership. Further, key managers may see their appointment to the partnership as a temporary career move, and remain more concerned with their loyalty to the parent company than with the partnership's success.

Finally, the management system infrastructure of partnerships may not be easily developed and made consistent. Again, partners start with different assumptions, and different organizational inheritances. For example, one partner may start from a tradition of decentralized decision-making where decisions are pushed to 'the lowest possible level' while the other partner may start from a tradition of functional reporting and centralized autocratic decision-making. Coming to some common position at the beginning of the relationship may already be difficult. Changing that position over time, and resetting management systems as a function of evolving strategic redirection needs is even more difficult.

These observations lead us to question the strategic change capabilities of most partnerships: changes that are difficult in the context of a single corporation are even more difficult at the intersection of two, or more corporations, each of which already has its own history, own perspectives and beliefs, human resource management traditions and practices, administrative systems, and management style. These differences make the joint evolution of strategy, be it progressive adaptation or more abrupt redirection, particularly difficult.

Different starting positions, in terms of skills and strategies, which make value creation possible, are also likely to make joint reactions to changed strategic conditions less likely: the separate interests of the two partners may lead them to decide on different reactions, particularly if the strategic importance of the partnership and the partner's willingness to commit resources to the partnership are strongly different. Strategic control issues may also take a different light depending on the strategic redirection, and thus become a stronger source of tension.

The implications of strategic redirection issues for the design and management of strategic partnerships are several. First, realism from the start in the objectives and strategies of the partnership are likely to be the best guarantee of stability. A commonly developed, well-understood and shared strategy with some robustness is most desirable. Yet, few partnerships may achieve that, largely because companies often come into partnerships in periods of technical change and turmoil. The appropriate strategy for the partnered activity, as well as the importance of the partnership in relation to other activities, may change abruptly in emerging technologies and emerging industries. A current example is the lesser emphasis on the 7J7 programme, between Boeing and a group of Japanese companies, to develop a 'propfan'-driven commercial airplane. While in the early 1980s confidence in the propfan technology and the forecasts of high oil prices made the fuel economies promised by the propfan look both desirable and feasible, by the late 1980s, slower propfan technology development and cheaper oil made the 7J7 programme a lot less important to Boeing. Further, Boeing had modernized its older generation 737 model, which continued to sell well.[21] Similarly, the evolution of the computer industry, with a rapid shift to microcomputers, the uncertain status and potential of the UNIX standard, the limited experience of international markets of both AT&T and Olivetti, made the development of a successful strategy a trial and error process which required many changes.[22] The partners found it difficult to adjust to this process.

Since partnerships are often vehicles used to develop new, less certain technologies, such as the propfan projects; to enter new business areas (e.g. computer systems of which both AT&T and Olivetti had only limited experience), and to enter new geographical markets, strategic stability and realism may not be expected at the beginning of every partnership. Quite to the contrary, many partnerships have to be framed by managers as evolving learning relationships, in which a priori detailed planning is just not practical. Yet, open-end learning-orientated relationships do not flourish easily in the context of large corporations. They challenge usual approaches to resource allocation and planning too directly.[23] Approaches to allow change, but to frame change in a clear context may thus be required. Contingent contracting and planned post-settlement settlements are two commonly used approaches to such issues in negotiating uncertain contracts.

Short of a robust, realistic, agreed-upon strategy, partners may provide for contingent contracts in their partnerships. Contingent clauses are activated if and when certain parameters change. Such clauses can be based on mutually accepted scenarios of possible changes, so the partnership is made resilient to possible, identified, but unlikely changes. Such contingent clauses have been standard practice in the raw material partnerships and in minerals' rights negotiations to account for wide fluctuations in raw material prices, and in end-product demand. Yet, to be effective, contingent clauses require either partnerships bound by a few well-defined, externally measured variables (such as raw material prices). When the variables possibly impacting a partnership's results are many, and their measurement cannot be stipulated, a priori contingent contracting becomes complex and uncertain. What works for oil exploration or bauxite extraction may not work for biotechnology discoveries or computer chips.

Beyond contingent contracting, partners may plan detailed post-settlement settlements in the context of a broad agreement, i.e. provide for the renegotiation of certain aspects of their partnership, such as transfer prices, if and when a set of parameters defined at the beginning of the partnership no longer applies. While this approach does not structure all the possible changes nor plans the joint responses to changes, at least it recognizes explicitly the possibility of changes. Typically, though, for post-settlement settlement to work, the partners must see the partnership more as an evolving relationship than as a contract to implement. The partners must be willing to renegotiate the contracts as the situation evolves.[24] Such willingness often stems from an in-depth involvement in the day-to-day management of the partnership, so that partners are comfortable enough with the relationship to see it evolve over time, and to abandon the safeguards provided by the initial agreement. An intermediate position may be provided by a broad memorandum of understanding, complemented by shorter-term contracts. Yet, if each contract renegotiation becomes a conflictual situation (e.g. on transfer prices), this may sour the quality of the relationship through frequent, difficult, painful, renegotiation exercises.

The strategic redirection and flexibility of partnerships may thus rest on a difficult balance: clarity and stability in aims; but some ambiguity in means, i.e. the willingness by the partners to enter an evolving relationship rather than to implement a fixed contract. Ambiguity may also favour collaboration: by not specifying a common valuation basis for partnerships, both partners may be under the impression that the partnership is particularly favourable to them. For instance, in a project we observed, between a technology leader in an industry and a partner from a nearby industrializing country, each partner was under the impression that the partnership was highly slanted in its favour. The technology leader had carefully avoided leakage of specific technologies, and was getting a lot of financial support and manufacturing process expertise from the partner. The partner from the NIC, unbeknown to the technology leader, was not particularly keen to obtain specific pieces of technology (which he believed he could acquire or develop elsewhere), but gave a high value to the opportunity to observe his partner's total product development process at close range. Both partners thought they had a very favourable relationship.

Beyond ambiguity and renegotiations between partners, the foundation of a joint venture, and the granting of some autonomy to such a joint venture may provide a vehicle to manage redirection. First, it constitutes a joint optimization structure for the partners, who become associated to joint profits. Second, it may develop its own management structures, tools, and processes matching the strategic requirements it faces. This may remove part of the difficulty of making two different sets of management processes interface through a partnership, a frequent cause of problems and failures. The autonomy of a joint venture may be constrained, though, not only by the parents' desire for strategic control discussed in the first section of this paper, but also the feasible operating autonomy of the venture. One partnership we analysed in the chemical industry was administered through a joint venture, but the joint venture's operations were closely imbricated into its parents' petrochemical processing sites. Critical aspects of differentiation, on manufacturing costs, personnel policies, and investment priorities were thus critically dependent on the parents' own policies. The joint venture remained a 'notional' company, but did not have the capability to adjust to changing strategic demands. Further, with parents of different nationalities and of different corporate cultures, any adjustment could only be a slow negotiated process.

Joint ventures thus may not be the full answer unless they are given enough strategic autonomy and allowed sufficient operating differentiation to face the challenge of the joint task in the most appropriate ways. How joint ventures are managed thus conditions their capabilities for flexibility.

In summary, to create the possibility of strategic change in partnerships requires that relative power issues between the partners be addressed successfully and that the governance structure of the partnership – from stable contracts to flexible joint ventures – be adjusted to the needs for change. Considering partnerships as relationships rather than contracts, and thus as evolving exchanges, provides management with the perspective which allows partnerships to withstand strategic redirection, and even to achieve flexibility.

Flexibility

In MNCs, the flexibility required by the dual needs for integration and responsiveness is achieved by creating an advocacy process within the company, between managers who are most sensitive to various aspects of the environment; most typically between product-focused and market-focused managers. Depending on the nature of the decisions at hand, the advocacy process will identify the most adequate response, and the balance of responsiveness and integration required in implementing such a response.

Nothing, in principle, prevents a partnership from achieving such flexibility. To a large extent, whether flexibility is achieved depends on the capabilities of the partner firms to make joint decisions successfully. In turn, the difficulty of making joint decisions may depend on time pressures, on the intensity of the interface between the two companies, and on the ability of the partners to reassess the values of their contributions and benefits in the context of shifting outcomes.

Rather than take a view of partnership based on form (i.e.

equity-non-equity, contract-joint venture, etc.) as a starting point, it is useful to start with a view based on the nature of the task facing the partners. The more the task requirements call for flexibility, the more the governance structure of the partnership needs to embody provisions to allow for such flexibility. In other words, we need a categorization of partnership based on the underlying task structure, not on the legal form of the relationship.

While it is difficult to specify the great variety of underlying task structures beyond some general ideas of 'complexity', a few dimensions influenced most critically the need for flexibility in the partnership we observed. These dimensions are the predictability of outcomes, the nature of task interdependences, and the time pressures faces by the partnership.

1. Predictability of outcome

The ability to predict the outcome of a partnership varies greatly from situation to situation. First, the desired objective can be more or less stable. Space exploration partnerships may have almost totally certain desired outcomes; the design of a space probe to explore a planet may be quite well specified technically, as the timing of its use. So can the European particle accelerator, despite all the bargaining between partners about location and funding of the joint effort. As one moves from public sector to commercial research, the issues become more complex. Competition may unfold in unexpected ways which question the stability of the objective. For instance, in large long-term projects, such as the Philips-Siemens partnership on 'megachip' development, it is difficult to maintain a stable goal in the face of rapidly evolving semi-conductor market needs, shifting technological opportunities and accelerating Japanese competition. Technological choices, and their outcomes, are much harder to predict than for space exploration.

Manufacturing and supply partnerships, although they do not face the same technological uncertainty, may also need much flexibility — J2T, for example, constantly faces a series of difficult choices concerning, among others, the following critical issues:

— product policy (e.g. whether to manufacture a wide assortment of high-end VCRs or a narrower range of low-end VCRs, which face much more intense price competition but can also be made more efficiently in longer series),
— product development choices and co-ordination (e.g. Do the partners come to a common product range or not? What is feasible given diverse market requirements?),
— manufacturing volumes and costs, v. other sources,

— supply of components, and choice of subcontractors,
— product standards,
— transfer pricing.

In a volatile market, where product life cycles seldom exceed eighteen months, where competition is intense, and where distributors are very powerful, the issues listed above need constant reassessment. Yet the decisions made regarding them define the outcomes of the partnership from the standpoint of JVC, Thomson, and Thorn. The volatility of the partnership's key performance parameters calls for much flexibility in the management of J2T and a keen sense of trade-offs between responding to the specific market needs of various partners and achieving efficiency in manufacturing.

2. Nature of the required partners' interface

The task structure in an international partnership may call for more or less interdependence between the partners. In some partnerships, the task allocation may be specified at the beginning of the relationship and call for very little interdependence over time, following a phase of joint task design. Some of the partnerships in the aerospace industry may have had these characteristics: following an overall design phase, detailed engineering tasks were apportioned to different manufacturers and subcontractors according to their share in the joint programme, domains of expertise and future manufacturing responsibilities. The joint venture between SNECMA and General Electric to design and manufacture the CFM56 jet engine, benefited from such a situation. Early on it was relatively easy to allocate and partition discrete development tasks between the partners. Once the engine was in service though, the insight gained from operational experience had to be shared between the partners, and common improvements to performance developed, leading to a more interdependent relationship between General Electric and SNECMA as the engine went through its life cycle and as new versions were developed. Partnerships in the pharmaceutical industry may also have some of these characteristics, where one company develops a drug for another up to a certain stage, and then gives manufacturing rights to the other company.

Conversely, complex interdependent R&D alliances, or manufacturing collaborations such as J2T, or even broader multibusiness multifunction collaborations, such the AT&T-Olivetti relationship, may require more interdependence between the partners. Partnerships that involve the design of systems — for instance computers, the hardware for which is developed and produced by Fujitsu, and the software developed by ICL — may also require more inter-dependencies between partners. Reciprocal and pooled interdependencies are the most critical. More interdependent tasks between partners, when the outcome is not easily predictable and the tasks cannot easily be planned from the outset, call for more flexibility.

3. Time pressures

Partnerships may differ substantially in time horizon and need for fast action. R&D in pharmaceuticals, for instance, is a slow process anyway, spanning many years. Partnerships may be run with relatively less frequent adjustments than in faster-moving industries such as semiconductors or consumer electronics. Time pressures call for more flexible, faster responses, and a more active management of the partnership. The J2T management board, for example, with representatives of the three partner companies met monthly, and sometimes more often in Europe or in Japan. And, following the 1987 acquisition of Thorn's consumer electronics manufacturing interests by Thomson, even that was found too slow and cumbersome, and the J2T management structure was reorganized to provide for faster decisions and reactions to competitive moves.

These three dimensions, unpredictability of outcomes and outcome values, interdependencies of tasks, and time pressure capture the essence of the need for flexibility.

Again, we can compare this fast-moving situation with the CFM56 joint venture, in which things evolved much more slowly, partly because jet engines have very long development and product life cycles, and partly because, early on, there were no volume applications for the CFM56 (in the late 1970s the CFM56 programme was nearly cancelled for lack of a market, while a huge market developed later with the KC135 remotorization programmes, the Boeing 737-300 and Airbus A320).

The capabilities of several partnerships we observed fell short of the needs for flexibility that these partnerships faced. Partnerships faced difficulties when partners' expectations had to change rapidly to face new circumstances. First, unless some mutual learning could take place, partners reinforced their prior expectations in the face of new circumstances, rather than revising their expectations. Cognitive dissonance and uncertainty triggered these reactions. Second, unexpected changes created tensions in the balance of contributions and the valuation of outcomes. Joint ventures, by creating a common (albeit partial) optimization structure allowed a more flexible adjustment than contractual relations.

Purely contractual agreements offer little flexibility, unless they are constantly renegotiated, a cumbersome and often irritating process. Contracts, though, by limiting the partners' commitment can be terminated at a relatively low cost. Flexibility may thus be achieved through belonging to a network of companies, engaging in flexible short-term contracts, provided these companies know each other well enough to limit transaction costs.[25] This has been characteristic of the usual OEM relationships in the US and, to some extent, Europe, particularly in some industries, such as textiles.

Joint ventures, which create a common optimization structure between partners, allow for more flexibility, provided the conflicts between partners' strategic control and joint venture autonomy do not stifle such flexibility. One cannot thus consider the legal form only. The internal governance mechanisms, be they contractual (e.g. the contingent clauses discussed in the previous section) or managerial (e.g. the by-laws of a joint venture), and the ways in which these governance mechanisms are used, are as critical to the flexibility of the partnership as its broad legal and fiscal form.

Further, as in fully-owned operations, needs for control, change, and flexibility conflict within partnerships. The partners' desire for control may limit their willingness to be flexible in seeking adjustment. Misplaced emphasis on the negotiation of partnerships, and benign neglect of their day-to-day management may also have very negative consequences, with operating managers taking partnerships into uncharted direction in their concern for seeing them succeed. Lack of attention to day-to-day implementation issues may also lead to growing asymmetry in the partnership, with one partner encroaching into the other set(s) of skills and competences and gaining the upper hand in the relationship. To achieve flexibility, while maintaining control may thus require the active involvement of management in the monitoring of a partnership as an ongoing relationship.

Conclusion

Our tentative examination of partnerships as an alternative to organic or acquisition internalization yields mixed results. While, in principle, strategic control, strategic redirection, and flexibility issues can be addressed in partnerships, the added difficulties brought about by partnerships, in particular partnerships between competitors, lead us to question the viability of partnerships as a durable alternative to fully-owned growth.

Our tentative evidence suggests that most partnerships may be intrinsically unstable, bound to fall back towards mere OEM relationships between buyers and sellers, or to evolve into a single operating entity with a common strategy and shared vision and goals. Whether this single entity results from a merger between operations, or from the existence of a stable relatively autonomous joint venture, it is characterized by strategic unity and flexibility.

Notes and References

1 C. K. Prahalad and Y. Doz, *The Multinational Mission: Balancing Local Demands and Global Vision* (New York: The Free Press, 1987), and Y. Doz, 'International industries: fragmentation versus globalization' in B. R. Guile and H. Brooks (eds), *Technology and Global Industry: Companies and Nations in the World Economy* (Washington, DC: National Academy Press, 1987).

2 Y. Doz and C. K. Prahalad, 'A process model of strategic redirection in large complex firms: The case of multinational corporations' in A. Pettigrew (ed.), *The Management of Strategic Change* (Oxford: Basil Blackwell, 1987).

3 Y. Doz, 'Government policies and global industries', in M. E. Porter (ed.), *Competition in Global Industries* (Boston, Mass: Harvard University Press, 1986).

4 C. K. Prahalad and Y. Doz, *The Multinational Mission: Balancing Local Demands and Global Vision* (op. cit.), chapter 6.

5 S. Ghoshal and N. Nohria, 'Multinational corporations as differentiated networks', INSEAD Working Paper 87/13, and C. K. Prahalad and Y. Doz *The Multinational Mission* (op. cit.), chapter 7.

6 G. Hamel and C. K. Prahalad, 'Do you really have a global strategy?' in *Harvard Business Review*, July–August 1985, and Y. Doz and C. K. Prahalad, *The Multinational Mission* (op. cit.), chapters 3 and 6.

7 See Bettis, Porter, Prahalad.

8 J. R. Atwood, 'The Export Administration Act and the Dresser Industries Case', *Law and Policy in International Business* 15, no. 4, 1983.

9 Y. Doz, *Government Control and Multinational Management: Power Systems and Telecommunications Equipment* (New York: Praeger Special Studies, 1979).

10 See L. G. Franko, *Joint Venture Survival in Multinational Corporations* (New York: Praeger, 1971); see also J. M. Stopford and L. T. Wells, *Managing the Multinational Enterprise* (New York: Basic Books, 1972); and C. K. Prahalad, 'The strategic process in a multinational corporation', doctoral dissertation, Harvard Business School, 1975).

11 Peter Lorange, 'Co-operative ventures in multinational settings', (unpublished working paper), (Wharton School, University of Pennsylvania, 1985), and K. R. Harrigan, 'Joint ventures and competitive strategy', *Strategic Management Journal*, 9, 1988.

12 Partnerships most often combine scale and skill dimensions, as partners combine operations both to achieve higher scale and to learn from each other. Yet, as the strategic control issues stemming from scale and from skill dimensions differ significantly, it is useful to treat them separately.

13 For more detailed discussions of these issues, see G. Hamel, Y. Doz, C. K. Prahalad, 'Collaborate with your competitors and win', *Harvard Business Review* (Jan.–Feb., 1989) and Y. Doz and A. Shuen, 'From intent to outcome: a process framework for partnerships' (INSEAD Working Paper No. 88/46).

14 P. Lorange, ibid.

15 For a discussion of specialized assets and commitments in partnerships see D. Teece, 'Profiting from technological innovation: implications for integration' in D. J. Teece (ed.) *The Competitive Challenge* (Cambridge, Mass: Ballinger, 1987).

16 V. Pucik, 'Joint ventures with the Japanese: the key role of HRM', *Euro Asia Business Review*, vol. 6, no. 4, Oct. 1987 and R. B. Peterson and M. S. Schwind, 'A comparative study of personnel problems in international companies and joint ventures in Japan', in *Journal of International Business Studies*, vol. 8, no. 4, 1977.

17 M. Lyles, 'Learning among joint venture sophisticated firms, E. Contrastor and P. Lorange, *Co-operative Strategies in International Business* (Lexington, Mass: Lexington Books, 1988).

18 P. Lorange, ibid.

19 Y. Doz and C. K. Prahalad, 'An approach to strategic control in MNCs', *Sloan Management Review*, Summer 1981, pp. 5–13; Y. Doz and C. K. Prahalad, 'Headquarters influence and strategic control in MNCs', *Sloan Management Review*, Fall 1981, pp. 15–29; and Y. Doz and C. K. Prahalad, 'A process model of strategic redirection in large complex firms: the case of multinational corporations' in A. Pettigrew (ed.), (op. cit.).

20 For an example see M. Horwitch, *Clipped Wings* (Cambridge, Mass: MIT Press, 198?).

21 D. C. Mowery and N. Rosenberg, 'Commercial aircraft: co-operation and competition between the U.S. and Japan' in *California Management Review*, 27, no. 4, Summer 1985.

22 Researchers' interviews at Olivetti and AT&T.

23 For a more detailed discussion of these issues, see Y. Doz, 'Value creation through technology collaboration', *Aussenwirtschaft*, 43, 1988, pp. 175–190.

24 Even in the absence of strategic change, over time partners are likely to develop a better mutual understanding, a more realistic assessment of the potential value of their contribution, of the conditions needed for value creation, a greater appreciation of each others' *modus operandi* and cultures, as well as (hopefully) more trust. This may usefully lead them to renegotiate their agreements to improve effectiveness (i.e. the value created for each partner) over time.

25 See, for instance, S. Mariotti and G.-C.- Cainarca, 'The evolution of transaction governance in the textile-clothing industry', *Journal of Economic Behaviour and Organisation* 7 (1986), pp. 351–374.

Chapter six

Effective strategic planning processes in the multinational corporation

Peter Lorange and Gilbert Probst

(Based on a paper given at an EIASM conference, 'The Management of the MNC', in Brussels, June 1987)

Introduction

Most multinational corporations (MNCs) that want to remain truly excellent and continue to be successful will have little choice, we shall claim, but to be firmly committed to a strategic process approach for coping with the international or global business opportunities and threats. Approaching international success through applying a strategic process seems necessary in order to stay competitive and remain at the cutting edge. The alternative, it seems, is that an MNC might run the risk of slowing down and become relegated to the role of a 'parochial' company. Loss of offensive momentum might be a likely result.

In this chapter we shall claim that strategic management processes can play a significant role in assisting corporations in their efforts to implement better global or multidomestic strategies. Our contention, however, is that most management processes, such as many strategic planning processes, unfortunately often fall short of offering realistic support for an effective international strategic focus.

Strategic planning has become an integral part of most MNCs' working modes. To a greater or lesser degree most MNCs have typically developed a quite tailormade mode of practising strategic planning, so that it might better work in their particular circumstances. Thus, we should not expect to see the emergence of widely shared, relatively standardized planning processes, nor should the problems inhibiting effective strategic management become very similar between companies' MNCs. Still, however, there are at least a few common dilemmas that tend to face many multinational corporations. In this chapter we shall elaborate on four such major sets of challenges that, in particular, may become critical for the MNC's strategy to be able to remain effective:

— The changing formality of an MNC's strategic planning process.

— Changing executive roles in the strategic planning process.
— Changing behavioural aspects of practising strategic planning.
— Changing integrative requirements facing the strategic planning process.

We shall thus attempt to offer new strategic process know-how, rather than to address the many emerging strategic content issues that face today's MNCs. We shall thus attempt to shed light on how the modern MNC's strategic planning systems should function for it to be better able to cope with today's emerging realities. Also, our discussion shall attempt to shed light on how strategic planning processes may look in the MNC of the future.

The changing formality of an MNC's strategic planning processes

Increasing complexity

Many will agree that we live in a world of increasing complexity, variety and dynamism and therefore with increasing uncertainty. Change is nothing new. Heraclitus, for instance, wrote: 'Nothing endures but change.' Nonetheless, strategic management and the challenges for strategic planning in MNCs seem to differ today from what we have experienced in the past. The rate of change has accelerated when it comes to many relevant dimensions: social, technological, economic, political, ecological, etc.

Examples of macroshifts that create new complexity, add to our picture of dynamism and accelerate change and uncertainty are:

— Balance shifts in economic and political power, from the Atlantic to the Pacific world.
— Shifts in basic values of managers, workers, customers, society, etc., when it comes to issues such as safety, environmental concerns, self-realization, etc.
— Dramatic alternations and oscillations between crises and hope, pessimism and optimism, in countries such as Brazil, India, the Philippines, and so on.
— Prices, interest rates and currencies that cannot easily be predicted.
— Ecological risks that are becoming exceedingly grave.
— The technological revolution continues to accelerate in most fields, such as information technology, bio-technology, materials sciences, etc., with the emergence of new challenges regarding how to master these new technologies.

— Massive convergence between the technologies of the computer business and the telecommunication's business, and between the biological and electronics sciences.

Complexity has, at least in part, grown beyond our capacity, and put strains on our ability to cope with it in traditional ways, with traditional instruments and methods (Gomez and Probst 1987). The emerging, more complex systems may have special characteristics that we have not yet fully understood. They may be highly interrelated, dynamic, multidimensional, based on a particularly high variety of behavioural modes, etc. The strategic planning systems of the future may increasingly have to be thought about along these lines. To illustrate, we see that problems and tasks often change so fast that solutions and agreed-upon strategies may rapidly become outdated – the environment or the context is no longer the same. The multinational corporation is thus in need of new strategic processes and methods that may allow for more immediate adaptiveness and quicker evolution.

The need for growth

Assessing today's strategic planning and strategic management practices, there seem to have developed certain biases. We emphasize a lot how to develop generic strategies in order to gain competitive advantages, but seem to have paid relatively less attention to delineating effective strategic working processes. The strategic analysis is relatively well developed, but becomes less effective due to lack of insight when it comes to delineating processes for achieving a sense of agreement among members of an organization regarding the analytic delineation and implementation of competitive strategies. In this chapter we shall point towards certain requirements that the typical MNC may have to face when it comes to strengthening management.

We shall propose that the MNC will typically have a need for a process emphasis, which focuses on how better to adapt to environmental opportunities, how to stimulate internal growth, and how to create organizational motivation to develop a more growth-oriented, opportunistic, revenue-generating strategy, preferably with a global point of view in mind. This, together with our initial observation regarding the added complexity in the environment, will lead us to propose in the next three sections a number of changes in the formal characteristics that we feel planning processes must face.

Strategic control and adaptability

Management control systems are, of course, a critical part of running a complex global business. Unfortunately, however, such processes can have several dysfunctional impacts on the development of global strategies (Lorange, Scott Morton, and Ghoshal 1987). First, control systems may tend to put relatively unilateral emphasis on monitoring short-term performance, thereby reinforcing a potential bias towards bottom line results. This can create mixed signals and doubts in the organization regarding the viability of building up global strategies in the longer term. Thus, a longer-term globally built perspective must be kept in mind to minimize possible misunderstanding – the control process should not distract from or disrupt the organization's longer-term global-strategic frame of mind.

It is also important that the management control process is sufficiently 'rich' to be able to cope realistically with multi-dimensional strategic circumstances. For instance, in a firm organized along global business lines, a uniform treatment of all country operations can lead to strategy implementation dysfunctionalities for the company's cadre of local managers across several businesses in a given country. Similarly, when controlling a multi-domestically organized firm, proper attention must also be given to a global assessment of the overall business seen in a global context.

For instance, when it comes to a firm which is organized along global business lines and which has several business operations located in a particular high-inflation country setting, there may be a natural propensity for each business to impose tight control of cash flows and to keep a heavy scrutiny on controlling the capital structure. By seeing all the firm's business activities in the country together, however, one might create an opportunity to take advantage of the interplay between short-term financing/borrowing/capital placement tactics and 'managed' ups and downs in the cash flow streams stemming from the various operations. Thus when, for instance, a major devaluation is expected, a phenomenon which normally can be anticipated by astute local management, it may make sense to intensify sales activities, accelerate the shipping of products through the distribution channels, and increase promotional efforts, so as to realize a temporary surge in positive cash flows. The additional liquidity can then be used as a basis for the other businesses to boost additional borrowing, so that the firm in total will gain from the devaluation. Financial tactical hedges may thus more than offset short-term disturbances in operations (Jacque and Lorange 1984).

Consider now a multidomestically organized firm which naturally pays strong attention to controlling each of its countries of operations. It may be hard however to detect shifts in growth patterns of its various businesses across the world. It is critical for the success of the company to pick the 'right' businesses to emphasize, i.e., the 'battlegrounds' which have the strongest future potentials and which can offer a relatively long-term basis to return the efforts expended to develop such businesses. Needless to say, it is also important to spot early signs of decline in growth rates in particular businesses. Monitoring underlying critical factors such as emergent technologies is probably key in this context. Another critical aspect of proactive strategic control is the systematic monitoring of news on a global basis regarding one's key competitors. It is again important to keep in mind that most control approaches might involve signals from one's local business managers on how they see a move from a given competitor. Such signals, seen in isolation, do not necessarily reveal a true picture of the underlying strategies of global competitors; they must be seen in an overall strategic context to highlight a clearer understanding of key competitors' strategies. Spotting and detecting major shifts in the global competitive arena is thus essential, but hard unless the multidomestic control system is strengthened in a multidimensional way.

Changing executive roles in the strategic planning process

The CEO's and upper management's roles: global visioning

A communication of upper management's global vision to the various business activities world-wide seems vital. It is crucial that the CEO is seen as a proponent of a global vision which is experienced as relevant throughout the organization. He must be able to communicate a meaningful message to a broader global constituency of executives. He will have to give prompt and meaningful feedback to an often rather heterogeneous group of business strategists located throughout the world. Above all, he must, in his projection of commitment to a global strategy, insist on a global level of ambition. He should dispel tendencies towards settling for more comfortable, parochial objectives. Thus, the CEO must pay particular attention to his 'inspirator' role in the global strategic planning process. To ensure a global vision a more passive and reactive approach is unlikely to work.

The time-spending patterns of the CEO must, in particular, be very carefully worked out so that his energy, in fact, is spent on creating global strategies. In this connection, it should be pointed out that the sum of a number of local initiatives from around the globe, put together into a corporate strategy, is not necessarily likely to add up to a global strategy as such. Thus, it can be a fallacy for the CEO to fall into the illusion that he is effectively pushing a global approach simply because he is making himself busy by travelling extensively world-wide. The CEO must spend his time and energy in gaining insight into what constitutes an over-lying global value-creating dimension. Strategic planning should be his ally in facilitating this, so that he does not lose track of such an overall vision.

Team participation by members throughout the multinational organization to achieve more creativity

A second commonly fertile area for improvement of the strategic planning process will be to put more emphasis on the delineating of how to make better use of creative, *ad hoc*, task forces in the strategic processes, with broader participation processes from talented executives from several countries. To see how such task forces may get formed, it is important to pay proper attention to whether the basic formal organizational structure is delineated along geographic lines or global business lines. If, for instance, each particular business is to be run as a global one, the conse-quence will be that in a given country there will be several global business strategies executed in parallel. If, on the other hand, each country will have its own integrated strategy, the consequence will be that 'global' business strategies will tend to become the multi-domestic sum of these country-based business strategies. The practical reality for most multinationals, however, is that both dimensions must be dealt with. The planning process may be structured in such a way that it helps to focus on the most dominant of these dimensions, but in addition allows for the establishing of task forces with *de facto* mandates to address the other dimension (Lorange 1980).

For instance, let us assume that we have a capital-intensive producer of various types of metal products. For such a company, one might argue that each of the basic metal types should be seen as a global business and have its separate global strategies. However, particular important regions such as the North American market also represent a critical strategic dimension. There might be a lot to gain by strategically co-ordinating, say, the North American activities between these global strategies. A task force with repre-sentation from each of the global business strategies might thus be formed to delineate the co-ordination needs, so that a North American strategy can also emerge.

For a globally operating food company, on the other hand, it would be typical that the country-based local consumer preferences often might tend to be key, and that therefore its international strategy might be largely developed on a multidomestic basis. However, it may be increasingly evident in this case too that global co-ordination of particular business strategies may also have to be pursued to ensure strategy consistency across the various country boundaries. Global task forces might be established for such businesses, with representatives for the most important countries involved, to work out how to address these strategic challenges.

To make strategic task forces of these types work effectively is, of course, not easy given both the complex tasks at hand and the heterogeneity and diversity of the committee's memberships. It is, of course, particularly hard to make the committees work when they draw on executives from across national boundaries (Hedlund 1980). It is therefore critical to get broad-based acceptance for what constitutes meaningful working forms of such executive task forces. One must be realistic about the fact that it typically will take a lot of time and energy for many executives to develop strategies in such a manner. Careful attention should be given to setting the agendas, to running the meetings efficiently, to scheduling the planning calendar and meetings in such a way that travel can be minimized, in short, to pay utmost attention to spending executives' time cost-efficiently. Choice of a good chairman for each committee also means much. To be effective, none the least politically, the committees should be given clear mandates, articulated from the CEO and backed up by his visible support. Why are these cross-organizational committees so critical? Probably the most important reason is that they can add the critical dimension of being effective 'think tanks'. They can help provide the necessary vitality and vision in the strategic thinking of the global corporation. Without such cross-functional, eclectic impetus to 'lift' executives out of their more narrow unidimensional strategic contexts, it is quite likely that the global strategy will become nothing more than the sum of various unidimensionally segmental business perspectives. The overall commitment by the members of the organizations to be willing to develop a truly meaningful, ambitious global strategy will hinge on their ability to see that this must be based on providing something more than the sum of the unidimensional strategies of each operating organizational entity, i.e., a multidimensional vision.

Changing behavioural aspects of practising strategic planning

Learning

Given the turbulence and complexity of the environmental contexts in which most multinationals operate, it seems to be particularly critical that an organization is able to strengthen its ability to learn from how well its present strategies are working. Through this gain of experience it might develop further those more successful aspects of the established strategies. Similarly, dimensions of the strategies that are not properly functioning can also be addressed.

To focus on the critical success factor may be a way to operationalize this learning. How can one better build up an understanding of how one's success might depend on the interplay with what is critical in the environment? One set of critical underlying success factors has to do with assessing potential shifts in the attractiveness of the business, globally or in the several multi-domestic contexts, depending on the type of business at hand: shifts in what drives its growth, industry structure changes, technological break-throughs, governmental impacts, and so on. Other success factors focus on how the strategic programmme implementation efforts are coming along: customer reactions and competitors' countermoves, again seen globally or multi-domestically depending on the type of business.

An attitude to look for 'early warning signals' seems to be an important dimension of such learning. The formidable challenge, of course, is to get the entire multinational organization activated on this. Where are those in the best position to know about the particular elements of critical success factors located? How can they communicate what they have under surveillance so that the firm actually registers new situations and settings, and does not 'throw away' signals from its global network?

It seems important in this respect to develop an 'experimentation-based' planning process which emphasizes experience building, and encourages the members of the organization around the world to learn through interacting in a shared probing, trial-and-error sense. Our attitude regarding how we see problems in a global community of executives may be critical when it comes to learning. Problems are certainly not objective phenomena in such global contexts, but rather perceived, constructed in different executives' minds. There are many ways to perceive the world — some more 'realistic' than others, depending on where we are. We must take advantage of this variety and eclecticism regarding how to see problems. It is a true opportunity for the MNC to learn, in this way, by making 'errors' based on global interpretation in one's striving towards adaptation and development. Learning thus means that we must not try to avoid conflicts, change, errors, noise, danger and risk-taking because of the diverse underlying backgrounds of the executives at hand (Argyris 1985). An MNC, for instance, must not try to trivialize, negate or oversee problems by imposing a headquarters or home-country sense of what is 'right'. There is a need for a global attitude to conflicts, openness, reflection, experiments and unlearning (Probst 1987). Seen this way, learning, adaptation and development go hand-in-hand in providing the MNC with a time advantage.

Learning to learn (Argyris and Schön 1978; Argyris 1985; Bateson 1972; Isenberg 1986) means having the ability to identify those mechanisms and principles that underlie learning processes, so that in new contexts it becomes more possible or easier to shorten learning and unlearning processes. For the complex MNC it may often not only be a question of what a system learns, but that it learns fast enough. For the MNC to embrace the many forces of change, to be prepared and trained to adapt and evolve in a context with growing complexity, a series of implications for the MNC's strategic planning approach can be pointed out:

— strive for a better interaction of the many diverse elements of a global strategy into a more comprehensive, holistic strategic management approach, i.e., a true shift from parts to whole; insistence on bringing a global or multidomestic focus to its conclusion;
— shifts from relatively strong emphasis on organizational structure to relatively more emphasis on management interaction processes, from 'organizational entities of subsidiaries' to 'global networks of executives' as a metaphor of understanding and learning (Gomez and Probst 1987).

Entrapment avoidance

Most MNCs will attempt to build up a strong commitment to their strategies. This is, of course, desirable and allows the MNC to build on its successes of the past along the lines just discussed. As has become evident too, however, it is also critical not to be trapped in one's own past successes, nor to become blind-folded. Key underlying assumptions may, for instance, be in need of change. Successful managers must always be ready to live up to this.

For the MNCs it seems particularly critical that the planning process should emphasize how to avoid being trapped in one's approaches of the past, so that one more rapidly can adapt to new opportunities and circumstances as they come along. Issues that may cause difficulties in this context have to do with prestige, organizational politics, ability to bring together *ad hoc* teams so that executives with 'fresh eyes' can become involved, development of an organizational culture which 'calls a spade a spade', etc. (Brockner *et al.* 1981; Lorange and Nelson 1987). Again, the multi-national variety of the MNC should be taken advantage of in order to achieve this. Sadly, many MNCs seem to do exactly the opposite, being entrapped in their own home-country cultures.

It is thus not sufficient for the MNC merely to idiosyncratically set strategies and to attempt to implement them according to a 'home-country mode'. One must also be prepared to make decisions about strategic 'disentrapment' processes, or alternative 'solutions' needed given the global multidimensionality. Can the MNC act upon its complex environments rather than belatedly react to them? The critical organizational blockage factors that have to be controlled to achieve this have to do with nationalistic, myopic host-country narrowness.

Human resources as the key strategic resource

Scarcity of strategic resources represents a major obstacle to successful strategy implementation in most MNCs. How, there-fore, can the MNC 'allocate' this scarce strategic resource? Emphasis on capital as the most assumed critical strategic resource has been quite typical in many MNCs' strategic processes. It seems clear, however, that the critical competence-base of the firm, as embodied in the MNC's managers and organizational teams, repre-sents a key precondition to value creation in the firms. Thus, it is important to 'allocate' this critical human resource in such a way that managers can best create value. These key management resources must of course then be backed up with the necessary capital. The entire global stack of executives represents the strategic resources. It would not be to the benefit of an MNC to limit its human resource management focus to executives from the home-country only – a common 'bias' in many MNCs' 'allocation' processes, however.

As already alluded to, the use of *ad hoc* management teams with relevant information, analytical ability and creativity is a critical way to activate the global talent pool (Hedlund 1980). These task forces can be assigned executives in such a way that complementary know-how can come together. The planning process should facilitate such global mobilization of relevant know-how for taking advantage of the opportunity at hand. Issues such as flexibility of management, creation of a stimulating professional atmosphere so as to have the ability to attract, develop and maintain managers who can 'produce' strategic results, etc., become critical.

In order for any resource to have strategic value it must be transferable. This is the case for financial funds, technologies, other know-hows – and, people. When it comes to considering the human capital as a strategic resource there are at least three aspects of transferability that the MNC must face up to. First, an executive must be able to transfer information, such as data describing the system, the environment, etc., so that he can analogously draw on this in a new business setting. Second, knowledge, such as instructions, methodologies, 'how-to-do-it', know-how for accomplishing implementation tasks, etc., must be transferable so that he can 'produce' in another, perhaps, geographic assignment. Third, understanding strategic insight must be 'transferable'. Why is a given phenomenon critical for explaining global strategic success more broadly? Why is a given global strategy appropriate under 'so and so' circumstances? Why does a normative strategic path make sense? The executive must thus be able to understand global strategy and how he can be able to contribute to it in different ways depending on his assignments.

Focus and simplicity

Many MNCs have pursued strategies which more or less by necessity have led to quite complex global business activity patterns, through diversification, geographic expansion, vertical integration of its value chain, acquisitions, etc. An MNC might question, however, whether its management teams have infinite capability to deal with such complexity. How much complexity can it handle? Does management's cognitive capacity become an issue?

The MNC's strategic process should be structured to be sensitive to cognitive capacity limitations when it comes to the individual managers involved. One should stay within reasonable limits of complexity. The planning process might therefore emphasize the need to make choices, set priorities, etc.

Commitment and communication

It is probably fair to assume that an MNC's strategy can better be developed and implemented under circumstances when the global management team of the organization is fully behind the strategy. Thus, the issue of participation in the strategic process, development of a sense of ownership, establishing a strong degree of commitment to the strategy becomes critical. Such a commitment must, of course, be a realistic one, not based on entrapment in wishful, unrealistic assumptions that do not have a basis in the reality of the day.

For most MNCs participation and communication will be a critical aspect of the strategic process. Executives from around the globe who need to be involved must actually become involved in relevant ways. Communication within the global managerial network must go on effectively, and be of good quality. There is probably nothing that can substitute for face-to-face communication when it comes to development of strategic commitment. This can however be exceedingly time-consuming and expensive in multinational settings. Still, such an 'investment' is necessary. Computer-based decision supports may, to some extent, help in the communication by simplifying the creation of a strong basic 'platform' from which all parties can better begin with their dialogue (Hagström 1987).

An entirely different dimension of participation and communication has to do with ensuring that the signals communicated through the strategic process are actually understood throughout the organization. In this context, it is probably critical to make sure that the parties involved actually realize what the particular communication at hand is all about: Is it brainstorming and thinking about potential future alternatives? Is it vision-setting? Is it analysis to narrow down strategic alternatives? Is it strategic decision-making? With the complexity of the strategic tasks of most MNCs in mind, to clarify the intention behind a particular communication exchange it is important that both parties see the interaction alike, so that the strategic planning process does not create crossed signals. To strive for a common organizational culture within the MNC can be very meaningful for providing a more realistic base for communication within the global network. Needless to say, it can be a real challenge to develop such an organizational community base within a large, complex and geographically dispersed MNC.

Flexibility, timing and opportunism

Strategic processes within MNCs may at times become exceedingly rigid. Thus, they easily end up creating an atmosphere of unrealism regarding how to actually execute particular strategic opportunities — in real life actual opportunities never come along as planned, of course. What planning can do, however, is to 'prepare' the MNC's organization to be ready for certain strategic moves, which can then be made faster. The organization can thus be preconditioned to act faster when the opportunity arises — timing and determination to move can be strengthened by developing a clearer understanding of why a certain strategic direction is important from a general strategic point of view. The planning process should therefore attempt to foster such readiness to be flexible and determined. In many MNCs, large and bureaucratic as they often are, it is exactly this lack of urgency to decide which can become a problem. Sluggishness and indecisiveness lead to opportunity losses.

Enhancement of flexibility is thus a key part of strategic management in today's MNCs. Flexibility as such is rather the result of self-organizing processes attempting to create 'mini-organizations' with their own autonomy within the large global network. Flexibility is not a need in itself but a means to enhance the ability to adapt and develop.

As noted, processes and methods for design and control of social systems paradoxically often hinder or reduce flexibility, creating a bureaucracy instead. Efforts to make an MNC's strategic planning system flexible thus typically involve having to fight bureaucratic management methods. To enhance flexibility therefore means that one has to search for ways to introduce innovative aspects so as to create new balance in the strategic process. The aim of such instruments — human resource management, job reassignments, promotions, incentives, structuring of organization, flexible control system, etc. — is to contribute towards a more open steering frame to promote and develop flexibility.

To create flexibility, i.e., to enhance the potential of adaptability and development, means to enlarge the MNC's ability to use knowledge to create wealth rather than to use wealth to create knowledge. Thus, as discussed, it is not money or technology as such that is the cause of an effective corporation. A consistently performing company differs from the rest through its people, organizational, planning and managerial systems. If money or technology alone were the cause, then there would be many more successful companies (Rada 1987). Flexibility imbedded in the people network of an organization is particularly critical for the MNC – both very hard to achieve, but also with very large potential pay-offs.

Changing integration requirements facing the strategic planning process

Looking at the emerging strategic process requirements from a metapoint of view, integration is key. This means that the MNC needs to pull together the many and diverse elements, dimensions, functions, etc., that constitute aspects of its strategic activities into one unifying system or process. The MNC's planning process of the future can thus also be seen as consisting of a set of concepts of integration:

Integration across different hierarchical levels – functional business, corporate, industry, society, etc.

Each strategic level yields profound strategic insights that cannot be dispensed with. It is important to recognize that each level's strategy is interrelated with the strategies of the other levels, and they must be seen together in a common context to be meaningful. This also means that the requirements for good strategic planning must be considered in such a hierarchically interrelated context. For instance, it will not suffice if learning is taking place at one level but not at the next – this can easily create friction and confusion. Similarly, considerations of focus and simplicity may well be met at one level, say when it comes to global or multi-domestic business strategies, but lack of synthesizing focus regarding overall global exposure and too much complexity in geographic exposure might still exist at the corporate level.

For didactic reasons it may well be helpful to differentiate between a normative, strategic hierarchy of levels and a formal operational organizational hierarchy of levels, the former being flatter in theory, the latter encompassing more hierarchical levels. But, in practice, this distinction may represent an increasingly indivisible concept. It becomes more and more important to integrate the many levels in the global organization more boldly to involve entrepreneurs, to flatten the pyramid, to spread responsibility, etc. (Peters and Waterman 1984; Pinchot 1985). Thus, the MNC's hierarchical integration should encompass fewer levels, allowing a *de facto* logic of hierarchical integration to have a chance. With the excessive hierarchical complexity of many MNCs it is ludicrous to expect that hierarchical integration can take place.

Integration across functional units, divisions, companies, countries, etc.

It is the integrated combination of all functional operations in a value-creating stream, such as, for instance, R&D, manufacturing, logistics, marketing, etc., that creates strategic value (Porter 1985). While a simple concept in principle, it can be a hard and difficult task in practice for an MNC with its far-flung global operations to

157

achieve satisfactory horizontal integration. More or less independently operating 'kingdoms' throughout the world may imply that relatively little strategic value creation may take place (Lorange 1980). Most strategic issues for the globally or multidomestically organized MNC are of a horizontal and not a vertical kind. Questions such as quality, customer services, productivity, etc. cut across most functional units in the global set up.

Therefore the MNC's strategic process must attempt to break down barriers to networking, teamwork, task forces and self-organizing groups. Again, the previously articulated requirements to good strategic planning processes should be applied in this context. For instance, commitment and communication seem particularly important to achieving horizontal focus. Entrapment avoidance, so as not to build barriers, similarly seems crucial.

Strategic processes thus have to harness the potential for strategic value creation across the MNC's organization by integrating everyday operating decisions and actions in a more strategic manner. Strategic management is thus again a task for and a process concerning the whole global organization. It is not, and cannot be, the province of functional strategist specialists.

It will typically be a too narrow and entrapping approach to concentrate on only one dimension of integration for creating strategic value, such as, for instance, only to emphasize global marketing integration, a global R&D focus, or a global manufacturing system. Rather, a particular function, in addition to having to be globally or multidomestically integrated on its own, should also be horizontally integrated with the other functions. It is thus a holistic, horizontal integration process, involving many individuals, elements, functions, dimensions, units, groups, etc.

Integration of vision and rationale

This might involve the analysis of parts and a synthesis of details into a whole, drawing on both the so-called 'right side', rational brain, and the 'left side', intuitive brain (Mintzberg 1986), or, on both management and leadership (Lamb 1987).

Global vision, cross-cultural intuition, cosmopolitan imagination, synthetic and holistic thinking are one side of the MNC's 'strategic management' coin. The rational understanding of the bottom-line of existing businesses throughout the world, the crisp analysis of the many geographic environments, financial analysis for the MNC, and the assessment of management potential in the global network, etc. represent the other side. It is a key challenge for strategic planning to facilitate a creative drive in all parts of the

MNC so that it can develop a global strategic focus which is both dynamic and realistic. Which management instruments and methods suit different system levels and parts so as to enhance and maintain flexibility and realism in the whole? How can one create a sense of appreciation for creativity and commitment to delivering results within local, regional, and global organizational entities, i.e., a broad integration of the two perspectives as complementary, not adversarial?

Integration of strategy-setting, implementation and incremental strategic control

Creating new strategies is one side of the coin; implementing and maintaining and evolving them through adaptation and development is the other. These are dual aspects of one indivisible strategic management task. Integration is critical to counteract the unrealistic notion of dichotomy between strategy formulation and implementation.

Setting strategies is often a painfully complex task. Strategies can, for instance, often only be realized if the entire 'critical mass' of the global management team not only gets enough information but also understands and supports what is meant to take place, through a process of communication, participation and commitment building. It is thus a continuous question who within the global network shall have to be informed about what, who should participate when? In short, how meaningfully to involve all in the process? Who shall, for instance, take immediate actions to implement and control various aspects of a particular global strategic initiative? Strategic processes that end up with grand global strategies without integrative assignments of responsibilities for execution of the plans, and without delineation of follow-up control modes, are probably quite useless. It is key for the MNC not only to develop plans but also to have critical implementation tasks and steps under control. Implementation implies incremental execution of the global grand strategies taking into account early warnings on subsequent changes concerning the environment, incorporating new opportunities, reassessing the management potential, facing up to shifts in the political scene, accepting shifts in social philosophy, etc. The actual manifested strategy will thus never turn out to be exactly like the formulated strategic intentions.

Strategic decisions taken in the present have effects in the future. Managing in turbulent times thus asks for flexibility in the design, control, and development of strategies. What this means is to build in provisions in the strategy development for alternative strategies, redundancy in the means and resources, early warning signals, etc., calling for close attention to integration and adherence to the various requirements to planning.

Integration of all people involved who have a stake

Strategic resources (key people, technologies, know-how, funds) must, in principle, as we have noted, be freely movable in order to have strategic value. Handling of strategic resources to get such flexibility is, however, often difficult to achieve without creating potentially significant stakeholder resentment. Typically, a wide variety of stakeholders, external and internal, are key participants in the MNC's strategic processes if strategic flexibility is to be maintained. Further, a number of new 'stakeholders' always emerge such as governmental agencies, labour unions, activist groups, etc. To identify which of those are becoming critical — to pick the 'right' stakeholder allies — is a difficult challenge for most MNCs. This calls for the ongoing integration of these new stakeholders in the MNC's strategic process, but in such a way to maintain focus, flexibility and commitment. Failure of meaningful integration of changing stakeholder groups can lead to a stifling of the corporation's strategic evolution.

The strategic planning process of the future multinational corporation must be based on value creation through people's information, know-how and understanding. It will be based on 'brains-organizations'. Growth must, above all, be achieved through interfacing among human resources in networks, both within the corporation itself as well as with key external stakeholders, such as customers, other competitors, etc. The MNC's planning process may, therefore, be seen more as a co-operative partnership activity among many actors and groups of stakeholders. One might expect such a planning process to be simultaneously both quite decentralized, centred around a number of relatively self-organized local entities, but also quite centralized in the sense that these entities will have to be sensibly pulled together when it comes to a common global strategic domain and vision.

Integration of one's own strategy with other companies' strategies

Co-operative strategic forms can be expected to play a major role in the future strategic planning (joint venture, licensing, franchising, etc.). These can also be integrated with other companies' competitive strategies, within the context of industry or sector strategies, etc.

As an example, let us consider the integration-effect from electronic micro-component technology as driving computer component and telecommunication companies to become suppliers of networks for processing digital information. One can expect that there will be more global alliances between these businesses, both to exploit new markets as well as to protect old ones. One can expect the emergence of an intriguing multidimensional pattern — to co-operate with someone else in one context but at the same time to compete with the very same firm in another context. A global strategic vision is, of course, critical for working out such patterns in a realistic manner.

Conclusions

We have argued that MNCs will have to re-examine the strategic processes they make use of along several dimensions. First, we have suggested that the way the formal delineation of strategic planning processes takes place may have to be re-examined. With the vast complexity facing the MNC, both in terms of internal activity patterns and environmental growth opportunities and threats, it will be a real challenge to show moderation regarding added formality and complexity in the strategic planning process. Simplicity and flexibility should be striven for so that the system can facilitate incremental changes and adaptation. Over-formalization should be avoided at all costs.

Second, executives' roles in MNCs' future strategic planning activities may be expected to shift, at least to a degree. Critical importance will be given to the human resource, i.e., the global network of executives constituting the MNC. It is 'wise allocations' of key executives within this network that will impact strategic success above all. Abilities of executives to work together in *ad hoc* team contexts within the network will also be key. The CEO's role in contributing to a common vision for the global network of executives will also matter. In total, we see a shift towards emphasis on people, a global network of executives, geocentric human resource considerations – and a relative lessening in emphasis on strategic plans formulated predominantly around financial variables.

In line with the above, the strategic process may also have to provide for more effective organizational learning and generation of commitment, as well as avoidance of entrapment in cherished, unrealistic strategies of the past.

Finally, the strategic planning processes of the excellent complex, multinational corporations will have to provide an integrative, centripetal focus, allowing the effects from the many critical requirements of the process to take place. Less consistently developed, mechanistic, overly rational strategic planning and analysis, on the other hand, is likely to lead to centrifugal, fragmenting effects — the very antithesis of strategic management.

References

Argyris, C. (1985) *Strategy, Change and Defensive Routines*, Marshfield: Pitman.

Argyris, C. and Schön, D. (1978) *Organizational Learning*, Reading: Addison-Wesley.

Bateson, G. (1972) *Steps to an Ecology of Mind*, New York: Ballantine.

Bartlett, C. A. (1984) 'Organization and control of global enterprise: influences, characteristics, and guidelines', Harvard Business School, Working Paper, Boston.

Brockner, J., Rubin, J., and Lang, E. (1981) 'Face-saving and entrapment', *Journal of Experimental Social Psychology*, vol. 17.

Gomez, P., and Probst, G. J. B. (1987) *Vernetztes Denken im Management*, Schweiz, Volksbakn, *Die Orientierung*, Nr. 89, Bern, partly published in 'Thinking in networks for management', IMI, Working Paper, Geneva, 1987.

Hagström, P. (1987) 'New information systems and the changing structure of MNC's', IIB, Working Paper, Stockholm School of Economics, Stockholm.

Hedlund, G. (1980) 'The role of foreign subsidiaries in strategic decision-making in Swedish multinationals', *Strategic Management Journal*, vol. 1, no. 1.

Isenberg, D. J. (1986) 'The structure and process of understanding: implications for managerial action', in H. P. Sims and D. A. Giola, *The Thinking Organization*, San Francisco: Jossey-Bass.

Jacque, L. and Lorange, P. (1984) 'The international control conundrum: the case of "hyperinflationary" subsidiaries', *Journal of International Business Studies*.

Lamb, R. B. (1987) *Running American Business*, New York: Basic Books.

Lorange, P. (1980) *Corporate Planning: An Executive Viewpoint*, Englewood Cliffs, NJ: Prentice-Hall.

Lorange, P. and Nelson, R. T. (1987) 'How to recognize and avoid organizational decline', *Sloan Management Review*, Spring.

Lorange, P., Scott Morton, M., and Ghoshal, S. (1987) *Strategic Control*, St Paul: West Publishing.

Lorange, P. (1983) 'Implementing strategic planning: an approach by two Philippine Companies', *The Wharton Annual*, vol. 8.

Mintzberg, H. (1986) 'Planning on the left side and managing on the right', *Harvard Business Review*, vol. 54, no. 4.

Peters, M. and Waterman, R. H. (1984) *In Search of Excellence*, New York: Harper & Row.

Pinchot, G. (1985) *Entrepreneuring*, New York: Harper & Row.

Porter, M. (1985) *Competitive Advantage*, New York: The Free Press.

Probst, G. J. B. (1987) *Selbst-Organisation*, Berlin: Parey.
Rada, J. F. (1987) *Information Technology and Services*, IMI, Working
  Paper.

Chapter seven

New information systems and the changing structure of MNCs

Peter Hagström

New global information systems are vital tools for MNCs trying to achieve overall organizational flexibility and co-ordination, in situations characterized by rigidity and disorder. Indeed, effective co-ordination is a requirement for flexibility.

New information systems directly and through enhanced strategic capabilities have an impact on organizational structure. As a rule, the impact sequence can be seen as a process, but with discernible phases. While initially stressing cost-cutting and improved control possibilities, in time focus tends to shift towards adding value through redeployment of resources. Presently, this more actively competitive way of exploiting new information systems appears to attract most attention. However, there is a strong case for taking stock of where these initial phases have left the MNC and for looking at what a third, more integrative phase may hold in store.

This paper attempts to give a non-technical overview of the issues involved as they affect multinational organization. At the end of the day, the balance is found to tilt in favour of multinationals becoming more 'permeable', as systems extend outside the organization, and more co-ordinated, as the same systems foster integration. In short, the multinational will have increased possibilities to mobilize geographically dispersed resources for the activities that create most value.

The initial argument is twofold. First, the introduction of company-wide, on-line information systems (IS) significantly increases the administrative capabilities of existing organizations. Second, and more important, it adds significantly to the number of possible alternative organizational solutions in a given situation. The latter point follows from three qualitative attributes of IS. New possibilities to un- and rebundle activities mean that firms are given novel choices concerning where in the organization – if at all – an activity should be performed. Establishing new links permits new

164

scale economies within the organization and opens for access to totally new service markets. These new links can also be used as a competitive tool vertically as well as horizontally. Furthermore, IS forge standardization of existing and new information flows, improving the possibilities for controlling varied and dispersed activities. These attributes are reviewed in the second section of the paper, following a brief discussion of a few points of terminology set out in the first section.

The paper draws on the experience of Swedish multinationals, for which the small home market contributed to an early and extensive internationalization. Today, it is not uncommon that their foreign sales exceed, say, 85 per cent of total sales.[1] The fragmented nature of the home region has prompted European multinationals in general, and Swedish multinationals in particular, to very early development of in-house capabilities regarding international information systems. The third section is devoted to the experience of one Swedish multinational, SKF. The choice of SKF rests on the company being an early adopter and leading-edge user of IS.

In the fourth section, a more general interpretation of IS-related organizational change is offered. The identified attributes of IS are related to three sequential phases, focusing in turn on cutting costs, increasing revenue, and maintaining integration.

In the fifth and final section, some general conclusions are suggested, casting some doubt on the orthodox application of traditional organizational principles. IS are found to favour mixed organizations by stimulating functional specialization and undermining traditional vertical links.

1. What is 'IS'?

Just mentioning 'information systems' one runs the risk of inviting an extremely unruly set of interpretations. From the outset, we therefore need to distance ourselves, on the one hand, from more or less fanciful views of the new 'information economy/society' (e.g. Masuda 1984; Martin 1981; Toffler 1980), and, on the other, from a more technically oriented tradition, which treats computer-based information systems as being within the purview only of a separate function (or department) in organizations. The perceived technical complexity associated with information technology has tended to leave the field wide open to people with a strong technical and/or data processing background. We propose to steer clear of both Scylla and Charybdis by choosing to discuss new information systems from a corporate level perspective.

A very common line of reasoning, which arrives at the conclusion of an infrastructure in the making, takes the development of the microprocessor as its starting point. By virtue of its wide-ranging flexibility of application, the microprocessor can then be termed a new 'heartland technology' (Gershuny and Miles 1983). Related advances in communications technology have subsequently given rise to the so-called 'telematics' infrastructure.[2] However, there is more to (tele)communications than mere transmission. A suggestive formulation that has gained wide acceptance is that of 'three islands of technology' (office automation, telecommunications, and data processing) merging, increasingly being linked in physical networks (McKenney and McFarlan 1982, and expanded in McFarlan and McKenney 1983). With variations, this theme basically boils down to hardware manufacturers from the three industries offering increasingly comprehensive communications packages as a result of product innovations blurring industry boundaries.

This development is fuelled by the *de facto* breakdown of transmission monopolies. Transmission is disappearing as the bottleneck, where control can be enforced by legal means. Economies of scale in transmission are rapidly decreasing, as are communications costs in real terms. Rapid improvements in existing services and the advent of a whole host of new services have eroded the capacity of government regulation to provide reliable entry barriers. The defences of the traditional PTT (Post, Telephone, and Telegraph authority) high ground have been undermined.[3] So, to the industry quandary we can add a regulatory one. Both have tended to obscure more than clarify the strategic and organizational impact of IS.

The approach chosen here is as pragmatic as it is non-technical: when referring to 'information systems' (IS), we think of global real-time (or near-real-time) data systems. The implication is quite simply that it is possible to connect each part of the organization to the information system(s), regardless of its geographical or hierarchical location, and that transmission of information will be immediate, or almost immediate. The transfer is handled through a variety of dedicated networks, or logical networks. In terms of information-carrying capacity, ordinary (voice) telephone systems and various data networks have most practical significance at present. It is the latter category – data communications networks – which in effect constitutes the 'new infrastructure' as commonly understood.

Organizing a corporate-wide information systems infrastructure typically involves decisions at least concerning the following aspects:

— Geographical spread of the network (including location of processing nodes).
— Internal and external access (in the latter case regarding both the possibility of parties external to the firm accessing internal applications and employees of the firm accessing external applications).
— Capacity (transmission speed, volume, etc.).
— Availability (in time and whether use is interactive or not).
— Quality and reliability (transmission errors and robustness of links).
— Confidentiality.

These aspects are not independent of one another. For example, the degree of vulnerability is in part a function of the geographical extension and the level of external access. However, below we deal only with the first two items (geographical spread and access), as they are most relevant for our purposes. The latter four are largely technical in nature. Higher levels of performance can be had at a price. Technical design choices do not alter the conceptual discussion in the remainder of the paper.

The networks of corporations are normally referred to as 'private information networks'. 'Private' relates to control over the network, though not necessarily connected with ownership. From the user end, wholly owned networks are in practice limited to LANs (Local Area Networks) – normally users connected within a building or a set of adjacent buildings. Over long distances, communication is handled over leased lines, the switched telephone network or special purpose lines, usually public data networks. Corporations with geographically dispersed activities tend to build networks with elements from all of these. Although a public transmission network may be used, it is possible to define exclusive user groups. A corporation can thus control access (thereby also choosing if and with whom to share information). For all intents and purposes, the information infrastructure is perceived by the user as a proprietary network. In spite of some regulatory complications, these communications networks readily extend across international boundaries.

2. A change of degree or of kind?

Commonly, new (data) communications are perceived only as a replacement on the margin for slower, more expensive, and more error-prone methods of transferring information, like telex and telephone (cf. UNCTC 1982 and OECD 1983). However, the difference is more fundamental. The new information systems constitute a new infrastructure in a wider sense; a new transport system for mass transport of (information) services or activities. As such, the information systems are akin to other, more well-known and familiar transport systems like railroads and air transport. Innovations in communications that took place in the nineteenth century paved the way for exploitation of economies of integration in both production and distribution, which, in turn, underpinned the evolution of the multiplant, multiproduct firm as we now know it (cf. Chandler 1962 and 1977). Here, the advent of new information systems is seen as a necessary, but not sufficient condition for some kinds of organizational change. The impact of IS will tend to operate through furnishing MNCs with enhanced strategic capabilities. Clearly, IS will improve the MNC capability of optimizing the network advantages inherent in being multinational (cf. Kogut 1983). They will also ease the trade-offs between international integration and local responsiveness (cf. Doz 1986).

At least three fundamental attributes of IS offer new strategic possibilities and directly influence organizational structure. They are:

— the very concept of a 'system' implies a certain measure of standardization,
— activities can be un- and rebundled, and
— new links can be established, within the organization as well as to its environment.

Although strongly interconnected, these specific attributes are discussed in turn.

Standardization

The larger and more complex information flows permitted by IS require standardization. This goes beyond technical compatibility and relates also to content, i.e. what information is transmitted and how it is presented. Such standardization can be a cohesive influence on the organization. This is clearly demonstrated by Electrolux (the world's largest white goods manufacturer) that explicitly uses computer-based reporting systems as a prime integrative mechanism *vis-à-vis* foreign acquisitions. Actually, Boddy and Buchanan (1986) very perceptively, but only in passing (p. 24), suggest the term 'control technology' for information technology.

The need to standardize, or 'containerize', information tends to result in better use of information already within the organization, in practice adding value to existing information. Improved possibilities for transportation and aggregation have led to quicker reporting procedures and to a better general overview. It is possible to spot something going wrong much quicker, permitting speedier corrective measures.

The latter point has several facets to it. First, there are the benefits from, for instance, being able to stop cost-overruns on a development project much earlier. Another case is being able to monitor competitors and their behaviour with less of a timelag. Traditional hierarchical transfer of such information (e.g. from a sales subsidiary in a distant market) has often proved to be too slow, at least in the experience of several Swedish MNCs. Besides, standardization also induces routinization, which in this case adds to the capability of giving prompt competitive responses. Lastly, a very similar example regarding quality control is how Electrolux has been able to make great savings as a result of the faster and more efficient feedback from the service organization to production.

Standardization normally evokes images of streamlining, but can also be viewed as a policy to keep options open. It facilitates potential future information-exchange spanning different activities within the corporation, as well as with external parties.

Un- and rebundling

Similar to the way transport innovations made dispersed component manufacture and subsequent assembly commonplace in manufacturing, the IS infrastructure creates possibilities for un- and rebundling of information-based activities. These activities constitute approximately half of the labour costs in one large Swedish engineering products MNC (Fries 1984). Of the remaining half, half again was indirect production work, also with high information-processing content.

Increased scope for functional specialization within companies is particularly noticeable in the finance area. Expertise and information can be concentrated, and capital management rationalized. Via information systems, the finance function is linked both vertically and horizontally to other organizational units. Improved overview and centralization lead to increased overall financial control. At the same time, the finance function can become more independent by becoming a significant actor in its own right on the (financial) market. The capability to eliminate the role of banks as intermediaries places additional demands on the company's own information collection and external connections.

Other, similar examples of activities that are frequently centralized using IS in order to capture new scale economies are purchasing, order handling, inventory control, and transport logistics. Centralization does not necessarily imply that the activity is located at the top management level or even in the home country, which is why concentration is in some sense a better word.

Another aspect of possible un- and rebundling of activities relates to the provision of totally new services made feasible through the advent of IS. New services can provide price information on activities carried out in-house, possibly prompting externalization of uncompetitive activities. A good illustration is corporate reporting systems commonly available externally. A service vendor with a communications network can offer, say, the unbundled service of consolidation of reports rebundled with a limited transmission service. Conversely, new, initially 'internal', services may lead to external sales. Volvo's electronic mail system, 'MEMO', has, for instance, become a very profitable product for the car-maker. It has been sold internationally to more than 300 large companies.

As unbundled information-based activities become more or less insensitive to distance, MNCs can also further exploit the international division of labour. An analogy is the electric power grid, which freed production from its historical dependence on locally available energy resources. IS can ease the constraints of localized availability of stored knowledge and of information-processing abilities. The only requirement is that the local subsidiary, as an example, can 'plug into' the corporate information system.

Moreover, MNCs can improve their bargaining position *vis-à-vis* host governments. In principle, a manaufacturing subsidiary can be relieved of most of the functions that are not directly linked to production (technically, even production control can be handled remotely). Specialized functions can then more easily be located where most efficient. For example, American Airlines has processed flight coupons in Barbados since 1984, having the Barbados operations connected to the US by a high-speed data link (*Financial Times*, 19 May, 1987). In short, MNCs can become even more foot-loose, with IS facilitating both entry to and exit from geographical markets.

New links

That a new communications infrastructure creates new links within the organization as well as to external data bases is fairly straight-forward. The idea of using information systems as a competitive tool in relation to customers and suppliers (by adding to product value for the former and by creating switching costs for both) has also been extensively discussed (e.g. by McFarlan 1984 and Porter and Millar 1985). Indeed, it is not uncommon (e.g. Rockart and Scott Morton 1984) to carry the argument so far as to claim that these, mainly vertical, applications drive corporate strategy and organizational structure.

Our argument stops at regarding IS as a necessary condition, but is not confined to the two end points in a firm's vertical chain of activities only. Links of a more horizontal nature must also be allowed for. Two extensions to the standard argument come to mind. The first is possible externalization/internalization both of support activities and of different sequential activities along the firm's vertical chain. In these cases, the new external links are an integral part of service provision and can connect a company to totally new kinds of suppliers and customers. Just consider services like on-line management of internal shipments or of travel and expense accounts, which can be purchased or sold on the market by, say, an industrial firm.

The second extension is co-operative systems or agreements, often involving competitors. External links can support both permanent and temporary co-operative ventures. Experience suggests that multilateral ventures are more stable, e.g. the joint airline seat reservation system SITA (Société International de Télécommunications Aéronautiques), than bilateral ones. The cost in competitive terms of ending up outside a multilateral system is often higher as alternative systems are few, if any.

3. The case of SKF

Changing the perspective slightly to that of one company, an excellent candidate for closer scrutiny is SKF. The company is a very early adopter of new information systems, is heavily internationalized, and operates in a relatively stable (competitive) environment. The aim in this section is to describe the salient features of SKF's development as they relate to IS for subsequent interpretation in section four.[4]

Background

SKF dates from the turn of the century and was created around a path-breaking product invention – the double-row, self-aligning ball-bearing from 1907. Superior technology and quality, combined with a small home market created forceful incentives for geographical expansion in the very first years of operation. Strong foreign demand allowed the company to command premium prices, in turn used to finance the setting up of first sales, then production subsidiaries abroad. By the outbreak of World War I, SKF had manufacturing subsidiaries in Great Britain and Germany, an assembly plant in France, sales subsidiaries in all the major markets in Europe as well as in the US, and sales agents in far away places like Australia. Backward vertical integration remained a home country endeavour. In 1916 SKF bought its first steel works and a major foundry for bearing houses.

Diversification has remained limited (and mostly related), and SKF today derives 83 per cent of its total sales of approximately US$3 bn (SEK 20 bn) from bearings. The world market share of about 20 per cent makes SKF the industry leader. The three largest manufacturing units are all located outside Sweden (in West Germany, Italy and the US, respectively). Actually, Sweden only accounts for 12 per cent of employment and 5 per cent of sales, further underlining the limited significance of the original home market for SKF. The foreign subsidiaries of Swedish MNCs have traditionally been strong and independent entities, and SKF is no exception.[5]

Enter competition

The internationally relatively small, little diversified, and informally run SKF remained on a steady path of geographical expansion until the mid-1960s. Gradually, however, the technological lead had eroded and international competition intensified. Demand growth slowed and new, notably Japanese, competitors appeared on the international scene. SKF's competitive response was to rationalize, cutting production and capital costs. Inventories and the product range were dramatically reduced. Production was specialized to individual plants by allocating it according to the dimensions of standard roller bearings, permitting a change from batch to continuous production.[6]

A production co-ordination and inventory system, GFSS (Global Forecasting and Supply System), was decided upon *circa* 1971. The technical bias of SKF management had fostered a receptive attitude towards new information technology. However, the intended attendant on-line integrated system failed, in spite of repeated attempts, and was dropped in favour of less ambitious temporary solutions. Computer tapes were criss-crossing Europe by courier delivery. GFSS finally came into full swing only when supported by direct data communications, successively established 1974−76, which was still very early by any standard. It all evolved into a fully-fledged, self-operated, private data communications network by 1979.

The system is run from the Forecasting and Supply Office (FSO) located in Belgium, where SKF has no manufacturing. The location was in part chosen for reasons of communications, in part to avoid a powerful subsidiary (or the head office) dominating it. The pivotal operational role played by FSO is also reflected in the attention paid both to board representation and staffing. Corporate management and the half dozen most important subsidiaries claim their share of each. The fact that subsidiary presidents sit on the board gives FSO additional credibility and contributes to the integration originally sought.

GFSS has since been improved upon and further developed. It has also been followed by a whole host of other systems, all operating on the information systems infrastructure initially supported by GFSS. The systems have proliferated over the years and now cover most activities. It is important to note, however, that they have been developed per function (e.g. the Group Finance Information System) and are not integrated into any one, giant system. This is also valid for sequential activities along the value chain. Here, systems tend to overlap 'neighbouring' functions (e.g. production and shipping). In addition, the systems are both local (e.g. a Factory Administration System or Domestic Customer Service System) and company-wide (e.g. the Group Management System or the International Customer Service System), but can be accessed through the same systems infrastructure.

Later systems development and maintenance have more and more come to be left to operative units, which separately or in groups assume the responsibility (and economic risk) for improvements in old or the creation of new systems. Most of the computer processing needed has been done jointly in the same computer, in spite of the geographical dispersion and temporal instability of project groups. Official company policy to decentralize IS development is, however, subject to corporate guidelines and stringent regulations on standards for hardware, databases, communications, and the applications that are intended for more than local use only. In addition, both initiation and participation in decentralized systems development require prior central approval.

Centralization can be illustrated by the financial function, where several activities (e.g. internal payments, currency management, cash management, corporate borrowing) have been concentrated to a separate, wholly-owned company, SKF International AB, since 1974. The backbone of this operation is the Group Finance Information System. SKF now also makes a point of being a market actor and having the same information systems as the banks themselves have.[7]

An interesting example of a solution 'in-between' is the organization of R&D. Basic research is to a large extent carried out at the SKF Engineering and Research Centre in the Netherlands (where 20–25 per cent of total R&D is performed). ERC is connected on-line with all major subsidiaries in Europe, where R&D (with the stress on the 'D') is carried out according to their respective product mandates. Co-ordination concerns one function only within the bearing business and centralization (or concentration) is only partial.

Opening up

The stress on rationalization and specialization has slowly given way to a phase characterized by the opening up of information systems externally.

On the input side, SKF is generally a very important customer. A notable, albeit economically not very significant, example is the direct ordering of hand-held tools from Tingströms, a wholesaler/distributor in Gothenburg. Within the framework of yearly agreements between SKF and Tingströms, orders can be placed directly from the shop floor. The system became fully operational *circa* 1984. Initially perceived as a cost-cutting measure (quicker ordering, pushing inventories onto Tingströms), it also had the unintended effect of replacing *ex ante* control through authorization with *ex post* control through delegation. Individual purchasing decisions were decentralized as a result of superiors being convinced of having gained instant and better overview of the Tingströms-SKF relationship. Integration at the operative level thus lessened the need for staff to co-ordinate activities directly.

An additional aspect of the Tingströms example (and of opening up) is that the on-line ordering is shared with Volvo. Tingströms is in effect a joint captive supplier. On-line search for many items can in fact go on automatically through to Tingströms's own suppliers. Sharing is thus another alternative in the new make/buy decisions discussed above.

Of a toally different magnitude was SKF's divestiture of its specialty steel division in 1986. SKF has so far retained 50 per cent ownership of a new joint venture company, but it is very probable that we are witnessing the beginning of a phased withdrawal, a vertical (ownership) disintegration move. The new Ovako Steel AB is, however, maintained as a captive supplier by SKF, in no small part as a result of information systems integration. The steel company remains firmly within the SKF information infrastructure. The old SKF half of the company still houses two out of a total of eight major data processing centres, which are connected in the SKF communications network. As SKF has found novel ways of keeping strong supplier links, traditional input-good vertical integration thus has become less of a concern.

Turning to the output side, SKF's leverage is normally much smaller. Approximately two-thirds of bearing output goes directly to customers in industries such as automobiles (17 per cent of the total), trucks (9 per cent), heavy industry (9 per cent), and engineering (20 per cent). Powerful customers are not new to SKF. In 1935, Volvo, its car producing subsidiary, was spun off in order not to upset other car producers among SKF's customers. Today, the effect of opening up previously internal systems has, for SKF, more been one of adapting, rather than calling the shots. Actually, internal standardization of systems is a prerequisite for being flexible regarding communication links with (large) customers. This SKF has experience with most of the original equipment manufacturers (OEMs), especially the transportation equipment manufacturers.

Another example of external accommodation is the SKF participation in ODETTE (the Organization for Data Exchange by Teletransmission in Europe). ODETTE will organize the linking of European components and motor vehicle manufacturers in order to achieve a uniform set of standards for direct ordering; also illustrating the evolution of a co-operative system's development.

Naturally, SKF already offers customers on-line connection, allowing direct ordering and immediate information on delivery details. It is notable that more than 300 bearings customers have already been linked to the SKF private communications network and that this has been done in parallel with, but at a significantly faster pace than, the connection of the SKF sales subsidiaries (the last of which are still not hooked-up).

Additional features offered to customers are the use of SKF software packages, where, for instance, technical design software has a strong tendency to be biased toward the use of SKF products. In competitive terms, this is more important in relation to smaller customers, as they will be more dependent on the SKF systems. Even those customers who cannot be accommodated with a direct connection have the opportunity of using SKF design software. It is available on tape or diskette and is known as the SKF 'CADalog', since it includes the standard product catalogue as well.

Distributors, taking one-third of bearing sales, are fairly dependent on SKF as a supplier (with the exception of the Asia/Pacific region). SKF started connecting distributors on-line in 1981 in the UK. Substantial savings and improved customer service were achieved, very much at the instigation of SKF. In spite of UK distributors of industrial goods being fairly large and national in coverage, SKF leverage is great. Paradoxically, the leverage has increased with the rationalization of distribution. The leaner the physical distribution, the greater the possibility that the supplier can by-pass the distributor. SKF has chosen to keep its traditional distributors, for the moment, apparently being satisfied with their improved performance.

As we have seen above, SKF has so far concentrated on improving and upgrading, rather than changing, existing customer links. This is also reflected in the recent (1987) reorganization of the bearing business, where the area-based divisions were replaced by customer-based divisions, each with world-wide responsibility. The other 'business areas' (in SKF parlance) — 'Component Systems' and 'Tools' — remain as global product divisions.

4. Taking the long view

Stepping back and describing the SKF experience in more general terms can add content to the bundling, standardization and new links dimensions in section two above. In order to capture parallel changes in these dimensions, the description is structured along a sequential development comprising three phases. These can be labelled defensive, offensive, and integrative respectively. Significant overlap makes the phases less than ideally distinct, but explicitly introducing time is both illustrative and practical. Experimentation and learning in the organization, on the one hand, and competition, on the other, propel the process. Cognitive limits of management and of the organization as well as implementation lags are retarding influences.[8]

These are general considerations and, indeed, there is reason to believe that this describes a fairly typical sequence, although the phases are modelled on SKF's experience. The phases proposed are not mutually exclusive situations, but represent differences in focus and build on each other.

Sequential action pattern

Areas of IS potential	Defensive	Offensive	Integrative
Activities	Unbundle	Specialize	Rebundle
Links	Internal	Competitive	Co-operative
Standardization	Functional	Corporate	Extra-corporate

Phase one: defensive

Tracing the developments by column, the initial, supply-driven technological change is usually harnessed as an instrument of rationalization of simple routine tasks. Accompanying standardization is very much determined by the nature of these tasks. The obvious line of action is to trim the existing organization with a cost-cutting programme. This typical, mostly defensive response is characterized by the stress placed on control, as evidenced by IS first being used for accounting data. As a rule, systems for accounting, reporting, payroll and the like are the first to be computerized. Simple information-processing tasks (aggregation, repetitive calculation, etc.) and subsequent retrieval are easily separated out from many activities in the firm; activities are unbundled.

Partial centralization of shared activities normally follows, in turn yielding additional benefits like economies of scale through co-ordination not only within, but also across businesses. An obvious example of this is the common and early centralization of the finance function in MNCs.

The information systems introduced are primarily designed to improve vertical information flows within the organization. IS either allow for the organization to expand its tasks, or for a leaner organization to carry out the same tasks as before (cf. Galbraith 1973 and 1977). The effects on organizational structure will tend to be slight, but the organization may be reduced in size.

The classical predictions made by Leavitt and Whisler (1958) about dramatically increased centralization of decision-making and of a considerable reduction in middle management as a result of introducing computers are, with hindsight, clearly an overstatement. Still, the predicted direction of change tallies quite well with the 'defensive response' outlined here. Child (1984) also finds merit with the recentralization argument. However, by stressing the better possibilities for control and integration through IS, Child refines the line of reasoning and concludes that what is to be expected are smaller, more cohesive management structures in general. He sees IS supporting a centralization or decentralization of decision making as a matter of choice, but with most organizations opting for the former, at least in Britain.

SKF chose both partial and temporary centralization. A snapshot of SKF in the mid-1970s would show a clear tendency toward centralization of· some shared activities. Examples of this are the Engineering and Research Centre established in 1972, SKF International (finance) AB in 1974, SKF Dataservice AB in 1975, and SKF Reinsurance Co. Ltd in 1976. Also, when GFSS was introduced, there was a pronounced centralization of decision-making to headquarters. Many very simple decisions, normally made at factory middle management level, were referred to head-quarters. This situation continued for half a year to a year. Responsibility has since been pushed down the organization again. Central control – in general, and of production and supply in particular – was, however, clearly strengthened and expanded with GFSS. Interestingly enough, control can also take on a slightly different form as evidenced by centralization to FSO in Belgium.

This change over time within the same organization may go quite some way in explaining the often conflicting findings on whether the introduction of modern information systems leads to centralization or decentralization in organizations.[9]

Phase two: offensive

Moving on to actively exploiting the strategic opportunities implies redeploying resources across activities and geographically. In short, the firm decides to do new things and/or to do them differently. Using Thompson's (1967) more general terminology, the firm makes new claim to domain; an offensive strategic response.

IS naturally become even more of a corporate issue. The competitive potential of IS tends to be addressed more directly. Specialization is generally pushed further. Horizontal information flows increase in importance both as a result of interdependencies between loci of specialized knowledge and as a result of the need for different parts of the organization to access the corporate databases by then building up. Links are established with suppliers and customers, including suppliers of externalized activities and customers of previously only internal services. The stress on cutting costs gives way to a more revenue-oriented use of IS.

For SKF, the overlap between the offensive and the defensive phases is evident, especially from the introduction of GFSS, both a defensive and an offensive move. Rationalization was extreme, involving not only, for example, reduction of inventories and other buffers but also both raising of service levels (e.g. improved delivery performance) for customers and considerable geographical redeployment of resources.

SKF would have preferred to move more slowly, which may have been prudent given the four to five years of problems the company experienced when trying to set up a proprietary corporate telecommunications network. Moreover, it is interesting to note that strengthened internal control – a feature of the defensive phase – was deemed so important that an external supplier (General Electric

Information Services) was engaged to run a corporate reporting system rather than waiting for SKF's own telecommunications network to come on stream.

SKF was forced off the mark early by the competition, quickly going into what has here been labelled the offensive phase. The strong and early competitive pressure – relative to that of many other industries at the time – thus provided the impetus for SKF becoming an innovator in the use of new information systems. This reputation SKF has managed to maintain. For instance, systems originally developed for internal use have been sold to other major Swedish MNCs, although SKF has chosen not to do so actively. SKF was, moreover, very swift in realizing the opportunities of connecting both customers and suppliers on-line to its own systems. In addition, SKF is – to our knowledge – one of the very first major companies to offer something like the 'CADalog' widely to its customers.

Returning to the issue of centralization versus decentralization, the issue is further complicated since *ex ante* control mainly through authorization can be eliminated, as seen in the Tingströms example. Raising the demands on formalization of information flows through standardization and allowing for nearly instant monitoring of the activities of lower levels mean that delegation of authority can be achieved simultaneously with increased hands-on-control for higher levels in the organization. The 'losers' are middle-level managers, who owe their *raison d'être* to aggregation and processing of mainly control-related information. On balance, the peripheral parts of the organization probably stand to gain most in terms of increased autonomy during the second phase. This follows from the possibility for outlying units – in the widest sense – to access information previously only available centrally.

Phase three: integration

Here, we leave the comparatively well-trodden paths of experience and attempt to gauge the present and to look a bit ahead. Imminent and ongoing developments at SKF remain elusive for obvious reasons, but at least the contours of a third, more integrative phase can be discerned.

No major new system seems to be in the offing, perhaps barring the much heralded PC-80 (Production Concept for the 1980s) project, which is a system for continuous production requiring personnel for day shifts only. Production lines in operation can now be found, for example, in Italy and in Sweden. Very interestingly, PC-80 appears to make production more of a continuous flow as presently discrete production activities are integrated, simultaneously with being a more flexible production system, permitting shorter production runs. Thus, the extreme specialization of production that replaced local full-range production, stands to be succeeded by a system that combines the two. Local production and trans-shipment can become more of day-to-day operational alternatives.

Also, SKF products will continue to get 'softer', both in terms of technical support and embodied technology. There appears to be a stronger emphasis on further developing the traditional bearing business in SKF, e.g. by offering enhanced products (and not only increased service levels for standard products), like the rather recent complete hub units for automobiles. This can be taken further. Consider a situation where, say, CGR Roulements (one of the SKF French subsidiaries) is developing a bearing application jointly with a customer. Apart from local input, this development project could involve external database searches in the US, testing at ERC in Holland, computer job entry to a mainframe in Gothenburg, etc; all carried out within a very limited time frame. Each of these activities is highly specialized and performed at widely dispersed geographical locations, but from the client's vantage point together they form a new, rebundled product, where the resultant custom-made bearing itself is but a part.

The explicit ambitions to serve customers directly with technical applications imply a further opening toward and adaptation to customers' systems. Elaborate linking of companies' systems will increasingly be co-operative in nature – SKF's participation in ODETTE being a good example. In order to accommodate these types of ventures, standardization will have to be carried well outside the individual corporation. Having gone through two rounds of heavy-handed systems standardization, SKF is well poised for continued external adaptation.

The systems themselves are integrative, in that they forge 'communities of users', and become even more so as usage matures. As can be seen from SKF, these 'communities' will, however, be very different since there are general corporate systems (e.g. electronic mail), corporate systems within one function (e.g. finance), systems for one product area (e.g. the bearing product database), subsidiary level systems (e.g. a local administrative system), etc. In addition, these systems can accommodate temporary groupings, like systems development as previously exemplified.

Moreover, the 'communities' and their attendant systems can provide a strong element of stability, both internally and in relation to customers, suppliers, and other external parties. In so far as they have a logical motivation for their existence, the systems tend to remain, also during times of internal turmoil (like during a major reorganization).

Different 'communities' are also reflected organizationally. In SKF's formal structure, most common organizational principles can readily be traced: divisions on the same level are either product- or customer-based, subsidiaries were until very recently arranged by area, and functional (staff) units − like finance − are in effect very much on a par with the formal divisions. In addition, some specialized subsidiaries (like proprietary engineering) report directly to headquarters in the mother−daughter tradition. Complementing organizational bodies without formal authority or responsibility tends to reinforce functional co-ordination (e.g. the Finance Directors' Board and the Information Systems Board). It is clear that the new information systems have facilitated the management of this *de facto* 'mixed' organization structure. Indeed, the systems constitute a necessary condition for such a mixed structure to be practically feasible. In addition, the systems can define and redefine roles not covered by the formal organization.

But integration by way of system access is carried further. Increased external linkages make the organization more opaque. The new information systems, in effect, further integrate the company with the environment.

The increased scope for control and co-ordination brought about by IS cannot alone counteract the centrifugal forces unleashed by the same systems. Achieving integration within a company like SKF demands emphasis also on human systems. This is indicated by the new recruitment policy, under which SKF in 1986 hired 250 young economists and technicians with the ambition of making them 'SKF men and women'. Integration may become a skill *per se*, but that discussion lies outside the scope of the present paper.

5. Making a virtue out of necessity?

New information systems offer novel possibilities to un- and rebundle activities, thus changing the rules of the game. Exploiting opportunities to reconfigure activities, organizations become more permeable as a result of new external vertical and horizontal communications links. Activities beside the main lines of business can become market actors in their own right, like financial services. Customers can directly initiate production runs if the required items are not found in the host company's inventory. In turn, the new external links bring an additional impetus for standardization also of internal information flows, since external parties will have to be accommodated within the corporate communications infrastructure. But the systems are in themselves integrative, and create stability in a 'permeable' MNC. The suspicion is, however, that this counterweight is not enough, but will have to be complemented with other integrative measures.

Being 'permeable' does not exclude the possibility of the MNC being grouped under new headings such as the transnational organization (Bartlett 1986) or the heterarchy (Hedlund 1986). It does, however, recast the issues in a slightly different mould. The information infrastructure can support a multi-centre organization like the heterarchy, but it can also make interfaces with the environment more opaque by in itself offering a wider-ranging choice of links with the environment.

The increased scope for improving both control and co-ordination increases the tolerance for 'mixed' forms of organization. We have, for instance, seen a reassertion of the functional dimension in MNCs. But a full revival is probably not feasible, since a traditional functional organization still would be too unresponsive for truly international competition.

Global product divisions are also becoming less of an imperative. The threshold size of a manageable organization has increased with the advent of new information systems. In addition, traditional vertical (ownership) linkages appear to have been weakened, further undermining the rationale for global product divisions. This is another side of permeability, as information links can, in some instances, constitute an alternative to ownership.

New information systems can help mitigate some of the drawbacks of orthodox organizational forms by making new combinations feasible. This increased freedom of choice goes further than traditional matrix overlays, since the latter are only two-dimensional. Ideally, the 'mixed' organizational structure could capture some of the advantages inherent in several organizational forms without having to impose those organizational dimensions throughout the corporation.

Lastly, the organizational flexibility also has a dynamic quality. MNCs can become more footloose, and not only as to where activities are performed, but also as to which activities are performed. A traditional explanation for the existence of MNCs rests on their superior capability to arbitrage across imperfect markets. New information systems improve upon this capability.

Notes

1 This is true of, for instance, Alfa-Lavel (separator and food-processing systems), Astra (pharmaceuticals), Atlas Copco (mining equipment), Iggesund and NCB (both forestry products), Sandvik (specialty steel and tools), SKF (bearings), and Uddeholm (specialty steel).

2 The term 'telematics' originates from the French (*télématique*) and has been popularized by Nora and Minc (1978). In a different type of work, Pool (1983) inspires caution by providing an excellent opportunity to contrast contemporary forecasts with later, actual development.

3 For an interesting exchange of views involving different interested parties, see OECD (1980).

4 The sources for the material on SKF are mainly press reports and official company material. The present discussion has neither been officially authorized nor sanctioned by SKF. A more extensive version of the SKF case is found in Hagström (1987).

5 See Hedlund (1984) and Hedlund and Åman (1983) for an elaboration of the more general 'Swedish Model'.

6 For a detailed study of the rationalization of production in the industry, see Wolf (1985).

7 One discrepancy here is that these activities have so far not been located abroad, which is otherwise the standard, given the restrictions imposed by Swedish foreign currency regulations.

8 For a good treatment both of learning and of implementation lags in relation to new office technology, see Pava (1983), who sets the problem in a socio-tech framework and introduces the stage of 'deliberation' in this type of decision-making. Lorange, Scott Morton, and Ghoshal (1986) explicitly address the issue of limitations of managerial cognition and new information systems, but in a broader fashion. They point to the need for managerial information systems to expand the capability for managers to deal with complex phenomena in general, and not just – as discussed here – IS itself being a complex area.

9 For a review of some empirical findings, see Robey (1977). His concluding argument that computerized systems are neutral in this respect does, however, differ from the one made here (where centralization and decentralization effects instead are found to vary more systematically across time and type of activity).

References

Bartlett, C. A. (1986) 'Building and managing the transnational: the new organizational challenge', in Porter, M. E. (ed.), *Competition in Global Industries*, Boston, Mass: Harvard Business School Press.

Boddy, D. and Buchanan, D. A. (1986) *Managing New Technology*, Oxford: Basil Blackwell Ltd.

Chandler, A. D., Jr. (1962) *Strategy and Structure*, Cambridge, Mass: The MIT Press.

—— (1977) *The Visible Hand*, Cambridge, Mass: The Belknap Press of Harvard University Press.

Child, J. (1984) 'New technology and developments in management organization', *Omega*, vol. 12, No. 3.

Doz, Y. (1986) *Strategic Management in Multinational Companies*, Oxford: Pergamon Press.

The Financial Times, 19 May 1987.

Fries, H. (1984) 'Datateknik och koncernstyrning – fyra fallstudier', in G. Eliasson *et al. Hur styrs storföretag?* Stockholm: Industriens Utredningsinstitut (The Industrial Institute for Economic and Social Research) & Liber Förlag.

Galbraith, J. (1973) *Designing Complex Organizations*, Reading, Mass: Addison-Wesley Publishing Company.

—— (1977) *Organization Design*, Reading, Mass: Addison-Wesley Publishing Company.

Gershuny, J. I. and Miles, I. D. (1983) *The New Service Economy: The Transformation of Employment in Industrial Societies*, London: Frances Pinter.

Hagström, P. (1987) 'Linking new information systems to corporate strategy and structure: the SKF experience', Research Paper 87/11, Institute of International Business, Stockholm School of Economics.

Hedlund, G. (1984) 'Organization in-between: the evolution of the mother–daughter structure of managing foreign subsidiaries in Swedish MNCs', *Journal of International Business Studies*, vol. 15, No. 2.

—— (1986) 'The hypermodern MNC — a heterarchy?', *Human Resource Management*, vol. 25, No. 1.

Hedlund, G. and Åman, P. (1983) *Managing Relationships with Foreign Subsidiaries*, Stockholm: Sveriges Mekanförbund.

Kogut, B. (1983) 'Foreign direct investment as a sequential process', in Kindleberger, C. P. and Audretsch, D. (eds), *The Multinational Corporation in the 1980s*, Cambridge, Mass: The MIT Press.

Leavitt, H. J. and Whisler, T. L. (1958) 'Management in the 1980s', *Harvard Business Review*, vol. 36, No. 6, November/December.

Lorange, P., Scott Morton, M. F., and Ghoshal, S. (1986) *Strategic Control Systems*, St Paul, Minn: West Publishing Company.

McFarlan, F. W. (1984) 'Information technology changes the way you compete', *Harvard Business Review*, vol. 62, No. 3, May/June.

McFarlan, F. W. and McKenney, J. L. (1983) *Corporate Information Systems Management: The Issues Facing Senior Executives*, Homewood, Ill: Richard D. Irwin, Inc.

McKenney, J. L. and McFarlan, F. W. (1982) 'The information archipelago – maps and bridges', *Harvard Business Review*, vol. 60, No. 5, September/October.

Martin, J. (1981) *Telematic Society*, Englewood Cliffs, NJ: Prentice-Hall, Inc.

Masuda, Y. (1984) *Informationssamhället* (translation from: The Information Society, Tokyo: Institute for the Information Society), Malmö: Liber Förlag.

Nora, S. and Minc, A. (1978) *L'informatisation de la société*, Paris: La Documentation Francaise and Editions du Seuil.

OECD (1980) *Policy Implications of Data Network Developments in the OECD Area*, Paris: OECD.

—— (1983) 'Trade in information, computer, and communications services', *Committee for Information, Computer and Communications Policy*, ICCP(83)12, Paris.

Pava, C. H. P. (1983) *Managing New Office Technology: An Organizational Strategy*, New York: The Free Press.

Pool, Ithiel de Sola (1983) *Forecasting the Telephone: A Retrospective Technology Assessment*, Norwood, NJ: Ablex Publishing Corporation.

Porter, M. E. and Millar, V. E. (1985) 'How information gives you competitive advantage', *Harvard Business Review*, vol. 63, No. 4, July/August.

Robey, D. (1977) 'Computers and management structure: some empirical findings re-examined', *Human Relations*, vol. 30, No. 11.

Rockart, J. F. and Scott Morton, M. (1984) 'Implications of changes in information technology for corporate strategy', *Interfaces*, vol. 14, No. 1.

Thompson, J. D. (1967) *Organizations in Action*, New York: McGraw Hill Book Company.

Toffler, A. (1980) *The Third Wave*, London: Collins.

United Nations (1982) 'Transnational corporations and transborder data flows: a technical paper', *United Nations Centre on Transnational Corporations*, ST/CTC/23, New York.

Wolf, B. M. (1985) 'The bearing industry: rationalization in Europe', in Casson, M. (ed.) *Multinationals and World Trade*, London: Allen & Unwin.

Chapter eight

Rediscovering functions in the MNC: the role of expertise in firms' responses to shifting exchange rates

Donald R. Lessard and Nitin Nohria

Confronted by a turbulent global macroeconomy, intense global competition, and ever-changing product market conditions, multi-national corporations (MNCs) are being forced to become more responsive, flexible and innovative. This often requires strategic and organizational redirection.

Strategically, it is important to understand the distinctive competitive implications of these complex environments. There are strategic considerations that arise from global competition in a turbulent macroeconomy that are very different from those in the context of domestic or multidomestic competition. Research that develops this view contends that the structure (technology, product mix, geographic location and value added) of the cost and revenue streams of an MNC relative to its global competition determines (1) the strength and sustainability of its competitive posture (e.g. global versus multidomestic) in international product markets; and (2) its vulnerability to fluctuations in the macroeconomy. For instance, if a firm's costs are primarily in dollars and its main competitors' primarily in yen, and both compete in similar international product markets, then the exchange rate regime between 1981 and mid-1985 (when the dollar was very strong) had very different competitive implications when contrasted with the exchange rate regime between 1985–1987 (when the dollar became much weaker).[1]

Organizationally, in keeping with Chandler's by now classic norms that structure must follow strategy, several researchers have focused on the complex differentiation and integration that MNCs must exhibit in such a global economy in order to be both responsive to the different product and geographic market contexts and still exploit the advantages of scope and scale afforded by the distributed resource and organizational capabilities of the MNC and its unique potential for global rationalization and integration. This dual focus on local responsiveness and global integration has led to

186

the articulation of several idealized organizational structures for the MNC, such as the global matrix, the transnational corporation, the heterarchy, and the horizontal MNC.[2] A common theme in all these models is the emphasis placed on differentiated roles for the various sub-units of the MNC and on various mechanisms that lead to global co-ordination.

In this chapter we examine this general relationship between the strategic implications of turbulent global business environments and the organizational structure of MNCs in the specific context of how MNCs respond to volatile exchange rates. Shifts in exchange rates not only change the reference currency value of a firm's foreign currency denominated assets and liabilities (so-called transaction and translation exposures) and foreign profit streams, but also shift the relative prices of the firm's inputs and outputs and, in the case of global competitors with different cost structures, their competitive position (so-called operating exposure).[3]

For example, a US consumer goods manufacturer with a fully integrated subsidiary in France faced two potentially offsetting dollar profit effects when the franc fell to a low against the dollar in 1985 (or when it subsequently rose in 1986). On the one hand, its French franc profit stream translated or converted into fewer dollars. On the other hand, its costs fell relative to firms with a smaller proportion of their actual or potential production in France, allowing several possible sources of improvement in franc profits depending on the structure of global competition. If the firm faced other competitors in France or adjacent countries with a lower proportion of French costs, it had the option of using its lower costs to improve margins or gain share.[4] If it were concerned about its competition in the US, it also might have been able to use its low-cost French base to substitute for US production or to bring products into the US that it had hitherto not sold there.

As this example highlights, firms not only need to estimate and hedge their foreign exchange denominated exposures, but also to respond to shifts in exchange rates by adjusting operating parameters. Moreover, the nature of exchange rate determination makes accurate forecasting of such shifts extremely difficult and, perhaps, futile. Consequently, exchange rate fluctuations can have a dramatic impact on a multinational corporation's operations and finances.

This context, therefore, serves as an extremely useful lens through which one may examine the strategy-structure relationship in MNCs in the context of increasingly complex, turbulent, and volatile global business conditions. It also redresses the neglect of expert functions, such as finance, in existing discussions of the organization of MNCs that for the most part have focused on geographic versus product or corporate versus subsidiary considerations.[5] Our focus on how MNCs respond to volatile exchange rates leads to two basic points of departure from the existing literature.

First, while we acknowledge that formal models provide valuable insights regarding the strategic implications of turbulent global environments and the appropriate response to complex problems such as volatile exchange rates, we contend that an unrealistic assumption made by these models is that the complete information and expertise relevant to the solution of the problem is available to a single rational agent acting in the best interests of the organization as a whole.[6] In reality this information and expertise is often distributed very widely among different agents and decision makers in an organization who may even have competing interests. For instance, in responding to the problems posed by exchange rate volatility, there are finance experts, marketing and pricing experts, production management experts, and international business experts, all of whom have only partial information and expertise necessary for the rational solution proposed by the formal models. Thus, the issue of managing expert tasks must increasingly be recognized as involving a broad set of expertise distributed throughout the corporation as opposed to being a narrow functional problem. This requires revisiting the role of functional experts in MNCs.

Our second point of departure from the existing literature is that this is not an organizational problem that can be solved by a priori design. As opposed to proposing a deliberate pattern of differentiation and integration specifying who should talk to whom, about what, when, and how, we attempt to locate organizational processes that facilitate the recognition, linkage, and diffusion of widely distributed expertise in a flexible way. It is difficult to solve the problem of responding to volatile exchange rates by a priori design because the firm must be responsive to specific changes (events) and the competitive interactions that flow from these events; all of which do not follow from any well-defined temporal pattern and hence cannot be incorporated into a routine or a finite set of contingency plans.

Drawing an analogy with the well-known fable of the five blind men and the elephant brings our points of departure into sharper focus. Our first point of departure follows from the moral of the fable that the five blind men, each analogous to a different organizational expert, are better off once they recognize that by sharing their individual and separate expertise they will arrive at a better understanding of the animal they are trying to describe. Our second point of departure involves an extrapolation of the fable. If it were known with certainty that the only problem the five blind men were going to be required to solve was that of describing a specific animal such as the elephant, it would be possible for someone who knew the outlines of an elephant to specify a priori the ideal organizational structure (no doubt, some form of matrix) that must exist in order for the blind men to describe the elephant accurately. However, if the nature of the beast to be described is constantly changing – today an elephant and tomorrow a pig – as is inevitably the case in a turbulent and volatile global economy, the organizational problem is rendered far more complex. Clearly there is no deterministic organizational solution, so what is required is a more flexible context that permits the blind men, or analogously the different organizational experts, to recognize, share, and diffuse their differentiated expertise. Furthermore, the organization needs mechanisms that not only help link the expertise relevant to a particular situation, but preserve and further develop the differentiated knowledge and expertise that is required to address the different aspects of such complex problems.

This chapter is organized to expand on the above issues as follows. In Section I we briefly articulate the nature of the task of coping with volatile exchange rates in the context of global competition. This is done with a view to highlighting the highly distributed information and expertise that is required to address the problem. In Section II, based on field research in several organizations, we develop a descriptive model of the major factors that shape corporate responses to exchange rate volatility. In Section III, we conclude by describing the key elements of the 'emergent matrix' organization that we have observed and by offering a brief set of normative observations based on our identification of best practice among the firms we studied.

I. The expert task – coping with volatile exchange rates

Impact of volatile exchange rates under global competition

A major difference between multidomestic and global competition is the impact of exchange rates on the operations of a multinational firm. Under multidomestic competition, markets are national in scope and, typically, a substantial proportion of value added is local. Thus, exchange rate shifts do not significantly change the relative costs of firms operating in a particular market. As a result, firms' revenues and costs move together in response to shifts in exchange rates, and profits from foreign operations, when converted into dollars,[7] move roughly proportionally with exchange rates.[8] Further, operating decisions regarding pricing and output, for example, should be unaffected by these changes.

In contrast, under global competition, there will be a tendency toward world prices and larger proportions of firms' value added are likely to be concentrated in particular countries. Thus, unless all firms have the same geographic patterns of value added, shifts in exchange rates will change their relative costs and profit margins. With the emergence of non-US global competitors, this is almost bound to be the case.[9] In this situation, the profits of foreign operations may respond either more or less than one-for-one with shifts in exchange rates and the profits of operations in the US may be affected as well. Further, operating decisions should be altered in response to such shifts. Even where prices remain localized through local regulation, product differentiation, or other factors that enable firms to maintain cross-border price-discrimination, the optimal competitive strategies of firms with different configurations are likely to shift.

The responsiveness of operating profits to shifts in exchange rates, then, is comprised of two effects: a conversion effect and a competitive effect. The conversion effect is the proportional adjustment of foreign currency operating profits into the reference currency (dollars for US-based firms). By definition, it applies only to foreign operations. The competitive effect, in contrast, is the response of local currency operating profits to exchange rate shifts resulting from the interaction of the various competitors' supply and price responses. It applies to both domestic and overseas activities. While the conversion effect may create headaches for treasurers and controllers, the competitive effect, since it requires adjustments in operating decisions, also affects and increases the complexity of the operating manager's job.

Potential firm responses to volatile exchange rates

Management of financial exposures (or of the conversion component of operating exposures) involves several stages very similar to those involved in portfolio management. These are (1) estimating positions or exposures, (2) simulating possible outcomes (including anticipated speculative returns, if any) and (3) taking appropriate offsetting positions, all of which take place in anticipation of exchange rate shifts. These are shown in the left-hand column of Figure 8.1. But coping with the competitive impacts of exchange rate volatility also includes an operational element, since the impact of exchange rate movements on a firm depends in large part on its tactics subsequent to the shift; and the range of possible tactics in turn depends on the configuration of the firms' assets in anticipation of possible exchange rate shifts.

Thus, to the three steps noted above, three more must be added, as shown in the right-hand column of Figure 8.1: (1a) adjusting asset configuration and organization structure to enhance the range of possible responses (2a) altering operating tactics in anticipation of imminent exchange rate shifts and (3a) aligning operating tactics in response to exchange rate changes. These elements of coping with exchange rate exposures in the operating domain involve much greater interdependency across time frames than the simpler financial functions.

Each of these steps may involve elements in more than one activity domain, typically several. For purposes of simplicity in this discussion, the various domains of activity are defined at a highly aggregated level – marketing/pricing, production/sourcing, and finance/contracting. Further, these responses may be contained within a single organizational unit, e.g. corporate staff or a single country-centred subsidiary, or they may cut across two or more such units. Finally, the temporal dimension is divided into three stylized phases – strategic/anticipatory, tactical/anticipatory, and tactical/reactive. These are specified in Figure 8.2 and discussed at greater length below.

Strategic/anticipatory

At a strategic/anticipatory level, firms have both business and financial options for exploiting and protecting themselves from exchange rate fluctuations. For instance, with regard to the configuration of production and sourcing networks, firms face three generic strategies to cope with future exchange rate volatility. These are: (1) configure individual businesses to have the flexibility to increase production and sourcing in countries that become low cost due to swings in exchange rates; (2) configure individual businesses to reduce operating exposure by matching costs and revenues, and (3) select a portfolio of businesses with offsetting exposures.

The first option, that of configuring operations to increase flexibility, can actually increase a firm's expected operating profits as well as reduce its variability.[10] The other two can at best reduce variability with no reduction in expected operating profits and, often, will result in some reduction in expected operating profits. The reason for this in the case of configuring individual businesses to match the currency dimensions of revenues and costs, is that such matching typically will require some departures from the

Figure 8.1 Dimensions of response

Type of Exposure	Financial	Operating
Time Frame		
Strategic/ Anticipatory	**Assess Exposures** **Simulate Outcomes** **Select Positions**	**Assess exposures** **Simulate outcomes** *Adjust configuration* *Simulate outcomes* **Select Positions**
Tactical/ Anticipatory	**Fine Tune Positions**	*Fine Tune Market and Production Plans*
Tactical/ Reactive	**Unwind Active Positions**	*Align Marketing and Production Plans*
Reflective	**Compute Results**	**Compute Results** *Compute Contribution*

Figure 8.2 Corporate responses by function and timing

Function / Timing	Finance	Marketing	Production	Control
Strategic/ Anticipatory	Estimate (range of) future exchange rates Core liability strategy Hedging Strategy	Segmentation Product strategy Pricing Strategy	Plant location/ configuration Technology/ factor choices Sourcing Strategy	Determine locus of responsibility Measurement strategy
Tactical/ Anticipatory	Estimate Exposures Hedge positions	Set prices, mix Set terms	Production loading Sourcing	Set planning rate, budget expectations Assess possible outcomes
Tactical/ reactive	Unwind active positions	Adjust prices Adjust mix	Adjust loading Adjust sourcing	Adjust expectations
Reflective	Assess Performance	Assess response/ performance	Assess response/ performance	Assess/response performance

optimum configuration in terms of scale and location advantages. Similarly, selecting a portfolio of businesses with offsetting exposures is likely to lead to increased administrative costs and reduced efficiency associated with managing diverse businesses without other synergistic linkages. With all three strategies, firms must consider the expected level of real exchange rates over quite long periods. Such estimates typically are based on a presumed tendency of exchange rates to return toward purchasing power parity, although some firms implicitly or explicitly take current levels as the best long-run forecasts.

Firms face a similar set of choices in their marketing strategy – the degree of product differentiation, the extent to which segments are identified or reinforced within national boundaries, and so on – which affect both their exposures to exchange rate shifts and their ability to respond to such shifts.

The firm also has several financing/contracting options available to it. These include offsetting their operating exposures with financial exposures, such as those created by matching long-dated forwards (or, equivalently, foreign currency borrowing), swaps, or currency options. None of these is exact, since they are keyed to nominal rather than real exchange rates, but they have the advantage that when competitively priced they reduce the variability of operating profits with little or no reduction in the anticipated level of such profits.

Tactical/anticipatory

Given a particular competitive configuration and projection of exchange rates, firms must set prices and determine production loading and sourcing over the coming planning period. In the short run, these decisions typically will involve a balancing act between vaguely understood limits to sustainable price differentials across countries and the impact of local currency price shifts on demand and hence profits or, in the case of production, the trade-off between current cost differentials and the cost of switching locations. Further, given the emergence of global oligopolies in many industries, pricing decisions must reflect anticipations of competitor actions or reactions. Estimating these reactions is likely to be complicated by the fact that competitors differ significantly in the currency composition of their costs and, perhaps more importantly, in the currency eyeglasses they wear.

Tactical/reactive

The same set of issues arise in event rather than calendar time in response to an unanticipated shift in exchange rates. Volatile industry. Sudden shifts in exchange rates require adjustments to prior decisions regarding pricing, output, and sourcing. These actions must be spontaneous, quick, and flexible in order to minimize losses or quickly capitalize on opportunities that may arise. They are further complicated by the fact that they no longer follow an orderly time frame and typically must be based on fragmentary, noisy information. Again, strategic interactions among various competitors are likely to be critical factors. These features preclude time-consuming, detailed analysis, yet also imply that intuitive responses are likely to be incorrect. This places a premium on a prior identification of appropriate contingent responses.

Based on the preceding discussion of the task of coping with volatile exchange rates in MNCs, it should be readily apparent that this activity involves information, expertise, and actions that span across multiple business domains and time frames. Therefore, conceptualizing the response of MNCs to this task as one that involves only the finance function is clearly inadequate. Instead, to further our understanding of this phenomenon we need to proceed by first understanding more carefully the various factors that influence corporate responses to this complex task. This descriptive understanding is a necessary precondition for managerially relevant prescriptions and is the task to which we turn in the next section.

II. A descriptive model of the factors influencing corporate response to volatile exchange rates

In order to understand corporate practice, and in particular to determine how firms have dealt with the information and organizational complexities of the exchange rate problem, we conducted in-depth interviews with managers in four firms and less intensive interviews with another six firms.[11] The firms interviewed included high-technology-based global manufacturers, global manufacturers with medium-level technologies and high recurring costs, and providers of financial services. Eight of these firms were from the US, two were Japanese. Whenever possible, we interviewed foreign exchange 'experts', usually members of the corporate staff, as well as their organizational 'clients', typically general managers of operating units. Our interviews in firms usually involved a half day, but they ranged from a two-hour discussion to more than fifteen individual interviews of more than four days in total. The interviews were open-ended, but our major lines of inquiry were guided by the existing literature on the management of similar complex problems and the literature on the management of the MNC discussed earlier in this paper.

Summary of the descriptive model

Our descriptive model of the factors that influence a firm's response to volatile exchange rates, which in turn affects corporate performance, is schematically represented in Figure 8.3. Three basic factors are at the core of this model: (1) The definition of the problem of coping with volatile exchange rates which is determined by the environmental context, the business strategy, the frames employed by individual managers, and the broad corporate frame; (2) The organizational context in terms of the formal structure of responsibility and authority and the co-ordination mechanisms that relate to the various components of the overall task; and (3) The information and control system which includes the control, performance appraisal and incentive system for both individual managers and corporate units.

In addition to these three general factors it is important to remember the important influence of the firm's administrative history, its corporate culture, and the particular vehicle it chooses to implement changes in the corporate response to volatile exchange rates. We will now elaborate on the theoretical and empirical rationale for the different aspects of this model.

Definition of the response

In principle, if one had complete information on all aspects of the relevant strategic environmental context and the firms' position in it, such as the structure of the cost and revenue streams relative to the competition, there exists for every firm, and possibly every business within a firm, a definition of the feasible set of responses to exchange rate that maximizes the (present) value of its cash flows. However, the near impossibility of accurately forecasting exchange rates and the complexities involved in specifying their impact and the appropriate organizational response makes the way an organization understands or 'frames' the task of coping with exchange rates an important determinant of the nature and quality of their response.[12]

There are various dimensions along which individuals, or the firm through an established routine, may characterize the exchange rate context and the appropriate responses to it. Three dimensions of this framing are of particular importance: (i) framing of the broad exchange rate environment, (ii) framing of the impact of exchange rate volatility, and (ii) framing of the appropriate actions firms must take to cope with volatile exchange rates.

196

Figure 8.3 Determinants of firms' responses to volatile exchange rates: a descriptive model

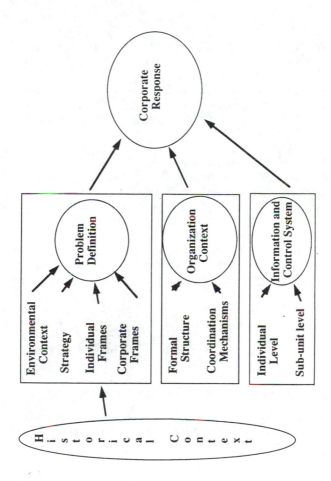

Framing of the broad exchange rate environment

Theoretically, a key issue here is the extent to which the volatility of exchange rates is acknowledged or suppressed.[13] A closely related issue is whether the firm believes that it can 'beat the market', or that the market is 'efficient'[14] as reflected in views on the dynamics of exchange rates, such as purchasing power parity or momentum models.[15] In our empirical research, in almost every instance, managers felt that the volatility they had experienced in recent years in exchange rates was likely to remain an integral feature of the international business environment. While most had a general belief that exchange rates did tend in a secular sense towards purchasing power parity, they felt that short- and intermediate-run volatility was so great that the general trend was not very important in comparison.

In stark contrast to this generally shared view of the broad exchange rate environment at the individual level, firms we studied had very different routines that characterized their overall framing of the exchange rate environment. In several firms, for instance, no formal forecasts were made and, as a result, the implicit reference rates used were the current spot rates. In another firm, the forecast used as the reference point for defining corporate responses was a short-term single-point forecast, based on near term forward rates, which was updated every month. In a Japanese firm we studied, in contrast, the forecast that served as the reference point was the worst-case scenario over the product planning horizon. In yet another firm, the rate used for key decisions was a periodically updated 'long-term parity level' that often diverged substantially from current rates. One can readily imagine how these corporate differences in the framing of the exchange rate environment also influenced the definition of responses in these cases.

Framing of the impact of exchange rate volatility

Traditionally, the problem of coping with exchange rate changes has been viewed as minimizing exchange rate losses, and in some cases seeking to gain on the upside, typically focusing on financial assets and liabilities. As has been noted elsewhere (Lessard 1986), framing the problem as one of financial risk management is deficient in the context of global competition in two regards. First, it is concerned primarily with deciding whether to hedge or retain particular exposures arising from operations, rather than seeing to it that this exposure and its impact on expected operating profits have been factored into operating decisions. In fact, to the extent that it includes a speculative element by factoring possible gains into the hedging decision, it differs little from staking the assistant treasurer with a sum of money to be used to speculate on stock options, pork bellies, or gold. Second, it tends to focus on exposures that lead to identifiable foreign exchange losses, neglecting the more critical, but harder to measure comparative effects. This further leads to responses being framed with less operational and strategic content than is desired under conditions of global competition.

Most managers we interviewed recognized the enormous competitive significance of volatile exchange rates and the operating and strategic implications in addition to the straightforward financial or contractual exposures. However, the degree of sophistication they showed in framing the operational and strategic impact varied. Some had only a vague, undifferentiated notion of these impacts, while others categorized various businesses in terms of the nature and degree of pricing responses and cost shifts. In some cases, the perception of a relatively undifferentiated operating exposure appeared to reflect a reality of largely local pricing which limited the exchange effect to the conversion of the local profit stream. However, in another firm there clearly were differences in the extent to which pricing of, say, service and products was determined by local versus global factors, yet no clear articulation of these differences was provided by either financial or operating managers. In yet another firm, some business unit managers had quite a clear sense of the nature and degree of operating exposure in their domain, yet even though these varied substantially across units, there was no evidence of a general corporate awareness of these differences.

The framing of exchange rate impacts was often narrowly focused on particular business activities or decisions where exchange rates had a critical impact rather than on the larger, less explicit exposures of the firm as a whole. As a result, firms with, say, Japanese yen cost exposures from the sourcing of a few components would emphasize these despite the fact that they faced Japanese competition virtually across the board in their product markets.

Framing of the appropriate actions

The greatest variation in framing among individual managers was in their definition of the appropriate organization actions that were needed to cope with volatile exchange rates. Several firms explicitly or implicitly assumed that the appropriate response was financial, and that 'good' treasury management would obviate the need for a broader operational response. In one such case, for instance, the treasury foreign exchange management function was conceived as a profit centre that should profit from astute foreign exchange transactions, whether or not these transactions bore any relation to the overall exposure of the firm.[16] In another, the treasury sought to hedge the full exposure at all times, but most of the internal communication between finance and operations centred on reconciliation of differences between observed exchange rate impacts and hedging gains and losses. In yet other cases, including the two Japanese firms, operations managers viewed themselves as carrying the ball with little linkage to financial responses. In only a minority of firms could senior managers, finance managers, and operating managers articulate a view that included both sets of responses and appropriate co-ordination between them.[17]

Another distinctly different framing of the appropriate response was really an incremental shift in the traditional financial view. Recognizing that economic exposures were broader than financial exposures, the view here was that operating managers should be made aware of such economic exposures and be asked to report those exposures so that they could be adequately hedged with the increasingly sophisticated financial instruments available for these purposes. In this view what was required was awareness and control.

As opposed to these finance-oriented views, several firms had framed the problem in operational terms. The critical issue in most cases was not what should be done under particular circumstances, but to structure a process that would bring to bear the appropriate expertise on specific decisions regarding responses to shifting circumstances. In one case, a manager felt that the only way one could truly cope with exchange rates was by developing a rich cadre of 'international business' managers who could think through appropriate responses on the spot. In his view, operating in volatile global environments required a fundamentally different world view than operating in domestic environments. The solution, in his opinion was, therefore, not one of formulating strategy, because there was no clear calculus which one could employ that would be appropriate for each turn in the environment. Instead, the organizational solution lay in the development of managers who intimately understood the complex nature of the problems posed by volatile global environments and could, therefore, use this informed world view to address strategic issues as and when they arose. Therefore, the key organization mechanisms, in his view, were learning and education. In the same firm though, it was the view of another manager that the appropriate organizational response was to try and explicitly model the contingencies of exchange rate volatility in the strategic planning process – both short and long term. In this sense, formal strategic analysis and contingency planning were the required organizational responses. Neither view was widely adopted by the firm.

In another set of firms, however, the appropriate organizational response was seen as requiring the creation of special purpose organizations – typically task forces with members drawn from the relevant functions and organizational units – to build expertise and relate it to the various responses. The view in these firms was that this problem, although complex, was amenable to structured analysis and that the key issue was creating a network to develop, link, and diffuse the expertise present in different parts of the organization.

In addition to the impact of differences in individual and corporate frames on the definition of the firm's responses to exchange rate, the strategy adopted by the firm or the business unit is also a major determinant of this definition. For instance, a strategy of aggressive growth by building market share is certain to result in a different definition of response than a strategy of making maximum profit without necessarily growing. In one of our companies, the fall of the dollar was on the one hand viewed as an opportunity to penetrate and build market share in critical markets such as France and Germany, and on the other hand a time for getting larger profits in less critical markets such as Singapore.

Organizational context

The preceding discussion of the definition of the exchange rate problem focused on the analytical and cognitive dimensions of the management of this complex activity. It described the factors that drive differences in the way firms define what should be done to manage in an environment of volatile exchange rates. The organizational context influences how firms respond to volatile exchange rates. Two aspects of the organizational context need to be discussed: (i) Formal structure of responsibility, and (ii) Co-ordination and linkage mechanisms.

Formal structure

The formal structure defines the locus of responsibility and authority for various aspects of how a firm responds to exchange rate volatility. It is likely to be closely related to the way the problem is framed. However, it is not easy to devise a formal structure to deal with volatile exchange rates. Dividing responsibility and authority among staff, geographic, and business units can be a difficult balancing act. All three steps of financial foreign exchange risk management must lie within the traditional realm of corporate treasury. However, the responsibility for strategic and tactical operational aspects must lie with operating units and, possibly, corporate planning staff. Also the authority to carry out specific functions may be separated from the responsibility for those functions. Financing decisions, for example, may be a major determinant of a business unit's exposure, but the authority may reside with the corporate treasury. A mismatch is most likely where the overall problem is partially or improperly framed.

In our empirical research, there was a widely shared view that coping with volatile exchange rates required the utilization of several different knowledge bases and skills that resided in different parts of the corporation. Corporate staff and functional experts in the international treasury, control, and co-ordination units as well as operating managers were each considered to possess skills and information necessary but not sufficient for handling the expert task of coping with volatile exchange rates.

In one company that had recently moved from a functional to a product-based organization, a complex division of responsibility and authority had evolved to couple the operating knowledge base of the line operations with the functional skills that, due to the administrative heritage of the corporation, resided in the corporate staff. Formally, the division of responsibility was clear. The corporate treasury was responsible for the corporate-wide financial exposures and the line managers for operating exposures. Increasingly though, these clear lines of responsibility were getting blurred with the corporate treasury taking a more active role in working with line organizations to identify and manage operating exposures. The difference of authority is similarly being shared. Authority for operating decisions does not reside solely with the line managers but is shared by corporate staff responsible for such functions as the rationalization of production and transfer pricing. This division of responsibility and authority is not in the form of a formal matrix, but more in the form of a set of networked and interlinked actors that need to share expertise and negotiate differences and decision-making authority.[18] Interestingly, despite this understanding of the cross-functional nature of the problem, the predominant organizational response was to leave the co-ordination and most of the execution of exchange rate responses to the manager of foreign exchange in the treasury unit. This tended to limit the response to financial ones, and also to reinforce the information gathering and control aspects of the task over the provision of assistance or guidance to operating units. This case clearly shows the enormous difficulties in creating an organizational structure that is responsive to the task of coping with volatile exchange rates.

The two firms that in our judgement were most successful, however, adopted more integrative patterns. One firm, which had determined that it had few valid operating responses, nevertheless incorporated exchange rate scenario analysis into its strategic planning, including the presentation on a quarterly basis to senior management of possible exchange rate impacts. Another, which faced large exposures and felt it could feasibly respond in finance, production, and marketing, instituted a task force that included members from finance, planning, pricing, production, and sourcing. This team obtained and maintained sponsorship at the top executive level and insinuated itself into ongoing strategic and operating decision-making wherever it determined that exchange rates were an important factor. Over time, though, some of its functions were spun off to operating units and, perhaps more importantly, members from various parts of the organization cycled in and out of the team, dispersing expertise and broadening the team's network.

Co-ordination and linkage mechanisms

As emphasized earlier, the task of responding to volatile exchange rates requires a highly complex set of interactions both across organization units/centres of expertise and over time. Centred around the recognition that coping with volatile exchange rates requires tapping multiple bases of expertise and competence that resides in different parts of the organization, we observed several different patterns of interaction and information flows. These may be organized and discussed under two basic types: (1) patterns associated with the discovery and dissemination of the relevant existing stocks of knowledge; and (2) patterns for the coupling of the relevant knowledge bases.

The discovery and dissemination of relevant knowledge

Several approaches were observed to accomplish this purpose. One involved the redefinition of a specialized knowledge base to highlight aspects that may be of relevance to other parts of the corporation. Thus, in one case, the manager in charge of the foreign treasury operations had redefined his knowledge base to include operational exposure management, such as the ability to bear the risks of all contractual exposures that were brought to his notice, to advise operating managers on decisions such as cross-border inter-firm financial agreements. To facilitate the recognition of this expertise he was advertising this new capacity by circulating memos throughout the corporation and searching for a few visible cases to solve which would then serve to make his claims credible. Similar attempts were being made by other corporate functions such as finance and management information services.

Another approach to discovery and dissemination of expertise involved internal training and education programmes. For instance, one firm had started a regular international management education programme which was staffed by internal and external 'faculty'. In other cases, key individuals had taken a special initiative to educate others. For instance, the manager, described earlier, who felt that the corporate solution to cope with volatile exchange rates was to create the consummate international business manager had also taken it upon himself to go on-the-road, giving lectures on pricing strategies to various operating managers in subsidiaries of the company throughout the world.

A third approach was the expert consultant who 'called' on operating managers to offer expertise on this issue. All these approaches, though, were premised on the shared notion that successful response to exchange rate volatility required creating awareness of the problem and the location of the expertise in the corporation that might help solve various aspects of it.

The coupling of the relevant knowledge bases

Several organizational mechanisms were being set in place to facilitate the coupling of the dispersed knowledge bases. For instance, in one approach, as part of the regular planning process, teams which comprised line and corporate staff members were being asked to develop strategic plans together to promote the coupling of different information and analytical skills. The scope of the strategic plans was correspondingly enlarged and teams were required explicitly to consider exchange rate contingencies among several others.

A second approach designed to promote coupling of knowledge bases involved internal quasi-markets for specialized expertise. For example, finance specialists were placed as consultants within line operations who were billed for the specialists' services and shared in their evaluations. This was described as an attempt to develop information linkages between operations and corporate staff that facilitated the coupling and full utilization of the knowledge that resided in the corporation. Several innovative organizational solutions were attributed to this organizational linkage. For example, one financial analyst, asked to update product profitability calculations, noted that the standard rules of thumb for allocating sales overheads bore no relation to the actual allocation of sales effort. The analyst then tracked actual sales efforts and recomputed the profit calculations with major differences. This procedure is now being replicated by financial analysts in other line organizations.

In yet another approach, a permanent foreign exchange task force was set up that included within its purview all international outsourcing decisions as well as major capital investments. This group first obtained a role in these operating decisions after a major sourcing decision resulted in significant currency-related losses, and gradually became institutionalized by the naming of one member from the procurement function.

Information and control systems

The final determinant of corporate responses to volatile exchange rates is the information and control system used to measure and reward individual and organizational unit performance. For instance, a critical issue faced by most firms is how to get finance 'experts' to contribute to operating decisions rather than restricting attention to their own limited domains. Here we saw various mechanisms at work, ranging from the 'matrixing' of finance staffers into operating organizations to explicit monetary performance targets tied to contributions to 'other peoples' ' areas of responsibility. In the majority of firms, finance staffers were formally assigned to operating groups, with the operating unit sharing in their evaluation. Further, in one of these firms senior corporate financial staffers' profit goals were tied to their contributions (savings or value-added) to operations as acknowledged by operating unit managers. Thus, they were operating as results-based consulting profit centres.

Another dimension of control is the way that exchange-rate related variances are computed and evaluated. The typical process with US firms, borne out in our interviews, is to plan at a projected exchange rate and then seek to link subsequent profit variations to changes in exchange rates. The Japanese firms in the sample used a radically different technique, planning operations at a pessimistic rate (180 when the yen was at 220, 140 when it was at 180, etc). Only one of the firms surveyed had explicit mechanisms for identifying before-the-fact specific responses to different contingencies and tracking, after the fact, the timeliness and accuracy of those responses.

Situational factors

In addition to these three basic determinants of a firm's response to volatile exchange rates, we observed several differences that could be attributed to situational factors which cannot be generalized but operate on a company-by-company basis. Perhaps the most important of these situational factors was the administrative history of the firm. For instance, one of the firms had only recently changed from a functional to a line-of-business structure. The background of the finance group which was one of the most powerful groups in the functional era is central to an understanding of the firm's response to volatile exchange rates. Another important situational factor was the vehicle or forum different firms had chosen to address this increasingly important problem. For instance, in one company there was a high-powered, multi-disciplinary task force that had been given charge to develop a company-wide practice and in another the process was being dominated by an individual with a background in international finance. The response of these two companies was influenced to a great degree by these choices.

In this section we developed a theoretically and empirically grounded descriptive model of the determinants of corporate responses to volatile exchange rates. Little attempt was made in this section to explicitly identify best practice along each of these dimensions. We do this briefly in our conclusions.

III. Conclusions

This research has focused on one activity (or related set of activities) within MNCs – coping with volatile exchange rates – in order to learn how these firms deal with the complexity presented not only by the contradictory needs of focusing both along product and geographic lines, but also developing expertise in particular domains whose application is diffused throughout the firm with varying degrees of intensity over time in response to environmental turbulence. We clearly have succeeded in establishing that the activity is a complex one, but we also believe that we have developed a more fine-grained view of complexity than that usually presented and have identified and described various cognitive and organizational factors that appear to influence the timeliness and quality of firms' responses to this complexity.

This chapter represents a step towards a fuller understanding of the importance of expertise and expert functions in coping with the complex problems thrown up by a turbulent global economy.

Furthermore, this rediscovery of expert functions broadens and extends the currently favoured structural conception of matrix organizations so that instead of emphasizing patterns of differentiation and integration based on a priori logic, more attention is accorded to emergent and less formal patterns of co-ordination and linkage. Indeed, the organizational form this view represents is sufficiently distinct from existing conceptions of matrix organizations that we label it the 'emergent matrix' to call attention to the fact that differentiated expertise represents a critical set of third dimensions in many organizations, but that these are largely self-designing and self-integrating.

While our observations are still incomplete, and thus we have not been able to link formally observed behaviours to various cognitive and organizational measures or factors, we believe that we have identified some of the key linkages and have begun to be able to spot 'best practice' in various aspects of the activity.

In particular, we find that the overall framing or 'vision' of the problem, coupled with an understanding of the constraints to various responses implicit in the firms' overall strategy, structure, and systems, is a critical factor in successful responses. We also find that an expert group explicitly charged with helping line managers cope with exchange rates is an important element in success. Finally, we find that the most successful firms create incentives for these experts to support line managers in their decisions, and not just to be successful transactional profit centres.

Framing

Three aspects of successful firms' framing stand out. The first is the recognition that coping with volatile exchange rates requires an options-like perspective, that it cannot be 'structured away' by any amount of a priori analysis or planning. The second is that 'finance cannot do it all', that regardless of the sophistication of the treasury function, it at best can reduce fluctuations in profits resulting from exchange rate swings. Treasury expertise cannot substitute for the business judgement required as circumstances change, nor can it be expected through astute trading to earn back losses incurred in operations. The third is that appropriate responses often involve the linking of normally differentiated functions and, hence, require 'going out of ordinary channels' with special structures and systems.

While a few experts in the firm may develop this understanding on their own or through consultants, external seminars, or discussions with peers in other firms, extending it to a large constituency requires special efforts. We observed several successful mechanisms including 'rehearsing' exchange rate impacts and responses within ongoing management processes, classifying various activities in terms of their sensitivity and response potential, and varying the 'currency frame'.

Rehearsing differs from contingency planning in that it involves those who must take actions as well as the expert group framing the problem. As one finance staffer put it, 'our job is not to tell (operations) how to respond, but to ask the right questions' to make sure that these considerations are taken into account. Therefore, it must also compete successfully with the variety of other demands placed on line managers and appears to work best when it is embedded in other ongoing management processes. Among those contexts we observed were evaluations of investment and outsourcing decisions, annual planning and budgeting, and quarterly reviews of projected and realized performance with senior management.

Rules of thumb for classifying activities, e.g. pricing in particular market segments or the production of particular components, in terms of the degree of potential and desired response to exchange rate shifts serve two purposes. First, they reduce complexity by allowing firms and managers to ignore exchange rate responses in a large number of activities where shifts might 'cause you to smile or cry but not change what you are doing'. Second, they provide experts and line managers with 'templates' to recognize similarities and, hence, to learn better from experience and link reactions.

Varying the currency frame helps managers identify biases arising from their own money illusion, the fact that business measurements implicitly assume that the numeraire or currency yardstick being used is constant over time. Managers in a dollar-based firm, for example, will typically perceive currency impacts as something that primarily affect foreign exchange operations even if competitive effects are substantial in the home market. As a result, they often overlook home responses such as raising dollar prices when the dollar is relatively weak. In several firms the currency group reported raising questions such as 'what would we do differently if we were a German firm, or if we used the SDR[19] as a unit of account?' Some had taken the further step of plotting prices and costs in various currencies in order to understand better their currency dimensions. One had gone so far as to begin discussing shifting the organization's currency reference point to SDRs in order to place US operations in the same currency context as all others.

Organization

It is unrealistic either to centralize operational foreign exchange management in one unit or diffuse it throughout the organization. None of the firms we studied, with the exception of one where all critical pricing and production decisions were made by a small group at the top, succeeded in having a full framing of operational responses to shifting exchange rates permeate the full range of managerial levels and functions involved in the response and, therefore, had to rely on an expert cadre for this purpose. In some cases, this cadre sought to act as a catalyst, linking itself into the relevant areas of activity. In more cases, though, it sought to maintain its own isolated expert function.

The most successful firms in our sample created units to deal with operational exchange rate impacts and responses other than the traditional forex group in treasury. In several cases this was a task force that cut across functional lines, in one a planning group, and in another a special purpose unit in treasury separate from the transactional foreign exchange group. Those firms that left the coordination of operational exposure to a transaction-oriented foreign exchange group at best appeared to hedge these exposures well, though they provided little support for operating responses. At worst these groups' interactions with the rest of the firm centred on reconciling actual and budgeted hedging results.

Systems

As a general rule, organization alone is not sufficient and firms' control and information systems must be aligned with the organization for success. This certainly appears to be the case with the management of operational exposure. Those more successful firms with special-purpose structures also provided strong incentives for experts to support line managers, in several cases going so far as to set profit targets that had to be met from 'identified improvements' in line units attested to by line managers. In other firms, these incentives were more informal, with the task force receiving top-level sponsorship and having its impact observed by senior management. Those units, in contrast, with transactions-based financial goals (gains on foreign exchange trading) did little other than that, although in at least one firm the chief foreign exchange manager personally pursued both types of goals.

Effective management in the context of volatile exchange rates requires a number of elements, the most important of which appears to a clear framing of the problem that the firm is seeking to solve. This framing must be supported by organizational structures that foster the development and diffusion of relevant expertise and a set of incentive and control systems that support these tasks.

Notes

1 See, for instance, Hout, Porter, and Rudden (1980), Kogut (1985), Porter (1986), and Bartlett and Ghoshal (1987a,b) for general statements of the unique problems posed by global competition, and Lessard (1986) and Lessard and Lightstone (1986) for problems posed by macroeconomic volatility, such as exchange rate shifts in the context of global competition.
2 See Bartlett (1986) and Bartlett and Ghoshal (1986) for a discussion of the transnational; Hedlund (1986) for a discussion of the concept of organization as a heterarchy; Poynter and White (1989) for a discussion of the dual-focus firm.
3 For a discussion of the linkage between exchange rates and prices see Dornbusch (1987).
4 The issue of whether a firm should use its currency-derived cost advantage to gain margin or share depends on a number of factors, including the anticipated permanence of the exchange rate shift, the degree of customer loyalty, and the overall elasticity of demand for the good. For a discussion of these points see, for example, Krugman (1987).
5 Other expert functions include technological innovation, which has been addressed, among others, by Bartlett and Ghoshal (1989) in chapter 9 of this volume, competitor scanning (see e.g. Ghoshal and Westney (1988)), and marketing research.
6 This critique is similar to Bower's (1970) critique of the usefulness of formal models in financial theory for understanding the management of the resource allocation process in large, multi-unit, multi-product firms.
7 Since US firms represent our point of reference, our discussion is organized in 'dollar' terms. The basic arguments, of course, are fully general and can just as easily be translated into other reference currencies.
8 In more technical terms, given a change in the real exchange rate, the demand and supply curves facing the firm will remain unchanged in the local currency (adjusted for inflation). Hence the optimal output and local currency price will remain unchanged, as will local currency profit. From a dollar perspective, of course, both curves will shift by the same amount, and the dollar profit will change in proportion to the change in the exchange rate.
9 Under these circumstances, a change in the real exchange rate will result in a relative shift of demand and supply curves, regardless of the reference currency of the firm. This implies that the optimal price and volume will change as well.
10 Recent developments in financial economics have stressed that volatility is not simply a negative situation to be avoided or hedged, but that

it may also create valuable options for active management response. In the case of operating exposure, for example, a firm with manufacturing flexibility could actually increase its average profits over time by switching production from one country to another in line with real exchange rate fluctuations.

11 The research project is still in progress. The final results will be based on interviews with 15 to 20 firms and a questionnaire survey of a larger number of firms. Some of the initial interviews were part of a masters' thesis research undertaken during the 1986–1987 and 1987–1988 academic years.

12 This importance of strategic issue diagnosis and the way the environment is framed by organizational members have been emphasized by Dutton and Jackson (1987).

13 One extreme can be caricatured as 'pseudocertainty', where firms forecast future exchange rates and act as if these forecasts will materialize. The other extreme believes that forecasting is difficult if not impossible and, as a consequence, considers a range of scenarios.

14 See Oxelheim and Wihlborg (1987) for a discussion of the relationship between beliefs regarding the efficiency of various markets and the relevant response set.

15 For an interesting discussion of alternative models of exchange rate behaviour which arise from alternative frames that might be employed by analysts, see Frankel and Froot (1987).

16 This firm has subsequently abandoned this 'transactions' model and has instituted a more passive hedging function, coupled with a much greater emphasis on operational responses.

17 One firm that framed the problem very well recognized that it had few degrees of operating freedom given the structure of its costs and markets and, hence, the appropriate responses were essentially financial. This insight, however, appeared to have important implications for general management perceptions of the health of the business, in contrast to firms that focused on the financial component because they had not fully articulated its linkages with operational responses.

18 Subsequently, this firm has begun to create task forces to tackle some of these issues.

19 The special drawing right of the IMF, a (roughly) trade-weighted basket of the five major currencies.

References

Bartlett, Christopher (1986) 'Building and managing the transnational', in M. Porter (ed.) *Competition in Global Industries*, Boston: Harvard Business School Press.

and Ghoshal, Sumantra (1986) 'Tap your subsidiaries for global reach', *Harvard Business Review*, July/August.

(1987a) 'Managing across borders: New strategic requirements', *Sloan Management Review*, Summer.

(1987b) 'Managing across borders: new organizational responses', *Sloan Management Review*, Fall.

Bower, Joseph (1970) 'Planning within the firm', *American Economic Review 60*.

Dornbusch, Rudiger (1987) 'Exchange rates and prices', *American Economic Review*, May.

Dutton, Jane and Jackson, Susan (1987) 'Categorizing strategic issues: links to organizational action', *Academy of Management Review*, January.

Frankel, Jeffrey and Froot, Kenneth (1986) 'The dollar as a speculative bubble: a tale of chartists and fundamentalists', Wallenberg Papers on International Finance, vol. 1, No. 1.

Ghoshal, Sumantra and Westney, D. Eleanor (1988) 'Competitor analysis in large corporations: adding value to information', MIT Sloan School working paper.

Hedlund, Gunnar (1986) 'The hypermodern MNC: towards a heterarchy', *Human Resource Management*, Fall.

Hekman, Christine (1986) 'Don't blame currency values for strategic errors: protecting competitive position by correctly assessing foreign exchange exposure', *Midland Corporate Finance Journal*, Fall.

Hout, Thomas, Porter, Michael, and Rudden, Ellen (1980) 'How global companies win out', *Harvard Business Review*, September–October.

Kogut, Bruce (1985) 'Designing global strategies: profiting from operational flexibility', *Sloan Management Review*, Fall.

Krugman, Paul (1987) 'Pricing to market when the exchange rate changes', in Sven Arndt and David Richardson (eds) *Real-Financial Linkages Among Open Economies*, Cambridge, MA: MIT Press.

Lessard, Donald (1986) 'Finance and global competition: exploiting financial scope and coping with volatile exchange rates', in Porter (1986).

—— and Lightstone, John (1986) 'Volatile exchange rates can put operations at risk', *Harvard Business Review*, July–August.

—— and Sharp, David (1984) 'Measuring the performance of operations subject to exchange rate fluctuations', *Midland Corporate Finance Journal*, Fall.

Oxelheim, Lars, and Wihlborg, Clas (1987) *Macroeconomic Uncertainty: International Risks and Opportunities for the Corporation*, Chichester: John Wiley.

Porter, Michael (1986) *Competition in Global Industries*, Boston: Harvard Business School Press.

Poynter, Thomas and White, Roderick (1989) 'The strategic management of multi-national subsidiaries', (Chapter 4 this volume).

Part three

Innovation and R&D in the MNC

Chapter nine

Managing innovation in the transnational corporation

Christopher A. Bartlett and Sumantra Ghoshal

Philips has long held a leading position in the mature but profitable electric shaver business. Its Philishave is sold world-wide, but has particularly strong sales in Europe and North America. In recent years, this rather traditional and stable product category has been shaken up by several product innovations brought to market primarily by Japanese companies trying to fight their way into an established business with new clearly differentiated product ideas. The most important innovations have been in the area of miniaturization, rechargeability, and most radically, the concept of wet shaving with an electric razor.

For Philips, the new technologies and product market concepts were important trends that had to be fully understood and closely monitored, and in this task Philips' Japanese subsidiary had a critical role. However, the subsidiary had neither the technological capabilities nor the marketing expertise to develop the appropriate response to these events, and had to pass its data on to the product group and development laboratories in Europe to decide what actions Philips should take and to undertake the actual technological development. Finally, while the company had to consider introducing a new product in Japan, its competitive exposure was far greater in Europe and the United States. It was vital to introduce the new product in these locations and the co-operation of the local subsidiaries was necessary to protect Philips' global leadership position in this business.

This example, one of the thirty-eight cases that we documented in some detail in the course of a large research project involving extensive discussion with over 230 managers in nine large companies,[1] illustrates the complexity of managing the innovative process in today's multinational corporations. Not only must the company have sensing, responding and implementing capabilities around the globe, it must be able to co-ordinate those activities and link them in a flexible yet efficient manner, despite the fact that interdependent units may be separated by enormous physical and cultural distances.

Innovations as the key source of global competitive advantage

Scholarly research on international corporations has long identified innovations as the *raison d'être* of multinationals. A firm invests abroad to make more profits out of innovations embodied in the products it has developed for the domestic market. The ticket for a firm to invest and manage its affairs in many different countries is its ability to innovate, i.e. to develop new products and processes, and to create an organization through which it can appropriate the benefits of its innovations more advantageously by operating as a multinational rather than selling or licensing its technology.[2]

In the current international environment, a company's ability to innovate is rapidly becoming the primary source of its ability to compete successfully. While once MNCs gained competitive advantage by exploiting global scale economies or arbitraging imperfections in the world's labour, materials or capital markets, such advantages have tended to erode over time. In most industries today, MNCs no longer compete primarily with numerous national companies, but with a handful of other giants who tend to be comparable in terms of size and geographic diversity. In this battle, having achieved global scale, international resource access and world-wide market position is no longer sufficient – many other MNCs will match such assets. The new winners are the companies that are sensitive to market or technological trends no matter where they occur, creatively responsive to the opportunities and threats they perceive world-wide, and able to exploit their new ideas and products globally in a rapid and efficient manner. Meanwhile, companies that are insensitive, unresponsive, or slow are falling victim to the rising costs of R&D, the narrowing technology gap between countries and companies and the shortening of product life cycles.

The different multinational innovation processes

World-wide competition has not only made innovations more important for MNCs, it has also made it necessary for them to find new ways of creating innovations. Traditionally, most MNCs have adopted one or both of two classic innovation processes. The first of these is what we describe as the 'centre-for-global' innovation process: sensing a new opportunity in the home country, using the centralized resources of the parent company to create a new product or process, and exploiting it world-wide. The other traditional process we have labelled 'local-for-local' innovation process: national subsidiaries of MNCs using their own resources and capabilities to create innovations that respond to the needs of their own environments.

While most MNCs have tried to develop elements of both processes, the tension that exists between them normally means that one will become the primary source of innovations in any particular company. Quite naturally, the centre-for-global process has been dominant in MNCs adopting what has been described elsewhere as the 'centralized hub' mode of operations while local-for-local innovations have been common in the 'decentralized federation' organizations.[3]

These traditional innovation processes also reflect the traditional mentalities of these two types of companies. The centre-for-global process tends to be associated with what may be described as the extreme global mentality which sees the diversity of international environments as an inconvenience whose effects must be minimized. Thus, these organizations modify their centre-for-global innovations reluctantly and only minimally to meet specific needs. On the other hand, the archetypal multinational mentality underlies the local-for-local innovation process wherein complete conformity to local needs is seen as an unavoidable price of admission to the market. To somewhat caricature these multinational mentalities, if the first reflects minimum compromise to meet local needs, the second implies unquestioning capitulation to the whims and fancies of local customers.[4]

In recent years, however, some of these traditional management attitudes have been changing. As a result, the innovative processes in some MNCs have been evolving. In the course of documenting innovation cases in our nine core companies, we have seen how successful MNCs are developing and managing some new ways of creating new products, technologies, and even administrative systems. These new approaches tend to fall into two broad categories which we have labelled 'locally-leveraged' and 'globally-linked' innovation processes. The first involves utilizing the resources of a national subsidiary to create innovations not only for the local market but also for exploitation on a world-wide basis. The second pools the resources and capabilities of many different components of the MNC – at both the headquarters and the subsidiary level – to create and implement an innovation jointly. In this process, each unit contributes its own unique resources to develop a truly collaborative response to a globally perceived opportunity.

Both of these new and much less frequently implemented innovative processes imply a very different attitude on the part of management – an attitude that constitutes what we call the transnational mentality. Rather than viewing the differences among international environments and the diversity of local demands as liabilities, managers with the transnational mentality see them as one of the company's greatest assets. By being exposed to a diversity of consumer needs, market trends, technological breakthroughs, and government demands, a company has a greater chance of stimulating new ideas internally.[5] By operating in different environments world-wide, the company has access to a broader range of resources and capabilities (particularly the scarcest resource of all – creative people) and is able to enhance its capacity for innovative response. Many companies in our sample tried to create new products, processes, and administrative systems through the two new innovation processes but it seemed that in the absence of this transnational mentality, such efforts rarely succeeded.

Some of the companies we studied, however, were in the midst of a transition to this transnational mentality. They were beginning to synthesize their learning from exposure to diverse environments. The new mentality led them to a new set of management processes that could integrate and focus their dispersed organizational capabilities, and thereby unlock the power of the new innovation processes. Why and how they have succeeded while many others have failed is the main topic of our discussion in this chapter.

Managing innovations in MNCs: the management challenge

While locally-leveraged and globally-linked innovations are becoming increasingly important, they are not substitutes for the more traditional innovation processes. In a competitive environment in which the ability to innovate is becoming the critical differentiating capability between the winners and losers, companies are recognizing the need to maximize the number of ways in which they can develop innovative products and processes. But as they try to develop all four of these innovative processes, managers have become aware of the advantages and disadvantages of each, and also of their mutually debilitating characteristics.

Centre-for-global innovations: risk of market insensitivity

Centre-for-global innovations are necessary because certain key capabilities of the MNC must, of necessity, remain at the headquarters both because of the administrative need to protect certain core competencies of the company, and also to achieve economies of specialization and scale in the R&D activity. A good example is provided by Ericsson's development of the AXE digital switch.

Impetus for this came from early sensing of both shifting market needs and emerging technological changes. The loss of an expected order from the Australian Post Office combined with the excitement generated in a trade show by the new digital switch developed by CIT-Alcatel, then a small French competitor virtually unknown outside its home country, set in motion a formal review process within Ericsson's headquarters. The review resulted in a proposal for developing a radically new switching system based on new concepts and a new technology. The potential for such a product was high, but the costs and risks were also enormous. The new product was estimated to require over £50 million and about 2,000 man-years of development effort and take at least five years before it could be offered in the market. Even if the design turned out to be spectacular, diverting all available development resources during the intervening period could erode the company's competitive position beyond repair.

In sharp contrast to almost all the 'Principles of Innovation' proposed by Peter Drucker in his book *Innovation and Entrepreneurship*, corporate managers of Ericsson decided to place their bet on the proposal for the AXE switch, as the new product came to be called. They provided full authority and all resources so that Ellemtel, the R&D joint venture of Ericsson and the Swedish telecommunications administration, could develop the product as quickly as possible. For over four years, the technological resources of the company were devoted exclusively to this task. The development was carried out entirely in Sweden, and by 1976 the company had the first AXE switch in operation. By 1984, the system was installed in fifty-nine countries around the world.

The need to centralize the development process was driven by three main forces. First, management wanted to have control over a technology that was going to be at the very core of the company's long-term competitiveness. The cost of unco-ordinated or duplicated development in such a product is astronomical. Second, the effort required close integration between hardware and software development, and subsequently between the development and manufacturing functions. Such close co-ordination could best be provided at a central location. Finally, in a rapidly changing competitive environment, Ericsson knew it had to develop its new switch rapidly if it was to respond to tenders that had begun to specify digital capabilities. Centralizing development reduced the time and inefficiencies associated with more dispersed efforts.

The major risk of such a centralized development process is that the resulting innovations may be insensitive to market needs and may also be difficult to implement because of resistance from the subsidiaries in accepting a central solution. Ericsson was able to avoid many of these problems by seconding to the development a group of engineers from their Australian subsidiary who had recent and direct market experience in responding to the demands of one of the first tenders in the world to specify digital switching capabilities. Other companies, however, were not so fortunate and experienced some of the problems of centre-for-global innovation. For example, NEC designed NEAC 61 as a global digital switch, but with the primary objective of meeting the requirements of the US market. However, while the Japanese engineers at the corporate headquarters had excellent technical skills, they were not totally familiar with the highly sophisticated and complex software requirements of the independent telephone operating companies in the US. The result was that while everyone applauded the switch for the capabilities of its hardware, early sales suffered since the software did not meet some specific needs of end users that were significantly different from those of Japanese customers.

Local-for-local innovations: risk of needless differentiation

Local-for-local innovations are essential for responsiveness to the unique attributes of each of the different national environments in which the MNC operates. Current fascination with globalization of markets tends to overlook the fact that while the forces of globalization have certainly strengthened in many industries, the need for responsiveness to national demands and local differences has not disappeared, and often has increased. For example, Unilever faces numerous pressures to develop globally standardized products. The cost and sophistication of R&D is increasing, economies of globally integrated operations are available, and competitive battles with major MNCs like P&G are forcing global responses. Yet, Unilever's ability to sense and respond in innovative ways to local needs and opportunities has been a major corporate asset. While advanced laundry detergents did not sell well in huge markets like India, where much of the laundry was done in streams, a local development that allowed synthetic detergents to be compressed into solid tablet form gave the company a product that could capture much of the bar soap market. Similarly, in Turkey, while the company's margarine products did not sell well, an innovative application of Unilever's expertise in edible fats allowed the local company to develop a that competed with the traditional local clarified butter product, ghee.

But, on the negative side, such innovations may also reflect the efforts of national subsidiaries to differentiate themselves to retain their identity and autonomy, without any real need, and may impose differentiation costs without any significant benefits. Also, they may lead to considerable reinvention of the wheel as each subsidiary finds its own solution to common problems. In the course of interviewing managers in the different companies, we came across scores of instances of such limitations of local-to-local innovations. In Philips, for example, the British subsidiary spent a large amount of resources to create a new TV chassis that would be specially suitable for the local market. The final product was almost indistinguishable from the standard European chassis that headquarters managers were trying to implement, and resulted in the company having to operate five instead of four television set factories in Europe. While this may have been an objective of the managers in the national organization, it clearly compromised Philips' overall efficiency and competitiveness.

Locally-leveraged innovations: NIH risk

Locally-leveraged innovations permit management to take the most creative resources and innovate developments from its subsidiaries world-wide, and allow the whole company to benefit from them. In so doing, the company is often able to take the responses to market trends that emerge in one location and use them to lead similar trends in other locations. This kind of innovation requires management to develop and control a process of world-wide learning, but in so doing it allows the company substantially to leverage its world-wide innovative resources.

For example, Proctor and Gamble created the fabric softener product category with a brand called Downy in the US and Lenor in Europe. Unilever's entrant in this fast-growing segment was Comfort, but after years of effort it had done little to shake P&G's dominant first mover advantage. Then, its German subsidiary developed a new brand with a product position and marketing strategy that proved enormously successful in gaining market share rapidly. Management soon recognized that at the heart of the success of Kusshelveich (literally Teddy soft) was the bear that the Germans had developed as the product's symbol and identity. Consumer research showed that not only did the bear do an excellent job in communicating the desired image of softness, it also evoked strong recognition and trusting association in consumers that gave

221

the advertising promise great credibility. The German brand (appropriately translated) and their product market strategy were successfully transferred to other markets throughout Europe and eventually to the US where the teddy bear spokesman rapidly helped Snuggle to build a 25 per cent share in P&G's home market where Unilever's Comfort had been struggling for a decade.

Yet local innovations are not always so easily transferred. The main impediments include attempts to transfer products or processes that are unsuited to the new environment, the lack of suitable co-ordinating and transfer mechanisms (a particular problem with much of the technology transfer), and the barriers presented by the NIH syndrome.[6]

Despite the outstandingly successful transfer of its bear fabric softener, Unilever management was unable to transfer a zero phosphate detergent product developed by its German subsidiary to other European subsidiaries. Insisting that its market needs were different, the French subsidiary proceeded with its own zero-P project. Product co-ordination managers at the central office believed that a NIH attitude was at least as important a factor, particularly in an environment where national companies were struggling to maintain their local R&D budgets against pressures from the centre for more co-ordination.

Globally-linked innovation: co-ordination cost

The globally-linked innovation process is the one most suited to an environment in which the stimulus for an innovation is distant from the company's response capability, or where the resources and capabilities of several organizational units can contribute to developing the most innovative response to a sensed opportunity. By creating flexible linkages that allow the efforts of multiple units to be combined, a company can create synergies that can significantly leverage its innovation process. Like locally-leveraged innovations, the globally-linked process captures the MNC's potential scope economies and harnesses the benefits of world-wide learning.

One of the best examples we observed of this mode of innovation was the way in which Proctor and Gamble developed its global liquid detergent. When Unilever's US success with Wisk demonstrated the potential of the heavy duty liquid detergent category, P&G and Colgate rushed to the market with competitive products (Era and Dynamo respectively), but with limited success. All three companies tested their products in Europe, but due to different washing practices and the superior performance of European powder detergents which contained levels of enzymes, bleach and phosphates not permitted in the US, the new liquids failed in all these test situations.

But P&G's European scientists remained convinced they could enhance the performance of the liquid to match the local powders. After seven years of work they developed a bleach substitute, a fatty acid with water softening capabilities equivalent to phosphate, and a means to give enzymes stability in liquid form. Their new product beat the leading powder in blind tests, and the product was launched as Vizir, establishing the heavy duty liquid segment in Europe.

Meanwhile, researchers in the US had been working on a new liquid to replace Era which had failed to establish a satisfactory share against Wisk. The challenge for liquids in the US was to deal with the high-clay soil content in dirty clothes, and this group was working on improving builders, the ingredients that prevent redisposition of dirt in the wash. Also during this period, the company's International Technology Co-ordination group was working with P&G's subsidiary in Japan and had developed a more robust surfacant (the ingredient that removes greasy stain) making the liquid more effective in the cold water washes that were common in Japan. Each unit had developed effective responses to its local needs, yet none of them was co-operating to share its breakthroughs.

When the company's head of R&D for Europe was promoted to the top coporate research job, one of his primary objectives was to develop more co-ordination and co-operation among the diverse local-for-local development efforts. Through several important organizational changes, he was able to develop the means for co-operation, and the world liquid project became a test case. Plans to launch Omni, the new liquid the US group had been working on, were shelved until the innovations from Europe and Japan could be incorporated. Similarly, the Japanese and Europeans picked up on the new developments from the other laboratories. The result was the launch of Liquid Tide in the US (a brand that was able to challenge market leader Wisk), the successful launch of Liquid Cheer in Japan, and Liquid Ariel in Europe. All of these products incorporated the best of the developments created in response to European, American, and Japanese needs.

But this process also has its own limitations. It requires a degree of internal co-ordination that may be extremely expensive and wasteful. The complex interlinkages among different organizational components that are necessary to facilitate this process can also overwhelm a company because of ambiguity and excessive diffusion of authority. One of the companies participating in our study estimated that a new system of periodic meetings that had been instituted for more effective integration of its European production plants resulted in company managers having to spend 2,581 person-days in one year just on travel and in being physically present to attend the meetings. Similarly, ITT faced enormous problems in attempting to develop its System 12 digital telecommunications switch through a collaborative effort of its different European subsidiaries. Trying to co-ordinate the efforts of the different units that were responsible for developing different components of the switch proved to be extremely time consuming and costly, leading to delays and budget overruns. This effort to create a globally-linked innovation may well have been responsible for the failures that led to the company's exit from this business which has traditionally been its primary activity.

The management challenge

The challenge for MNC managers, therefore, is not one of promoting one or the other of these different innovation processes, but to find organizational systems and processes that will simultaneously facilitate all the different processes. In other words, they must, at one and the same time, enhance the effectiveness of central innovations, improve the efficiency of local innovations, and create conditions that will make the newer forms of transnational innovations feasible. To do so, however, requires that the companies overcome two related but different problems. First, for each innovation process, they must avoid the different pathologies we have described. Second, to develop innovations simultaneously through all the different processes, they must find ways to overcome the contradictions among the organizational factors that facilitate these processes.

None of the companies in our sample had solved both problems fully. However, some of them had developed special competencies in managing one or the other of the different innovation processes and in overcoming the pathologies of those processes. Their experiences suggest some ways in which MNC managers can overcome the first problem and these are described in the next part of this chapter.

A few of these companies had also made some progress in overcoming the inherent contradictions among the different processes. A special system of internal differentiation in the roles and responsibilities of different organizational units appeared to lie at the core of the solution they were in the process of developing.

Instead of finding ways so that each unit could contribute equally to all the different processes, those companies were systematically differentiating among the units based on their capabilities and needs, and were creating an internally differentiated organization so that each unit could have attributes that facilitated its participation in the particular innovation process to which it could make the greatest contribution. In the concluding part of the chapter, we draw some lessons from the emerging practices of these companies to suggest how multinational managers can build an overall organizational system for creating and exploiting the local, central, and two transnational innovation processes.

Making central innovations effective: lessons from Matsushita

The key strength on which Japan's Matsushita Electric Company has built the global leadership position of its well-known Panasonic and National brands in the highly competitive consumer electronics industry is its ability to create central innovations and to exploit them quickly and efficiently throughout its world-wide operations. This is not to say that it does not employ some of the other modes of innovation, but, of all the companies we surveyed, Matsushita is the champion manager of central innovations. As we tried to identify the organizational mechanisms that distinguish Matsushita's way of managing central innovations from those of the others, three factors stood out as the most important explanations of its outstanding success in managing this innovation process: gaining the input of subsidiaries into the process, ensuring development efforts are linked to market needs, and managing responsibility transfers from development to manufacturing and to marketing.

Gaining subsidiary input: multiple linkages

The two most important problems facing a company innovating centrally are that those developing the new product or process may not understand market needs, or that those required to implement the new product introduction are not committed to it. (Philips learned both lessons very well when it tried to introduce its technologically superb V2000 video recorder in competition with Matsushita's VHS system and Sony's Beta format.) Matsushita managers are very conscious of this problem and spend a great deal of time building multiple linkages between headquarters and overseas subsidiaries designed not only to give headquarters managers a better understanding of country-level needs and opportunities, but also to give subsidiary managers greater access to and involvement in headquarters' product development processes.

Matsushita recognizes the importance of market sensing as a stimulus to innovation and does not want its centrally driven development process to reduce its environmental sensitivity. Rather than trying to limit the number of linkages between headquarters and subsidiaries, or focus them through a single point, as many companies do for the sake of efficiency, Matsushita tries to preserve the different perspectives, priorities, and even prejudices, of its diverse groups world-wide, and ensure that they have linkages to those in the headquarters who can represent and defend their views.

The organizational systems and processes that connect different parts of the Matsushita organization in Japan with the video department of MESA, the US subsidiary of the company, are illustrative of these multifaceted interlinkages. The Vice President in charge of this department has his roots in Matsushita Electric Trading Company (METC), the organization which has overall responsibility for Matsushita's overseas business. Although formally posted to the United States, he continues to be a member of the senior management committee of METC and spends about a third of his time in Japan. This allows him to be a full member of the top management team of METC that finalizes overall product strategy for the US market, including priorities for new product development. In his role as the V.P. of MESA, he ensures that the local operation implements the agreed video strategy effectively. The General Manager of this department is a company veteran who has worked for fourteen years in the video product division of the corporate headquarters of Matsushita Electric, the production and domestic marketing company in Japan. He maintains strong connections with the central product division and acts as its link to the local US market. Two levels below the department's general manager is the Assistant Product Manager, the junior-most expatriate in the organization. Having spent five years in the company's main VCR plant in Japan, he acts as the local representative of the factory and handles all day-to-day communication with factory personnel.

None of these linkages is accidental. They are deliberately created and maintained and they reflect the company's open acknowledgement that the parent company is not one homogeneous entity, but a collectivity of different constituencies and interests, each of which is legitimate and necessary. Collectively, these multiple linkages enhance the subsidiary's ability to influence key headquarters decisions relating to its market, and particularly decisions about product specifications and design. The mutiple links not only allow local management to reflect its local market needs, they also give headquarters managers the ability to co-ordinate and control implementation of their strategies and plans, including those of implementing their innovations.

Linking development to needs: market mechanisms

But Matsushita's efforts to ensure innovations are linked to market needs does not stop at the input stage. The company has created an integrative process that ensures that the researchers and technologists are not sheltered from the pressures, constraints and demands felt by managers in the front line of the operations. One of the key elements in achieving this difficult organizational task is the company's willingness to employ internal 'market mechanisms' for directing and regulating the activities of central researchers and development engineers. Because the system is unique, we will describe some of its key characteristics.

Research projects undertaken by the central research laboratories (CRL) of Matsushita can be categorized into two broad groups. The first group consists of 'company total projects' which involve developing technologies that are important for Matsushita's long-term strategic position and that may be applicable across many different product divisions. Such projects are decided jointly by the research laboratories, the product divisions, and top management of the company, and are funded directly by the corporate Board. The second group of CRL research projects consists of relatively smaller projects which are relevant to the activities of particular product divisions. The budget for such research activities, which amounts to approximately half of the total research budget of the company, is allocated not to the research laboratories but to the product divisions. This creates an interesting situation in which technologically driven and market-led ideas can compete for attention. Each year, the product divisions suggest a set of research projects that they would like to sponsor. At the same time, the various research laboratories hold annual exhibitions and meetings and also write specific proposals to highlight research projects that they would like to undertake. The Engineering and Development groups of the product divisions mediate the subsequent contracting and negotiation process through which the expertise and interests of the laboratories and the needs of the product divisions are finally matched. Specific projects are sponsored by the divisions and are allocated to the laboratories or research groups of their choice, along with requisite funds and other resources.

The system creates intense competition for projects (and the budgets that go with them) among the research groups, and it is this mechanism that forces researchers to keep a close market orientation. At the same time the product divisions are conscious that it is their money being spent on product development and they become less inclined to make unreasonable or uneconomical demands of R&D.[7]

The market mechanism also works to determine annual product styling and features. Each year the company has its merchandising meetings, which are in effect, giant internal trade shows. Senior marketing managers from Matsushita's sales companies world-wide visit their supplying divisions and see on display the proposed product line for the new model year. Relying on their under-standing of their individual markets, these managers pick and choose among proposed models, order specific modifications for their local markets, or simply refuse to take products they feel are unsuitable. Individual products or even entire lines might have to be redesigned as a result of input from the hundreds of managers at the merchandizing meeting.

Managing responsibility transfer: personnel flow

In local-for-local innovations, the task of transferring responsi-bility from research to manufacturing and finally to marketing is facilitated by the smaller size and closer proximity of the units responsible for each stage of activity. This is not so where large central units take the lead role in the development of new products and processes, and Matsushita has built some creative means for managing these transitions. The systems rely heavily on the transfer of people. First, the careers of research engineers are structured so as to ensure that a majority of them spend about five to eight years in the central research laboratories engaged in pure research, then another five years in the product divisions in applied research and development, and finally in a direct operational function, usually production, wherein they take up line management positions for the rest of their working lives.[8] More importantly, each engineer usually makes the transition from one department to the next along with the transfer of the major project on which he has been working.

In other companies we surveyed it was not uncommon for research engineers to move to development, but not with their projects, thereby depriving the companies of one of the most important and immediate benefits of such moves. We also saw no other examples of engineers routinely taking the next step of actually moving to the production function. This last step, however, is perhaps the most critical in integrating research and production both in terms of building a network that connects managers across these two functions, and also for transferring a set of common values that facilitates implementation of central innovations.

Another mechanism that integrates production and research in Matsushita works in the opposite direction. Wherever possible the company tries to identify the manager who will head the production task for a new product under development and makes him a full-time member of the research team from the initial stage of the development process. This system not only injects direct production expertise into the development team, but also facilitates transfer of the innovation, once the design is completed. Matsushita also uses this mechanism as a way of transferring product expertise from headquarters to its world-wide sales subsidiaries. Although this is a common practice among many multinationals, in Matsushita it has additional significance because of the importance of internationalizing management as well as its products.

Making local innovations efficient: lessons from Philips

If Matsushita is the champion manager of central innovation, Philips, its arch rival in the consumer electronics business, is the master of local innovations. Again, this does not imply that they have not been successful at central innovations. Indeed, the company has a long list of products and processes that were developed in their Central Research Laboratories that extends from their earliest ventures in light bulbs to today's latest innovations in laser disc technology. In the present context, however, we would like to focus attention on why and how Philips has been able to foster a process of innovation at the national organization level to a degree unmatched by any other company of comparable size, diversity and maturity.

The first colour TV set of the company was produced and sold not in Europe, where the parent company is located, but in Canada, where the market had closely followed the US lead in introducing colour transmission. The K6 chassis introduced in Canada was designed in the company's central research laboratory in Holland, but the local subsidiary had played a major role in the development process and had an even greater input in designing the production system. The first stereo colour TV set of the company was developed by the Australian subsidiary; teletext TV sets were created by its British subsidiary; 'smart cards' by its French subsidiary, a programmed word-processing typewriter by North

American Philips; the list of local-for-local innovations in Philips is endless.

Philips' ability to create such local innovations has been due in part to the administrative history that shaped the company's growth, and in part to a strong philosophy and explicit strategic choice to respond to the local market needs. The net result has been that, over a period of time, the company has accumulated substantial resources in its different national organizations which, in conjunction with the relatively high level of decentralization of authority, has made dispersed entrepreneurship one of its key organizational assets. Out of the many different factors that have facilitated local-for-local innovations in Philips, there are three that appear to have been the most significant – the company's use of a cadre of entrepreneurial expatriates, an organization that forced tight functional integration within a subsidiary, and the historical dispersion of resources and authority.[9]

A cadre of entrepreneurial expatriates

Expatriate positions, particularly in the larger subsidiaries, have been very attractive for Philips managers for several reasons. With only 6 to 8 per cent of its total sales comes from Holland, many of the different national subsidiaries of the company have contributed much larger shares of the company's total revenues than the parent company. As a result, foreign operations have enjoyed relatively high organizational status compared to most companies of similar size with headquarters in the United States, Japan, or even the larger countries in Europe. Further, because of the importance of its foreign operations, the formal management development system of Philips has always required considerable international experience as a prerequisite for top corporate positions. Finally, Eindhoven, the small town in a rural setting that serves as the corporate headquarters of the company, is far from the sophisticated and cosmopolitan world centres that host many of its foreign subsidiaries. After living in London, New York, Sydney, or Paris, many managers find it hard to return to Eindhoven. Collectively, all these factors have led to the best and the brightest of Philips managers spending most of their careers in different national operations. This cadre of entrepreneurial expatriate managers has been an important facilitator of local-for-local innovations in the company.

Further, unlike companies such as Matsushita or NEC where an expatriate manager spends a tour of duty of three to five years in a particular national subsidiary and then returns to the headquarters, expatriate managers in Philips spend a large part of their careers abroad continuously, working for two to three years each in a number of different subsidiaries. This difference in the career systems results in very different attitudes on the part of these managers. In Philips, the expatriate managers follow each other into assignments and develop close relations among themselves. They tend to identify strongly with the national organization's point of view, and this shared identity makes them part of a distinct subculture within the company. In companies such as Matsushita, on the other hand, there is very little interaction among the expatriate managers in the different subsidiaries, and they tend to see themselves as part of the parent company temporarily on assignment in a foreign company. One result of these differences is that expatriate managers in Matsushita are far more likely to take a custodial approach which resists any local changes to standard products and policies, while expatriate managers in Philips, despite being just as socialized into the overall corporate culture of the company, are much more willing to be advocates of local views and to defend against the imposition of corporate ideas on national organizations.[10] This willingness to 'rock the boat' and openness to experimentation and change is the characteristic that fuels local innovations.

Furthermore, by creating this kind of environment in the national organization, Philips has had little difficulty in attracting very capable local management. In contrast to the experience in many Japanese companies where local managers have felt excluded from a decision-making process that encompasses headquarters management and the local expatriates only, local managers in Philips feel their ideas are listened to and defended in headquarters. This too, creates a supportive environment for local innovations.

Integration of technical and marketing functions within each subsidiary

Historically, the top management in all national subsidiaries of Philips consisted not of an individual CEO but a committee made up of the heads of the technical, commercial, and finance functions. This system of three-headed management had a long history in Philips, stemming from the functional independence of the two Philips brothers, one an engineer and the other a salesman. Although this management philosophy has recently been modified to a system which emphasizes individual authority and account-ability, the long tradition of shared responsibilities and joint decision-making has left a legacy of many different mechanisms for functional integration at multiple levels. These integrative mechanisms within each subsidiary enhance the efficiency of local-for-local innovations in Philips[11] just the same way that various means of cross-functional integration within the corporate head-quarters facilitate centre-for-global innovations in Matsushita.

In most subsidiaries, these integration mechanisms exist at three organizational levels. First, for each project, there is an article team that consists of relatively junior managers belonging to the com-mercial and technical functions. It is the responsibility of this team to evolve product policies and to prepare annual sales plans and budgets. At times, sub-article teams may be formed to supervise day-to-day working, and to carry out special projects, such as pre-paring capital investment plans should major new investments be felt necessary for effectively manufacturing and marketing a new product.

A second tier of cross-functional co-ordination takes place at the product group level, through the group management team, which again consists of both technical and commercial representatives. This team meets once a month to review results, suggest corrective actions, and resolve any interfunctional differences. Keeping control and conflict resolution at this low level facilitates sensitive and rapid responses to initiatives and ideas generated at the local level.

The highest level co-ordination forum within the subsidiary is the senior management committee (SMC) consisting of the top com-mercial, technical, and financial managers in the subsidiary. Acting essentially as a local board, the SMC provides an overall unity of effort among the different functional groups within the local unit, and ensures that the national unit retains primary responsibility for its own strategies and priorities. Again, the effect is to provide local management with a forum in which actions can be decided and issues resolved without escalation for approval or arbitration.

Dispersed resources and decentralized authority

Finally, perhaps the most important facilitator of local innovations in Philips is the dispersal of its organizational assets and resources, and the very high level of dencentralization of authority which respectively enable and empower subsidiary managers to experi-ment and to seek novel solutions to local problems.

The decentralized organization structure and management philo-sophy have deep roots. From its inception in 1891, Philips has recognized the need to expand its operation beyond its small domestic market. In those early days, however, transport and communications barriers forced management to decentralize operations and delegate responsibilities within its far-flung empire. The forces of decentralization were reinforced by the protectionist pressures of the 1930s that made it practically impossible to ship products or components across different countries within Europe. During World War II, even R&D capabilities were dispersed to avoid the possibility of their falling into enemy hands and many corporate managers left Holland reducing the parent company's control of the world-wide operations. For all these historical reasons, Philips' national organizations developed a degree of autonomy and self-sufficiency that was rare among companies of its size and complexity.

It is said that for an innovation to arise, two factors are necessary. First, the innovation must be desirable for the local managers. Second, it must be feasible for them to create it.[12] Dispersed managerial and technological resources and effective integration among them have made local innovations feasible for Philips subsidiaries. Local autonomy and decentralized control over those resources, coupled with the leadership of a highly entrepreneurial group of expatriate managers have made such indications desirable for them.

Making transnational innovations feasible: lessons from L. M. Ericsson

Innovations are created by applying required resources to exploit an opportunity, or to overcome a threat. In multinational corporations, however, the location of the opportunity (or threat) is often different from the location of the appropriate response resources. The transnational innovation processes (locally-leveraged or globally-linked) use linkages among different units of the organization to leverage existing resources and capabilities, irrespective of their locations, to exploit any new opportunity that arises in any part of the dispersed multinational company.

Among the companies we studied, there were several that were in the process of developing such organizational capabilities. A few appeared to have become quite effective in managing the required linkages and processes, and we were able to identify three organizational characteristics that seemed most helpful in facilitating the new integrated innovation processes. The first was an interdependence of resources and responsibilities among organizational units, the second was a set of strong cross-unit integrating devices, and the last was a pervasive management attitude of strong corporate identification and well-developed world-wide perspectives.

Interdependence of resources and responsibilities

Perhaps the most important requirement for facilitating global innovations is a need for the organizational configuration to be based on a principle of reciprocal dependence among units. Such an interdependence of resources and responsibilities breaks down the hierarchy between local and global interests by making the sharing of resources, ideas and opportunities a self-enforcing norm. To illustrate how such a basic characteristic or organizational configuration can influence a company's process of innovation, let us contrast the way in which ITT, NEC and L. M. Ericsson developed the electronic digital switch that would be the core product for each company's telecommunications business in the 1980s and beyond.

From its beginnings, in 1920, as a Puerto Rican telephone company, ITT built its world-wide operation on an objective described in the 1924 annual report as being 'to develop truly national systems operated by the nationals of each company'. For half a century ITT's national 'systems houses', as they were called within the company, committed themselves to meeting local interests and market needs. All but the smallest systems houses were established as fully integrated, self-sufficient units with responsibility for developing, manufacturing, marketing, installing and servicing their own products. All major innovations had their origins in the powerful and independent national companies, and even a product as important to the company's world-wide success as the highly regarded Pentaconta electromechanical switch was developed by ITT's French subsidiary.

These powerful, independent, and entrepreneurial national companies became the source of many important innovations, but management had never been able to co-ordinate or integrate the diverse efforts very effectively. After enormous frustrations in trying to co-ordinate development efforts and technical standards on the company's production in the electromechanical then early electronic (SPC) exchange switches, management recognized that establishing collaborative processes and co-ordinated efforts was all but impossible in an organization in which the key units were so strongly independent and autonomous. Yet the increasing cost of developing a new switch, and the shortening life cycle of successive generations of technology were forcing the company to take a more integrated approach.

The first sign that exchange switches built on a digital technology might replace recently introduced analog signal processing products occurred in the United States in the late 1970s when Northern Telecom's switch started creating what became referred to as 'digital fever' in North America. Despite the fact that ITT's British and French companies held the original patents for the process of sampling analog signals to convert them into digital form, European markets were being converted to ITT's existing analog switch and the local subsidiaries showed no interest in further developing and applying their pioneering digital research. At headquarters, the company's general technical director saw this as an opportunity to seize the initiative and create a company standard for this product that could then be developed in a co-ordinated global fashion. Consequently he assigned a team at the company's small Connecticut research centre to work on the project. But within a year, the Europeans were interested (and concerned) enough to send their own team of engineers to work with the headquarters group on the new System 12 switch. Their market knowledge and development experience allowed them to bend the researchers' global specifications better to reflect European needs. Soon after they convinced the company to take the responsibility for System 12 out of the hands of 'theoretical researchers in Connecticut' and transfer it to 'practical engineers close to the market'.

But the company wanted to ensure that the original work was not dissipated, diverted, and adapted by local systems houses, and created an International Telecommunications Center (ITC) in Brussels to lead, co-ordinate and control the development process of the System 12 switch. But the newly formed group and the staff managers responsible for it soon found they were no match for the powerful systems houses and the well-entrenched line managers who ran them. Although ITC management was able to allocate some development tasks and keep control over some standards, the large systems houses generally refused to rely on others for the development of critical parts of the system or accept standards that did not fit with their view of local needs. As a result, duplication of effort and divergence of specifications began to emerge, and the cost of developing the switch ballooned to over US $1 bn. The biggest problems appeared when the company decided to take System 12 into the US market. In true ITT tradition, the US business wanted to assert its independence and launched a major new R&D effort, despite appeals from the chief technological officer that they risked developing System 13. After years of effort and hundreds of millions of dollars in costs, ITT acknowledged it was withdrawing from the US market. The largest and most successful international telecommunications company in the world was blocked from its home country by the inability to transfer and apply its leading edge technology in a timely fashion. It was a failure that eventually led to ITT's withdrawal from direct involvement in telecommunications.

If effective global innovation was blocked by the extreme independence of the organizational units in ITT, it was impeded in NEC by the strong dependence of national subsidiaries on the parent company. Like ITT, NEC managers first detected 'digital fever' in the US market. The Japanese manager in charge of the US company recognized the importance of this trend early but did not have the resources, the capability or the authority to take much action. His role was one of selling corporate products and developing a beachhead in the US market. In Japan, technical managers were wary about a supposed trend to digitalization that they saw nowhere else world-wide (they called it a passing fad). They were sceptical about the claims of digital's technological superiority, and they were hesitant about beginning developmental work on a new switch that would compete with NEC's existing electromechanical and electronic products.

When the US managers finally were able to elicit sufficient support, the new NEAC 61 digital switch was developed almost entirely by headquarters personnel. Even in deciding which features to design into the new product, the central engineering group tended to discount the requests of the North American sales company and rely on data gathered in their own staff's field trips to US customers. Although the NEAC 61 was regarded as having good hardware, its software was thought to be unadapted to US needs. Sales did not meet expectations.

Both ITT and NEC have recognized the limitations of their independent and dependent organization systems and have begun to adapt them. But the process of building organizational interdependence is a slow and difficult one that must be constantly monitored and adjusted. In our sample of companies, L. M. Ericsson was by far the most consistent and experienced practitioner of creating and managing a delicate balance of inter-unit interdependency. The way in which it did so suggests the value of a constant readjustment of responsibilities and relationships as a way of adapting to changing strategic needs while maintaining a dynamic system of mutual dependence.

Like ITT, Ericsson had built during the 1920s and 1930s a substantial world-wide network of operations sensitive and responsive to local national environments; but like NEC, it had a strong home market base and a parent company technological, manufacturing, and market capability that was available to support those companies. Keeping the balance between and among these units has been a consistent company objective. In the late 1930s, when management became concerned that the growing independence of its offshore companies was causing divergence in technology, duplication of effort, and inefficiency in the sourcing patterns, they pulled sales and distribution control to headquarters and began consolidating responsibilities under product divisions. In the early 1950s, when these divisions showed signs of isolation and short-term focus, corporate staff functions were given more power, particularly in R&D. This led to the company's development of a crossbar switch that was an industry leader. As the product design and manufacturing technology for this product became well understood and fully documented, Ericsson management was able to respond to the demands of increasingly sophisticated and aggressive host governments, and transfer more manufacturing capacity and technological know-how abroad. Because assembly of crossbar switches was so labour intensive, it could often be done more efficiently abroad, and offshore sourcing of components and sub-assemblies increased.

Following half a century of constant ebb and flow in the centralization and decentralization of various responsibilities, Ericsson had no hesitation and little difficulty in adjusting tasks and responsibilities in response to the coming of electronic switching in the 1970s. Development efforts and manufacturing responsibilities were pulled back to Sweden, but where national capabilities, expertise or experience could be useful in the corporate effort, the appropriate local personnel were seconded to headquarters. In this way, the work the Australian subsidiary had done on a digital group selector was incorporated into the company's AXE digital switch. The AXE was designed knowing that local modifications would be necessary. As a modular system with very clear specifications, it allowed national companies to make necessary adaptations without compromising the integrity of the system. Similarly, in manufacturing, Ericsson's global computer-aided design and manufacturing system has allowed the delegation of component design and production to any national unit without the parent losing control.

With such central control, Ericsson has been willing to delegate substantial design, development, and manufacturing responsibilities to its subsidiaries and in recent years, the interdependence of units has increased. Primary responsibility for global development of peripheral products has been delegated (for example, Italy is the centre for transmission system development, Finland has mobile telephones, and Australia develops the rural switch). Further, headquarters has given some of these units responsibility for handling certain export markets (e.g. Italy's role in Africa). Increasingly, the company is moving even advanced software development offshore to subsidiary companies with access to more software engineers than it has in Stockholm.

By changing responsibilities, shifting assets and modifying relationships in response to evolving environmental demands and strategic priorities, Ericsson has maintained a dynamic interdependence between its operating units that has allowed it to develop entrepreneurial and innovative subsidiary companies that work within a corporate framework defined by a knowledgeable and creative headquarters group. This kind of interdependence, while hard to achieve rapidly, is the basis for global innovations.

Inter-unit integrating devices

We have shown how central innovations require strong integrating mechanisms at headquarters, and how local innovations are facilitated by co-ordinative capabilities within national units. The two newer global innovation processes need a different kind of integration process — one that operates across units. Such organizational positions and devices are more difficult to develop and manage than the inter-unit mechanisms, and an examination of the approach taken by L. M. Ericsson may provide some insight into how it can be achieved.

Unlike ITT, where relationship among national companies was often competitive and where headquarter–subsidiary interactions were often of an adversarial nature, L. M. Ericsson has been able to develop an organizational climate that is more co-operative and collaborative. This is essential if units are to work together to develop and implement innovations, but is not easily achieved. There are three important pillars to Ericsson's success in inter-unit integration — a clearly defined and tightly controlled set of operating systems, a people-linking process employing such devices as temporary assignments and joint teams, and inter-unit decision forums, particularly subsidiary boards, where views can be exchanged and differences resolved.

Ericsson management feels strongly that its most effective integrating device is strong central control over key elements of its strategic operation. Unlike ITT, Ericsson has not had strong or sophisticated administrative systems (it only introduced strategic plans in 1983), but its operating systems have been carefully developed. As indicated earlier, AXEs product specifications are tightly controlled and the CAD/CAM systems allow close central co-ordination of manufacturing. Rather than causing a centralization of decision-making, management argues that these strong operating systems allow them to delegate much more freely; knowing that local decisions will not be inconsistent with or detrimental to the overall interests.

But, in addition to strong systems, inter-unit co-operation requires good interpersonal relations, and Ericsson has developed these with a long-standing policy of transferring large numbers of people back and forth between headquarters and subsidiaries.[13] It differs from the more common transfer patterns in both direction and intensity, as a comparison with NEC's transfer process will demonstrate. Where NEC may transfer a new technology through a few key managers, Ericsson will send a team of 50 or 100 engineers for a year or two; while NEC's flow is primarily from headquarters to subsidiary, Ericsson's is a balanced two-way flow with people coming to the parent not only to learn but also to bring their expertise; and while NEC's transfers are predominantly Japanese, Ericsson's multidirectional process involves all nationalities.

Australian technicians seconded to Stockholm in the mid-1970s to bring their experience with digital switching into the development of AXE developed enduring relationships that helped in the subsequent joint development of a rural switch in Australia a decade later. Confidences built when an Italian team of 40 spent 18 months in Sweden to learn about electronic switching in the early 1970s provided the basis for greater decentralization of AXE software development and a delegated responsibility for developing the transmission systems.

But any organization in which there are shared tasks and joint responsibilities will require additional decision-making and conflict-resolving forums. In Ericsson, often divergent objectives and interests of the parent company and the local subsidiary are exchanged in the national company's board meetings. Unlike many companies whose local boards are pro forma bodies whose activities are designed solely to satisfy national legal requirements, Ericsson uses its local boards as legitimate forums for communicating objectives, resolving differences and making decisions. At least one and often several senior corporate managers are members of each board and subsidiary board meetings become an important means for co-ordinating activities and channelling local ideas and innovations across national lines.

National competence, world-wide perspective

If there is one clear lesson from ITT's experience with the development of its System 12, it is that a company cannot innovate globally if its managers identify primarily with local parochial interests and objectives. But NEC's experience shows that when management has no ability to defend national perspectives and respond to local opportunities, global innovation is equally difficult. One of the important organizational characteristics Ericsson has been able to develop over the years has been a management attitude that is simultaneously locally sensitive, and globally conscious.

At the Stockholm headquarters, managers will emphasize the importance of developing strong country operations, not only to capture sales that require responsiveness to national needs, but also to tap into the resources that are available through world-wide operation. Coming from a small home country where it already hires over a third of the graduating electrical and electronics engineers, Ericsson is very conscious of the need to develop skills and capture ideas wherever they operate in the world. But, at the same time, local managers see themselves as part of the world-wide Ericsson group rather than as independent, autonomous units. Constant transfers and working on joint teams over the years has helped broaden many manager's perspectives from local to global, but giving local units systemwide mandates for products has confirmed their identity with the company's world-wide operations.

Managing innovation in the transnational

As we highlighted earlier in the chapter, the challenge of managing innovation in world-wide organizations is two-fold: first, management must enhance the efficiency and effectiveness of each of the different innovation processes and, second, it must create conditions that allow innovations to come about through all the different processes simultaneously.

In the preceding part of the chapter, we have described some of the ways in which managers can achieve the first of these two tasks. However, to benefit from these specific suggestions we have made, managers must also ensure that efforts to strengthen one of the innovation processes do not drive out the others. And this task of achieving simultaneity of the different innovation processes often proves to be the great challenge because of the dilemma that organizational attributes which facilitate one of the innovation processes often tend to impede the others.

The organizational dilemma

Consider, for example, the organizational attributes that are required to facilitate local-for-local and centre-for-global innovations. As we have illustrated, the former process requires that national subsidiaries have certain slack resources, and the requisite autonomy for deployment of those resources for creating local innovations. But such independent and resource-rich subsidiaries also tend to become victims of what Rosabeth Kanter, the Harvard sociologist and author of best selling *Changemasters* calls the 'entrepreneurial trap' — a mentality in which 'the need to be the source, the originator, leads people to push their own ideas single-mindedly'. This mentality impedes the subsidiary's ability and willingness to adopt centre-for-global innovations. Philips has long suffered from this problem, just as companies like Matsushita have suffered from the reverse problem of sheer incapability or lack the motivation wherein perceived or actual scarcity of slack resources and local authority in the national organizations have led to efficient adoption of centre-for-global innovations, but have constrained the company's ability to facilitate local-for-local innovations.

Overcoming the dilemma: the transnational organization

At the core of this dilemma lies an assumption that managers of most multinational companies make about their international organization: they assume that organizational structure and management processes must be symmetric and homogeneous. This assumption is common to companies with what we have described as the global and the multinational mentalities and appears to be extremely widespread in practice.

Although there are wide differences in importance of operations in major markets like Germany, Japan, or the United States compared with subsidiaries in Argentina, Malaysia, or Nigeria, for example, most multinationals treat their foreign subsidiaries in a remarkably uniform manner. One executive we talked to termed this approach 'the UN model of multinational management'. While the functions carried out by the different subsidiaries may be different, they are administratively created as similar and equal. Thus, it is common to see managers express subsidiary roles and responsibilities in the same general terms, apply their planning and control systems uniformly world-wide, involve country managers to a like degree in product development, and evaluate them against standardized criteria. This norm of symmetry and uniformity is inherent in the family metaphor that multinationals, irrespective of their origin, use persistently: Subsidiaries are children of the parent, and therefore there should be no discrimination – read differentiation – among them.

This symmetrical and homogeneous organizational approach encourages management to envision two roles in the multinational company: a local role for each subsidiary, and a global role for the headquarters. As a result, the relationship between the headquarters and the subsidiaries is also viewed in unidimensional terms. It is assumed that the relationship must be based on either dependence or independence of the subsidiary and, therefore, on either local autonomy or central control.

These assumptions and their administrative consequences constrain the flexibility of most multinational companies and imprison them into an either/or choice between central and local innovations. The very simplicity and clarity in these traditional organizational systems prevent the companies from developing the relatively more complex global innovation processes we have described and from achieving the even more difficult task of facilitating all the different local, central, and global innovation processes simultaneously.

These limitations of the symmetrical and homogeneous mode of operations have become increasingly clear to multinational corporations, and in many of the companies we surveyed, we found managers experimenting with alternative ways to manage their world-wide operations. And as we reviewed these various approaches, we saw a new pattern emerging that suggested a significantly different model of international organization based on some important new assumptions and beliefs. This organizational model we call the transnational and we have described the key characteristics of such organizations in a separate paper.[14] However, one attribute of the transnational – its ability and willingness to explicitly differentiate the roles and responsibilities of its different national subsidiaries – is of particular importance to our present discussions since this attribute appears to allow such companies to break out of central/local dilemma and to create an organizational infrastructure for managing central, local, and global innovations simultaneously and effectively.

Differentiated subsidiary roles for different innovation processes

In most industries, a few key markets lead the industry's evolution. They are often the largest, most sophisticated and most competitive markets in which the nature of impending global changes is first mirrored. Results of competitive battles in such markets usually have a great deal of influence on the future world-wide competitive positions of firms. In the telecommunications switching business, for example, the United States is perhaps the principal lead market in the world. In the consumer electronics industry, in contrast, Japan, the United States, and a few of the major European markets share the lead position.

These are the markets that provide the stimuli for most global products and processes of a multinational company. Local innovations in such markets become useful elsewhere as the environmental characteristics that stimulated such innovations diffuse to other locations. Similarly, the technological, competitive, and market-sensing processes that are required as inputs for centre-for-global and globally-linked innovations must also be provided by local operations in these lead markets. Relatively speaking, the sensing task for global innovations is much less intense in other 'follower' markets in which the company operates.

While the sensing opportunities lie outside the company and are determined by the strategic importance of different national environments, capabilities required to respond to the stimuli through development of new products or processes lie inside the organization and are determined by the company's administrative history. Further, while environmental opportunities are footloose, shifting from location to location, organizational resources are not easily transferable within the same company due to various administrative, regulatory and other reasons. The result is a situation of environment-resource mismatches: The company accumulates excessive resources in some environments that are relatively non-critical, and very limited or even no resources in some critical lead markets that offer the greatest opportunities and challenges.

Such environment-resource mismatches are pervasive in multinationals. Ericsson has significant technological capabilities in Australia and Italy – relatively insignificant markets in the global telecommunications business – but almost no presence in the United States which not only represents almost 40 per cent of the world's telecommunications equipment demand, but is the source of much of the new technology. Procter and Gamble is strong in the United States and Europe, but not in Japan where important consumer product innovations have occurred recently and where a major global competitor is emerging. Matsushita has appropriate technological and managerial resources in Japan and the United States, but not in Europe – a huge market, and home of arch rival, Philips.

These differences in external environments and internal capabilities imply some significant differences in the contributions that different subsidiaries can potentially make to the different innovational processes we have described. Thus, instead of either choosing to facilitate innovativeness or adoption in all subsidiaries, or seeking to find the non-existent grand compromise between the two, managers of transnational companies allocate different roles to their different operating units, based on the contributions the units can make to the different innovation processes. While none of the companies we studied had developed an explicit set of criteria for allocation of such differentiated roles, Figure 9.1 shows a simple framework for such differentiation that reflects some of the norms that appeared implicitly to guide their various approaches.[15]

Figure 9.1   Managing innovations in the transnational organization

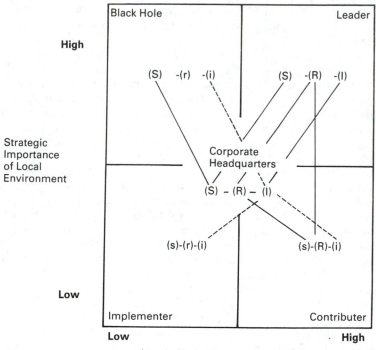

Some subsidiaries which are located in challenging and stimulating environments and which possess high levels of technological and managerial capabilities, are allocated the role we label as

strategic leaders and these subsidiaries serve as the transnational's innovative spark plugs.[16] They create local-for-local innovations, many of which are subsequently diffused to the rest of the organization as locally-leveraged innovations as the new technologies, tastes or business practices that first emerge in their environment diffuse around the world. Similarly, like the German organization of P&G that led the development of Vizir, they play key roles in creating globally-linked innovations. They also contribute to centre-for-global innovations, providing headquarters managers with the early warning signals of an emerging market need or opportunity and by serving as a learning ground for central managers to test their ideas and fine-tune their responses.

If, however, the subsidiary in a critical market does not have adequate internal capabilities to exercise the lead role, it can be designated the sensor role of serving as a scanning and monitoring unit to direct the global innovation processes. Such, for example, has been the role played by the Japanese subsidiaries of many North American companies, and of the US subsidiaries of many Japanese companies.

National subsidiaries with relatively high levels of resources in nonstrategic markets can, in the traditional organization forms of the multinational, become a major source of disruption for the global strategies of the companies. The normal tendency in such units is to utilize the excess resources to demand and justify greater local differentiation and autonomy.[17] In the transnational organization, these subsidiaries are allocated the contributor role through which these excess resources are channelled to global rather than local tasks. Specific tasks with regard to centre-for-global or globally-linked innovations are farmed out to them and their primary contribution to the company's innovation processes becomes one of response rather than sensing.

Finally, organizations with relatively low levels of resources in relatively non-strategic markets are allocated the implementer role, in which their principal task is seen as one of adapting and implementing central and global innovations in the local context, creating in this process such local innovations as the adaptation task may require.

It is important to note, however, that these roles apply to specific businesses, functions, and product lines only, and not to all the activities of the subsidiary. Thus, a particular subsidiary may play a lead role for a specific product and an implementer or contributor role for others. For example, the UK subsidiary of Philips plays the lead role for the company's teletext TV sets, but an implementer role in the compact disc player business.[18]

Recognition of these differences in the potentials of its different organizational units to contribute to the different innovation processes lead to a set of clear norms in the transnational for deciding where and at what scale they should build the sensing, response, and implementation capabilities that are required to support the different innovation processes. In Figure 9.1 we provide a schematic representation of how such capabilities may be configured and linked within the transnational organization so as to enhance the overall innovation capacity of the company.

In the implementer subsidiaries, each of these capabilities may be built only to the extent that they are required to execute local tasks, including the task of creating and implementing local-for-local innovations. Such local level capabilities are represented by small letters in the diagram with (s), (r), and (i) standing for sensing, response, and implementation, respectively.

In the leader subsidiaries, in contrast, each of these capabilities is required in global scale to support its global roles. Recall, however, that these roles apply to specific businesses, functions, or product lines only, and not for all the activities of the subsidiary, and the global scale sensing, response, and implementation capabilities (represented by capital letters, (S), (R), and (I) respectively) are built in these units only with regard to the specific activities for which they carry the leadership role. Thus, if the French national organization in Philips is given this role for the 'smart card' business, the unit is made responsible for scanning the world-wide technological, competitive, and market environments of this business and not just the environment in France. Similarly, adequate development resources are also provided within the subsidiary to support its 'world product mandate', and appropriate production and marketing capabilities are also established locally so that the unit can serve as a world-scale source for the product as well as the driver for the company's global strategy for this business.

The sensor is not a viable strategic role, and the company's long-term goal should be to build up adequate resources and capabilities in such subsidiaries so that they can assume a leadership role in the relevant business. This process, however, is difficult and requires a long period of time. In the meanwhile such subsidiaries can and must serve as key sources of intelligence; collecting, interpreting, and circulating critical technological and competitive information on developments in its environment. Given the strategic importance and complexity of its local environment, this task requires a high level of sensing capability. Thus, while its response and implementation capabilities may be built up over time, advanced scanning capabilities must be built in such locations on high priority to support their global sensor roles.

The innovation process, however, requires that these dispersed and differentiated capabilities be interlinked so that the sensing, response, and implementation processes can function both sequentially and interactively. Thus, the sensing capabilities of the leader and the sensor subsidiaries must be linked by establishing mechanisms to ensure that intelligence acquired by the latter is passed on to the former. Similarly, the response capabilities of the contributor must also be integrated with those of the leader so as to capture the excess slack in the contributor organization to support the global level tasks that are carried out by the leader.[19] Even the implementation capabilities of the different subsidiaries may be interlinked, or they may be connected via the headquarters since all subsidiaries other than the leader carry only local-level responsibilities for this task.

In our description of the system we have assumed a situation where a national subsidiary plays the leadership role. However, this is not always necessary and the headquarters can and must play the leadership role for certain businesses, and in those cases the linkage among the dispersed sensing, response, and implementation capabilities must be established with the headquarters playing the nodal role. Even otherwise, in most companies, the centre retains the responsibilities for overall strategic direction and co-ordination, and has advanced sensing, response, and implementation capabilities either by design or as a result of historical evolution. Therefore, even for those activities for which the leadership role is allocated to a national subsidiary, the central capabilities must be linked with those of the leader to sustain the overall co-ordination role of the headquarters.

Let us illustrate how such a system might function. In L. M. Ericsson, the Australian subsidiary carries the leadership role for small rural switches built and marketed by the company. For this business, both the headquarters and the Italian subsidiary of the company act as sensors and as contributors. To support this way of operations, the Australian subsidiary has built a highly developed scanning capability and closely monitors world-wide developments in this particular business. The company also has a centralized scanning unit in Stockholm, and this unit passes on to Australia any information on the rural switch market that may come to its attention. Similarly, some of the development engineers in Italy are allocated specific tasks for designing rural switches and they, in effect, work for the Australian subsidiary, despite being located physically in Italy. The development process is co-ordinated through the company's CAD/CAM system which serves as the linking device for the response task. The headquarters co-ordinates the design activities being carried out in Italy and Australia, but the Australian subsidiary drives the entire process and considers itself responsible for the overall task of designing and developing new products to support this small but profitable business of the company.

Conclusion: organizational capability is key

In the course of our study, we found that managers in many companies see the task of managing innovations as one of committing the greatest possible resources for creating new products and processes. This view implied that creating innovations was a specialized function performed in isolation from the mainstream of company activities and that the role of top management was one of resource allocation. Innovation could be improved if R&D budgets were increased, or, if the allocation of funds was made more efficient.

The emerging transnational companies, on the other hand, take a very different view of this task. More than increasing resources or developing new capabilities, we found that managers in these companies consider the challenge to be one of enhancing and leveraging the company's existing assets; rather than focusing the innovative responsibility on a specialized group, they see the task to be one of involving all units of the organization in the process; and instead of developing one highly efficient process of innovation, they recognize the need to manage and integrate multiple processes.

In short, the challenge is much more one of developing organizational capabilities than one related to technological skills or resource allocation. Indeed, the two new transnational innovative processes are based on the ability to leverage existing innovative resources and capabilities by capturing synergies in their combined application or gaining scale and scope economies through broader exploitation of innovations. And to provide just one dramatic illustration of how organizational capabilities may triumph over resource commitments, recall that spending well over US $1 bn on the development of its digital switch did not assure ITT success over L. M. Ericsson who spent only a third of that amount.

Notes

1 This research project consisted of three phases. The first aimed at identifying and describing the key challenges that are being faced by managers of multinational corporations and to document 'leading practice' in coping with these challenges. This was also the hypothesis-generating phase and the sample was selected to represent the greatest variety of strategic and organizational situations. We chose three industries: consumer electronics, branded packaged products, and telecommunications switching. Each of these businesses was highly international but represented a very different set of key strategic demands. The first offered the greatest benefits of globalization, the forces of national responsiveness were particularly strong in the second, and the third represented the situation where both global and local forces were strong. Within each industry, we selected a group of firms that represented the greatest variety of administrative heritages including differences in nationality, internationalization history, and corporate culture. Philips, Matsushita, and GE in consumer electronics; Kao, Procter and Gamble, and Unilever in branded packaged products, and ITT, NEC, and L. M. Ericsson in telecommunications switching were the obvious choices.

Figure 9.2   Sample: choice of industries and companies

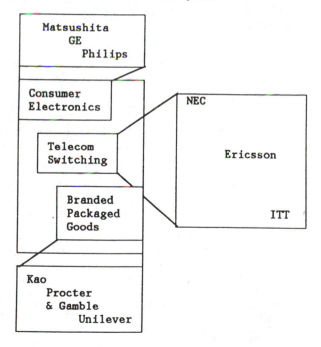

Figure 9.2 provides a schematic representation of our sample in terms of the strategic characteristics of the industries, and the competitive postures of the firms. In this representation, we adopt the Global Integration–National Responsiveness framework proposed by Prahalad (1975) and subsequently developed by Doz (1979), Prahalad and Doz (1981), and Doz, Bartlett, and Prahalad (1981). For each box, the vertical axis represents the strength of globalizing forces in the industry or the extent of global integration in the company's strategic posture, and the horizontal axis represents the need for national responsiveness in the business or the extent of local differentiation in the company's overall competitive strategy (for a more detailed description of the strategic demands of these industries and administrative heritages of the companies, see Bartlett and Ghoshal 1987:a).

In each of these companies, we tried to identify as many specific cases of innovations as possible, and to document the participants' views on the organizational factors that facilitated or impeded the innovation process. To this end, we interviewed about 230 managers in these companies, both at their corporate headquarters and also in their national subsidiaries in the US, UK, Germany, France, Italy, Taiwan, Singapore, Japan, Australia, and Brazil. None of the interviews lasted less than an hour, and some took as long as three to five hours. We also collected and analysed internal documents relating to the histories of these innovations. This effort led to identification of thirty-eight innovation cases which form the key data base for this article (these innovations have been listed and briefly described in Ghoshal 1987b).

In the next phase of the project, we conducted detailed questionnaire surveys in three of the nine companies. The principle objective of the survey was to carry out a preliminary test of some of the hypotheses that were generated from the first phase of clinical research, also to define the hypotheses more precisely, and to develop suitable instruments for testing them more rigorously. Approximately 160 managers from NEC, Philips, and Matsushita participated in the survey, the results of which broadly confirmed most of the ideas that were generated from the first phase of the study (see Ghoshal and Bartlett 1987a and b).

Finally, in the third phase of the study, the hypotheses were tested through a large sample mailed questionnaire survey that yielded usable data from sixty-six of the largest US and European multinational corporations.

The overall findings of the project are being reported in our book, *Managing Across Borders: The Transnational Solution* (Harvard Business School Press, 1989).

2. This argument is implicit in the Product Cycle Theory proposed by Vernon (1966). It has been stated more explicitly in the internationalization and appropriability theories of foreign direct investment: see Buckley and Casson (1976), Rugman (1982), and Calvet (1981).

3. See Bartlett (1986) for descriptions of centralized hub and decentralized federation modes of multinational operations. In the centralized hub

mode, the key assets and capabilities of the company and key value-adding activities, such as product development and manufacturing, are retained at the centre, or are tightly controlled from the centre. The national subsidiaries of centralized hub organizations act primarily as delivery pipelines to supply centrally manufactured global products to the local markets, and their roles are limited to local sales and service tasks. In contrast, in companies operating in the decentralized federation mode, key assets and capabilities of the multinational are dispersed among the different subsidiaries, each of which is allowed to develop as a self-contained and autonomous operation that is able to respond to local demands and opportunities. In a loose sense, the centralized hub mode supports what Porter (1986) calls a 'pure global' strategy, while the decentralized federation corresponds to what he describes as the 'multidomestic' strategy.

4 See Levitt (1983) for an interesting, if somewhat provocative, discussion of these two mentalities.

5 Vernon (1980) has highlighted the potential advantages that could accrue to a multinational through such a global scanning capability. The same point has also been made by Kogut (1983) and a number of other scholars in the field of international management.

6 The Not-Invented-Here (NIH) syndrome refers to the resistance of managers to accept ideas or solutions that have been generated elsewhere, and not by them. For a discussion and elaboration of this syndrome, see Katz and Allen (1982).

7 Westney and Sakakibara (1985) have observed a similar system of internal quasi-markets governing the interface between R&D and operating units in a number of other Japanese companies.

8 See Westney and Sakakibara (1985) for a more detailed discussion of these transitions in the careers of research personnel in Japanese companies, and for a comparison of American and Japanese practices in this regard.

9 The organizational form we have described as the decentralized federation shares many common features with the mother-daughter organization that Franko (1976) described as representative of many large European multinationals. Hedlund (1984) showed that national subsidiaries of such companies typically develop strong and entrepreneurial local management teams and also accumulate relatively high levels of local resources – two attributes that we propose are key to the ability of such companies to foster local-for-local innovations.

10 See Van Mannen and Schein (1979) for a rich and theory-grounded discussion on how such differences in socialization processes and career systems can influence managers' attitudes towards change and innovation.

11 Much of the earlier research on organizational innovation has been focused on innovations that are conceived, created, and implemented within individual sub-units of large and multi-unit organizations. Burns and Stalker (1961), for example, state this explicitly: 'The twenty concerns which were subject of these studies were not all separately

constituted business companies . . . (some of them) were small parts of the parent organization. . . . This is why we have used "concern" as a generic term.' Other researchers have similarly observed a district sales office of General Electric, or a department in the headquarters of 3M, or a divisional data processing office of Polaroid, but not the overall configuration of any of these companies. In essence, therefore, these studies have focused on what we call local-for-local innovations. And most of them have identified internal integration, local slack and decentralized authority as key factors that facilitate such innovations in organizations that have been variously described as 'organic', 'integrative', or simply 'excellent' (see, for example, Burns and Stalker 1962; Peters and Waterman 1982; Kanter 1983). To this extent, our findings regarding the factors that make local innovations efficient fully conform to the conclusions reached by earlier researchers. A major point of departure in our study, however, is that we view such local innovations as one of many different processes through which innovations may come about in complex organizations and suggest that the organizational factors that facilitate the different innovation processes are not only different, but may also be mutually contradictory.

12 See Mohr (1969).

13 The use of personnel transfers as an integration mechanism in multinational companies has been highlighted by many scholars, most notably by Edstrom and Galbraith (1977).

14 See Bartlett (1986) for a broad description of the transnational organization. Subsequently, some key attributes of such organizations have been described and illustrated in Bartlett and Ghoshal (1987:b). Based on their own research in a wide range of companies, a number of other researchers have also identified this emerging trend of a very different organizational model being adopted by some major multinational companies around the world – a model that has been variously described as the multi-focal organization (Prahalad and Doz 1987), the hierarchy (Hedlund 1986) and the horizontal organization (White and Poynter in this volume). While there are some considerable differences among these different organizational models, there are also some significant similarities. In essence, all these observations point towards the emergence of a more complex organizational form in multinational companies, with significantly higher levels of internal differentiation and integration that are supported through the simultaneous use of a wide variety of structures and management processes.

15 Refer to Bartlett and Ghoshal (1986) for a more detailed description of these different roles of national subsidiaries and for some suggestion on how these roles can be allocated and managed.

16 Rugman and Poynter (1982) have observed a similar phenomenon in the trend toward assigning 'global product mandates' to mature national subsidiaries.

17 The potential of such a disruptive role being played by resource-rich subsidiaries in noncritical environments has been highlighted by White

and Poynter (1984) based on their study of the Canadian subsidiaries of a number of large multinational corporations.

18 This is an extremely important point that we have elaborated in Bartlett and Ghoshal (1986) and therefore do not discuss in this paper. If the roles are not differentiated by product lines or businesses, a few subsidiaries will come to play the lead role in general while others will become implementers for all tasks. This can have some adverse motivational consequences, not unlike those described by Haspeslagh (1982) for companies that embraced the portfolio concept uncritically and allocated star roles to some businesses and cash cow, question mark, or dog roles to others.

19 The response capability can be of many different kinds: research and development, manufacturing, marketing, and general management competencies are but some of the capabilities that may be required to respond to a specific situation. In the specific context of R&D capabilities, the need for such linkages among dispersed facilities has been emphasized by Håkanson (see his paper, chapter 10 of this volume) and also by Ronstadt (1977).

References

Bartlett, C. A. (1986) 'Building and managing the transnational: the new organizational challenge', in M. E. Porter (ed.), *Competition in Global Industries*, Boston: Harvard Business School Press.

Bartlett, C. A. and Ghoshal, S. (1986) 'Tap your subsidiaries for global reach', *Harvard Business Review*, vol. 64, No. 6, November–December.

—— (1987a) 'Managing across borders: new strategic requirements', *Sloan Management Review*, Summer.

—— (1987b) 'Managing across borders: new organizational responses', *Sloan Management Review*, Fall.

Buckley, P. J. and Casson, M. (1976) *The Future of Multinational Enterprise*, London: Macmillan.

Burns, T. and Stalker, G. M. (1961) *The Management of Innovation*, London: Tavistock.

Calvert, A. L. (1981) 'A synthesis of foreign direct investment theories and theories of the multinational firm', *Journal of International Business Studies*, Spring–Summer.

Doz, Y. L. (1979) *Government Control and Multinational Strategic Management*, New York: Praeger.

Doz, Y. L., Bartlett, C. A., and Prahalad, C. K. (1981) 'Global competitive pressures and host country demands: managing tensions in MNCs', *California Management Review*, Spring.

Drucker, P. F. (1985) *Innovation and Entrepreneurship*, New York: Harper & Row.

Edstrom, E. and Galbraith, J. R. (1977) 'Transfer of managers as a coordination and control strategy in multinational organizations', *Administrative Science Quarterly*, June.

Franko, L. G. (1976) *The European Multinationals*, London: Harper & Row.

Ghoshal, S. and Bartlett, C. A. (1987a) 'Innovation processes in multinational corporations', unpublished manuscript, Fontainebleau, France: INSEAD.

(1987b) 'Creation, adoption, and diffusion of innovations by subsidiaries of multinational corporations', unpublished manuscript, Fontainebleau, France: INSEAD.

Haspeslagh, P. (1982) 'Portfolio planning: uses and limits', *Harvard Business Review*, (January–February): 58–73.

Hedlund, G. (1984) 'Organization in-between: the evolution of the mother-daughter structure of managing foreign subsidiaries in Swedish MNCs', *Journal of International Business Studies*, Fall, vol. 15, No. 2.

(1986) 'The hypermodern MNC – a heterarchy?', *Human Resource Management*, Spring, vol. 25, No. 1.

Kanter, R. M. (1983) *The Change Masters*, New York: Simon & Schuster.

Katz, R. and Allen, T. J. (1982) 'Investigating the not invented here (NIH) Syndrome: a look at the performance, tenure, and communication patterns of 50 R&D project groups', *R&D Management*, 12.

Kogut, B. (1983) 'Foreign direct investment as a sequential process', in C. P. Kindelberger and D. B. Audretsch (eds), *The Multinational Corporation in the 1980s*, Cambridge, MA: MIT Press.

Levitt, T. (1983) 'The globalization of markets', *Harvard Business Review*, May–June: 92–102.

Mohr, L. B. (1969) 'Determinants of innovation in organizations', *American Political Science Review*, 63: 111–28.

Peters, T. J. and Waterman, R. H. (1982) *In Search of Excellence*, New York: Harper & Row.

Porter, M. E. (1986) 'Competition in global industries: a conceptual framework', in M. E. Porter (ed.), *Competition in global industries*, Boston: Harvard Business School Press.

Prahalad, C. K. (1975) 'The strategic process in a multinational corporation', unpublished doctoral dissertation, Graduate School of Business Administration, Harvard University, Boston.

Prahalad, C. K. and Doz, Y. L. (1981) 'An approach to strategic control in MNCs', *Sloan Management Review*, 22, No. 4, Summer.

(1987) *The Multinational Mission: Balancing Local Demands and Global Vision*, New York: Free Press.

Ronstadt, R. C. (1977) *Research and Development Abroad by US Multinationals*, New York: Praeger.

Rugman, A. M. and Poynter, T. A. (1982) 'World product mandate: how will multinationals respond?', *Business Quarterly*, October.

Van Mannen, J. and Schien, E. H. (1979) 'Toward a theory of organizational socialization', in B. Shaw (ed.), *Research in Organizational Behavior*, JAI Press.

Westney, D. E. and Sakakibara, K. (1985) 'The role of Japan-based R&D in global technology strategy', *Technology in Society*, No. 7.

White, R. E. and Poynter, T. A. (1984) 'Strategies for foreign-owned subsidiaries in Canada', *Business Quarterly*, Summer.

Vernon, R. (1966) 'International investment and international trade in the

product cycle', *Quarterly Journal of Economics*, May.
Vernon, R. (1980) 'Gone are the cash cows of yesteryear', *Harvard Business Review*, November–December.

Chapter ten

International decentralization of R&D – the organizational challenges

Lars Håkanson

Introduction

For a considerable time, conventional wisdom has held that multi-national corporations tend to centralize R&D to the home country, in the vicinity of major production units and the corporate head office. However, empirical evidence is mounting to suggest that this may no longer be so. Indeed, in many multinational companies, foreign volumes and shares of R&D expenditures seem to be rapidly increasing.

In most MNCs, foreign R&D volumes tended in the past to be low and directed mainly to local markets. As a rule, foreign R&D units enjoyed relative freedom and were allowed to operate without much costly co-ordination. Today, companies face new pressures for international co-ordination and control of R&D. Co-ordination is required to avoid duplication of effort, to reduce product differentiation, to facilitate technology transfer and to ensure the technical and market compatibility of products and components developed at different locations but sold as parts of total systems.

The increasing geographical decentralization of R&D has major ramifications not only for the organization and control of the R&D function *per se* but also for the design of overall corporate structures and control systems. Indeed, in many companies, these developments reinforce an on-going transformation of strategic modes of operation.

Drawing on the results of a study of international R&D management in four Swedish MNCs (Håkanson and Zander 1986), this paper outlines some of the changes being implemented to meet the emerging organizational challenges and speculates about their possible consequences. The patterns observed are believed to be reasonably typical for that significant portion of Swedish industry which is organized by highly internationalized MNCs with a moderate degree of product diversification, selling technologically advanced systems and products, primarily on industrial markets. Moreover, Swedish companies share many characteristics with MNCs based in other European countries (Franko 1976; Hedlund and Åman 1984). Hence, it is reasonable to assume that similar tendencies operate also in other companies, especially those with small home markets.

Background

During the last two decades, Swedish MNCs – both inadvertently and by design – moved away from the traditional 'decentralized federation' type of organization. Slowly, companies moved away from 'polycentric' attitudes and modes of operation towards Perlmutter's (1969) 'geocentric' ideal. In Bartlett's (1986) terminology, they were increasingly approaching 'integrated network' structures. Whereas in the past, intra-group linkages largely consisted of financial flows and technology transfers between the parent and individual subsidiaries, complex flows of technology, finance, people, and materials now tie subsidiaries both to one another and to the parent. Several forces jointly brought about this change:

International rationalization of production

With the establishment of free trade within the European Communities and the European Free Trade Association, subsidiaries originally set up as miniature replica plants to serve national markets were able to serve larger market areas. Concurrently, Swedish companies were confronting new environmental forces. Technological maturity and intensified competition reduced the possibilities of obtaining premium prices by means of differentiation. To maintain profit margins, costs had to be reduced through more efficient exploitation of economies of scale and specialization in production, marketing, and logistics. (Cf. Doz 1978; Flaherty 1986).

In consequence, many Swedish companies concentrated manufacture of certain products or components to specialized factories. Frequently, such specialized units were given continental, or sometimes global, responsibility not only for production but also for R&D and marketing relating to its area of specialization. Such changes were sometimes reflected in formal organization structures, e.g. product divisions headquartered abroad – but this seems to be the exception rather than the rule.

International rationalization of production resulted in a dramatic

Figure 10.1 Material flows 1955 and 1985 in a major Swedish multinational company

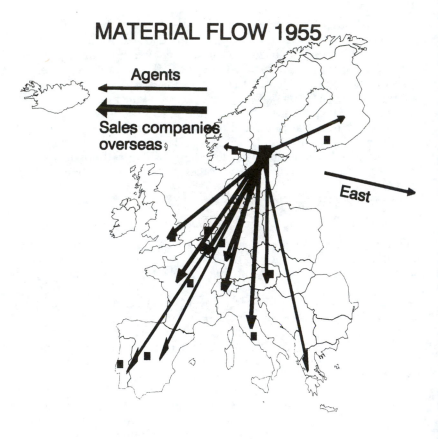

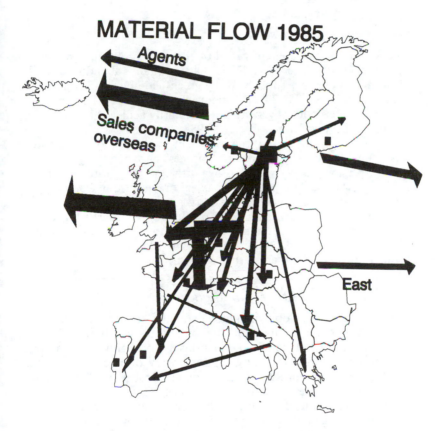

MATERIAL FLOW 1985

increase in the volume of intra-group cross border flows of goods and materials (Figure 10.1). However, it also brought both geographical and organizational decentralization of strategically significant decisions and functions. Technical know-how and other strategic expertise were no longer solely in the realm of the corporate head office, inducing a much higher degree of subsidiary involvement not only in implementation, but also in the formulation of corporate strategy.

Growth through acquisitions

These tendencies were reinforced by the growth strategies pursued. By the 1970s, Swedish MNCs had virtually abandoned their historical preference for growth by greenfield investments (Hörnell and Vahlne 1986: 35–37). On increasingly mature and competitive markets, international growth was primarily achieved by means of acquisitions (Swedenborg, *et al.*, 1988).

Although acquired entities were in various ways integrated into the overall organization, this process hastened the geographical dispersion of R&D and other strategic corporate functions. Often – whether for political reasons or because it would entail unnecessary waste of valuable resources – acquired competencies in R&D, technologically advanced production or marketing could neither be abandoned nor transferred to the parent. Instead, companies were becoming increasingly dependent on foreign sources of know-how and other strategic assets.

Other forces for R&D decentralization

The granting of 'global product mandates' as part of an international rationalization of production and the addition of foreign R&D laboratories through acquisitions are probably the two most important factors accounting for the observed increase in volume and share of foreign R&D (Håkanson and Nobel 1989). However, several other forces strengthen this tendency:

The spontaneous development of foreign subsidiaries has tended to widen the geographical basis for the creation of firm, specific advantages. Foreign manufacturing units, originally set up as mere market outlets, in time acquire their own technical, managerial and marketing expertise. Thus, engineering capabilities acquired to perform routine technical activities – service, maintenance and customization of products to individual buyer needs – often evolve into proper R&D. In the words of Steele (1975: 212), 'there is an almost irresistible creepage from production engineering upstream into design and development'. For entrepreneurial subsidiary managers this is a means both to exploit local market opportunities and to attract and retain qualified technical personnel (Ronstadt 1978, Håkanson 1981).

Before being taken over by another Swedish group, a Swedish electrical engineering company with extensive international operations had suffered a long period of financial difficulties. As R&D had been cut back, foreign subsidiaries slowly found the stream of new technology from Sweden drying up. In response to competitors' introduction of new products, several subsidiary managers started shifting engineering capacity from technical service and customization into proper R&D.

Historically, in consequence of loose control systems and high subsidiary autonomy, local R&D capabilities could often be established without the explicit consent of headquarters. Today, tight labour market conditions for qualified engineers make it increasingly necessary to exploit such technical capacity, regardless of location.

It is estimated that two major Swedish companies, ASEA and Ericsson, could alone recruit 150 per cent of all electronics engineer graduates in Swedish. Although electronics is an extreme example, in other expanding areas such as biotechnology, problems are similar. Thus, Astra, a major Swedish pharmaceutical company, recently announced the establishment of a biotechnological research unit in India, tapping into the large pool of underutilized technical expertise available in this country.

Furthermore, new technologies are not everywhere available but grow in 'pockets of innovation' around the world. Some technology-based companies have therefore established R&D units abroad to act as strategic 'listening posts'. Others have done so in order to establish closer ties to technically demanding and risk-willing customers, not present on the home market.

In the Swedish gas company AGA, one of the seven companies that dominate the world gas industry, R&D have traditionally been concentrated to corporate laboratories outside Stockholm. The development effort is directed to finding new applications for industrial gases. R&D projects are, as a rule, carried out in close cooperation with customers. In consequence, AGA's R&D capabilities closely mirror the structure of Swedish industry, with superior know-how of gas applications in the paper and pulp industry, mechanical engineering, etc.

On the other hand, AGA commands only weak capabilities in industries not well developed in Sweden. Recently, this fact led AGA to neglect for a long time developments in the electronics industry, where gas applications were becoming increasingly important. Recognizing the danger of a too narrow focus on the Swedish market, AGA has begun to expand R&D in some selected subsidiaries, notably in the U.S.

Differentiation of control

The developments outlined above have tended to strengthen the capabilities of foreign subsidiaries in relation to headquarters. However, the process has affected some subsidiaries more than others, increasing the diversity of foreign subsidiary 'roles'. This makes it increasingly impossible to run foreign subsidiaries according to standard systems; incentives, control systems and degrees of autonomy must be differentiated.

The manager of the Italian subsidiary of a major Swedish engineering company has in less than 10 years, in stiff competition with a major U.S. multinational, captured some 60 per cent of the market. In the process, with the aid of a local financier, the Italian subsidiary has grown to become 'a group within the group', encompassing several companies, one dedicated solely to R&D. By virtue of his success – the Italian operations are extremely profitable – the local subsidiary manager commands a degree of autonomy envied by his colleagues in sister companies around the world. As perceived at headquarters, the issue is not how to control activities in the subsidiary, but how to exploit its entrepreneurial capability to the benefit of the group as a whole.

As emphasized by Bartlett and Ghoshal (1986), systems and procedures for the management of foreign operations must be designed so as to allow for differences in local capabilities and strategic importance. This is one prerequisite for the competence and entrepreneurial initiatives of foreign subsidiaries to be efficiently exploited.

The need for organizational differentiation is reinforced by new strategic imperatives. Historically, Swedish companies tended to pursue strategies emphasizing 'national responsiveness' to local customer needs and government regulations. Now, they are increasingly forced to pursue 'multi-focal strategies', i.e. attempting to increase efficiency through 'multinational integration', while maintaining a high degree of local responsiveness (Doz 1986).

The imperatives for differentiated control systems are strong and increasing. However, such systems inherently threaten the ability of corporate management to maintain an overview of the total activities of the group. Unless coupled with strong integrating mechanisms, differentiation can easily lead to corporate 'atomization', with units acting without co-ordination and common goals.

A model of organizational evolution

The trends outlined above, implying a continuing geographical decentralization of R&D and strategic decision-making, can be seen as a logical extension of international growth processes dating back to the beginning of the century (Figure 10.2). Combinations of internal and external forces have led companies to locate increasing parts − sometimes whole links − of their value chains abroad.

In Swedish MNCs, mother-daughter structures, with subsidiaries reporting directly to the head office, were the prevailing mode of organization for many decades. The inherited model of management was characterized by strong and highly autonomous subsidiaries, loosely co-ordinated through informal networks of personal contacts between corporate top management and the general managers of major subsidiaries (Hedlund and Åman 1984).

However, stagnating global demand and increasing competitive pressures on maturing product-markets forced corporations to increase efficiency. Specialization and the pursuit of scale economies in all links of the value chain became an imperative. As outlined above, traditional polycentric structures, with more or less autonomous and self-contained subsidiaries had to be abandoned. Interdependence between units increased as did the volume and complexity of intra-company flows of money, people, goods and information. In combination with growing product diversity and continued international expansion, these tendencies made it increasingly difficult to maintain central control within existing organizational structures.

In an initial response to these problems, many Swedish MNCs attempted to strengthen central control over foreign operations. Tighter and more effective formal control systems were introduced and many companies moved towards 'global structures'. Product divisions were given explicit responsibility for foreign operations, where possible, through separate subsidiary organizations (Hedlund and Åman 1984).

However, results tended to be disappointing. Increasing central control undermined the authority of foreign subsidiary management. Strategic decisions were shifted away from the market place

Figure 10.2   A model of organizational evolution

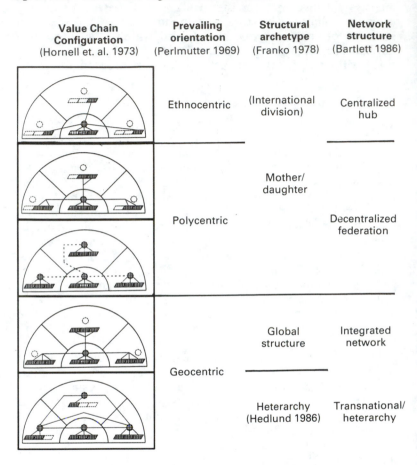

Value Chain Configuration (Hornell et. al. 1973)	Prevailing orientation (Perlmutter 1969)	Structural archetype (Franko 1978)	Network structure (Bartlett 1986)
	Ethnocentric	(International division)	Centralized hub
	Polycentric	Mother/ daughter	Decentralized federation
	Geocentric	Global structure	Integrated network
		Heterarchy (Hedlund 1986)	Transnational/ heterarchy

into home-based product divisions, often with insufficient managerial staff and lacking international experience. Foreign managerial initiatives were stifled while divisional staff were struggling, often unsuccessfully, to introduce central control of diverse international operations.

As the management of a Swedish MNC decided to survey the R&D capabilities of an acquired company with extensive international operations of its own, it was found that central R&D laboratories in Sweden almost totally lacked vital competence in electronics. However, strong R&D units with electronics competence had developed in Canada, Brazil and Italy. Partly due to recruitment problems, it was judged impossible – at least in the short run – to create the required capacity in Sweden.

Faced with the problem of running an R&D organization dispersed over three continents, the company decided to designate the subsidiaries in Canada, Brazil and Italy as 'R&D centers', with group resonsibility for R&D in designated areas. The product group manager at divisional headquarters was charged with coordination.

The response had not been expected. Foreign subsidiary managers felt that their right to take R&D initiatives had been removed. R&D activities were cut back in expectation of central funding and central directives. However, lacking technical capacity and being far removed from the market, the Swedish product division was in no position to provide guidelines or specifications for R&D. Furthermore, no provisions for central funding of R&D had been made.

Within a few months, the policy was totally reversed. Foreign subsidiaries now have explicit responsibility for R&D and authority to embark on any project judged profitable. If the local market should be too small, joint projects with sister companies in other countries can be set up. As a subsidiary decides to embark on a project, others are forbidden by headquarters to pursue similar projects. To facilitate coordination and information exchange between subsidiaries, the Swedish product manager participates in reference group meetings, where R&D projects are monitored. However, he has no formal authority to overrule local decisions.

The introduction of 'global product divisions' and other global structures, usually encompassing some matrix element, solved some of the problems but helped to create others. Increasingly, companies find that traditional hierarchical structures and organization principles no longer work. In consequence, we today see many companies engaged in experimentation, seeking new organizational alternatives.

The process has just started and it would be premature to draw firm conclusions as to its outcome. However, a world-wide organization with tasks and functions allocated among specialized units may suggest decentralizing responsibility for strategy formulation and business development. As suggested by Bartlett (1986) and Hedlund (1986), the MNC of the future may have to be organized along quite different 'heterarchical' or 'transnational' lines – adopting 'geocentric' modes of operations as suggested by Perlmutter (1969).

If the above diagnosis is correct, the themes of the papers collected in this volume attain special interest. It is tempting to hope that, in this instance, academics may be able to contribute to the development of business practice. However, many of the new organizational concepts proposed remain as yet rather speculative, although they do go beyond the common academic habit of codifying practices and ideas already well established in the business community.

The contributions to this book suggest an emerging consensus that something akin to a 'new organizational paradigm' is in the making. However, the exact nature of such a paradigm remains to be more clearly defined. Such clarification requires both development of theoretically well-defined concepts and operationalization of these concepts. Only then will it be possible to arrive at testable propositions that – if supported in empirical research – can be the basis of normative prescriptions.

Thus, in spite of normative overtones, it should be stressed that the framework outlined below should properly be seen as a set of largely unsubstantiated hypotheses. It is the object of planned empirical research to establish its possible validity and to identify modifying contingencies and the character of those systems and procedures that would be needed to sustain it. Nevertheless, it is believed that defining the major functions that must be met in an emerging new 'organizational paradigm' is a step towards the generation of empirically verifiable propositions.

A central aspect of the new 'organizational paradigm' is the reformulation of the roles of corporate management and managers in divisions and subsidiaries. Changing roles and responsibilities, in turn, imply changes in capacities and incentive structures as well as in the mechanisms for co-ordination and control, in short, a new strategic balance. In this context, focusing on the R&D function is particularly enlightening because of its strategic significance.

Changing roles of corporate R&D staff

The degree of control exercised by central R&D managers and the corporate head office will be considerably less than in traditional hierarchical structures with most R&D conducted centrally. Instead of being the main supplier of new technology, finance and strategic initiatives, the central task of the head office may shift towards maintenance of network balance and strategic direction, i.e. ensuring that strategies are pursued that conform to overall corporate goals. Corporate staff must also ensure that systems for co-ordinating a dispersed R&D organization and for maintaining necessary links with other functions are developed and maintained.

Rather than being at the top of the organizational hierarchy, central R&D will tend to become more of a staff unit, providing support to the R&D units of the group. A main aspect will be to facilitate information flows to ensure that important knowledge is shared and technical and marketing competencies are fully exploited.

However, the co-ordinative function does not imply responsibility for the control of world-wide R&D. Corporate staff usually lacks the level of technical competence required for detailed control. If it attempts this task, it runs the risk of developing into little more than an expensive bureaucracy.

The absence of clearly defined line authority can easily place central R&D management in a difficult position, with unclear roles and functions. Hence, it is vital that these be clearly defined and appreciated by the rest of the organization. The central task of top management, of which corporate R&D staff forms a part, is to monitor the portfolio of activities to ensure that efforts are efficiently pursued that support overall corporate strategy. In an integrated heterarchical network, the accomplishment of this task involves the development, monitoring, and maintenance of three interdependent aspects of corporate structure: (1) network balance, (2) strategic direction, and (3) corporate infrastructure.

Maintaining network balance

Headquarters must manage the distribution of tasks and capabilities in the group. This is of vital importance since this distribution will determine the power structure of the organization. The role and domain of each unit must be defined to avoid intra-organizational conflict, uneconomic duplication of effort and unintentional strategic action.

Careful allocation of tasks and functions between units –

matching the technical capability of individual R&D units with areas of specialization – not only determines the distribution of strategic power but is also necessary to minimize the need for close and costly co-ordination.

During World War II, due to government pressure and the difficulty of maintaining control from Sweden, SKF's 12 manufacturing centers developed very independently, each extending its product range to meet military needs and intensifying its own R&D program.

A policy of very loose coordination between major subsidiaries was continued until the end of the 1960s. Then, following the introduction of a divisional organization, a so-called Global Forecasting and Supply System was implemented, permitting world-scale coordination of production.

The product range of the subsidiaries – each traditionally having produced a full range of ball and roller bearings – was reduced, permitting considerable scale economies through longer production runs and automated production processes.

Concurrently, the R&D activities of the group were reorganized. R&D in the major subsidiaries were cut back and concentrated on defined areas of specialization. In 1972, a corporate Engineering Research Centre (ERC) was established near Utrecht in Holland. The Dutch location was chosen not only because of its central location, but also because of the absence of any major manufacturing unit in Holland. In this way ERC, which now conducts some 20 per cent of SKF's R&D, could establish a 'neutral' position in the group. The corporate character of ERC was also emphasized by being incorporated as a joint venture, with the five major European subsidiaries owning equal shares.

It should be emphasized that 'maintenance of network balance' is a dynamic task. Roles and tasks evolve over time as units acquire new technical capabilities and respond to environmental changes. Domains cannot be defined in a 'once-and-for-all' fashion but are subject to regular redefinitions, often initiated in a bottom-up fashion. However, to maintain integration, role changes should be explicit and not be allowed to evolve in an uncontrolled, haphazard way.

Maintaining strategic direction

The most central task of corporate technical staff is to monitor the formulation and implementation of R&D strategies. In this task, technical staff acts as a liaison between top management and the

R&D organization, translating strategic intentions into actual R&D programmes and explicating technological options and opportunities in the strategy formulation process.

In order to prevent uncontrolled strategic drift, budgeting procedures attain special significance. Thus, total R&D budgets for the entire group should be prepared regularly, not so much as instruments of control as a means to monitor the strategic direction of R&D efforts. This, in turn, requires that central guidlines on accounting and reporting principles be laid down and communicated to all R&D units.

In one interview, the technical director at corporate headquarters of a Swedish multinational with R&D conducted in separate establishments on four continents lamented: 'We occasionally compute a corporate R&D budget by summing the budgets of the individual R&D units. But the result is always so terrible that we immediately put it away. Besides the figures are not comparable anyway.'

In private conversation, the CEO of a major Swedish multinational complained that he had absolutely no idea how the group's R&D budget was spent. He had recently sent out a questionnaire to all R&D performing units. The purpose was to collect data on the distribution of R&D expenditures between product groups and technologies. Regular reporting routines contained no such information.

In some companies, central technical staff will be responsible for R&D in a corporate laboratory, generally focusing on long-range research and projects falling outside present business areas. In others, central technical staff will be responsible for initiating long-term and special projects undertaken by decentralized units on behalf of the entire group. In either case, to avoid excessive orientation towards minor improvements and adaptations with secure and rapid pay-offs – a common danger with R&D decentralized to divisions and other profit centres – corporate funds should be available for long-term research and other projects of common interest to the corporation. The problem is especially acute in the case of local-for-global innovations (Ghoshal and Bartlett 1987), i.e. when a local subsidiary performs R&D to the benefit of the group as a whole.

A Swedish MNC in the engineering industry performs R&D in separate establishments on several continents. To reduce the need and costs of coordination each has been assigned group responsibility for part of the product range. Problems appear when the

U.S. subsidiary – in response to the depressed local market – decides to cut back on its R&D expenditures. Sister companies in other parts of the world, where sales develop more favorably, in vain await the appearance of a new product generation. Clearly, some common system for allocating R&D costs must be devised.

Maintaining corporate infrastructure

In an integrated network organization, management of information flows is of critical importance. Whereas federative hierarchies are dominated by two-way information flows between head-quarters and subsidiaries, an 'integrated network' organization is characterized by far more complex communication patterns, with considerable lateral contacts between subsidiaries. To support efficient communication patterns, corporate headquarters must not only develop and maintain facilities and rules for formal communication but must also promote the establishment of informal communication networks and personal contacts.

Formal communication networks

In order to facilitate the transfer of information and technology, standard procedures must be established regarding accounting guidelines, methods of documentation, standards for blueprints, spare parts numbers and a host of other technical details. Moreover, these standards must be continually updated and maintained.

The introduction of corporate-wide on-line computer systems and computer aided methods for design and archiving often acts as an important catalyst for such standardization. Maintaining corporate data banks and regulating access to technical and other information are also tasks for the central staff.

In SAB NIFE, a Swedish electrical engineering company, the introduction of a Computer Aided Design system, to which major subsidiaries have on-line access, has not only led to a much greater degree of coordination and standardization but also to a redefinition of roles and responsibilities. Central R&D in Sweden now concentrate on long term developments of general interest to the group. R&D projects may be taken to the prototype stage but are then transferred to subsidiaries for detailed design and implementation in accordance with specific market needs.

Informal communication networks

In spite of the rapid development and pervasive impact of new communications technologies, efficient exchange of information will have to rely heavily on personal face-to-face communication for the foreseeable future. By its very nature, the transfer of strategically significant information and technological know-how involves demonstrations, negotiations and common problem-solving – activities that require direct personal contact.

Furthermore, personal contacts are often vital in the exploitation of R&D results. Again and again, during the course of our interviews, we found examples of significant new technical developments which had been transferred between units because of *ad hoc* personal contacts. 'By coincidence, we learnt that the subsidiary in country X had solved this problem in a very inventive way.' Similarly, new ideas and unexpected synergies often emerge as different competencies and technical skills meet.

Many of these types of contact cannot be formalized in organizational structures and systems. They are often of an *ad hoc* nature, involving new combinations of persons and knowledge, the needs for which cannot easily be foreseen. Hence, an important task for corporate management is to facilitate and encourage the creation of informal contact networks linking managers in different parts of the world. Rotation of managers, short-term foreign assignments, cross-divisional and cross-subsidiary conferences are some of the means of forging such networks.

Changing roles for divisional R&D staff

In Swedish relatedly diversified corporations, a natural consequence of the creation of profit-responsible product divisions has been the decentralization of the bulk of the corporate R&D effort to divisions. An advantage of this organizational structure has been to separate R&D for different products. In R&D units responsible for several product groups, it is often difficult to combine R&D in areas characterized by small projects and rapid adaptations with large time-consuming projects. In Swedish MNCs, the current tendency is to strengthen the position of divisions and product managers (Hedlund and Åman 1984). To an increasing extent subsidiaries report to divisions rather than to the CEO. In countries where the volume of operations does not warrant the establishment of several subsidiaries, and divisions 'share' a common market outlet, subsidiaries are organized so as to give each division a direct counterpart in the local organization.

271

As argued above, strengthening the role and authority of divisions can be hazardous in companies where subsidiaries traditionally have enjoyed a great deal of autonomy. Defining a properly balanced role for divisional staff can be a critical issue, as suggested by recent Swedish experience.

Three interrelated functions appear to be of special significance for divisional R&D staff: (1) to ensure functional and geographical co-ordination, (2) to establish and enforce quality standards, and (3) to optimally mobilize resources.

Co-ordination

Even with a high degree of specialization between units, co-ordination of R&D within product areas is required. The purpose of co-ordination is twofold: (1) to avoid unnecessary duplication of effort and (2) to ensure that available capabilities and locally developed initiatives are efficiently exploited. The task of managing the R&D portfolio within a specific product area usually rests with divisional management who are responsible for organizing Product Councils and other procedures for screening, carrying out pre-studies and selecting new project ideas.

With specialized R&D units, not all of these activities have to be carried out centrally (i.e. individual R&D units may well establish their own systems for the selection and implementation of new projects). However, divisional management should monitor these activities in order to maintain the balance of the project portfolio. This requires high technical competence on the part of divisional R&D staff, lest the initiative for product development gravitates to product managers with special competence in particular product areas.

Enforcing quality standards

In a heterachical organization, co-ordination of work processes ('throughput') must largely rely on informal integrative mechanisms. However, as a rule, these mechanisms permit only weak opportunities for central control and must often be combined with strong control of output.

> One of the major tasks of SKF's Engineering Research Centre, besides long term research, is to develop common standards for products and procedures. It also performs extensive testing and quality control of all products manufactured in SKF's plants across the world.

Hence, a central task of divisional staff is to enforce quality standards, including products developed by subsidiaries. As a rule, this requires that the division has access to modern testing facilities in order to check that components and finished products meet technical specifications. One of the most efficient ways to uphold quality standards — an exceedingly important task in a decentralized organization with high autonomy in peripheral units – is to require all production units regularly to send random specimens of components and finished products for central testing. With decentralized testing, specifications tend to be adjusted to the results achieved, rather than the other way around.

Mobilization of resources

A central task in an integrated network structure is to maintain and encourage the entrepreneurial capabilities of foreign subsidiary managers, while simultaneously integrating subsidiary actions more fully with the rest of the group. This is the only way to exploit fully the technical and managerial competence available. However, co-ordinative mechanisms must not become an administrative burden for subsidiaries, but rather support their pursuit of new business opportunities and their implementation of corporate strategies.

A divisional manager with responsibility for a widely decentralized R&D organization explained how projects were monitored and controlled by means of monthly progress reports. However, his response as to the efficiency of the system was hardly convincing: 'What do we do with the 30–40 monthly progress reports we get from subsidiaries? Well, that is a good question. I guess we file them.'

In many companies, Product Councils and similar reference groups fulfil several vital functions. They form a focus for information about the technical activities of the group and are also important for the formation of informal contacts. They are also an important means to exploit foreign technical and market know-how and can be used to achieve understanding for and commitment to corporate strategy.

For this reason, a wide representation in Product Councils – e.g. marketing and technical managers from all major subsidiaries – is important. Although rotating membership in Product Councils is a mechanism for widening representation, this solution is usually not optimal since it tends to obstruct the continuity and stability required to make effective long-term decisions.

In spite of the many advantages of comprehensive representations in divisional Product Councils, it is often difficult to convene very large meetings. There is then an apparent danger that fundamental decisions can be delayed. Sometimes, the efficiency of Product Councils can be increased by creating several smaller groups, each responsible for a particular product area. Moreover, local R&D managers can perhaps be given wider authority to start new projects or make changes in existing operations. Such decisions can later be confirmed or altered but help local R&D to maintain momentum.

A critical issue in an integrated network structure is the design of systems and mechanisms for evaluating and rewarding foreign subsidiary performance. In a 'decentralized federation', it is reasonable to evaluate each subsidiary on the basis of its performance in the local market. However, with the high degree of interdependence characteristic of an 'integrated network', this may lead to inappropriate sub-optimization. Mechanisms must therefore be found to evaluate subsidiary contributions to overall corporate goals. An example of such a mechanism is letting the salaries of foreign subsidiary managers be determined, in part, by overall corporate performance.

As indicated above, product development is an area where the issue of evaluation and reward systems is particularly relevant. As a rule, divisional management should encourage foreign subsidiaries to exploit locally developed new products through sister companies throughout the world. Active involvement of divisional staff may be necessary to detect possibilities for the international exploitation of local innovations and to remove possible obstacles to an efficient flow of technology. Thus, clear rules regarding transfer pricing, internal licences and the financing of R&D must be established.

Changing roles of foreign subsidiary management

The role of the foreign subsidiary manager will, of course, vary both with the size and significance of the local market and with the extent to which the subsidiary commands strategically significant resources. Some subsidiaries will take an active lead in formulating strategy, others contribute special resources while some will be assigned a more passive role as 'implementors' (Bartlett and Ghoshal 1986).

Nevertheless, a set of three common functions can be identified: (1) developing the allocated domain, (2) maintaining corporate integration, and (3) environment scanning.

Developing the allocated domain

Foreign subsidiary managers should be explicitly charged with – and rewarded for the active development of their companies' realm of activities. The often quoted argument of Hayes and Abernathy (1980) regarding the dangers of short-term profit maximization in profit-responsible divisions applies equally to foreign subsidiaries. Often entrepreneurial activity on the part of a foreign subsidiary manager is viewed with suspicion. Since new business development is always to the detriment of short-term profits, foreign subsidiary managers – unless protected by very high profitability – generally find a tendency on the part of headquarters to restrain local entrepreneurial efforts. Since such activities are inherently risky, their encouragement presupposes a high degree of mutual trust, i.e. headquarters must be sure that money is not being squandered on hopeless projects and subsidiary managers must feel confident of the right to fail. This fact points to the central role of recruitment, long-time employment and socialization processes in 'heterarchical' structures (Hedlund 1986).

As a rule, only a minority of foreign subsidiaries will be large enough to be able to support a local R&D unit. However, where such units exist, line authority for their activities should rest with local management, possibly shared with divisional R&D. In order to remain flexible and to be able to respond to local business opportunities, local influence on decisions must be strong. Whenever central units are involved, the decision process for new projects tends to be very lengthy. Hence, such involvement should only be reserved for projects of corporate significance.

Maintaining corporate integration

The value placed on entrepreneurial initiatives must be combined with a clear understanding on the part of foreign subsidiary managers that, as part of a corporate network, they will be expected to take decisions with a view to the total activities of the group, actively contribute to the formulation of corporate strategy, and maintain close liaison with other operating units. In many companies, this will require a major change in strategic orientation on part of foreign subsidiary management, traditionally accustomed to a high degree of autonomy and an almost exclusive focus on activities on the local market.

The R&D manager in a British subsidiary, explaining why the exterior design of locally developed products only partially met corporate standards, differing in minor details of lines and

275

colours: 'They did not ask for my opinion when the new standards were developed at headquarters. If the norms suit me, I use
them – if they don't, I do not see that I have to.'

Myopic attitudes will not change easily and a new outlook may
have to await the arrival of a new generation of managers. However, the design of information and reward systems, rotation of
managers and the introduction of common fora for strategy formulation may go some way to promote efficient integration of
dispersed units.

Environment scanning

In a rapidly changing environment, corporate headquarters must
enlist foreign subsidiary managers to monitor market developments, keep track of technological changes and watch competitors'
moves. The managers of major foreign subsidiaries must actively
participate in the strategy formulation process, keep an eye open
for possible acquisitions and detect new business opportunities
(Hedlund 1980).

As of now, few Swedish companies have developed formalized
systems for scanning technological and market developments.
Instead, they seem to rely on informal means to monitor the activities of competitors and analyse customer needs, etc. In
consequence, there is very little systematic knowledge to guide
strategy formulation and implementation.

Today, the responsibility for scanning usually rests with the
marketing function at divisional headquarters. Since information
obtained from subsidiaries as part of normal operations is felt to be
too filtered and largely irrelevant, extensive travelling on the part
of many marketing managers is often the main mechanism for
obtaining relevant information. Foreign subsidiary managers often
appear to submit information only on direct request from headquarters.

Strengthening the scanning function is an important means both
for obtaining information about technological and marketing
developments and for improving the capacity to exploit new ideas
and initiatives in the subsidiaries. In large multinationals, active in
very many countries, it may not be possible to systematically
engage all foreign subsidiaries. But major ones on strategic markets
should be given explicit responsibility for technical and market
scanning.

Summary

Analysing the way that multinational corporations organize and manage international R&D operations throws interesting light on the problems of co-ordinating and directing complex operations of strategic importance. Solving these problems attains special significance if one accepts that encouragement of innovativeness and entrepreneurship throughout the corporation is a major means to attain competitive advantage, and that such encouragement is rarely compatible with strong central control. Indeed, it often requires explicit changes in role definitions and reward systems.

This article suggests that the emerging literature on the organization of complex MNCs provides some important clues regarding the means to solve the problems inherent in international R&D management. However, it is also argued that the concepts proposed in this literature remain as yet too vaguely defined to constitute effective guidance to practising managers. The article is an attempt to contribute to the pursuit of operational concepts and testable propositions. It does so by addressing the question how roles and tasks of R&D managers at different positions will be affected as corporate networks increase in complexity and strategic responsibility becomes increasingly decentralized.

References

Bartlett, C. A. (1984/1986) 'Building and managing the transnational: The new organizational challenges', in M. E. Porter (ed.), *Competition in Gobal Industries*, Boston, MA: Harvard Business School Press.

Bartlett, C. A. and Ghoshal, S. (1986) 'Tap your subsidiaries for global reach', *Harvard Business Review*, vol. 64.

Doz, Y. L. (1978) 'Managing manufacturing rationalization within multinational corporations', *Columbia Journal of World Business*, vol. 13.

—— (1986) *Strategic Management in Multinational Companies*, Oxford: Pergamon.

Flaherty, M. T. (1986) 'Coordinating international manufacturing and technology', in M. E. Porter (ed.), *Competition in Global Industries*, Boston, MA: Harvard Business School Press.

Franko, L. G. (1976) *The European Multinational*, London: Harper & Row.

Ghoshal, S. and Bartlett, C. A. (1987) 'Organizing for innovation: Case of the multinational corporation', *INSEAD Working Paper*, 87/04.

Hayes, R. H. and Abernathy, W. J. (1980) 'Managing our way to economic decline', *Harvard Business Review*, vol. 58, No. 4.

Hedlund, G. (1980) 'The role of foreign subsidiaries in strategic decision-making in Swedish multinational corporations', *Strategic Management Journal*, vol. 1.

(1986) 'The hypermodern MNC – a heterarchy?', *Human Resource Management*, vol. 25.

Hedlund, G. and Åman, P. (1984) *Managing Relationships with Foreign Subsidiaries*, Stockholm: Sveriges Mekanförbund.

Håkanson, L. (1981) 'Organization and evolution of foreign R&D in Swedish multinationals', *Geografiska annaler, Ser. B.*, vol. 63.

Håkanson, L. and Zander, U. (1986) *Managing International Research & Development*, Stockholm: Sveriges Mekanförbund.

Håkanson, L. and Nobel, R. (1989) 'Overseas research and development in Swedish multinationals', *Institute of International Business*, Research paper, 89/3.

Hörnell, E. and Vahlne, J.-E. (1986) *Multinationals: The Swedish Case*, London: Croom Helm.

Perlmutter, H. V. (1969) 'The tortuous evolution of the multinational corporation', *Columbia Journal of World Business*, vol. 4.

Ronstadt, R. C. (1978) 'International R&D: the establishment and evolution of research and development abroad by seven U.S. multinationals', *Journal of International Business Studies*, vol. 9.

Steele, L. W. (1975) *Innovation in Big Business*, New York: Elsevier.

Swedenborg, B., Johansson-Grahn, G. and Kinnwall, M. (1988) *Den svenska industrins utlandsinvesteringar, 1960–1986*, Stockholm: Industriens utredningsinstitut.

Chapter eleven

Internal and external linkages in the MNC: the case of R&D subsidiaries in Japan

D. Eleanor Westney

(Paper presented at an EIASM conference, 'The Management of the MNC', in Brussels, June 1987)

The challenge of strengthening, diversifying, and exploiting the cross-border linkages within the multinational corporation has recently emerged as one of the dominant themes in the field of international business. Competitive pressures are driving MNC managers to try to increase cross-border co-ordination in order to exploit potential economies of scale and locational advantages and to realize potential scope advantages by applying innovations and know-how generated in one sub-unit elsewhere in the organization.[1] And in a dynamic context, where existing products and processes are being modified and new products introduced, cross-border co-ordination requires increasingly dense cross-border interaction. The emphasis on cross-border co-ordination extends to the arena of linkages with other firms, as the longstanding resort to local joint ventures with single-country partners is being overshadowed by global strategic alliances with other MNCs.[2]

The increasing density of cross-border linkages within the MNC generates increasing pressure toward convergence in the organizational patterns of headquarters and the various sub-units in an array of countries.[3] Some of this convergence is the result of deliberate design, as it is in MNCs that have moved to global product organizations that reach into subsidiaries to realign their organization more closely with that of headquarters. Even more is the unanticipated consequence of the growing reliance on socialization – on shared conceptual maps and ongoing interactions – as a control strategy.[4]

Yet the pressures for convergence contend with pulls towards variation. As the extensive literature on MNCs emphasizes, subsidiaries in different countries are subject to different national regulatory regimes and embedded in different national cultures; they each bear a different legacy from their historical development over time; they also have varying strategic mandates, depending both on that history and on the resource environments of their respective societies. In addition, they are located in networks linking them to other organizations within their own society, and these linkages differ across societies both in density and kind.

Therefore the focus on managing the internal linkages of the MNC must be complemented by awareness of how the effective operation of those linkages is constrained by the organizational variation among subsidiaries and the external networks in which each subsidiary is embedded. This means understanding how organizational changes will affect the subsidiary and its networks. If, for example, a subsidiary in Brazil has followed the organizational patterns and human resource development systems of local Brazilian firms, will significant changes become necessary as its level of co-ordination with European subsidiaries and with its North American parent increases? If these changes are made, making it more similar to the patterns in those other sub-units, will that have negative effects on its capacity to function effectively in Brazil? And if new patterns are modelled on those developed in the social context of another country, how can their inevitable modifications as they are adapted to their new organizational and social environment be anticipated and planned for? The MNC dilemma of reconciling the benefits of local tailoring with those of global standardization in products and in strategies has been joined by the organizational dilemma of local versus standardized organizational patterns. And in this dilemma, finding ways of combining variation and standardization is even more complex than in the arenas of products and strategies.

This paper explores the sources and implications for organization design of the potentially competing pressures toward convergence and divergence within the MNC in the context of one function, R&D, and in one society, Japan. A growing number of North American and European MNCs have recently decided to establish R&D laboratories in that country, both to adapt their products to the demands of the Japanese market, the world's second largest, and to tap into Japan's growing scientific and technical resources for application in their global technology strategies.[5] Although one funtion in a single country may seem a rather small window through which to view so large an issue, there are several factors that make it a revealing one. R&D is a function where both intra-organizational linkages with other functions and with R&D elsewhere in the MNC and inter-organizational linkages with local sources of scientific and technical expertise and knowledge are of critical importance. In consequence, the organizational dilemma of local and global co-ordination and integration is cast into high relief, although since the facilities are so new (many are still in the planning stage) the outcome remains uncertain. Moreover, for most firms the establishment of Japan-based R&D facilities means adding a new function in that country, rather than expanding or modifying an existing function, and consequently the constraints of established organizational patterns are not of major importance. Finally, the dominant features of R&D organization in large Japanese corporations and the distinctive features of Japan's technology system (including technical labour markets, the role of universities, and patterns of inter-firm co-operation in R&D)[6] raise some formidable challenges not only to cross-subsidiary co-ordination but even to the survival of a Japan-based R&D function in the MNC.

The next section briefly looks at some of the perspectives in the international management field that can be brought to bear on these issues. This is followed by an examination of the dominant patterns of R&D human resource development systems and research management systems within large Japanese firms, which provide the local model for the new facility. The final section then addresses the question of how the MNC can make the necessary choices between those patterns and its own as it moves to establish an R&D facility in Japan.

1. Localization, standardization, and co-ordination in MNC organization

As any text on organization management points out, multinational corporations, almost by definition, contain higher levels of internal organizational variety than do domestic firms, even those of a comparable scale, because their subsidiaries are located in very different social and political environments. Explanations for the variations across subsidiaries have focused on four major categories of variables: national culture, national regulatory regimes, institutional legacy of the subsidiary, and strategic intent. Recent developments in theories of organization-environment interactions suggest that we can usefully add a fifth category: the pulls toward similarity within each society in structures and processes induced by the inter-organizational linkages sustained by each sub-unit.

The analysis of national culture has focused on societally-induced values, norms, and expectations held by individuals. Therefore advocates of the importance of national culture in the organization of the MNC have tended to emphasize the necessity of conforming to local culture, particularly in its modes of interpersonal interaction and its motivation structures. Because the organizational patterns dominant in the local environment provide the most parsimonious set of indicators of these cultural patterns and how they affect work organization, adapting to local culture has usually been interpreted to mean adopting the behavioural norms and organizational patterns that prevail in large local organizations.[7]

National regulatory regimes impose a different set of constraints on organizational structures and processes, particularly in terms of setting conditions of employment, ownership, and the range of activities in which the MNC can or should engage. In the case of R&D in Japan, however, this particular perspective is of little direct relevance to questions of how to organize a Japan-based subsidiary. Japanese government regulation makes a significant Japan-based R&D capacity a condition for participation by foreign firms in government-sponsored research programmes such as the Fifth Generation Computer project, but no regulatory constraints determine how that facility should be organized. Indeed, the theme of most recent work on national regulatory regimes and the MNC has been the extent of the activities performed within the boundaries of a given nation, rather than on how those activities are organized.[8] The third category for explaining variation within MNCs focuses on variations in societies' resource environments and on the consequent variation across subsidiaries in their strategic intents.[9] This perspective is useful in explaining why MNCs are setting up R&D facilities in Japan: the combination of the richness of local scientific and technical resources, the need to keep abreast of Japan-based global competitors in technology, the importance and distinctiveness of the Japanese market, the dynamism of Japanese science and technology as its research community moves to an increased emphasis on generating new knowledge. But like the recent work on regulatory regimes and the MNC, it addresses the issues of what parts of the firm's value-added chain and product line should be located within a country, rather than of how to design the local organization.

The fourth category, the influence of institutional legacy on current organizational patterns, might also seem to be of little relevance, given that for most firms the Japan-based R&D facilities are new, and therefore are not directly constrained by a legacy of previously institutionalized patterns. However, this perspective is important in understanding the MNC context of the new Japanese R&D facilities, especially in terms of the nature and extent of non-R&D activities that the MNC performs in Japan. Several MNCs that are setting up R&D labs in Japan have extensive local marketing organizations, but do their manufacturing either off-shore or through Japanese OEMs. And given that Japan is now one of the world's highest-cost manufacturing sites, MNCs are often reluctant to commit themselves to major investments in manufacturing in Japan in the near future. In such a context, many new R&D labs will be in the somewhat unusual position of handing over the technology they develop either to another part of the MNC or to another firm within Japan.

Moreover, few of these MNCs have already built a significant technical presence in Japan that could serve as a base for the development of more value-added research activities. In a study of the internationalization of R&D in seven US MNCs before 1973, Robert Ronstadt identified four kinds of foreign R&D units:

1. Technology Transfer Units (TTUs): to facilitate the transfer of the parent's technology to the subsidiary, and to provide local technical services;
2. Indigenous Technology Units (ITUs): to develop new products for the local market, drawing on local technology;
3. Global Technology Units (GTUs): to develop new products and processes for world markets;
4. Corporate Technology Units (CTUs): to generate basic technology for use by the corporate parent.[10]

Each type of unit has distinctive linkages with the local subsidiary, the parent organization, and with local sources of technology. Ronstadt has focused on the first two kinds of linkage, but clearly the strength of the ties with local centres of science and technology varies across the four roles. The ties are virtually non-existent for a TTU, whose primary technical linkages are with the parent. They will be stronger for an ITU, which will probably (although not necessarily) draw to some extent on local sources of technology to develop products tailored to the local market – although it is quite conceivable that the ties to the local marketing function may be more important than ties to the local scientific and technical community. The ties will probably be strongest for the GTU and the CTU, since the primary motivation for a firm's establishing such a unit is to tap into local sources of science and technology that are not adequately accessible from outside the country.

Given the relatively low level of the manufacturing presence of foreign multinationals in Japan, even their TTUs have been extremely small, and very few have built R&D units beyond that level.[11] However, most of the new labs have multiple roles from their inception: they are expected to be ITUs, GTUs, and CTUs. This multiple mandate creates some complex problems. Ronstadt's study identified a clear evolutionary pattern: over time, the TTUs tended to evolve into ITUs, and a subset of the ITUs evolved into GTUs. CTUs tended, where they were successful, to develop GTU and ITU roles. The moving force in these changes came from the subsidiary. In the present case, these 'natural' evolutionary processes are being pre-empted by the urgency of the MNC commitment to multiple strategic intents within Japan.

The prospect of handing over technology either across national borders or across company boundaries and the multiple roles of the R&D units have implications for organization that are best explored through a focus on the internal and external linkages of the organization. An important strand in this framework is the concept of 'isomorphism'. Theories of organizational isomorphism posit that there are strong pressures for increasing similarity across organizations within an organizational field, a concept that is the sociological analogue of the industry: 'those organizations that, in the aggregate, constitute a recognized area of institutional life: key suppliers, resource and product consumers, regulatory agencies, and other organizations that produce similar services or products.'[12]

Three major premises undergird the work on isomorphism. First, the ease of interorganizational interaction increases with similarity in organizational structures and processes.[13] Therefore there is a strong tendency for the patterns of organizations that occupy central positions in resource allocation networks to be emulated by those with whom they interact, either because the central organization makes such emulation a condition of interaction, or because the less powerful organizations see emulation as a strategy that can increase their access to resources. Second, emulation of other organizations is also spurred by management's use of organizational change not only to increase legitimacy and acceptibility in the eyes of external constituencies, but also as a powerful internal signaling device, to increase legitimacy and enhance commitment among employees and internal stakeholders. In such cases there are strong inducements to turn to organizational models that are strongly established within the immediate environment.[14] Finally, because in complex organizational systems there is great uncertainty about what patterns are producing certain desired outcomes, managers are likely to look for models to other firms that are perceived as successful. This tendency is reinforced by the growth of the 'management industry' of the business press, consultants, and management schools and schools of public affairs, all of whom generate strictures on 'best practice' and thrive on the identification of 'exemplar' organizations, thereby producing what can be seen either as a growing and increasingly shared sophistication about organizational practice, or as a growing tendency to fads and bandwagons, depending on one's degree of cynicism.

If one applies the isomorphism paradigm to the MNC, one can portray the MNC subsidiary as subject to two potentially conflicting pulls toward emulation: those within the MNC itself, and those within the society in which the subsidiary is located. The organizational patterns of each MNC system as a whole are in most cases likely to be shaped by the patterns dominant in the home society of the headquarters. But the structures and processes of the organizations which dominate resource allocation within a subsidiary's own society are likely to differ substantially from those dominant within the MNC's home society. Several authors have discussed the problems created for the MNC headquarters if a subsidiary's dependence on it for resources (financial, technical, or personnel) diminishes over time. Most writers have put the difficulties in terms of an increase in the autonomy of the subsidiary. The isomorphism paradigm suggests that in addition, as the subsidiary draws more resources from its immediate environment, it becomes subject to a changing set of isomorphic pressures. To the extent that these produce organizational patterns that depart substantially from those of the parent, co-ordination difficulties will increase. Regarding it simply as an issue of management autonomy and control, therefore, may be to miss an important dimension of organizational change.

In addition, the internal constituents of the subsidiary are apt to have a different set of expectations about patterns that confer enhanced legitimacy and increase commitment than do the internal constituents of the home country headquarters. If matrix organization is widely recognized as an 'advanced' organizational form in the United States, for example, employees of the home country organization of a US-based MNC are more likely to regard a move to a matrix structure positively than are subsidiary employees in a country where matrix organization has not been widely introduced. Such issues have been addressed by the MNC literature largely in terms of differences in culture; the isomorphism paradigm directs attention more to the specific organizational patterns that dominate an organizational field within a society than to the more general value orientations of individual employees.

This emphasis on the important influence of the organization's external linkages is an important complement to the current focus on internal linkages within the multinational corporation; it also focuses more attention on the organizational implications of both kinds of linkage. Both are important perspectives in helping MNC managers make decisions about organizational design in subsidiaries.

R&D facilities in Japan provide a case in point. Their managers confront four interrelated challenges: setting the R&D agenda; building a human resource development system; establishing a research management system; and building the 'knowledge networks' with the Japanese organizations that are sources of scientific and technical information and stimuli to innovation. In facing the last three issues, they must decide whether to follow the patterns of their own organization, to emulate those which prevail in comparable organizations in Japan, or to compromise in some fashion between the two. To the extent that the established patterns of R&D in the multinational resemble the dominant Japanese patterns, the MNC faces relatively few problems in deciding how to design its HRD and research management systems in the Japanese context. But to the extent that its own patterns are different from the prevailing Japanese model, then managers face no small difficulty in making these decisions.

The following section summarizes the main features of R&D organization in large Japanese firms, as a background for assessing how MNC managers can make decisions about how important a model these should be for their own organization.

2. Organizational and interorganizational patterns of R&D in Japan[15]

In Japan, there are greater similarities in the structures and processes of large-scale organizations across industries and across sectors than is the case in societies whose industrial development was less compressed in time. As a result, it is possible to speak of 'Japanese' patterns of organization in large firms without as much danger of over-generalization as is the case with the United States and Europe, although of course there are still important differences across individual firms and between firms and government and university structures. In R&D, there are a number of commonalties across large firms, especially in human resource development systems. These are shaped in large part by the general HRD systems of large Japanese firms (the recruitment of new graduates, long-term employment, standardized rewards, and so on) but have some distinctive features produced by the nature of Japanese technical labour markets.

In Japan, as in most societies, the universities are the major source of scientific and technical personnel. In Japan, however, the leading universities play a more important role in allocating technical people to firms than in most highly industrialized societies. Especially for the Master's graduates, who constitute the lion's share of the recruits to R&D laboratories, the professors at the élite universities allocate their students among a core group of leading companies in the industry. The professor writes one recommendation letter to one leading company for each of his Master's students; the company will as a matter of course hire that student; and students do not feel free to approach a major company to which the professor has not written. For the Bachelor's graduates, who are recruited into divisional labs, the university placement offices are the most influential channel for guiding students into firms. The professors and the placement offices therefore assume considerable responsibility in evaluating firms to make sure that they provide secure and predictable career ladders for their recruits. In other words, they favour the large, established companies over smaller firms. This is one of the strong 'isomorphic' pulls on R&D organization in Japan: firms with aspirations to recruit Master's graduates from the élite universities must conform to certain organizational patterns of long-term commitment to employees, sustained commitment to spending on R&D in large and well-equipped laboratories, and a sustained relationship with the élite universities.

The number of mid-career recruits into the R&D organization of large firms is very small compared to most western societies. In principle, large firms do not recruit from other organizations in either managerial or research positions. However, there are perhaps more exceptions for R&D than for any other function. Under certain circumstances – such as expansion into new research areas, or extremely rapid growth in a certain field, or a 'hole' in the cohorts from which project leaders are chosen because an earlier economic slow-down contracted recruitment in the past – the firm will go to the élite universities, government laboratories, or public corporations such as NTT or NHK (but not, be it noted, to competing firms) to hire researchers in their early or mid-thirties. A recent study of fifteen leading firms in eight industries found that of a total intake of 2,400 researchers in 1984, only 90 (3.7 per cent) were mid-career recruits. The ratio of mid-career hires was highest in the heavy machinery industry, where the firms were making strenuous efforts to develop new business fields; five of the fifteen firms hired no mid-career researchers at all.[16]

Given this heavy reliance on new graduates, firms can and do put their R&D hires through a standardized entry-level training programme. Nearly all large firms combine the training of their research recruits with that of their managerial recruits, in several months of full-time training that includes intensive education about the company as a whole and rotation across functions (in Oki Electric Company, for example, both managerial and technical recruits even spend some time in a retail store selling Oki products, to provide them with direct exposure to customers).

Given the difficulties of hiring mid-career researchers, and given the nature of Japanese university education, companies also seem to assume greater responsibility for training researchers in Japan. Graduates of Japanese science and engineering departments are less likely then their US counterparts to have experienced internships or summer jobs in companies or to have industry-related research experience within the university lab. Education also tends to be more general and theoretical. As a result, R&D managers in Japan say that it takes about two years of primarily on-the-job training to bring a Master's graduate up to the level of making an independent contribution to research projects. But while on-the-job training by more experienced researchers remains the primary vehicle for enhancing the skills of the new researcher, off-the-job training is also significant. A 1979 survey of off-the-job training practices in leading Japanese firms found that over the previous three years 6.4 per cent had been dispatched to other companies or industrial associations on research projects with a training agenda; 5.7 per cent had studied at the graduate school of a foreign university or engaged in a co-operative research project overseas, and 9.7 per cent had enrolled in graduate courses at a Japanese university or been sent on temporary assignment to an outside research organiza-tion.[17] The practices of sending researchers to external research organizations and other firms as part of an HRD strategy is wide-spread. Although systematic comparison is not possible without similar data for US firms, the use of external assignments as a training mechanism seems more widespread in Japan.

The entry-level training programme also provides the company with an opportunity to assess the potential of each recruit, and initial job assignments are made at least in part on the basis of per-formance in training. But evaluation is a long-term process. One common characteristic of large Japanese firms is that the time frame for the evaluation of their researchers as well as of their managerial employees is from five to ten years. During this period, most firms provide their researchers with virtually no formal evaluation feedback. Researchers have no access to their annual evaluation reports, and there are few companies that formalize per-formance assessments. The companies rely instead on the intense interaction between superior and subordinates to provide constant informal signals. This is in marked contrast to the prevailing patterns in US research organizations, where formal performance appraisals and feedback interviews are standard. In both the US and Japanese systems research managers and project leaders have significant responsibility for fostering the development of their subordinates. In the United States, however, the emphasis tends to fall on formal evaluation and feedback procedures; in Japan, on informal interactions.

This, in turn, is linked to a pervasive difference between the reward structures of the two systems. Most US R&D organizations use some form of performance-based compensation, and an important function of the formal feedback procedures is to justify to each researcher the size of his or her pay package for the next year. Large Japanese firms, on the other hand, have a highly standardized salary and promotion structure, where outstanding achievement is not rewarded by significant pay increases. Salaries are virtually uniform across functions and areas, with seniority being the prime determinant of income.

This standardized reward system facilitates the transfer of research personnel that is a key feature of career structures and technology transfer in many large Japanese firms. In most leading firms, technology is transferred from R&D to manufacturing by transferring one of the project members to a divisional laboratory or engineering facility attached to the manufacturing division. In many firms this is not a temporary transfer but the next move on a career ladder that will eventually move into line management. Since nearly all researchers follow this career line, the move is generally accepted if not welcomed, even by those researchers who regret leaving advanced development work. The personnel transfers that are the primary vehicle for technology transfer exemplify one of the principal general features of the Japanese HRD system in R&D. In Japan, the locus of responsibility for the individual researchers' career clearly lies with the company. From the initial training through the assignment of researchers to projects and to post-entry training, the responsibility for planning a career that makes the best use of each individual's abilities (the best use for the company, not · necessarily the individual) rests with the company. Yet this does not seem to require larger personnel departments in Japanese R&D organization; the guidance comes from R&D managers themselves, rather than from personnel specialists.

Less systematic information is available on project management systems in Japanese firms than on HRD systems. The mode of technology transfer (linked as it is to HRD systems) is the clearest – the movement of researchers from the project through the production process. This pattern has been facilitated by the expansion of development facilities attached to product lines or to regional manufacturing facilities over the last ten years. Not only has the enhancement of the technical capability at the manufacturing facility helped in incremental product and process innovations; it has enabled the firms to hold down the size of their central R&D facilities, most of which have grown very little over the last decade. The relatively small size of the central lab in turn fosters the ongoing reliance on informal means of project monitoring. Compared to US firms, Japanese central R&D laboratories have fewer formal systems for scheduling and checking on research projects. However, the open office systems and the consequent daily communication enable research managers to keep a close informal watch on the progress of various projects.

A recent study comparing Japanese and US computer firms produced the following points of contrast in project management: Japanese firms exhibited greater reliance on informal methods of monitoring projects; less weight is given to technical expertise in the selection of project leaders and more to seniority, past experience in successful projects, and administrative ability; and there is a longer period of 'pre-project' work (exploratory research before formal project commitment) and a corresponding level of slack built into research budgets to accommodate it.[18]

Finally, the 'knowledge networks' in the Japanese technology system – the linkages across the various organizations that are sources of scientific and technical knowledge and expertise – differ somewhat from those in the United States and Europe. Universities are of more importance as a source of personnel than as centres of research. However, they remain important centres of information about developments in the research community, in part because employees of large firms and government laboratories generally maintain regular contact with their former professors, and in part because the professors in the élite universities are themselves participants in government technology advisory committees and projects.

Firms in Japan are also likely to have an extended portfolio of joint research projects: with other firms, with government labs, and even (somewhat surprisingly in view of the widespread belief in the poverty of the research capacity of Japanese universities) with Japanese universities. Most of the attention paid to inter-firm R&D projects has focused on the large-scale government-sponsored projects that bring together competitors to work together under a single project structure, such as the VLSI project, or the Fifth Generation Computer project. However, firms participate much more extensively in joint projects with their suppliers or with client

Table 11.1 Joint research projects in Japanese firms

(unit = research project)

| Firm | Research partner | | | | | | Total |
	A Japanese universities	B Foreign universities	C Think tanks	D Other companies	E Government and public laboratories	F Foreign companies	
Materials and chemicals							
Kyowa Hakko	60	0	0	3–5	8–10	3–5	74–80
Konishiroku	2–3	1–2	4–5	4–5	–	4–5	15–20
Daikin	10	2–3	0	10	5	5	32–33
Daido	5–10	1–2	–	10–20	5–10	–	21–42
Dainippon Ink	10	1–2	10	20–30	6–8	4–5	51–65
Consumer products							
Kao	40–50	8–10	3–4	10–15	8–10	–	68–89
Nisshin	10–12	2–3	1–2	14–15	3–5	3–4	36–46
Meiji	10–12	2–3	1–2	14–15	3–5	3–4	36–46
Snow	40–50	3–4	–	5–10	5–10	2–3	55–77
Lion	20–30	3–5	–	10–15	10–15	5–10	68–105
Machinery and equipment							
Kubota	6–10	2–5	–	10–15	10	–	28–40
Nippon Kogyo	30–40	4–5	–	10	10	–	54–65
Hochiki	5–6	–	1–1	2–3	1–2	1	10–14
Yanmar	4–5	1–2	–	3–5	2	2–3	12–17
Electrical							
Sumitomo El.	40–50	3–4	25–30	30–40	10–15	–	108–139
Toshiba	60	2–3	–	–	–	1–2	63–65
Hitachi	20–30	30–40	30–40	5–10	40–50	5–10	130–180
Construction							
Shimizu	15–20	3–5	5–10	50–60	10–15	–	93–125
Takenaka	4–5	1–2	–	20–30	4–5	–	29–42
Electric power							
Tohoku Denryoku	40	–	15	150	5	–	210

firms (Table 11.1).[19] These projects help direct the research strategy of the firm, they provide new experience for researchers, and they leverage the research capacity of the individual firm.

Too little public information or research exists concerning the operation of these projects, but they seem to run the gamut from small projects with relatively little interaction between the two firms to truly joint research, with an exchange of researchers and frequent problem-solving meetings. Those projects that involve the exchange of researchers are also a part of the HRD programmes of the firm. The exchange of researchers and close interfirm co-ordination on R&D projects are facilitated by the similarities in career structures, reward systems, and project management practices across Japanese firms. Especially critical are what Yoshino and Lifson have dubbed (in the context of Japanese trading companies) 'parellel hierarchies', that is, structures by which 'people who entered each bureaucracy can be expected to have contemporaries who entered the others in the same year and who are at approximately the same levels of responsibility and discretion.'[20]

One last feature of the 'knowledge networks' of Japanese R&D organization should be noted, and that is the strong professional orientation among researchers. Western writers on the Japanese technology system have asserted that professional orientation is relatively weak among researchers in Japan's large corporations, given the system of lifetime employment and their presumably strong company orientation.[21] However, the comparative study of the computer industry referred to above found that researchers in the Japanese firms were more likely than their US counterparts to belong to professional associations, attend professional meetings, and to feel that their company encouraged them to publish their research results. The importance of the professional associations in the knowledge networks in Japan has been overlooked in the western-language literature on the Japanese technology system; it should not be overlooked by the western firm entering Japan with R&D facilities.

The portrayal of the patterns of R&D in Japanese firms would be incomplete without some assessment of the direction of change. The dynamic evolution of R&D from the early 1950s, when most leading firms in Japan established their first research organizations, has continued to the present day. The current trend of change is the identification of basic research and the generation of original technology as major national priorities by both government and private industry. This has led to growing criticism of the rigidities of R&D careers and organization as a legacy of an earlier stage of manufacturing-oriented R&D. The parallel hierarchies and standardized organizational careers that have so facilitated the internal transfer of technology from the lab to the factory, collaborative inter-firm research, and the exchange of researchers across companies is increasingly criticized as stifling individual creativity and discouraging lifetime commitments to research.

The Japanese press, younger Japanese researchers, and Japanese R&D managers are engaged in increasing discussion of the desirability of mid-career recruitment, performance-based evaluation and reward systems, promotion by technical achievement rather than seniority, and greater variety of careers within R&D to allow for more specialized and longer-term technical ladders. There is growing scrutiny of personnel practices in US and European research organizations that foster basic research and major technology breakthroughs.[22] Yet despite some very conscious but isolated emulation of certain western patterns (such as the 'blue sky room' at Canon's central research laboratory), there has so far been little actual change in the overall organization of R&D. This in itself sugests the strength of the systemic supports for the current patterns, whose standardization facilitates both internal technology transfer and inter-firm co-operative research. It is, in fact, unclear what the direction and extent of future change will be, and this adds yet another dimension of complexity for MNC managers: emulating the patterns dominant in Japan today may mean adopting an obsolescing model.

3. Organization design in the R&D subunit in Japan

The concept of national culture as the major determinant of organization would suggest that all MNCs face a common set of constraints and expectations in setting up R&D facilities in Japan, based on 'Japanese-style management'. On the other hand, both the perspective that urges the importance of a strategic mandate to fit the local and the corporate environments and the isomorphism perspective argue for considerable variation across MNCs, depending on the actual and anticipated networks of the Japanese subunit.

In the simplest terms, the emulation of the MNC corporate patterns of R&D organization in the Japanese lab would be most appropriate under the following conditions:

(a) when the technology generated by the local R&D organization is routinely transferred across borders to other parts of the MNC;

(b) when linkages between the local lab and corporate R&D are dense and sustained;

(c) when organizational patterns are seen as a critical element of the firm's competitive advantage (the most vivid contemporary example is not in R&D but in manufacturing: Japanese auto firms have invested heavily in training blue-collar workers in their distinctive production systems).

These conditions are most likely when the Japanese lab is developing technology for use in the MNC's global markets (GTU) or is generating basic research for further development in the corporate lab (CTU).

On the other hand, emulation of locally dominant patterns will be favoured:

(i) when technology is routinely transferred to local manufacturing operations:

(ii) when linkages with local R&D organizations and the local scientific and technical community are dense and sustained.

These conditions are most likely when the lab is focusing on developing technology for use in the Japanese market.

However, in fact the Japanese R&D facility may well be faced with conditions of both types. Technology may be transferred both to local and to offshore manufacturing facilities (as is increasingly the case for IBM-Japan, in the face of the rapidly appreciating yen). The local lab may also be trying simultaneously to develop close linkages with corporate R&D and with local R&D organizations, as it must when it is playing the combined role of an ITU, a GTU, and a CTU, and when its technical capacity is brought to critical mass by leveraging it with co-operative projects with the corporate lab and with local partners or 'strategic allies'. The importance of such leveraging strategies, in turn, is reinforced by the peculiar difficulties of recruitment in Japan's technical labour markets. These three processes – recruiting, leveraging technical capacity, and technology transfer – are of critical importance in deciding how (as opposed to whether) to balance local and corporate organization models.

The R&D sub-unit will have to recruit in two markets that at first blush may seem to place contradictory demands on its organization. The recruitment of new graduates is controlled by professors and placement officers at the universities. Their principal criterion for directing students towards employers is the company's capacity for assuring them of a long-term career that provides the opportunity for the full development of their abilities. Many western employers equate this with 'lifetime employment' or job security, but it goes well beyond a commitment to keep an individual on a payroll. It demands a company that has the resources and the organization to enable the technical graduate to develop his capacities to the full. It also means a company which accepts its responsibility for the careers of its employees in the fullest sense of the word, and therefore usually implies a high measure of guidance and career structure.

On the other hand, mid-career recruits are likely to be those who are dissatisfied with the constraints of their careers in large Japanese firms and who want more choice in the direction of their careers. They are more apt to be attracted by a lower level of career structure.

One solution may be to develop a career structure in which autonomy and choice increase over time, and in which the 'Japanese' patterns of emphasizing the research manager's responsibility for developing the skills of junior people and research management's responsibility for overall career opportunities are combined with a 'western' pattern of soliciting greater involvement of individuals in planning their own careers and providing greater feedback on what the individual's attainable prospects might be.

Because of the relative newness of most of the MNC labs in Japan, clear career planning will be of critical importance. In the large Japanese firm young researchers can easily visualize the long-term contours of their careers by observing those of their older colleagues. The MNC lab that is 'ramping up' in staff and research agenda does not provide such models, and therefore the likely options have to be made explicit and the young researchers convinced that the R&D agenda of the facility will be set with one eye to the long-term implications for human resource development even as the other eye is firmly fixed on the immediate output of technology as a contribution to the overall strategy of the firm. Researchers will probably want evidence that the MNC has at least considered seriously what the people it is hiring today are likely to be doing in twenty years.

Reward structures are of course related to recruitment. The strengthening yen has made it increasingly difficult for US and European firms to consider trying to attract research staff simply by offering significantly higher salaries than the leading Japanese firms, even if that had been a viable option in the past. They can, however, offer inducements such as a performance-based reward system in which pay is less tightly coupled to seniority and rank than in Japanese firms, the prospect of a long-term research career (as opposed to the relatively early move into application and then line management of most Japanese firms), and overseas experience in the corporate labs or in western universities. This last also may be a useful way to develop the technical skills of the Japanese recruits (and it should be accompanied by a willingness to send such people to an intensive summer language programme abroad, as most Japanese firms do to prepare technical employees for overseas assignments).

Short-term assignments to the corporate lab can also provide a way of leveraging the capacity of the local lab, if they are part of a programme of joint research projects. Leveraging of some form is a necessity. In its early stages of development, the Japanese R&D subsidiary is relatively small, and yet to attract good people it must have a research agenda that includes challenging projects. The corporate lab can contribute to enhancing the Japanese lab's capacity to do such research in at least three ways:

(a) Joint projects, accompanied by an exchange of researchers on short-term assignment;
(b) Dispatching researchers from the corporate lab to work in the Japanese lab;
(c) Sending a senior, professionally established scientist from the corporate lab on short-term assignment (especially someone working in basic or very advanced areas) to interact with the Japanese scientific and technical community, raise the facility's visibility, and symbolize the MNC's commitment to Japan. To the extent that the Japanese lab is expected to be tightly coupled with the corporate lab in the long term, as well as in its early stages (i.e. to the extent that it has a CTU role), emulation of the corporate patterns will likely facilitate its development.

But in addition, the lab can leverage its capacity by drawing on outside organizations:

(a) Joint research projects with Japanese firms who are suppliers or customers, accompanied by an exchange of researchers;
(b) Joint projects with Japanese university professors, with the dispatch of one or more employees to the university lab;
(c) Joint projects with other MNC research subsidiaries in Japan. The ITU role is more likely to favour the ongoing resort to such strategies.

If both methods (corporate linkages and local linkages) are chosen – the likeliest strategy – then how can the lab deal with the potentially competing pulls on its organizational processes? More systematic empirical case research is clearly necessary before this question can be answered with any confidence, but one possibility is a combination of the following:

(a) A dual project management system, with one pattern (for projects with Japanese companies) that emulates the communications patterns, decision-making patterns, and role division of the Japanese system, and another that emulates the patterns of the corporate lab;
(b) training programmes that spell out for researchers in the local lab the differences between the two systems and the rationale behind each, in order to create 'ambidextrous' researchers who can function in both systems;
(c) an effort to involve the researchers themselves in self-conscious learning about which patterns facilitate which kinds of projects.

Finally, technology transfer across borders is an area where the experience of the corporate laboratory is critically important, and where corporate patterns should provide the model. Few Japanese firms have yet systematically developed methods of transferring technology directly from their Japanese labs to production operations overseas. The dominant mode is still to make the initial transfer to Japan-based production facilities, and then transfer the technology to facilities overseas after the learning process is virtually complete. North American and European firms are far more likely to have extensive experience in developing systems for cross-border technology transfer across functions.

Conclusion

In summary, the Japan-based R&D subsidiary faces some problems that are peculiar to the Japanese environment and to the existing level of foreign MNC presence there. But the dilemma of how to organize such a facility has general implications that go well beyond the country-specific application. The organizational structures and processes in any national subsidiary are strongly influenced by the kind and intensity of linkages within and across the boundaries of the MNC, and they in turn influence the efficiency and effectiveness of those linkages. As managers increasingly move to change those linkages, the theory and practice of international management must move to focus on their relationship to the MNC's organizational patterns at the corporate and local levels. The case of the emerging Japan-based R&D subsidiaries provides both a fascinating test in prospect for our existing theories and practices and a venue for improving them.

Notes and references

1 Christopher Bartlett and Sumantra Ghoshal, 'Tap your subsidiaries for global reach', *Harvard Business Review* 64–6 (1986): 87–94, and *Managing Across Borders: The Transnational Solution*, Boston: Harvard Business School Press, forthcoming.

2 See Farok Contractor and Peter Lorange (eds) *Cooperative Strategies in International Business*, Lexington, Mass: Lexington Books, 1988.

3 See, for example, M. Therese Flaherty, 'Coordinating International Manufacturing and Technology' pp. 83–109 in Michael P. Porter (ed.) *Competition in Global Industries*, Boston: Harvard Business School Press, 1986.

4 Yves Doz and C. K. Prahalad, 'Controlled variety: a challenge for human resource management in the MNC' in *Human Resource Management* 25–1 Spring 1986: 55–71; Gunnar Hedlund, 'The hypermodern MNC – a heterarchy?' in ibid: 9–35. An interesting aspect of these discussions is that the writers simultaneously assert the need for multinationals to expand their capacity to tolerate great internal variation in governance structures and other structural patterns.

5 The trend is most marked in the computer industry (Digital Equipment and Data-General); chemicals (Dupont, ICI, Ciba-Geigy, and W. R, Grace); and cases such as Eastman-Kodak, for whom Japanese firms have become formidable competitors.

6 See, for example, Hugh Patrick (ed.) *Japan's High Technology Industries*, Seattle: University of Washington Press, 1986; Ryuzo Sato, 'Japan's challenge to technological competition and its limitations', pp. 237–254 in Thomas A. Pugel (ed.) *Fragile Interdependence: Economic Issues in U.S. – Japanese Trade and Investment*, Lexington, Mass: Lexington Books, 1986; D. Eleanor Westney and Kiyonori Sakakibara, 'The role of Japan-based R&D in global technology strategy' in Mel Horwitch (ed.) *Technology in the Modern Corporation*, New York: Pergamon Press, 1986: 223–228.

7 This is clearly an oversimplified summary of an extensive and complex literature, much of which is ably summarized in a recent text by Simcha Ronen, *Comparative and Multinational Management*, New York: John Wiley & Sons, 1986. See also Gert Hofstede, *Culture's Consequences: International Differences in Work Related Values*, Beverly Hills: Sage, 1980; N. J. Adler, 'Cross-cultural management research: the ostrich and the trend' in *Academy of Management Review*, 1983 (8–3): 226–232.

8 Thomas A. Poynter, *Multinational Enterprises and Government Intervention*, London: Croom Helm, 1985; Yves Doz, 'Government Policies and Global Industries' pp. 225–266 in Michael E. Porter (ed.) *Competition in Global Industries*, Boston: Harvard Business School Press, 1986.

9 R. E. White and T. A. Poynter, 'Strategies for foreign-owned subsidiaries in Canada', *Business Quarterly*, Summer 1984; Sumantra Ghoshal and Nitin Nohria, 'Multinational corporations as differentiated networks', MIT Working Paper 1987; Bartlett and Ghoshal, forthcoming.

10 Robert C. Ronstadt, 'R&D abroad by U.S. Multinationals' in Robert Stobaugh and Louis T. Wells Jr. (eds), *Technology Crossing Borders: The Choice, Transfer, and Management of International Technology Flows*, Boston: Harvard Business School Press, 1984: 244.

11 The most important exception is IBM, which has gradually built its R&D capacity in Japan to the level of a GTU.

12 Paul J. DiMaggio and Walter W. Powell, 'The iron cage revisited: institutional isomorphism and collective rationality in organizational fields', *American Sociological Review* 1983, vol. 48, April: 148.

13 Empirical work in the field of international management has provided some supporting evidence for this: for example, Kathryn Harrigan's work on the importance of similarities across partners in K. R. Harrigan, *Strategies for Joint Ventures*, Lexington, Mass: Lexington Books, 1985, and Therese Flaherty's observation that 'it is easier and cheaper to coordinate operations which have more in common' in Porter (ed.) 1985, 'Coordinating international manufacturing and technology': 83–109.

14 John Meyer and Brian Rowan, 'Institutionalized organizations: formal organization as myth and ceremony', *American Journal of Sociology* 1977, vol. 83: 340–363.

15 The following section builds heavily on a research project comparing the organization and careers of engineers in the computer industry in Japan and the United States, which used interviews and questionnaires to compare the research organization of three US and three Japanese firms. See D. Eleanor Westney and Kiyonori Sakakibara, 'Comparative study of the training, careers, and organization of engineers in the computer industry in Japan and the United States', Working paper for the MIT-Japan Science and Technology Program, 1985. In addition, it draws on the growing Japanese-language literature on R&D organization, which is cited as appropriate in the text.

16 Seisaku kagaku kekyujo, *Gijutsu Kaihatsu sokushin no jōken chōsa hōkōkusho* (Report of an investigation of the advancement of technological development). Research report, March, 1986: 61–62.

17 Ibid.: 380.

18 Westney and Sakakibara, 1985. This contrasts with the speed with which formally announced projects are moved along. Subsequent interviews in firms in other industries suggest that these patterns characterize firms beyond the computer industry.

19 The data in Table 11.1 are compiled from information given by twenty of the thirty firms which provided dense descriptions of their R&D structures, a study of R&D in Japan by the Japan Management Association and published in Japanese as: Nihon Noritsu Kyokai, *Kenkyūjo Un'ei Kasseika Jitsurei Shū*, Tokyo: Nihon Noritsu Kyokai, 1987. The unit in the table is the research project.

20 M. Y. Yoshino and Thomas B. Lifson, *The Invisible Link: Japan's Sogo Shosha and the Organization of Trade*, Cambridge, Mass: MIT Press, 1986: 238–9.

21 See, for example, Gary R. Saxonhouse, 'Industrial policy and factor

markets: biotechnology in Japan and the U.S.', in Hugh Patrick (ed.) *Japan's High Technology Industries: Lessons and Limitations of Industrial Policy*, Seattle: University of Washington Press, 1986: 127–128.

22 For example, notes 15 and 16 are citations of a report by a study group on R&D organization that was set up by a Japanese foundation for scientific research: it conducted interviews at 22 Japanese companies and 10 US and European research organizations (including IBM, GTE, 3M, and MIT), and interviewed nine individuals with research experience in foreign institutions.

Part four

The concepts in use

Chapter twelve

Research on managing the multinational company – a practitioner's experiences

E. Ralph Biggadike

Similar to the multinational firms studied by the researchers reported in this book, Becton Dickinson has grappled with issues involving managers responsible for countries, Strategic Business Units (SBUs), both overseas and in the US, and functions. At times, the firm had to build up one perspective, worrying, as that was done, that the other perspectives were atrophying. How did managers achieve world-wide product competitiveness without giving up the country perspective? How were the company's experiences to be transferred around the world? Is there an alternative to the oscillation from one perspective to another? In this chapter, I will first set a historical context, then describe the problems, issues, and alternatives considered in 1985, the attempts in 1986 and 1987 to apply the transnational concept developed by these researchers and, finally, I will comment on the experience and how well this research helped.

In summary, the research has been most valuable in helping managers to understand and think through the multinational situation and to see an end-state, a strategic and organizational vision, which can help improve the company's world-wide competitive position. As the company turned to implementation, however, the managers found they needed additional help from the fields of human resources and organizational development. The researchers have not yet developed a theory of changing an organization to one or other of their end states. Some of their more recent work represents a beginning and I hope they move rapidly from describing existing situations in the leading multinationals to how less developed multinationals learn and change.

Historical context 1975–1985

Through the 1975–1985 period, Becton Dickinson competed in two broad areas of the health care industry: medical devices and supplies and diagnostic tests and systems. The best-known medical devices were needles, syringes, and thermometers. other devices included surgical blades, suctioning equipment, catheters and gloves. Diagnostics products included a line of microbiological products, immunodiagnostic products, and a variety of hematology products. Becton Dickinson's products were used irrespective of the health care setting – in hospitals, group practice, ambulatory care, HMO, clinic, laboratory, the home or physician's office.

The essence of the company's strategy has been to be the lowest cost producer in medical devices and supplies and to develop proprietary know-how in diagnostic tests. The company was the leader in most of the product-markets in which it competed. The form of organization was product divisions and groups. The planning, budgeting and evaluation system was an MBO-based budgeting system with each profit centre (i.e. the divisions) preparing five-year plans and annual budgets. Performance criteria were ROI, DCF and payback. The company's historic rate of eps growth was 15 per cent. Continuing this rate of growth was the company's fundamental financial objective and a cardinal element of the corporate strategy.

In 1975, following performance disappointments in 1973–75 as the economy bounced across its washboard of inflation and recession, senior executives became dissatisfied with the company's management system. The management-by-objective system, they believed, did not allow adequate control over strategic direction. Division presidents adopted corporate objectives as their own division objectives. But the divisions faced different market conditions and were in different stages of maturity. Division objectives should reflect these differences. Instead, presidents of profitable, established divisions tried to create new businesses to bring up their growth rates. Presidents of new ventures, on the other hand, pushed their units into profitability too soon, thereby sacrificing long-term competitive position.

Top management made a list of requirements for the kind of planning, budgeting and evaluation system the company needed in order to solve these problems. First, the system had to have a language that described the division's different strategic opportunities and encouraged evaluation on the basis of relative competitive position. Accounting language did not meet these requirements. Second, the system had to serve the operations needs of the divisions while also facilitating co-ordination of the whole corporate portfolio. Third, top management wanted a system that encouraged appropriate business strategies for each division and for seeing the financial implications of those strategies.

Company executives decided that the Arthur D. Little system, built around the concepts of Strategic Business Units (SBUs), stage of industry maturity, competitive position and differentiation in strategic roles for each SBU, met their requirements. The style by which Arthur D. Little suggested strategy be formulated was particularly appealing. The SBU managers, rather than consultants, top management or corporate planners, developed the strategy. They did this with guidance from a neutral, experienced strategy facilitator in group discussions called 'profiling sessions'. This style, top management concluded, fostered participation and commitment to the strategy among the SBU employees, put strategy formulation in the line, and made the division president the chief strategist.

SBUs and this management system were progressively introduced in the US between 1976 and 1979. The SBUs were overlaid on the existing organization of product divisions and initially were used to plan strategy only. Operations continued to be performed by the product divisions.

The international organization continued unchanged through this period – that is, international business continued to be handled by an international group and country branches or subsidiaries headed up by country managers. The international group used the MBO based budgeting system, with particular emphasis on annual budget control. Country managers put achievement of annual budget first. The country manager decided whether there were opportunities to export the company's US products to his country. Consequently, not all the company's products were marketed in each country in which we had a presence. Country managers and, often, the international group were reluctant to launch successful US products because initial launch costs would lower country profitability. Country managers argued that there was little demand for the US products they did not market or that the conversion effort would require too much investment. US division presidents complained that our country units behaved like ineffective distributors, refusing to make investments to build the business.

Much of the company's manufacturing was in the US; an important exception being the needles and syringes. US plants reported to the division presidents, overseas plants reported to country managers. Supply and demand of product was a continual source of problems and friction between the US supplying divisions and our country units. The supply divisions managed their own manufacturing variances and used overseas orders as fillers to help their own performance. Product specifications were in the main designed for the US market; a few exceptions occurred on products manufactured overseas. Country managers complained that our US divisions behaved like export skim opportunists. US division presidents took the position that demand in many countries was too small to worry about.

In 1980, senior company executives decided that we had to build strong competitive positions for most of our products in all European countries. We could not allow individual countries to decide which products to market. We could not allow individual US divisions to be inattentive to international opportunities. Several international competitors were extending their products throughout Europe. If successful, their European-wide strength could be used to attack our individual country positions, including the US. Above all, we thought that most European health care providers would find our products useful. Differences in medical practice from country to country were not so great that our products completely lacked customer value in some and were helpful in others.

At the same time, top management saw a need for increased co-ordination in world-wide manufacturing. Apart from problems of supply and demand, there was also concern about cost and quality standards at different locations.

The company introduced world-wide strategic management for certain products. The organizational design sought to achieve more centralized strategic management while also utilizing local country knowledge and expertise. World-wide SBU managers were appointed, usually the division president in the US. This person was given direct operating management responsibility in Europe and strategic co-ordination responsibility throughout the world. SBUs were formed in Europe to help create world-wide strategy and to build our competitive position in Europe. (They were not introduced elsewhere because our strategic focus was on Europe.) To help the new European SBUs fulfil this role, they were given status and resources. The head of each European SBU was given the title of president, and treated similarly to a division president in the US. This status level was higher than that accorded to our country managers. The European SBU presidents reported to the world-wide SBU managers (division presidents in the States). The reporting relationship of the sales force and marketing employees in each country was switched from the country manager to the European SBU president. This change was made to help integrate individual country knowledge in the world-wide strategy and to give the European SBU the power and control to apply the resources needed to implement the strategy in each country. In those European countries with plants, manufacturing reporting relationships were switched from the local country managers to the world-wide SBU managers in an attempt to seek greater quality and cost standardization. We started to stress European SBU P&Ls rather than country units P&Ls and encouraged losses where market conversion and building efforts were necessary.

The role of the country manager was defined as the primary representative of the company within a country. He was responsible for planning, financial, legal, personnel, and other related business activities of all local SBUs operating within the country. The country manager was usually the local head of the largest SBU. The country manager also represented the company in government relationships and public relations activities. Country managers reported to an area president (considered equal in status to a US division president), who reported to the international group president. When in the capacity of local head of an SBU, country managers reported to the European SBU president.

In the period 1980–1985, sales growth in Europe was spectacular and we achieved major improvements in competitive positions. The P&L picture was mixed, with profits in some years and losses in 1983–4, for a variety of reasons ranging from several European SBUs being in a build mode, slower than anticipated success in converting European markets to our products, higher overheads, and a stronger US dollar. Overall, company executives thought good strategic progress had been made in Europe but a number of problems and issues needed attention. To these, I now turn.

The problems and issues – 1985

I will describe these in three categories – problems and issues in our external environment, those in our organization, and, thirdly, our cost of management in Europe.

Environment

Principal issues in the world-wide health care environment in the mid 1980s were containing the cost of care, raising the quality and widening access. While efforts to control costs created greater pressures for efficiency, other actions to widen access, population growth and ageing, and technological breakthroughs provided both need and opportunities for new products. Being able to respond both efficiently and innovatively were becoming key bases of competition for medical device and diagnostic supply firms.

We were not so sure that we were as cost efficient and as innovative as we could be, or needed to be for that matter. A few plants overseas were performing to the standards of conditions in their country of location rather than world-wide quality and cost standards. We worried that, having made the up-front investment in converting countries to our devices and tests, we could be running the risk of losing the benefits to lower cost competitors and, in some partially protected markets, higher quality competitors. These concerns all pointed to global strategy and organization.

However, there were some differences in how individual nations were trying to contain costs, raise quality and widen access to health care, and there were important differences in medical practice and product usage. These differences pointed to the continued need for a country perspective. In sum, then, the external environment was placing even greater pressure for both global strategies and strong capability in local markets. Directionally, these environmental pressures were the same as five years earlier when the company extended its SBUs to Europe and maintained the country organization. But in magnitude, these pressures seemed to be mounting. We were not convinced that we had in place the right organization to handle these pressures.

Organization

Principal organizational issues concerned the amount of stress and conflict among our managers of countries, SBUs, and functions and the consequent cumbersome and insufficiently co-ordinated decision-making process. Country managers still smarted from their loss of influence in the early 1980s. They believed that their knowledge was not incorporated into strategies put together by our SBU managers. Indeed, they thought they were told about the strategy after it had been decided. Some thought that their ability to build a country team was severely limited by our SBU structure. They had less control over operations in their country because of the SBU reporting structure. To them what had started out as a device to build strategic position had taken operational control of product activities as well.

On the other hand, country managers and overseas SBU managers joined together to complain to our worldwide managers about back orders and insensitivity to country and regional customer preferences. They differed, however, on several key operational matters. For example, an overseas SBU manager wished to change a distributor for his product because of poor performance but, to the country manager, the distributor was doing a good job on the company's other products and he thought the change would damage the relationship. Another example was pricing because country managers were measured on a country P&L and SBU managers were motivated to build competitive position and manage an SBU (Multicountry) P&L. As for the concerns of country managers, SBU managers pointed to our high growth rate and wondered whether there was actually a problem. To the charge that they were not sufficiently incorporating country knowledge into their strategy, they argued that their sales and marketing managers in each country kept them informed of local sensitivity. And as for interfering in country operations, their position was that the sales forces reporting to them, were the primary tool for implementing the strategy, and they needed to manage the sales people closely.

Our US SBU heads believed they were expected to respond to every national or regional difference with no appreciation by our overseas managers of the financial and people investment required, the impact on costs, and the length of time needed to respond. Meanwhile, they claimed, building sales throughout the world of some of our existing products was inhibited by insufficient international selling and service resources. As for back orders, they argued that the role of inaccurate overseas sales forecasts was rarely recognized.

Three-way disagreements between countries, functions, and SBUs arose too. For example, a European SBU developed an incentive scheme for the sales force. This scheme was communicated to the head of the SBU marketing and sales force in each country. The local human resource manager found that the scheme was out of compliance with corporate policies and was considerably richer than incentive schemes in other SBUs. The country manager, worrying about morale throughout his entire organization and lack of compliance, bounced it back to the regional HR director who then took it up with the European SBU president and eventually, the regional president.

Top management concluded that we had to work on relationships and our decision-making process and seek big improvements in world-wide co-ordination. We were also about to step up our efforts in other parts of the world and wondered whether we should extend SBUs to other regions, maintain the existing country structure, or take another approach.

Cost of management

At this time, senior management was putting the entire company through rigorous analysis to reduce our costs. This effort was partially in response to the environmental pressures already described, and partially because, in 1983 and 1984, our corporate historical growth rate in earnings and sales had been broken. We were particularly curious about our costs in Europe. Not only had we made losses in 1983 and 1984, but European operating effectiveness, as assessed by the PIMS progamme of the Strategic Planning Institute, was weak. One hypothesis was that the triple organizational structure of countries, European headquarters, and SBUs had created high overhead costs which, to date at least, had not generated sufficient sales to justify it. Each country had an accounting staff to support country selling, a tax/finance/treasury staff to ensure local compliance with taxes, customs, and to handle foreign exchange, and an administrative staff to assist with forecasting, planning, and budgeting, and to manage human resources and compliance with local employment practices. Each of these functions was also represented in European headquarters, not only to provide advice to the countries but also to consolidate European operations and provide pan-European management of those topics governed by the EEC.

In summary, these problems and issues suggested to us that we had introduced SBUs to solve a strategic problem, that we had made good strategic progress but that we had also created organizational and cost of management problems. In addition, for the mid 1980s environment, we thought our strategies and operations were not sufficiently integrated but wondered how much further we could go without destroying our organizational capability in the countries.

The alternatives – 1985

Our first thought was to take a look at structure. We tried to clarify jobs and relationships by redrawing boxes and reporting lines. Unfortunately, it was not clear to us how these structural changes would improve working relationships and co-ordination. Indeed, it seemed possible that matters could be made worse because each structure proposal created winners and losers. Ideas proposed by a firm of consultants seemed to force us into choices that did not reflect the environmental demands. Solutions were posited as dichotomies: 'product versus geography' and 'centralization versus decentralization' for example. The most extreme of these was labelled 'Europe-the equal partner model' and stressed primacy of geography, strategic independence, and business equality with the US. This structural alternative would, we thought, drive our units further apart and seriously limit our ability to compete effectively.

We also came to the conclusion that the company was not ready for another restructuring and the accompanying turf battles. A structural change would focus our energies inwards when we really needed to be focusing on customers and competitors.

While we made one or two structural changes we concluded that we could make as good a case for one structural design as we could for another. All structural alternatives seemed arbitrary. And none of them offered both world-wide co-ordination and national representation. We took all this as a signal that we really did not have a good theory to guide us.

We turned to an approach that is reflected in this book. The global integration–national responsiveness grid described by Professor Bartlett evoked a favourable response among top management immediately. The forces favouring each explained very clearly why we had the kinds of problems outlined above. The three strategy and organizational options – global, multidomestic, and transnational[1] – offered reasonably clear visions of where we might head. The transnational concept seemed appropriate for parts of the health care industry because it recognized national and global imperatives. it stressed the validity of country, business, and functional points of view and provided a framework for figuring out when and how it is appropriate to co-ordinate them. Essentially, it described what we had been trying to do, though we had experienced the mix of success and problems outlined above. We particularly liked the suspicion about the power of structure to solve organizational problems as this mirrored our own experience. The transnational concept stresses people relationships rather than structure. The researchers emphasize that organizations should work on relationships first and deal with structure and systems later.

These researchers reject the notion of dichotomy in organization – one can, if appropriate, integrate the product and geographic points of view. Even better, the integration is not achieved by a matrix. Transnational is not the usual two-boss kind of matrix where many activities are managed jointly. Rather, one tries to keep the shared tasks at a minimum. As much as possible, one tries to give employees performing their daily tasks in R&D, production, and selling clearly defined jobs and simple reporting relationships. The matrix, if it exists at all, is in the minds of senior management. The researchers also reject the centralization/decentralization dichotomy. Some functions in a business might need to be centralized while others in the same business are decentralized. As the industry and strategy changes, one or more functions might have to change again. Thinking that one either had to decentralize or centralize a business unit was considered overly simplistic for the environment of the multinational company. Organization, to these researchers, is not symmetrical – one is free to manage differentially: by business, by function, and by country.

Introducing the research to managers

We decided to expose the ideas in this book to a broader set of our managers. We thought we had found a helpful multinational strategy and organizational framework and vision but we did not know whether our managers would think likewise. We also knew that to move from vision to action we had to involve our managers in working out the every-day operational details of behaving in a transnational manners.

We advised our managers that corporate headquarters did not have a structural solution in mind and we were not following the consultants' recommendations. Furthermore, top management stressed that any changes would be created in a participative manner. We stated that we had found a multinational strategy and organization framework which we wanted to share with them and obtain their reactions. We presented the transnational concept as probably appropriate to us at a general philosophical level but its full applicability had to be tested by them for each business.

In the last two years, we conducted five education conferences (three days each) for approximately 190 executives. In the case of Europe we also held a meeting to experiment with the complete cycle outlined in this book; (i) analyse industry; (ii) choose strategy; (iii) identify key tasks; and (iv) define roles, responsibilities, and relationships of each manager to get the tasks done. We had reasonably well-developed strategies and tasks and asked the European managers to try working on step (iv).

We did extend a structural overlay on the existing organization which we called world-wide teams. We formed a team for each of our major products. For some products, these teams were a reaffirmation of the world-wide SBU teams started in 1980 when we extended SBUs into Europe. Team membership included representatives of the three viewpoints – product, country/region, and function. Their primary charge was to formulate world-wide strategy and work on co-ordination. Other than that, their charge was left largely open. This role was narrower in scope than that of the world-wide teams introduced in 1980 which had both strategy and operations. The chairman was designed conceptually as coming from the lead market; in practice, all the team chairmen except one were from the US. The teams took the transnational concept as their overall strategic and organizational philosophy.

Each team has had several meetings. While agendas have varied widely, common topics included data gathering, strategy profiling, product design, selected operations issues (back orders for example), and budgetary decisions.

We had some managers, including some at the top, who already managed in a style similar to that suggested by the transnational concept. We relied on these managers to provide examples to the rest of the organization. Just by the way they went about their regular job, they modelled transnational behaviour on a daily basis. To them, differences in countries, SBUs, and functional points of view did not call for them to take sides but, rather, to take a strategic approach and seek a solution that was in the best company interest. We decided not to bring in outside consultants to help us because we had just had major involvements of consultants. We wanted to avoid the impression of 'yet another corporate programme', and we wanted managers to work on their problems themselves. Finally, we decided to increase our transfers of executives to other regions, to help them develop multiple perspectives. The surest education, meaning internalization of transnational ideas so as to change behaviour, would come from succeeding as a manager in other settings.

How did our managers react?

Initial reactions to the global integration–national responsiveness grid were good. It had an intuitive appeal to our managers. Studying the forces that favoured global integration or national responsiveness made the sources of their frustration clearer to them. At the same time, the idea that managers could choose the kind of strategy and organization – global, multidomestic, or transnational – they needed restored to managers a sense of control over their situation. 'It doesn't have to be this way', commented one of our managers and he captured the relief felt by many.

As one might expect, some reactions were motivated by self-interest. Managers tried to figure out the structural and power implications of the concepts. Country managers wondered if they would get their power back. SBU managers feared they might be about to lose control of the strategy. Functional managers were somewhat bemused, wondering whether these concepts applied to them or whether this was just another round in the country/SBU fight.

Suspicion was another reaction. Most managers thought that the educational conferences were merely a precursor to a major structural change which top management had already figured out. Most managers genuinely did not believe top management's claim that they did not have a structural design in mind, but rather, a process of management, a way of relating to each other to gain greater co-ordination. Further, many managers were uncomfortable with the view that if a structural change proved necessary they would be the ones to design it. Several middle managers said to senior managers, 'Why are you making this so complicated? Just tell us what the organization is to be and we'll get on with the job.'

Throughout the organization, there was hesitancy and uncertainty about how a transnational organization worked, or even if it could work. Most managers could not imagine a company made up of business units with different forms of organization. Worse, within a business, each function might be managed differently. That the organization would vary by business, by function, and by country seemed organizational anarchy. One manager said,'If I conclude that my people won't be able to handle the subtlety of this transnational then I'll manage by the global and make it work.'

Managers wondered frequently if top management was committed to the concept. This doubt, in turn, created a risky situation for them, subordinates in particular: would their experiments at applying the transnational be tolerated by their superiors? In effect, we were asking them to take a tremendous leap of faith. In the words of one manager, 'We're looking for signs that management was willing to nurture this transnational egg'. In the case of the transnational concept, these fears are particularly important because a transnational organizational change is difficult to achieve. It is an organization that requires a high degree of trust. To achieve interdependence, co-operation and co-ordination, each member of the organization has to be able to trust the other's use of data, accuracy in reporting, and judgement of situations.

Rather than finding organizational symmetry a disadvantage, as these researchers argue, some of our managers found the lack of it unsettling. The offered alternative, thinking of organizations in relationship and process terms, was not natural for them. Suggesting that they think of a transnational organization as more of a state of mind and type of managerial style was not regarded as particularly helpful. The same question kept popping up, 'But how do I know a transnational organization when I see one?' I have seen several discussions of the 'Yes, it is; No, it isn't' type about whether a particular unit or a decision was transnational. It seemed that if we could not describe a formal structure precisely then we did not have an organization.

World-wide teams

As the world-wide teams got formed and running, they provided a forum for airing these reactions. The teams served as a lightning rod for all the pent up frustrations and attitudes. The ebb and flow of enthusiasm, scepticism, collegiality, and polarization was played out in these teams. These teams also provided a task-oriented setting in which to work out these reactions and experiment with the transnational concept.

Several managers in the world-wide teams have reported that people are behaving larger than their responsibility; they are trying to think more broadly, less parochially. There has been less inclination to think of the seriousness of one's own problems and ignore the problems of others. Several instances of more timely co-operation have been cited. Proactively listening to people from different parts of the world has caused several R&D projects to be started which, it is thought, will help customers throughout the world. Better linkages among our manufacturing locations are occurring. Some employees feel their participation in decisions has increased – there is a heightened sense of involvement and influence. Some have observed that our managerial process is more transparent; the significant issues are getting on the table and debate is occurring.

Most teams have interpreted the transnational concept to mean that everybody has to get to know everybody better. This has been a valuable contribution in that it has increased respect for other people's opinions. One manager commented that it took each member about one year to truly appreciate the point of view of other functions and regions.

One of the major difficulties for the teams has been to define their role. In practice, we see roles that range from a world-wide operating committee to a strategy committee to a non-role. Some teams have worried that the real problem is to get the operating divisions around the world to implement the strategy. These teams report '95 per cent of our time is spent on how to get the things decided at the world-wide profile actually done'. Other teams have worried about the same topic but have taken the position that they cannot possibly get into implementation; their role is to foster communication.

Some teams have tried to define roles, responsibilities, and relationships of the team members and the operating units. This task is a very appropriate one for the teams, and exactly what the researchers recommend, but those that have tried it have struggled. One method, well meaning, but mechanistic in nature, consisted of a form with row variables representing decisions and column variables representing global, multidomestic, and transnational. Each person connected with the business was asked to vote how each decision should be treated. Another team inferred from talk within the company that the company had decided that the ideal organization form was transnational and so was treating all functions and all decisions as transnational. Upon being advised that the transnational was not ideal for all industries and businesses, other team leaders leapt to their defence by saying that the corporation had indicated that the transnational was the new corporate religion. Some teams had broken the decisions out in too fine detail thus making the task overly complex. They had then had difficulty in keeping the number of decisions to be managed on a shared basis to a few. Thus, the transnational concept became, to them, a matrix in which everything is shared. The intent of the transnational is the exact opposite but we had not succeeded in communicating this feature.

A difficulty for all has been to find the right balance between respecting all points of view and enforcing one particular viewpoint. One example of the former resulted in a strategic decision to permit a variety of product designs in different regions in an industry where global competitors offered standardized designs at very low prices. Each region was satisfied and the team thought they had behaved in a transnational manner. But, given the industry, it is unlikely that this decision was appropriate. We were learning that the transnational concept does not mean a loose federation of sovereign states – a sort of United Nations approach to multinational company strategy and organization.

Other managers have struggled with giving up a measure of control. As a group, our managers have previously described themselves as having high control needs, that is, they need to be in charge and to be seen to be in charge. A transnational organization is not an organization where control needs are satisfied. Rather, one has to gain satisfaction from guiding people, from sponsoring co-operative and collective action, from conducting a continual dialogue among managers and from participating in decisions and actions. Most of our managers were finding this style to be a big change, even a scary one. There are important personnel issues here: some managers may decide that this style is not for them and opt out.

In addition, they observed that the transnational managerial style takes so much time. But as one SBU president commented, 'You can't say I am going to listen to people around the world, ask for their ideas and then ignore their input'.

Membership of the world-wide teams has provoked considerable debate. In attempting to give representation to the functions, most teams ended up with a preponderance of Americans who reported to the team chairman, their division president. In the view of members from overseas, this created an unequal power structure within the team which resulted in a slant to the teams' discussions. In addition, we were not satisfied that we had given sufficient representation to the countries.

We continued to experience doubt among managers that our entire organization would operate with a transnational philosophy. We were hearing comments to the effect that, 'A problem is not a problem until the American Divisions experience it.' The notion of interdependence has proved particularly difficult to communicate. One manager commented, 'Interdependence existed for nine months of the year but it disappeared in the final quarter when the supplying division needed additional sales in the US to make their budget.' Some countries or regions continued to seek independence and behave as if they thought the correct solution was to go it alone. Some functions continued to behave dictatorially.

Reflections from OD and HR

After reflecting on the experiences described above, top management concluded in Spring, 1987 that we needed additional help to move us along. While pleased with improvements in co-ordination around the world, we realized much remained to be done. A lot of expectations had been raised and not yet met. Country managers wondered what, if anything, had changed. We still had a long way to go in spreading the ideas to lower levels. Some of the world-wide teams had stalled. No team had yet worked through the complete cycle of (i) industry; (ii) strategy; (iii) tasks, and (iv) roles, responsibilities, and relationships. It was clear that they needed help in this process, just as the researchers in this book suggest. We did not have a clear view of which SBUs were most suited to the global, multidomestic or transnational concepts. And, within each of these concepts, we had not developed appropriate decision-making processes.

Many managers were wondering about their managerial style and how they would exercise influence and power in the emerging organization. They saw the traditional sources of power conferred by formal structure eroding. The transnational concept suggested new sources of influence, namely the power of their ideas and their collaborative approach to decision making. But these sources were uncertain to them. They needed assistance in understanding that there are multiple sources of influence. On the other hand, our instinctively participative managers needed reminding that confusion could be caused by not being sufficiently directive. Transnational management meant more flexibiliy and participation but it did not mean total lack of structure and leadership.

Perhaps, most importantly, we saw signs that managers were focusing on the transnational without a clear view of why they were doing so. We had to stress continually that the objectives were better customer service and relative competitive positions. Somehow, though, these objectives got fuzzy as they attempted to work with the transnational ideas. The world-wide teams provided a task setting for their efforts but, apparently, not with sufficient clarity.

In the experiences related here, we saw all the familiar issues associated with people making individual and organizational change. Although the setting was multinational and the organizational concepts were relatively new, the problems involved in making change were old.

We turned to the fields of organization development and human resources. In our company, and many others, organization development – or process consultation – is regarded with less enthusiasm than in the 1960s, partly because of its preoccupation with technique and a lessening of a task orientation. But the original idea of organizational development is still very helpful: involve the people who need to change in working on the change. Or, to put it another way, to change people's behaviour, first change the behaviour – as opposed to changing attitudes first. And how does one do that? By asking them to tackle the problems and by providing them with facilitating skills to guide them through the process. We had given our people a vision, asked them to work on the problems of implementing that vision, but had not given them sufficient help in facilitation or process consultation, nor had we fully succeeded in linking their efforts to performance tasks.

Professor Beer, a human resources and organizational development specialist, expressed to us the factors involved in making organizational change in the formula below:

Change = (Dissatisfaction × Model × Process) > Cost of Change

His formula (he notes that versions of this formula were developed by other OD researchers) suggests that change will occur only when the cost of change to individual employees is outweighed by their level of dissatisfaction with the existing way of doing things; when there is a new model of organization which people think will solve the problems; and when there is a process for helping managers make the change.

As we analysed our experiences in the light of this formula, we thought we might have been somewhat low on D (dissatisfaction) and deficient in P (process). In thinking about dissatisfaction, we recalled that a few managers had told us that although there were many sources of frustration, they assumed that was natural for multinational operations and they had learned to manage them. It seemed possible that, although excited by the frameworks and visions in this book, the level of dissatisfaction was not high enough for some to justify grappling with the difficulties of implementing the transnational concept.

In thinking about the process variable in the formula, we recalled that we had deliberately provided little formal process assistance to our managers. We had wanted to avoid the continual involvement of consultants in organizational matters and get managers to work on the ideas themselves. But moving to the transnational, even at a philosophical level, is a fundamental change in organization and management. We concluded that we had provided insufficient facilitation help to our managers.

During this time, we were examining our human resource activities. We had a generalized concern that we needed to improve our human resource management. Our human resource planning effort does not complement our strategic planning activities in scale and comprehensiveness. We were not satisfied that we sufficiently considered the type of organization and skills we needed to execute a strategy. But in connection with the transnational concept we had a particular concern that our human resource practices were not conducive to an organization that was stressing co-ordination and interdependence more than before. Our practices had grown up during a time when our approach to employees had been more traditional. We needed to adjust other elements of our organization – compensation and evaluation systems, people development, and culture.

Next steps

In the fall of 1987, we commenced two parallel efforts. One provides process consultation assistance and the other is a thorough overhaul of our human resource practices. The process consultation effort started in Europe, at the request of the European Division President. At the time of writing, involved executives have taken a test to help assess their interpersonal orientation, discussed the results, talked about the characteristics of being a good team member, and talked about the process of management in Europe. Teams representing country managers, functions and SBUs are now working on their ideas for job definition, respective roles in different kinds of tasks and work relationships. These ideas will be explored in each business, throughout the world, one at a time initially. Each business will be guided through the four steps (industry analysis; strategy; tasks; roles, responsibilities and relationships).

As part of this effort, we are also doing more, recalling Professor Beer's change model, to increase dissatisfaction. Internally, we are giving a lot of attention to operating effectiveness and our cost of management. Externally, we have conducted customer surveys on quality and service which have indicated opportunities for improvement. Health care systems around the world continue to demand both quality and low cost. We set ambitious targets for improvement in quality, cost, innovation and service.

Our human resource practices are not as supportive as they could be in supporting an organization that is moving more and more to team work. We are developing a human resources 'profiling' process to analyse the HR implications of each unit's strategy. This approach will involve the managers in analysing and providing for human resource needs, just as we introduced strategy formulation into the company twelve years ago. Following the analysis of industry and consideration of strategy, managers will be guided through an assessment of human assets and skills and development of policies in reward systems, people development, and the design of work that supports the type of multinational strategy and organization they have chosen.

Commentary

The experiences described above raise the question: how do large numbers of people learn new ways of behaving? Our experiences suggest that having a model or vision and education in understanding that model is insufficient. In addition, we needed help on implementation. It is in this area of organizational learning where the researchers in this book still have some work to do. They have developed a theory of an ideal multinational organization, given certain industry and strategy characteristics. They have not yet developed a theory of multinational organizational learning and change.

Beer's organization development model, Change = (Dissatisfaction × Model × Process) > Cost of Change is helping us learn and change. In applying this formula to the multinational company, the model is the transnational, global or multidomestic concept. The formulation of this equation explicitly states that change efforts cannot rely on model alone. One needs also significant dissatisfaction among employees about the existing situation and a process of change to help them think through ways of improving the situation. The formula warns against reliance on vision, concepts, and frameworks.

The emphasis in Beer's approach is on doing, participation, and task accomplishments. Employees can gain assistance from models but may also end up creating their own. It is, if you will, a more inductive approach to organizational learning and change. In contrast, the deductive approach emphasizes analysis, choosing the right model, communicating it and then attitudes and behaviour will change.

The appeal of the deductive approach is precisely that it does provide a vision up front, a sense of direction. It facilitates the conceptual comprehension of the need for behavioural adaptation. And, as our experiences indicate, people at middle and lower levels can adjust their behaviour in the light of their understanding of top management's vision. But putting the model or vision up front is also potential for downfall because you may not be able to meet employee's expectations. Relying on model alone is dangerous: as this OD model says, if you try to change without having D and P in place, the cost of change is too high and the change effort will fail.

Furthermore, the OD formula illustrates that change in the multinational company requires a shared level of D (dissatisfaction) among multinational employees and a world-wide P (process) to assist them in making changes. It is not enough for the country managers to be dissatisfied: all the managers – country, overseas SBU, US SBU, and functional – must be similarly dissatisfied. If not, those managers who are least dissatisfied (or who are actually satisfied with the current situation) will simply drag and wait for the change efforts to go away. Similarly, one needs a process of change that is relevant world-wide. Planning a process, for example, that relies on shared involvement of both top-level employees and lower-level employees in the change effort may not work in all cultures.

If, with hindsight and help from OD, we see some deficiencies in our approach to introducing these concepts, we might ask: how did we make the improvements that have occurred? Because, as noted earlier, we think the ideas in this book have already helped our company.

The answer is the behaviour of top-line management. Of course, this will not be news, but our experiences provide perhaps an interesting reinforcement. It places top-management behaviour as part of the P (process) variable. The behaviour of our managers who were instinctively transnational in style provided real examples of 'how to do it' and evidence of commitment to the concept (equally, of course, those managers who were not instinctively transnational provided disconfirming evidence). They, more than anything else kept us reasonably on track and moving forward.

What would we have done differently in the light of this OD approach to organizational learning and change? In a couple of words, we would have focused earlier on tasks and facilitation. We would also have moved more rapidly in communicating these multinational frameworks and concepts to middle and lower level employees. At the least, this step would have created a common language throughout the company. We would also have tackled one business at a time, at least initially.

But, importantly, the sequencing would be different. Step one should be to establish a shared level of dissatisfaction among all the managers. To obtain everybody's dissatisfaction, the causes must be common to all. Focusing on country managers' dissatisfaction with their role or stating that the problem is how to achieve greater world-wide strategic co-ordination do not meet this criterion. Topics such as the high cost of management, raising our customer service levels, meeting unexpected customer opportunities, and responding to a competitive threat do meet this criterion. They are specific business tasks.

Step two is to assemble a group of people with responsibility and expertise in the area causing the dissatisfaction. Their charge is to tell top management what is wrong, why we have this problem, and what might be done to fix it. They are provided with a neutral process facilitator. They develop as a team and focus on the problems and tasks necessary to improve matters.

Step three is to expose them to relevant research models, frameworks, and concepts which take their data, experiences, opinions, and ideas and make them analytically tractable. By introducing research to them at this stage, the models can illuminate their own experience, provide them with some theory and shape their actions.

Paradoxically, this approach is similar to that used by the company successfully to introduce strategic planning ten years ago (explained earlier in the discussion of 'profiling sessions'). Our experience suggests that lack of a task orientation is why many staff activities fail in organization. By their training and experiences, staff people are comfortable with models and frameworks. The deductive approach is natural for them. But what is clear from our experiences and the OD formula is that managers needed action assistance and guidance. Without it the vision could have faded away. Another insight is that successful line managers may not be very skilled in the process of managing. Perhaps the more useful product staff employees can offer is process assistance to managers in applying concepts and models. Providing ways of conceptualizing and analysing the problems that are causing line managers to be 'dissatisfied' is not enough.

I turn now to the role of human resources management in helping organizations implement the transnational. This field covers four areas: employee influence – policies governing the extent to which and the mechanisms by which employee ideas are sought and communicated; human resource flow – policies on recruitment, development and promotion; reward systems – compensation policies; and work systems – the design of jobs and how work gets done. The central premise of the field is that these four policy areas should be consistent with each other and, collectively, consistent with the environment and strategy of the business.[2]

Consider what these policies are like in a traditional company. Employee influence is achieved by employees expressing their views through the 'chain of command' – employees say things like, 'I deal with my boss'. There will be an emphasis on clear reporting relationships. Human resource flow starts at the bottom and works up through the chain on the basis of functional competence. Reward systems will be characterized by 'pay for the job'. Work is organized on a functional, hierarchical basis.

Several of the policies in a traditional organization are not suited to a transnational. As we have seen, the transnational organization is characterized by flexibility, differentiation, interdependence, co-ordination and use of teams. Our experiences suggest we have to change employee influence policies so as to encourage employees to work across the chain of command on specific decisions. Employees will deal with their boss and at least two or three other people as well. Reporting relationships will not be as clear cut. Human resource flows will be through lateral moves – across functions and countries to help the development of multiple perspectives in a person. The ability to see many sides in an issue is as highly valued as functional competence. Reward systems will contain inducements to build relationships and to seek integrated decision-making. Devices such as gains sharing will be more common than in the traditional organization. Work systems will stress participation and foster team work. But this organization is not a happy-go-lucky club! Where we seem to be heading is towards a set of human resource policies that support the clarity and functional excellence of the traditional organization and the flexibility, participatory and multiple perspectives of the transnational.

It should be obvious that implementing the transnational concept is a major undertaking. Moving from cognition to action is no small step. Are we pleased that we are making the attempt? Unequivocally, yes. These researchers have identified what, I think, is the only hope of solving the perennial problems in multi-national companies. Structural solutions alone are incapable of combining the expertise and viewpoints of countries, overseas and US SBUs and functions. Multinational complexity and multiple perspectives on a decision can only be addressed by building good relationships among the managers and clearly identifying the strategy and tasks that have to be accomplished.

The researchers have also added a valuable piece to the strategy field. Let me illustrate by our own case. We already had in place a set of SBUs to foster a differentiated strategic approach; differentiated according to customer characteristics and bases of competition faced by each SBU. The reason SBUs had been introduced was to avoid a symmetrical and universal strategy for all the businesses in the company. Similarly, the transnational concept advocates a differentiated approach to organization, according to the strategic tasks that have to be accomplished by each business. The international and organization dimensions and an approach for building a differentiated organization are, in fact, missing from the various strategy formulation approaches, including ours.

Finally, these researchers have made us much more conscious of the potential to gain advantage from organizational capability. By this term, I refer to the ability to sense customer needs around the world, figure out a competitively superior response and then mobilize the organization to rapidly and effectively bring the response to world markets. We are thinking much more about the quality of our organization processes and our people, much more about achieving co-ordination, much more about communicating and sharing experience than we did before. We are used to seeking superior customer satisfaction through product design, quality, service, and low cost. But, as the researchers point out, these features can erode. A superior organizational capability, on the other hand, is much more difficult to imitate, simply because it takes so long to create. Organizational capability is built, not installed. This research has helped us see that.

Notes

1 I will use these terms throughout the chapter. Researchers in this book use a variety of terms but in their essence they are all directionally similar. For example, Heterarchical and Dual Focus are similar to the transnational ideas.

2 For a fuller discussion of these issues see *Managing Human Assets*, Beer *et al.*

Chapter thirteen

Building a dynamic intelligent network: lessons from the telecommunications revolution for the MNC organization of the future

Håkan Ledin

Introduction

For more than twenty-five years I worked with L. M. Ericcson, a Swedish multinational company specializing in telecommunications. Over this period I was responsible for: overseas manufacture; telecommunication systems and products; information systems; and finally, the US operations. My views are obviously heavily influenced by my experience in telecommunications as well as by operating in a very international organization. Early in my career I found a contradiction between the traditional organization and the way in which the job was executed. Initially, I related this to the specific complex character of the industry I was working in. Gradually, however I came to believe that the issue was more general and that the dilemma could often be overcome by understanding the 'informal organization'.

Very few outsiders understood how Ericcson functioned. There was always an organization chart describing a formal structure. However, this was of limited value when trying to understand how the company operated. Its business has always been very complex in products, technology, international scope (in 1900 90 per cent of the business was outside Sweden) and thus, in structure and composition of resources. As seen from inside, it was obvious that there existed many networks which had evolved over time and were changing continuously. They were never formalized. No one wanted to sanction the networks but preferred to keep them vague and let them evolve in response to changes in external and internal circumstances.

I have been a proponent of not formalizing the networks. However, I have also seen how the informal networks have been incapable of responding to fast and big changes. The reaction has been instead to rely on the formal organization, which has not been capable of solving the problems. All this has led me to believe that it is important to understand the informal organization better. A better understanding of the informal networks can help organizations and, in particular, MNCs to adjust to rapid changes in the environment.

In my efforts to understand the informal organization in MNCs, I have come to believe that a lot can be learned from telecommunications systems. They are complex, open, and built as vertical and horizontal networks. Their development is dynamic and they now represent a global network. In this respect telecommunications is ahead of and supporting businesses and industries as they grow global. Therefore, I believe that many analogies can be drawn from telecommunications networks when the evolution of multinational organizations is studied. Before exploring and explaining the analogy it is important to establish the basic elements of these telecommunications networks. There are some particular characteristics of the fast-changing global telecommunications networks that have important lessons for managers of multinational organizations.

From national systems to global intelligent networks

The telecommunications networks have undergone a dramatic development over the last twenty years. From nationally automatized systems, they are becoming one international on-line, real-time network serving well over 500 million subscribers. Networking capabilities have been vastly expanded. A key element therein has been system architecture – a must for the control of dynamic real-time systems. A recent development, as communication technology and computer technology start to merge, is the 'intelligent network' and 'open network architecture' approach. In the competitive and market driven US environment, a network of intelligent nodes supporting storage, processing and transportation is starting to evolve.

From hierarchical to horizontal networks

For a very long time a telecommunications network operated in accordance with its hierarchical structure, one layer of telephone exchanges (central offices in the US) on top of the other with the international one at the top. As markets have grown for the services, the network has become global and increasingly complex. The formal structure remains. From an operational point of view, however, it has become much flatter, the network is more horizontal than vertical. Calls can be routed from one part of the network to another without having to climb up and down through a hierarchy.

From mechanical to software-driven systems

In the evolution towards the 'intelligent network' the change towards software-driven systems is even more pronounced. This seems to be the only way to operate a very complex system which requires very fast response times, high reliability, and which can adapt quickly to a continuously changing environment. A hardware-driven, mechanical system has thus become a software driven, dynamic network.

These characteristics show considerable resemblance to the evolution of the organization of MNCs. It is, however, important to stress the fundamental difference between a complex technical system and an organization built of human beings. In the latter, motivation, values, power, politics, etc. play important roles. Therefore, the analogy can only help us build a conceptual framework within which those other factors of human behaviour have to be studied to further our understanding of the organization of the MNC of the future.

Another major difference is that when developing a technical system you can 'go back to the start'. In an organization, it is obvious that you cannot disregard earlier developments. The organization has to evolve to meet changes and new requirements.

In order to explore the nature and operation of Ericsson's informal organization, I found it useful to trace two management processes that related to the development of the company's digital switching system and to the evolution of the company's multinational operations through 'transfer of technology and know-how'.

The first is related to the development of an advanced switching system, AXE, and from this I drew lessons about the building and integration of an organizational network. The second is related to the transfer of technology and know-how and from this I drew lessons concerning the management of change and the operation of a world-wide organization, and in particular the importance of how to manage knowledge and information.

Building and integrating the organizational network – lessons from AXE

In my presentation of the AXE development, I will show how complex systems in a dynamic environment require new structure-

328

architecture, which emphasizes the horizontal flows rather than the hierarchy. The structure shown contains three levels; two are confined to the establishment of the system and to future changes in the system and the third to the ongoing operation of the system. When we translate this to the organization, the two former are identified as the strategic and tactical levels and the third as the operational level.

The AXE development represented a major change in the Ericsson organization. With examples, I will show how a change is implemented and the vital importance of the tactical level in this process.

In the system structure developed for AXE and here translated to an organization, focus is on knowledge and information as building blocks and main flows instead of physical assets and physical flows. The systems are software-driven which is vital for the horizontal flows.

Designing the network

In 1970, Ericsson had spent ten years trying without success to build telephone exchange switching systems incorporating computer technology. Conclusion: we were on the wrong track in merging telecommunication and computer technologies. The bold decision was to go back and start from zero. The system had to be functionally defined, i.e. software-derived and not hardware-derived. Earlier development (investments) was not to constrain the new approach.

The main reasons for the failure of the initial development were related to the basically hierarchical structure of the traditional telephone network, which was reflected by the same type of structure in the exchange systems. The rapid change of the environment, the market, had not been observed. In the 1960s one country after the other got fully automatic national networks and automatic international traffic started to emerge. The market grew rapidly as well as the complexity of the traffic. A hierarchical network could not cope with this and, therefore, the requirements on the switching systems had changed. Furthermore, the nature of computer software had not been understood. Functions implemented in software cut through the vertical hierarchical structure of the traditional electromechanical systems, in which the flows had to follow a fixed firmwired structure.

In the new effort overall responsibility was transferred from R&D to marketing. It was also decided to establish a completely new and independent organization, Ellemtel, for the development of AXE. In the beginning, twenty engineers spent two years to define the basic architecture, and they started by analysing the functions.

Systems are aggregates of functions

All systems contain functions; in complex systems they are many and of varying complexity. When specifying AXE, every function in the system had to be identified and defined. They were classified based upon complexity and frequency:

Figure 13.1 General nature of functions in a switching system

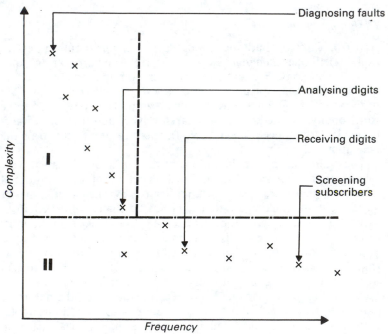

I CPU area – covers complex and low-frequency functions.
II RP area – covers low-complexity and frequent functions.

A central office system is supposed to run 24 hours per day for 25 years with two hours total down-time. Obviously, diagnostics and automatic repair are very complex but – hopefully – infrequent. On the other hand, as a subscriber, you expect to get a dial tone within 0.2 sec. Each subscriber has to be checked five times per second. In a telephone exchange with 20,000 subscribers this means 100,000 checks per second. Simple and frequent. It is my assumption that the functions of most systems show similar characteristics.

The two categories of functions executed in software differ in terms of demands on information, processing and in terms of optimal location. The ones that are complex require more processing power. With low frequency between the events this power is centralized to the central processing unit (CPU). The frequent functions require short response times and limited processing power. Therefore, they are moved as far out in the system as possible. They are executed in regional processors (RP). All functions are, however, not executed by software operating in processors (computers). A few simple functions stay very stable over time. It is more cost-effective to execute them in hardware (HW), which means that you give up the flexibility of a software solution.

Connecting functions – building system architecture

With a major part of the functions analysed, the development of the architecture started. It had to be a top-down approach. This meant that the purpose of the total system had to be defined before all the necessary functions belonging to that system were identified and defined.

Provocatively, it can be said that nobody at Ericsson had ever defined what a telephone exchange was. Over the years, the system had emerged in a bottom-up fashion. The mistake in the 1960s was to try to introduce computer technology in this bottom-up way. The development started with a limited set of functions, which were considered critical. Then one function after the other was added. As they were introduced, it became apparent that a hardware-derived architecture, with a hierarchical control structure, could not absorb software in an efficient way.

With this in mind, this is the architecture that was and still is the base for AXE. This is a multilevel architecture. The system comprises all functions required to operate a telephone exchange. They are divided into major groups, which are called sub-systems. One is the subcriber sub-system controlling all interfaces with the subscribers (the customers), another is the trunk sub-system controlling

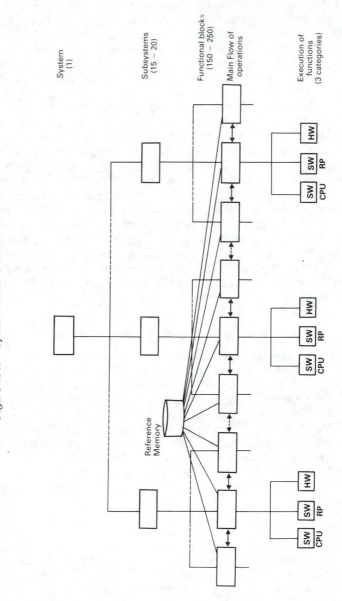

Figure 13.2 System architecture of AXE

all traffic to and from other central offices in the network. Thus the sub-systems represent the general organization of the functions to be executed. Each sub-system consists of functional blocks containing functions to be executed. Each one of these can be executed in three main ways:

Software, central processing unit (SW;CPU):

handles infrequent and complex functions which can involve many combinations of data and instructions and therefore require large processing capacity and flexibility. The CPU belongs to the system.

Software, regional processor (SW;RP):

handles frequent and simple functions which involve limited combinations of data and instructions and therefore require limited processing capacity and less flexibility. The RP belongs to the sub-system.

Hardware (HW):

handles functions which have well defined and stable environment. No flexibility is required and the probability of change is small. The main reason for executing a function in HW is cost and stability.

Key to success – functional level – operational flow

The key to the success of AXE lies at the functional block level. There is a maximum size of number of instructions handled by one block. The interfaces – language – between the blocks are very well defined and have to be adhered to by everybody working with the system. In a broad sense, software includes instructions and their flow and the data they are operating on. A lot of the data is used by several functional blocks. Data is added, deleted and changed as the network and subscribers evolve over time. To isolate these changes a reference memory was introduced separating the instruction (memory) from the data (memory). The reference memory always knows where the particular data is to be found. Data changes do not contaminate the instruction flow.

The interface rules and the reference memory make it possible to develop and handle the functional blocks independently of each other. The proof of the architecture came when 130 functional blocks, after three-and-half years, were put together as a telephone exchange. The system worked! A key was the fact that the multi-level architecture had been correctly designed. This is where all specifications for the system are established. The outcome is a horizontal flow of execution of functions. The multilevel or vertical structure is required for the building but not for the operations. Only when changes occur which require new or modified systems specifications do we have to go back to the vertical structure.

The conclusion is thus that the permanent operation of the system is horizontal and the vertical structure is used when building or changing the system.

Changing the system

Let us look at an example of such a change. In the late 1970s it was decided to use AXE as the switching unit in a new cellular mobile telephone system. This new application was so significant that it required the definition of new sub-systems, within the vertical structure. A set of functional blocks were developed and a few modifications were made on blocks belonging to some of the existing administrative sub-systems. Building on the very flexible and, at the same time, very stringent architecture of AXE a new product was born which has captured almost half the world market for cellular systems.

Building an organizational network

There are similarities between the system-architecture described and an organization built on human resources. However, one is predictable (except for software bugs and hardware failures) and technically controlled (experience shows that the human factor, however, still causes most problems in the system), and the other is less predictable, managerially and administratively controlled and operates in a dynamic environment. In the technical system it is possible to make a clear distinction between permanent operation and change. In an organization, e.g. an MNC, there are always changes going on. Therefore, the horizontal flow of permanent operations and the vertical structure are interacting all the time. One of management's major tasks is to control this interaction.

I will now try to apply the lesson learned from the design of a complex technical structure to an organization. In the background of Figure 13.3 we see the multilevel structure of AXE. Its four levels correspond to Chandler's general office (system) general offices (sub-systems), departmental headquarters (functional blocks) and field units (functions). (Chandler 1962). According to him, the first level deals with strategic long-term matters, the next with tactical day-to-day situations and the two remaining with implementation of the decisions. In Chandler's view this is a

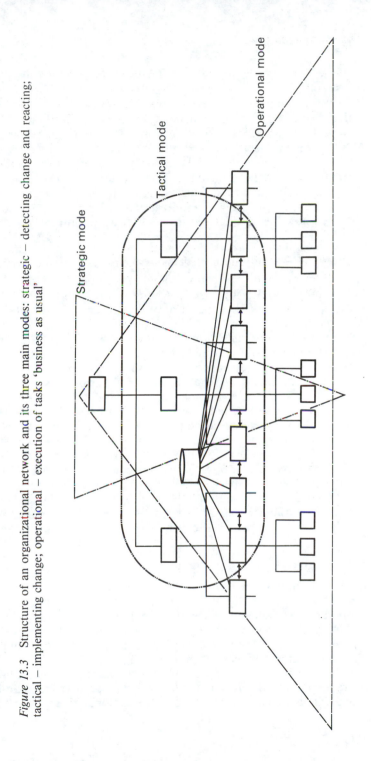

Figure 13.3 Structure of an organizational network and its three main modes: strategic – detecting change and reacting; tactical – implementing change; operational – execution of tasks 'business as usual'

vertical structure which does not, however, identify the need for horizontal flows, in particular at the two lowest levels.

As we saw in the AXE architecture, the vertical structure is only active when the system is being built or changed. We all know that organizations are continuously exposed to change in particular MNCs. There are activities going on continuously at the different levels and they are interacting. In such a dynamic organization where time is a vital dimension, I think it is more fruitful, however, to identify three basic modes instead of levels. These modes are the strategic, the tactical, and the operational. In Figure 13.3, I have indicated how they are related to the vertical structure.

Strategic mode – identify, change and react

In the strategic mode, focus is on identifying change and on searching for opportunities for change. Changes are related to the competitive position of the organization, requirements in order to maintain its position or opportunities to improve. Such changes involve modification, addition or deletion of sub-systems and their corresponding functional blocks.

In Figure 13.3 the strategic mode is shown as a pyramid turned upside down. It is obvious that the main responsibility is at the top of the structure. There are control systems to help management detect external and internal changes as well as more or less formal methods for strategic planning and search for new opportunities. In addition, there are many informal contacts and networks, which even reach the lower levels of the structure. This is not least the case where the need and opportunity for change are defined and solutions developed. Specifications for changes of the system and the sub-systems are the result of this process. As we will see later, the quality of these specifications and the plans for implementation are vital for the success of the change.

Tactical mode – implement change

Implementation of changes requires special resources and organization. This is the role of the tactical mode which takes the form of temporary project teams. They are organized across the traditional vertical structure and can be staffed from all levels. This mode has its centre in upper-middle management sub-systems and the upper level of functional blocks, as indicated in Figure 13.3.

The objective of the implementation is lasting changes at the operational level. Its units and components (departments, sections, groups, individuals) correspond to the functional blocks of AXE.

These blocks of AXE work with flexibility and efficiency because interfaces are well defined: there is a common language and a common reference memory of information on the entire network of blocks.

In the case of an organization, interfaces, common language, and common references are, however, more limited and less systematic. Very often, I have seen how changes are introduced in the vertical structure without good understanding of the impacts in the horizontal flow. The time to implement change becomes long and the final outcome can be much less successful than expected. It is fundamental to understand how change moves through the three basic modes. When we discuss transfer of technology, the process of change will be analysed further.

Operational mode – on-going execution of functions

At the end of a successful process the operational mode has been transformed so that it is more efficient in executing its old functions and routines and has learned to execute new ones. One important role of this mode is to deal with 'normal' changes, i.e. such changes as do not impact the system or sub-systems. One example is ongoing product development compared to completely new products. The more knowledge and information that is available in the operational mode the more changes it can learn to manage.

In Figure 13.3 this mode is represented by the large pyramid. Its base, the functional blocks and the flows, dominates, and this is where most of the resources of the organization are deployed. Therefore, the efficiency of the operational mode is decisive for the success of the organization. This mode is dominated by flows of software (instructions and data) and hardware (products) in the form of networks. Some of those are governed by well-established routines, but many are informal. When the informal networks work smoothly they make wonders, but they can also turn into sources of obstruction.

In the following I shall use the three modes to discuss the process of change that was parallel to the technical development of AXE. The same approach will be used in discussing transfer of technology.

Integrating the network

As we know today, AXE is an acknowledged success. Some say it is more of a marketing than a technical success. My opinion is, however, that it is an organizational success both in the development and industrialization stages.

Development of AXE: from strategic to tactical and to operational

The development of AXE took place in a completely new organization, Ellemtel, a joint venture between Ericsson and the Swedish Telephone administration. Its initial objective was the development of AXE and the very specific goal was to have a working prototype in 1976, the centenary of L. M. Ericsson as a company. Resources were added, primarily from the two owners, as the project evolved. The design of the architecture as described above was the strategic stage which laid the base for the tactical stage, a project organized in units corresponding to groups of functional blocks and units for the development of hardware as well as the processors to run software on. Thus the architecture of AXE also served as the structure of the organization of the development, but more importantly interfaces, the language, and design rules were so well defined that the units could work independently of each other and still in a very integrated fashion. The tactical project organization gradually turned into the operational organization which supports ongoing AXE development.

The objective of the company was to develop telecommunication systems and products. Its overall structure was, however, designed to support the development of very large and complex systems. When faced with the task of developing telephone instruments it failed. Such development required quick turn-around times for fast response to the market and very close co-operation with production and purchase to meet very tight cost objectives.

After the initial success, not even the development of complex systems worked well. A project to develop a large, very advanced PABX, private telephone exchange was a failure. Ellemtel now worked in the operational mode, the necessary severity and stringency of the strategic mode was relaxed and the development was not supported by the aggressive tactical mode. The operational role did not include the open and change-oriented networks and processes required for the development of a new product. Maybe an Ellemtel, which has to focus on and operate in the strategic and tactical modes, only has a limited efficient period of life. When it reaches the operational mode, it has to be started all over again.

Industrialization of AXE – a tactical project

Now let us take a look at the industrialization of AXE. In essence this involved the transfer of AXE from Ellemtel to Ericsson and the introduction of AXE into all functions of its organization. The strategic decision was to have this done within the established structure. All functions were to be impacted by the move from electromechanical technology, heavy in manufacturing, to electronics, heavy in software. This process started in scale in 1977. A project INDAX, industrialization of AXE, became the tactical mode. It cut through the vertical organization and was organized in eleven subprojects. Overall project leader was the head of the engineering function of the switching division of the parent company. As project leader he reported to a member of the corporate management. Except for a very small planning team, all participants had a function in the established operational organization. In a sense, they came to participate in two main networks, one tactical and the other operational. Although they had one job in the formal organization, they ran a parallel job in INDAX.

Saudi – the first commercial challenge – a tactical project

Soon, we got a tactical goal: an upcoming, very big tender in Saudi. Due to the very short delivery times the organization had to start to prepare itself at its own risk. In December, 1977, Ericsson was awarded the contract, the first large-scale commercial delivery of AXE. Five exchanges were to be put into service, within twelve months. A separate project team was established, but it had to rely heavily on INDAX. The existence of this project made it possible to find and implement new solutions and to make efficient short cuts. Few believed the delivery times could be met. They were, with two weeks' margin. Others believed that the priority and focus on Saudi would be detrimental for other projects. The reality was that the entire organization was pulled along.

The operational mode

INDAX and the Saudi project came to an end. The organization moved from tactical to operational mode. New networks had to replace or merge with old operational networks and processes. Aggressiveness met with resistance. The evolution slowed and the result was a mixture less efficient than what had been possible during the tactical phase. What this shows is the difficulties involved in moving from a very focused and visible tactical project with much management involvement to the 'business as usual' operational mode. Therefore this transition requires careful planning and managerial involvement.

Even if more could have been achieved, there is no doubt that AXE and the related restructuring of Ericsson has been very successful. The major reason is that it could benefit from an organic evolution through the modes, strategic, tactical, and operational.

Operating the global network: lessons from transfer of technology and know-how

We have seen that a dynamic evolution of an organization paralleled and supported the development of an advanced systems product. The last two decades have also seen a rapid development of international business. Multinational companies are growing more global in strategy and structure. Under pressure of time and competition the organizations have to be operated so that they can react to changes, and at the same time optimize the use of their resources.

In the preceding pages we have developed an organizational structure and identified three main modes of the organization. Also we have seen how they support changes and 'business as usual'. We shall now discuss the process of change in more detail. Through 'transfer of technology and know-how' (TT), a great deal of change takes place in international business, mostly within organizations but as strategic alliances become more common, organizational borders are also crossed. The evolution of Ericsson between 1965 and 1985 involved a lot of TT as more and more self-contained (but not independent) units were built. Production represented the most conspicuous and most systematized function. According to my experience, the main problem in TT is the lack of understanding of the complete operational flows; how the system is expanded and new subsystems are added; how the flows are linked to each other. Information is at the core of the problem; lack of information; lack of understanding of the lack of information; lack of knowledge at the sender end and, obviously, even more so at the receiver end. I have often defined our job as developing senders who could build receivers.

In an organization such as Ericsson's, the informal organization was always very strong. When transferring technology this had to be taken into account. Existing networks close to the production flows had to be brought into the process. New networks in a new country had to be developed and these had to connect into the networks at the parent company. The national – Swedish – informal organization had to be expanded into an international informal organization in a structured and systematic way.

It is important to identify the organizational evolution in connection with TT. At Ericsson the strategic decision was to establish local production in order to win new markets and to protect old ones. A product leaving any factory should meet the same quality standards. Productivity and efficiency should also meet the same standards except for differences due to the size of the operation in the country.

In order to help people to understand the process and their role in it, we used the following simplifed charts of the overall network:

Figure 13.4 Basic operational flows of product generation and product supply

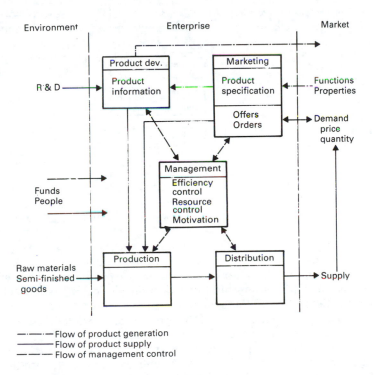

—·—·— Flow of product generation
————— Flow of product supply
— — — — Flow of management control

The objective when transferring technology and know-how is to build a long-term competitive operation, which means efficiency at the operational level. Figure 13.4 identifies the five main operational sub-systems of a business organization. The focus is, however, on the main flows, product generation and product supply, which are horizontal. They are supported by the management control systems, which are also linked to the vertical control structure. Tactical project organizations are not included as

341

Figure 13.5 Resource flow and control systems in the production activity

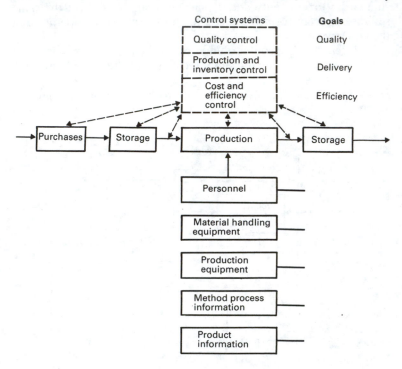

they are temporary by nature and active in the process of change of the system. Focusing on the flows also means that we emphasize interrelationships and linkages to the environment.

Let us look at the AXE-INDAX case as an example. The first step, development of AXE, involved marketing and product development, i.e. the product generation flow. INDAX tied it all together, adding sales to marketing and engineering to product development, and building the total product supply flow by getting AXE into production and distribution. New interrelationships and procedures had to be developed and implemented in order to get an efficient flow of software and hardware.

Production – a function in the network

Even if the particular TT was related to the production activity, it involved the entire organization. Many cases of TT have overlooked the need to build a complete product supply flow. There must always be a balance between all functions involved in the flow, including operational management. In order to make people understand the role of production in this flow, the function was described in Figure 13.5.

Focus on information and knowledge

The basic problem was that information and knowledge had grown over a long time. There was always someone to ask in the home organization. In theory, all inputs were available but nobody had ever thought about what would be required when the technology was to be transferred. Most people tend to focus on equipment and resources but a majority of the problems were – and are – related to the two boxes containing information. The control systems and the corresponding goals belong to the same category. They require definition of interfaces and development of a common language.

When the production transfer requirements started to accelerate in the second half of the 1960s, very little was available in the form of systems and goals. A small group of staff had the responsibility for implementing the strategy. All technology and know-how existed in the Swedish organization but had to be made available so that it could be transferred. The first step was to build a network that could support the overseas operations. The staff function with overall responsibility was only a small part of this network. People from all levels and functions were drawn into the network.

Building the control systems

At the start, the focus was on building the control systems and on establishing the corresponding goals. The existing systems had to be enhanced and new systems to be added. In this way the 'international language' for Ericsson's production function was developed as well as interfaces within a production unit and linkages to the Swedish production 'network'. In the early 1970s, after four years, the network was in place and it supported a very rapid and efficient expansion of production outside Sweden. This development also involved well systematized training methods and programmes.

One established goal was that products should meet the same quality requirements irrespective of where they were manufactured. This was achieved by the development of an implementation of a very elaborate quality audit system. Besides defining accepted standards it became the language for quality issues. Reports were received monthly, problems were identified and resolved quickly, often by phone and telex and in complicated cases by experts sent overseas.

When a new unit was built, experts were sent to establish the audit function. Quality was measured on an individual basis during the training of workers and thereafter continuously. The monthly results were displayed by department in the factory. Some of the best workers were promoted and trained to be quality auditors. As quality was measured it was also made part of the piece-rate. The importance of quality was well understood by the entire organization.

Change, time and goals

Any change requires time and evolves through different stages. In the case of TT, the period is usually several years. The production, in this case, goes through three major stages, preparation with strategic decisions in focus, rapid implementation and normal growth. This can be described with an S-curve, as in Figure 13.6.

Figure 13.6 Process of change (example: building a new production unit overseas)

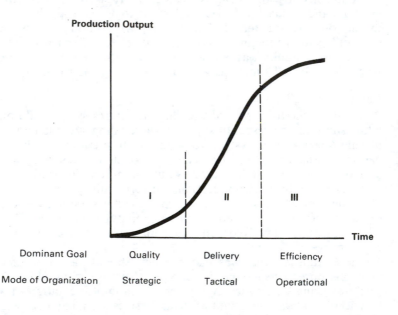

Three stages of change

The three stages also correspond to the three modes, strategic, tactical, and operational. In each stage one of the goals is dominant, although at the end of the process all three goals have to be met for the TT to be considered successful. Briefly, the three stages can be described as follows:

1. With the control and training systems in place this stage involved the detailed project plan and the selection and training of a project team. The responsibility remained with the group staff, which relied heavily on its Swedish network. At the end of this stage the site had been selected, construction started, equipment ordered and information had started to flow. The project team was transferred to the new country to start recruitment and training of key personnel. During this period, quality is in focus. This refers to quality in a broad sense, ultimately measured in quality of output, but relevant to inputs, selection and training of people as well as information transferred.

2. The project team was integrated as the production function of the local company. At this stage, the group staff still maintained major responsibility for the project. Detailed production plans were established. To support the rapid build-up experts were recruited from the Swedish network or from other well-established units in the group. Equipment was put in place and made operational. Human resources were recruited and trained.

   As a consequence of rapid expansion, delivery was the dominant goal. The co-ordination of increasing volumes of resources was crucial in order to meet established delivery schedules.

   Towards the end of this stage, the rate of build-up slowed down and approached the general growth rate of the local company of which the production had become a part. Experts went home. The responsibility for the function had been transferred to the local company and the role of the group staff became general support and control.

3. Production has become part of the local company and its evolution. It is as such part of the local network but still maintains strong links to the Swedish network through the common control systems as well as many relations between people. With organization and resources in place to meet normal growth, emphasis turns to productivity and efficiency while quality and

delivery are maintained. The group staff now performs normal staff functions. It receives reports, makes reviews, proposes and initiates actions for further improvements.

From time to time major changes take place, new product lines and/or new processes are introduced. Again, a process of change is initiated and part of the total network gets involved in a new project.

Globalization – network for continuous transfer of technology and know-how

As internal organizations evolve into global networks the capability to control TT becomes even more important. Initially, information and know-how flows in one direction, from parent to subsidiary. Knowledge is built at the receiving end and further enhanced by new information and learning. As this happens, information and know-how start to flow both ways. Gradually links are established, formally and informally, between units in the international organization. A fairly simple organization, on paper at least, develops into a global network. In the Ericsson case, this process started in the production function. As AXE was introduced in the market, it became necessary to go through the same process in TT in software development and engineering. The customers require local support centres when they buy and install complex systems such as AXE. As knowledge builds locally, these resources are not only used for local support but also in the on-going development of AXE.

In the late 1970s all development took place in Sweden. Today more than fifteen countries participate. A global network of development resources has been established. This evolution continues as major subsidiaries are given responsibility for marketing outside their national territories.

In this context of network building, it is interesting to see the disruption caused by a new organization of the Ericsson group, which was introduced in 1983. It was a traditional vertical structure, which did not take into consideration all existing networks, formal and informal, that constitute the operational flows of the organization. Only after several years is the new organization working properly.

TT is the way knowledge is grown and disseminated as MNCs grow into global networks. It is a time-consuming process which requires considerable management involvement. Problems arise due to, among other things, lack of proper language, efficient interfaces, and communication channels. Therefore, successful TT includes the establishment of networks and control systems which secure the continuous flow of technology and know-how. Only when this is achieved will the international organization be able to react to changes and to use its resources in a globally effective way.

Key resources – knowledge and information

As we have seen, knowledge and information are important to the success of complex and, in particular, international organizations. Over a century we have seen the centre of the economy move from agriculture through manufacturing, industry and distribution and now into 'information and services'. At the same time, scarce resources have become abundant. They may not be scarce in the traditional sense. There will rather be a scarcity in the competence to manage these resources in an efficient way, so that full value is added to products and services. Traditionally, this was taken care of by the organizational hierarchy. This will no longer be an effective way.

Impact of information technology

The management and organization of these key resources is heavily influenced by the information technology available. This has always been the case but is now more pronounced than ever, because of the rapid development of modern information technology. Computers started to appear in business organizations in the mid-fifties. The focus was on data processing in closed computer departments. Around 1970 it became apparent that so much information had been put into the computer systems that storage and retrieval had become a major problem. This initiated the development of database-technology. It took almost fifteen years to develop this into commercially mature products. Another response to the same problem was the introduction of the mini-computers which facilitated decentralization. Still the computer systems were closed systems.

In the early 1980s more advanced communication technology became available and the introduction of the personal computer accelerated dramatically. We will have achieved a third major stage of evolution when data processing, storage, and transportation will be integrated in open systems. This development will have a major impact on how organizations are built and operated. The technology now becoming available will not only support the evolution

347

Figure 13.7 Evolution of modern information technology

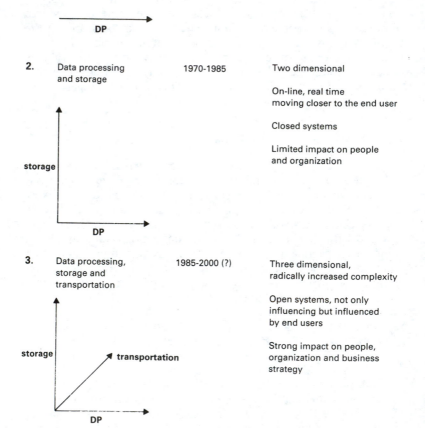

1. Data processing   1955-1970   One dimensional

Batch orientated

Closed systems

Minor impact on people
and organization

DP

2. Data processing   1970-1985   Two dimensional
and storage

On-line, real time
moving closer to the end user

Closed systems

Limited impact on people
and organization

storage

DP

3. Data processing,   1985-2000 (?)   Three dimensional,
storage and radically increased complexity
transportation

Open systems, not only
influencing but influenced
by end users

storage   transportation   Strong impact on people,
organization and business
strategy

DP

of networks, as described earlier, but make them virtually unavoidable. This represents a challenge and an opportunity to management.

In Figure 13.7, I have summarized the evolution of modern information technology. As can be seen it is becoming a three-dimensional problem.

Information only has a value if it is put to use. Human knowledge is required for this. Therefore, the information resource and the human resources are inherently coupled and synergetically linked. One cannot develop without the other. Even if artificial intelligence is on the horizon, a lot can be gained by organizations improving the use of already available resources. This is all the more important as available knowledge in all disciplines has increased dramatically for several decades and continues to do so.

What is the form of the system organization that can take full advantage of the valuable information and knowledge continuously becoming available? Putting it to use leads to progress, which generates change. The main challenge to management is to control change and the structure that supports ongoing changes at all levels in the organization.

Hierarchy will give place to networks

My experience tells me that a hierarchical structure will not be able to manage these changes. Nor do I think that the traditional informal organization will be a sufficient complement to the hierarchy. The traditional organization was hardware driven, focusing on the physical flow of products. In the future it will be software driven, i.e. focusing on the flow of information and on knowledge. This evolution resembles what has happened in the telecommunications network over the last 100 years. Three main stages can be identified:

1. Manual networks; rigid hierarchy controlled by hard-wired logic and with human operators executing the connections;
2. Automatic networks; electromechanical; same structure as manual but operators being replaced by electromechanical switches;
   Computer controlled; still same structure with logic being executed in computers in the switches. Hierarchy starting to break down and networks becoming horizontal;
3. Intelligent networks; corresponds to the third stage of IT (see Figure 13.7); storage and processing are handled in addition to transportation; intelligence is contained in switches but also

in large transaction-oriented databases and intelligent terminals. Public networks, private networks, voice networks, and data networks will all be interconnected. Networks for special services will evolve.

The second stage of the automatic network, computer-controlled, corresponds to the AXE development described earlier. Already in this case it was evident that the hierarchy could only serve as a conceptual framwork. The operational flows were horizontal.

This becomes even more pronounced in the intelligent network. We used the experience of the AXE structure to build a model of an organizational network (Figure 13.3). In this context the intelligent network consists of organizational networks being interconnected at the functional block level, i.e. an extended horizontal flow. As this happens, the traditional hierarchy becomes increasingly inefficient. To find solutions to this evolution will be a major challenge to management in the 1990s.

Conclusion

As the economy is moving into a stage dominated by information and service, new opportunities for gaining competitive advantage and adding value are created. An important factor is, as always, how resources are organized and managed. If we look at multi-national companies evolving into global organizations, the increasing complexity is obvious, as well as the fact that traditional organization structures − the hierarchy as well as the matrix − are too simple to relate to the real world. This development resembles what is happening in the intelligent network.

Heterarchy and management of intellectual assets

Trying to find a way to understand the present development of multinational organizations Hedlund (1985) introduces the term heterarchy, the meaning of which is 'that reality is organized non-hierarchically.' In the paper he concludes: 'The heterarchical prospect may seem too remote, or even silly, to people in successful hierarchies likely still to enjoy some time of harvesting the fruits of investments in a powerful organization for the maximum utiliza-tion of existing physical assets and know-how. It may seem less remote for people who have little alternative but directly to exploit the amazing global fluidity of capital, technology and people to develop *new* products, markets and competences.'

Bartlett and Ghoshal summarize: '. . . So national companies must not be regarded as just pipelines and expertise but recognized as sources of information and expertise that can build competitive advantage. The best way to exploit this resource is not through centralized direction and control but through a co-operative effort and co-option of dispersed capabilities. In such a relationship, the entrepreneurial spark plugs in the national units can flourish.'

Jaikumar (1986) concludes '. . . As noted before, the prime task of management once the system has been made reliable is not to categorize tasks or regiment workers but to create the fixed assets – the system and software – needed to make products. This calls for intelligent assets, not just pieces of hardware. Thus the new role of management in manufacturing is to create and nurture the project teams whose intellectual capabilities produce competitive advantage. What gets managed is intellectual assets, not equipment.'

These and many other recent articles arrive at the same conclusion; people and organizations have to be managed in new ways. Considering the complexity, new system structures have to be introduced. In the AXE case, a top-down approach was required in order to make it possible to build the system from the bottom, the functional blocks. As companies move to take full advantage of 'three-dimensional' information technology, I believe in a similar approach; a long-term strategy for restructuring is established top-down; the implementation has to understand and consider the bottom-up reality. No company organization can go back to zero as those designing AXE could. Therefore, it will require involvement and commitment by top management over a long period of change. The restructuring of the organization has to evolve through the three stages: strategic, tactical and operational.

Management of intellectual assets, information, and knowledge, in an environment will have to be characterized by change and will have to be dynamic. It will be handled through a structure of inter-related networks, strategic, tactical, and operational. The main flow are horizontal and they are interconnected by networks for planning, control and motivation. On each level, and particularly on the operational, many networks can be identified. A function, e.g. production, has its network through a multinational company; a subsidiary is structured in another dimension. The two networks have certain nodes, functional blocks, in common. Depending on the competence of management, these nodes can be points of conflict or points of opportunity to build more value.

Networks consist of nodes and links

Networks consist of nodes which are interconnected by links. The links perform the transport function and the nodes perform storing and processing, execution of routines as well as control functions. Value is thus added both in links and nodes. The smallest node is an individual or a small group of individuals. At the other end of the spectrum the functions of Figure 13.4 are also nodes, each very complex, in a simplified network. In between we find clusters of nodes and networks linking the clusters together. Figure 13.5 could be a general description of a node: input, information stored, processing capabilities, and output. In an efficient network each node could theoretically have total knowledge of all nodes and links in the system.

What types of questions does this network approach lead to?

- When is it more efficient to isolate nodes, networks and clusters? When and how should and could you promote interaction between these entities?
- How do you set goals and motivate in order to establish an entrepreneurial spirit in the nodes? How can they be promoted to take full advantage of information and knowledge available in other parts of the system?
- How can internal learning be an ongoing process whereby ambitions and achievements increase?
- How do you build systems to control the networks?
- How is career planning used in the building of strong networks? This seems to be a most important element in the organization of Japanese companies. On the operational level they seem to have very strong networks; so strong that they can incorporate the tactical level. This may be one reason why they can implement change very fast.

The network of intelligent nodes is at present a preliminary concept. It is in need of basic definitions, a language that makes it possible to build models, as well as to move between the model and real life in a fruitful way.

Some definitions may be derived from the field of complex information and communications systems. Others have to come from the organizational theories considering that intellectual assets rather than technical assets are the main building blocks.

I started to look for the informal organization in Ericsson, as the vertical hierarchy did not explain how the complex multinational company operated. It identified who is who and the formal positions, but still it did not explain how decisions were made, operations implemented and combined into flows of activities. As I was searching, the importance of networks, structured and unstructured, for 'business as usual' as well as change became clear.

In order to try to understand the relationship between the vertical structure and the networks, I have made an analogy with the ongoing development in telecommunication networks as they evolve from a hierarchy to a much more horizontal operating network. For such complex organizations as MNCs, a similar development is taking place. Management has to understand the structure and its networks and make them work to the full advantage of the organization and to support the evolution of new networks in order to respond to a dynamic environment.

The TT case very clearly shows how networks are built in a multinational company. It also shows how the process of change, through strategic, tactical and operational modes, has to be monitored, and the time it takes to build those networks. Furthermore, it stresses the vital importance of the capability to manage intellectual assets, knowledge, and information in the networks as well as in the process of change.

The informal organization contains many elements which, in a more structured way, can be used to build a network of intellectual assets. This is the organization that will be able to meet the challenge of global competition.

References

Bartlett, C. and Ghoshal, S. (1986) 'Tap your subsidiaries for global growth', *Harvard Business Review*, November–December.

Chandler, A. (1962) *Strategy and Structure*, Cambridge, MA: MIT Press.

Hedlund, G. (1985) *The Hypermodern MNC – a Heterarchy*, IIB, Stockholm School of Economics, research paper 85/5.

Jaikumar, R. (1986) 'Postindustrial manufacturing', *Harvard Business Review*, November–December.

Index